MW01602709

Emerging Horizons: Business and Society in the Post Pandemic Era

Emerging Horizons: Business and Society in the Post Pandemic Era

Editors

Brig. Dr. Rajiv Divekar
Dr. Komal Chopra
Dr. Smita Mehendale
Dr. Pravin Kumar Bhoyar

Routledge
Taylor & Francis Group

First published 2024
by Routledge
4 Park Square, Milton Park, Abingdon, Oxon OX14 4RN

and by Routledge
605 Third Avenue, New York, NY 10158

Routledge is an imprint of the Taylor & Francis Group, an informa business

© 2024 selection and editorial matter, Brig. Dr. Rajiv Divekar, Dr. Komal Chopra, Dr. Smita Mehendale, and Dr. Pravin Kumar Bhoyar; individual chapters, the contributors

The right of Brig. Dr. Rajiv Divekar, Dr. Komal Chopra, Dr. Smita Mehendale, and Dr. Pravin Kumar Bhoyar to be identified as the authors of the editorial material, and of the authors for their individual chapters, has been asserted in accordance with sections 77 and 78 of the Copyright, Designs and Patents Act 1988.

All rights reserved. No part of this book may be reprinted or reproduced or utilised in any form or by any electronic, mechanical, or other means, now known or hereafter invented, including photocopying and recording, or in any information storage or retrieval system, without permission in writing from the publishers.

Trademark notice: Product or corporate names may be trademarks or registered trademarks, and are used only for identification and explanation without intent to infringe.

British Library Cataloguing-in-Publication Data
A catalogue record for this book is available from the British Library

ISBN: 978-1-032-90822-9 (pbk)
ISBN: 978-1-003-55996-2 (ebk)

DOI: 10.4324/9781003559962

Typeset in Times LT Std
by Aditiinfosystems

Emerging Horizons: Business and Society in the Post Pandemic Era –
Brig. Dr. Rajiv Divekar et al. (eds)
© 2024 Taylor & Francis Group, London, ISBN 978-1-032-90822-9

Contents

Emerging Horizons: Business and Society in the Post Pandemic Era –
Brig. Dr. Rajiv Divekar et al. (eds)
© 2024 Taylor & Francis Group, London, ISBN 978-1-032-90822-9

List of Figures

Emerging Horizons: Business and Society in the Post Pandemic Era –
Brig. Dr. Rajiv Divekar et al. (eds)
© 2024 Taylor & Francis Group, London, ISBN 978-1-032-90822-9

List of Tables

Emerging Horizons: Business and Society in the Post Pandemic Era –
Brig. Dr. Rajiv Divekar et al. (eds)
© 2024 Taylor & Francis Group, London, ISBN 978-1-032-90822-9

Foreword

It is a pleasure to present the proceedings of the SIMSARC22 conference, focused on the theme "Pandemic to Endemic: Propositions for the Future." This year's conference brought together experts from around the world to discuss the challenges and opportunities as we move from a pandemic to an endemic phase of COVID-19. The theme highlights the need to rethink our approaches to health, economy, education, and social systems after the pandemic. The papers in this volume offer practical solutions and new ideas from the contributors. The insights and research presented here are intended to inform and inspire continued discourse and action towards a resilient and sustainable future.

Dr Kelvin Lee Yong Ming
School of Accounting & Finance
Faculty of Business & Law
Taylor's University, Malaysia

Foreword

Emerging Horizons: Business and Society in the Post Pandemic Era –
Brig. Dr. Rajiv Divekar et al. (eds)
© 2024 Taylor & Francis Group, London, ISBN 978-1-032-90822-9

Preface

The COVID-19 pandemic dominated our lives since its outbreak in the year 2020. The whole economy was disrupted, and businesses and society had to adapt to the new normal. Since the last two years, the release of different vaccines and the vaccination drive have helped to contain the pandemic to quite an extent. It is believed that irrespective of the different doses of vaccination and its impact on the citizens, the virus is here to stay and will translate into an endemic. An endemic situation is where the COVID-19 virus will be confined to certain people and regions. The COVID-19 pandemic drastically impacted businesses, which had to move from a physical mode to an online mode and hybrid mode. While several steps were taken to contain the pandemic, its lasting effect made organizations and society rethink the future. Organizations have moved from offline to hybrid mode and now work from home. The propositions in sales have changed from price to consumer well-being and convenience. Consumers have become health conscious. Healthcare has become a necessity, and healthcare companies are taking different steps to penetrate the market with immunity boosters. Education is now offered extensively through digital media and has become another alternative. The conference theme, "Pandemic to Endemic: Propositions for the Future," aims to identify the initiatives businesses and society will adopt for their sustained growth and development. The book provides research insights on how organizations should deal with endemic situations in different business areas. This book includes research in finance, marketing, human resources, healthcare, economics, education, and general management, such as leadership and decision-making.

Research in the area of marketing covers insights related to virtual reality, branding, entertainment, service quality, purchase decisions, and customer relationship management. One study explored the role of virtual reality (VR) on individuals' intention to visit destinations. The study found that VR significantly influences individuals' emotional involvement and mental imagery. Another study focused on the impact of emotional branding on consumers' buying behaviour towards AMUL dairy products: with particular reference to Vadodara City. This paper reflects the study undertaken to understand the response and how a consumer behaves in a particular situation when emotional branding is done by AMUL Dairy, with Vadodara City being the center for sampling. The paper sheds light on the impact of emotional branding on various aspects of developing a brand like AMUL and the adoption of this model by the dairy industry. Interesting research on the entertainment industry uncovered the challenges faced during the pandemic, like paused/ delayed productions, canceled shows, and economic crises, and discussed the well-being of the cast and crew.

Service quality is another critical area of marketing. A research paper presented at the conference discussed customer satisfaction of Delhi Metro commuters, indicating high satisfaction with cleanliness and security while suggesting the need for improvement in physical conditions, comfort, connectivity, information, availability and accessibility, price, and reliability. Over the years, the role of green marketing has gained significant importance. One study focused on customer awareness, intention, and purchase behavior in India regarding green marketing strategies and established positive associations between gender, age, education, consumer awareness, and intention. In the transition from pandemic to endemic, the relationship between shopper demography and online store preference makes an interesting study. One study examined the relationship between demographic characteristics and preference for a specific online store and found a significant association.

The volatility of the markets in the transition from pandemic to endemic has caught the attention of several researchers. The researchers have focused on different aspects of finance and economics. A study on profitability in Indian public sector banks revealed that profitability increased with an increase in the liquidity ratio, deposits ratio, capital adequacy ratio, asset quality, and asset management but decreased with an increase in the leverage ratio. These findings will assist bankers, policymakers, financiers, and investors in making better financial decisions and improve the nation's banking infrastructure. In economics, Quantum servitization catches the eye in the research field of servitization. A bibliometric analysis with detailed citations and network analysis gave a fair idea about leading researchers, universities, and their networks in this field. The P2P lending has also gained importance in the endemic situation. A study on this topic provided critical input for analyzing ventures in the P2P lending ecosystem and their valuations as diverse stakeholders in making critical financial decisions with long- and short-term impacts. Another interesting study emphasizes the role of financial literacy and the gender gap in financial decision-making. This research explores whether households in India have the intellect, capability, and knowledge to make well-informed and better decisions related to savings, investments, and borrowing decisions such as loans.

The pandemic and the endemic situation have made us realize the importance of healthcare. A study on anemia and health focuses on the population study of three districts of Amreli named Lathi, Liliya, and Babra in Gujarat, India. This study aims to recognize the impact of demographic factors on health, especially anemia, among rural people of the selected district. The endemic situation has also helped create social entrepreneurs, and extensive research is being conducted on sustainability for future community development.

The book will be helpful for various target groups. For the research community, it will help to understand current trends in research, re-look at the existing theories in different areas of study in the context of endemic situations, and identify new research areas. The book will help the academic community to incorporate research inputs in their classroom teaching, which helps to prepare students for their future careers. The behavioural changes amongst consumers and employees, like the high adoption of digital technology in all walks of life, have implications for business, which calls for deeper understanding and articulation of the phenomenon. The challenge of Covid 19 has led to the realization of the interconnectedness of various disciplines in management. During crises, academicians and industry looked for more holistic solutions with implications across countries. Any economic, social, medical, technological, process, or business innovation to protect or help in the progression of humanity and other life will see faster adoption than before. For industry practitioners, the book will provide information and guidance on how to adapt to global challenges. It will highlight the importance of good business practices and preparedness to respond and recover from crises. It will also encourage businesses to look for new opportunities amidst crisis. It will address the challenge from the lens of different management domains and propose holistic suggestions taking into account all stakeholders. The book will also benefit society by creating heightened awareness regarding the current state of affairs related to Covid-19 and help the general public deal with the future crisis. For policymakers, the book highlights the importance of investing in public health infrastructure to ensure the continuity of operations in the event of future outbreaks. It also provides concrete ideas for addressing the pandemic's long-term implications and preventing future outbreaks. It will bring to the forefront major lacuna in existing policy related to healthcare and identify the gaps that need to be addressed. The book will provide a comprehensive and practical guide for preparing for and addressing the long-term implications of the pandemic, benefiting all stakeholders involved in pandemic response and preparedness.

Emerging Horizons: Business and Society in the Post Pandemic Era –
Brig. Dr. Rajiv Divekar et al. (eds)
© 2024 Taylor & Francis Group, London, ISBN 978-1-032-90822-9

Acknowledgements

Symbiosis Institute of Management Studies would like to thanks the authors, editors, reviewers, and Ms Dipali More, organising secretary, for their constant support in publication process.

Emerging Horizons: Business and Society in the Post Pandemic Era –
Brig. Dr. Rajiv Divekar et al. (eds)
© 2024 Taylor & Francis Group, London, ISBN 978-1-032-90822-9

About the Editors

1. Brig. (Dr.) Rajiv Divekar

Brig (Dr.) Rajiv Divekar is the Director of Symbiosis Institute of Management Studies for the last 12 years. SIMS is amongst the top ranked B-schools in India which is over 27 years old. Prior to this he was Head of Faculty Strategic and Operational Studies at Army War College and Faculty member in Defence Strategic Studies at Defence Services Staff College, Wellington. He has done his PhD from Symbiosis International University. He is a M. Phil from D A V V University and MSc from Madras University. A Gold medallist in BE (civil), he has done his MBA specializing in Human Resource Management. He has rich experience of strategy, planning, logistics and human resource management based on his service with multinational teams as part of United Nations Force in both Somalia and Lebanon. He has served in Kargil and Leh on the LoC where he was responsible for the Logistics and Supply Chain Management for soldiers located on posts at 17,000- 22,000 feet in the Siachen Glacier.

He has a large number of research publications in National & International Journals & also in Scopus listed Journals. He is also a reviewer for a journal which is indexed in SCOPUS.

Under his leadership and guidance, SIMS has been organising an Annual International Research Conference for last 11 years. He teaches Strategy, Human Resource and Leadership to MBA students and has been invited to deliver talks at various organisations and institutes as also to deliver key note address in conferences.

He is a recipient of many awards in the field of education. He has been awarded "The Rashtriya Vidya Gaurav Gold Medal" by the Indian Solidarity Council, the "Rajiv Gandhi Education Excellence Award" by International Institute of Education and Management and the "Education Leadership Award" by Education Leadership Awards, Dubai.

2. Dr. Komal Chopra

Dr. Komal Chopra is an Associate Professor of Marketing at Symbiosis Institute of Management Studies, Symbiosis International (Deemed University), Pune, India. He has more than 16 years of experience in academics. Dr. Komal Chopra has taught subjects such as Retail Management, Consumer Behaviour, and

Essentials of Marketing to post-graduate students. He has conducted management development programmes for Godrej & Boyce, Wipro, John Deere, Cognizant and Directorate General of Resettlement, Government of India. He has also delivered guest sessions at the University of Witwatersrand, South Africa, and Kathmandu University. He has done research and consultancy projects for Ministry of Corporate Affairs, ICSSR, Tata Motors, Springer Nature and Bilcare Research. He has published many research papers in ABDC and Scopus ranked journals and is a reviewer for Asia Pacific Journal of Marketing and Logistics, International Journal of Emerging Markets, Sage OPEN, Emerald Emerging Markets Case Studies, International Journal of Retail & Distribution Management, Journal of Applied Research in Higher Education, Foresight and Health Education. He has also won the best research paper award at international conferences. He is a PhD guide at Symbiosis International (Deemed University) and PhD referee at the University of Witwatersrand, South Africa. He is an ISO 9001:2015 certified auditor and Co-Convener of SIMS Annual Research Conference.

3. Dr Smita Mehendale

Dr. Smita Mehendale is an Assistant Professor with Symbiosis Institute of Management Studies, Symbiosis International (Deemed University), Pune She has 18+ years of experience in diverse functions like finance, marketing and HR and across industries and educational institutions. She has worked in manufacturing, service sector and consultancy before stepping into academics. She has done her PhD from SPPU, Pune in online retailing. She teaches Research Methodology, Retail Management and Marketing Research at SIMS. She is passionate about training and has conducted sessions for FMCG, healthcare, financial services and educational institutions like Cargill, L&T, Nikita Distributers, SVM, St. Mira's, BMCC, SVIMS. She has presented numerous papers in international conferences and won best paper awards. She has conducted Faculty Development Programmes and is the co-convener of SIMSARC22

4. Dr. Pravin Kumar Bhoyar

Dr. Pravin Kumar Bhoyar is a Professor and Deputy Director at Symbiosis Institute of Management Studies (SIMS), Pune, for the last 17 years. His educational qualifications include BE (Production), an MBA and PhD. He has had 27 research papers published in national and international journals, including ABDC and Scopus. He, along with other researchers, has completed five research projects sponsored by the National Foundation for Corporate Governance (NFCG) over the last five years. His book, 'Effectiveness of FMCG Distribution Channels', was published in LAP LAMBERT Academic Publishing, Germany (2013 edition). Also, a case study — 'Millennium Company Ltd: Overcoming Tough Times' — was published in Emerald Markets Case Studies in 2014.

Emerging Horizons: Business and Society in the Post Pandemic Era –
Brig. Dr. Rajiv Divekar et al. (eds)
© *2024 Taylor & Francis Group, London, ISBN 978-1-032-90822-9*

1

Analyzing Profitability Drivers in Indian Public Sector Banks

Dinkar Nayak[1]
RBI Chair Professor (Rtd)
Faculty of Commerce,
The Maharaja Sayajirao University of Baroda

Rubina Barodawala[2]
Assistant Professor
School of Doctoral Research and Innovation
GLS University

ABSTRACT

This paper seeks to explore the complex network of factors affecting public sector banks' profitability in India. It aims to find the association between the equity returns (ROE) and the asset returns (ROA) with a host of independent variables with Indian banks over a period from January 2005 through December 2021. Through the use of panel data analysis, the study seeks to reveal some tough relationships that may be lurking beneath financial performance in these institutions.

The study offers persuasive interpretations of a rise in the liquidity ratio, deposits ratio, capital adequacy ratio, asset quality, and asset management which corresponds to a favorable trajectory in profitability. Besides, the analysis indicates a reverse relationship will emerge between profitability and debt.

This has an effect on being able to assist the key stakeholders such as bankers, regulators, financiers and investors in their decision-making processes, which would be far beyond the realms of the academic fraternity. A better understanding of these complexities and how they interrelate one with another will pave the way for these stakeholders to provide support in making informed decisions for a better financial health. Furthermore, the knowledge gained from this research is well-positioned to make a significant contribution toward improving the country's banking system and building a stronger and more resilient financial ecosystem.

KEYWORDS: Profitability ratios, Indian public sector banks, Panel data analysis
JEL Code: G20, G29

[1]dn_nayak2002@yahoo.com, [2]rubina150991@gmail.com

DOI: 10.4324/978100355996-1

1. Introduction

The Reserve Bank of India (RBI) has over the last three decades played a vital role in the implementation of banking reforms that will enhance efficiency, stability, effectiveness, and profitability in the banks. It has come up with a financial system that will be able to endure oscillations that may be encountered in the economy. The important objectives in implementing these reforms are twofold - upgrading the standard of regulations and instilling the competitive spirit among the banks to deliver their best performance. The RBI seeks to fortify banks with adequate resilience for mitigating risks and for safeguarding depositors and investors' interest, with a view to bolster regulatory frameworks. Simultaneously it incentivises banks by promoting a healthy competition causing them to operate with increased efficiency, innovation and adaptability towards altered market dynamics and also contributes vibrantly towards the economic growth and development in the country.

As a corollary of the Financial and banking reforms and liberalization, there has been intense competition, technological advancement, international integration, and the creation of new banking products. A market-based banking system was facilitated by the legislative change brought about by these reforms since it made it easier for foreign and private sector banks to operate in the country. All these developments must have had some effect on bank profitability and performance, it is logical to presume. Therefore, the management of banks as well as other stakeholders must understand the underlying causes that affect banks' profitability. Over the past few years, several significant developments have left a lasting impact on banking operations in India. These include issues such as non-performing assets (NPAs), the demonetization drive, the Digital India initiative, the rise of payment wallets, the implementation of the Goods and Services Tax (GST), and the establishment of payment banks. The public sector banks which have dominated the Indian scenario for decades are now facing the heat. The elements that affect bank profitability and the determinants of bank performance have drawn more attention to studies in the banking industry in general because of this. In the above backdrop, it has become essential to identify the bank-specific variables affecting the profitability of public sector banks in India since they cover almost 70 per cent of the banking operations in the country.

The paper unfolds as follows: first, it delves into a review of pertinent literature. Following this, the research methodology is elucidated, and subsequent sections offer results. Finally, concluding thoughts are presented to encapsulate the discussion.

2. Literature Review

Internal or bank-specific attributes and external or macroeconomic drivers make up the factors that affect a bank's profitability. The internal variables include the quality of the bank's assets, capitalization, non-traditional business lines, managerial capability, liquidity, and scale. On the other side, the external factors include inflation, economic growth, exchange rate, interest rate, and money supply. As bank-specific factors are asserted to be the primary factor affecting a bank's profitability in this paper we have considered these factors to analyze the impact of these factors on the profitability of the banks in India.

The examination of how financial factors impact the banks efficiency has its origins in the 1980s, with Amandeep (1983) employing regression analysis to meticulously analyze various factors influencing profitability. Amandeep applied trend analysis and ratio analysis to scrutinize the operations of India's scheduled commercial banks, identifying key factors that played a pivotal role in determining their profitability. In a parallel exploration, Mishra (1992) delved into the profitability dynamics of commercial banks, encompassing factors such as interest bearing income and non-interest bearing income, expenditure made on interest, labor costs, and other miscellaneous expenses. Mishra argued that the diminishing profitability observed in Indian commercial banks could be attributed to an escalation in fund preemption through liquidity ratios and cash reserve ratios, in comparison to income, advances, and total investments relative to interest revenue.

In their evaluation of Indian banks from 2004–2005, Satish et al. (2005) employed the CAMEL model to study the efficacy of 55 banks. Their findings suggested that the Indian banking system, driven by technological advancements, will exhibit robustness and an optimistic outlook for future growth. The authors have also expressed confidence that information technology will go a long way to fortify the banking system in the times ahead. Similarly, Bhayani (2006) utilized the CAMEL model to analyze the efficacy of newly established private banks. His investigation revealed that these private banks were performing satisfactorily within the Indian financial landscape.

Singla (2008) discussed the growth of India's banking sector and the important role played by financial management in doing so. He studied a total of sixteen banks over seven years highlighting the vital role of profitability during those years as compared to the previous years. Pat (2009) examined different groups of banks, highlighting financial ratios such as net profit, return on assets (ROA), and return on equity. The study observed enhancements in net profit margin, and return on assets and equity.

In contrast, Barua et al. (2017) found that factors other than profitability like market capitalisation, credit risk, ownership structure and leverage determine Indian banks viability. They also hinted at diminishing importance of banks' market capitalisation and profitability. Meanwhile, Brahmaiah and Ranajee (2018) considered a balanced panel dataset for the years 2005-2015 in their elaborate study. The independent variables, which represented various factors that influence the efficacy of commercial banks, were categorized into internal and external factors. Internal factors such as equity capital strength, operational efficiency, and the banking sector deposit-to-GDP ratio positively affect profitability. Conversely, factors such as cost of funds, consumer price index, credit risk, inflation and non-performing assets had an unfavorable influence on profitability. Al-Homaidi et al. (2018) in their study included factors that are related to banks along with considering macroeconomic variables to discern factors affecting the Indian commercial banks as a whole. Their study revealed that, all bank-specific characteristics except the number of branches had a positive and significant impact on profitability measured by net interest margin (NIM). In addition to this, their study also found that all macroeconomic variables considered in their study had large negative impacts on the profitability of Indian commercial banks.

Mahajan (2018) studied profitability in banks of India and concluded that around sixty per cent of variations in asset returns are explained by independent bank specific variables considered in the study. Kuknor and Rastogi (2021) studied the relationship between bank regulations on profitability and using non-performing assets on profitability of banks. The result derived using the panel analysis across Indian banks for five years showed a positive impact on regulations and negative impact on non-performing assets.

The studies discussed earlier have considered a myriad of micro and macro factors when examining the factors affecting bank profitability. The collective body of research underscores the nuanced influence of both internal and external factors on varying scales in shaping bank profitability. External determinants, rooted in industry and economic dynamics, stand independent of direct bank management, and significantly impact the overall performance and operation of the banking sector. Conversely, internal determinants constitute micro-level, factors that are specific to banks that have a pivotal impact in determining profitability.

Within the spectrum of findings, certain studies indicate a positive correlation between profitability of the banks and its determinants such as larger capital ratios, elevated interest rate margins, higher inflation rates, operational efficiency, and increased revenue generated out of non-interest income. Conversely, an adverse correlation is observed with higher credit risk and increased cost of capital. However, an alternative strand of research suggests that macroeconomic factors wield significant influence, exerting a detrimental effect on the profitability of Indian commercial banks.

Notably, the existing literature faces a lack of definitive consensus on the relationship between profitability and its drivers. Moreover, the most recent statistical data has not been fully integrated into the existing body of research to offer a contemporary reflection on the intricate interplay between profitability and its determinants. This study seeks to contribute by addressing this gap and providing a fresh perspective on the evolving dynamics of the relationship between profitability of the Indian commercial banks and its multifaceted drivers.

3. Methodology

All the public sector bank data ranging from 2005 to 2021 was collected from the resources provided by the Reserve bank of India on its official website.

Independent Variables:

Profitability

Profitability, as a key banking metric, signifies the prowess of an organization in deriving profit from its various business activities. It is one crucial indication of how management has been adept in the deployment of available resources to earn revenue. To define the performance in bank management, profits are the most significant. Hence, profitability of the banking industry is highly linked to the overall performance of the banks. This makes the profitability metrics such as Returns on Assets (ROA) and Returns on Equity (ROE), which indicate the bank's ability to create profit, important in ascertaining the robustness of any bank.

Dependent Variables:

Liquidity:

Liquidity reflects the ability of a bank to fulfill its financial commitments as and when they become fallen due. An optimum level of liquidity needs to be maintained since inadequate liquidity may lead to falling profit. The higher the liquidity ratio, the better will be the improved financial strength for the bank. This metric is assessed by calculating the ratio of liquid assets to total assets.

Leverage:

Leverage acts as an indicator of the indebtedness of a bank and its capacity to meet its financial commitments. The leverage ratio exposes the relationship between capital/assets of a bank and its debt. This ratio is of great importance as it impacts very highly on the financial profile of the bank and is measured as a ratio of total debt to total assets.

Deposits:

Bank deposits signify the funds entrusted with the financial institutions for safe custody and the banks reliance on deposited funds in relation to overall assets. This is measured as the ratio of the total deposits to the total assets.

Capital Adequacy Ratio:

The Capital Adequacy Ratio (CAR) is a core measure that ensures a bank's ability to meet obligations and moreover serves as a foundation for mitigating operational and credit risk. An appropriate CAR guarantees adequate capital not only regarding the absorption of losses but also promoting viability, thereby ensuring the safety of customers' money on deposit.

Asset Quality:

The quality of the assets is a key determination of the bank's financial strength. It depicts the percentage of non-performing assets (NPAs) in terms of total assets. Asset Quality provides insights into the risk profile of the bank and is expressed as the ratio of loans to total assets.

Asset Management:

Effective management is essential to the long-term viability and expansion of a bank. The future development of the company is determined by the decisions made by management, which are impacted by perceptions of risk. The ratio of operational income to total assets, or asset management, represents how well the bank is able to steer toward its objectives.

These factors, which include profitability, liquidity, leverage, deposits, capital adequacy, asset quality, and asset management, constitute an all-encompassing picture of a bank's financial health. The complex interactions among these variables characterize the operational and financial environment of a bank.

Model

The study intends to investigate the impact of liquidity, leverage, deposits, capital adequacy, asset quality, and asset management on the profitability of public sector banks in India with the help of pooled regression analysis.

Equation 1:

The relationship between asset returns and variables such asset quality (aq), capital adequacy (car), liquidity (lq), leverage (lv), and asset management (am) is established in the first equation. The model's equation is outlined as follows:

$$roa = \alpha + \beta_1(lq) + \beta_2(lv) + \beta_3(car) + \beta_4(aq) + \beta_5(am) + \varepsilon \qquad (1)$$

Equation 2:

The relationship between returns on equity and the following variables is shown by this equation: asset quality (aq), asset management (am), capital adequacy (car), liquidity (lq), and leverage (lv). The model's equation is presented below:

$$roe = \alpha + \beta_1(lq) + \beta_2(lv) + \beta_3(car) + \beta_4(aq) + \beta_5(am) + \varepsilon \qquad (2)$$

In each of the equations, α serves as the intercept, and β_1, β_2, and so forth, denote the coefficients corresponding to the independent variables. The term ε is the error term.

4. Results

The Hausman specification test results for both equations are shown in Table 1.1.

The null hypothesis in the Hausman test posits that the random effects model is the preferred choice, while the alternative hypothesis asserts the presence of

Table 1.1 Hausman's specification test

Profitability measure	Chi-Square Statistic	Probability
ROA	7.52	0.27
ROE	7.81	0.25

Source: Authors estimation

fixed effects. Examining the table reveals a p-value exceeding 0.05 (at a 5 percent confidence level), prompting the rejection of the null hypothesis. Consequently, it is inferred that the random effects model is more suitable in both scenarios under consideration. The findings of the selected model have been identified based on the outcomes of the Hausman test conducted for public sector banks.

Table 1.2 The panel data analysis findings of returns on assets and equities, random effects

Variables	ROA	ROE
Liquidity	5.59*	67*
Leverage	-8.58*	-125*
Deposits	6.46*	98.7
Capital Adequacy	0.23*	4.13*
Asset Quality	2.54*	44.4*
Asset Management	30.76*	43*

Note: * denotes significance at 5%,
Source: Authors estimation

The outcomes presented in Table 1.2 stem from the application of the Hausman test to the random effects model. These results shed light on the significance of various independent variables—namely, liquidity, leverage, deposits, capital adequacy, asset quality, and asset management—in relation to the dependent variable, returns on assets.

Examining returns to assets, each independent variable demonstrates statistical significance. A noteworthy observation is that a one-unit increase in liquidity is associated with a positive 5.59-unit change in asset returns. Conversely, a one-unit change in leverage is linked to a negative 8.58-unit change in asset returns. Similarly, a one-unit increase in deposits corresponds to a positive 6.46-unit change in returns to assets. Additionally, a one-unit change in capital adequacy yields a positive 0.23-unit change in asset returns. Notably, both asset quality and asset management exhibit positive changes of 2.54 units and 30.76 units, respectively, for a one-unit increase, in relation to asset returns.

Turning to returns on equities, all explanatory variables, except deposits, demonstrate statistical significance. The variables considered include liquidity, leverage, deposits, capital adequacy, asset quality, and asset management, with returns on assets as the response variable. As depicted in the table, a one-unit increase in liquidity corresponds to a substantial positive 67-unit change in returns to assets. Conversely, a one-unit change in leverage results in a notable negative 125-unit change in returns to assets. Moreover, a one-unit rise in capital adequacy results in a positive 4.13-unit change in asset returns. It's noteworthy that both asset quality and asset management exhibit positive changes of 44.4 units and 43 units, respectively, for a one-unit increase in relation to asset returns.

5. Conclusions

Significant problems and notable changes have been seen in the Indian banking industry such as demonization, financial fraud, and sustainability which have an impact on how well Indian banks perform. Additionally, the deteriorating profitability over the past few years and the upward trajectory of balance sheet indicators, particularly deposits, borrowings, loans, and advances, raise serious concerns about the performance of Indian banks. This study looked at bank-specific factors that affected the profitability of all Indian public sector banks from 2005 to 2021. As dependent factors, ROA and ROE were chosen, whereas the internal bank-specific factors that are liquidity, leverage, deposit, capital adequacy, asset quality, and asset management were chosen as independent variables.

The results show that factors specific to banks—like deposits, asset quality, asset management, liquidity, and capital—have a positive impact on returns on assets (ROA). When it comes to the bank-specific components of profitability of Indian public sector banks as measured by returns on equity, the results demonstrate that liquidity, capital adequacy, asset quality, and asset management have a positive impact on equity returns. Furthermore, there exists an inverse relationship between leverage and the return on equity (ROE), which gauges the financial viability of public sector banks in India.

The study's conclusions have important repercussions for different stakeholders, such as lawmakers, bankers, regulators, and academics. The statement underscores the significance of these stakeholders concentrating on the intrinsic components of banks, as they greatly influence the performance dynamics of public sector banks in India alongside the extrinsic factors.

The meticulous examination and administration of deposit and liquidity ratios need to receive increased focus in order to enhance the overall performance of Indian banks. Furthermore, stakeholders—bankers and regulators in particular—are encouraged to have more in-depth conversations about significant bank-specific criteria. This calls for expanding the equity financing portfolio as opposed to debt financing, decreasing the amount of money invested in operations, and effectively managing capital resources. Those who work in the banking sector, such as managers and bankers, are counseled to concentrate on the distinctive features that every bank has. Effective management practices and the prudent use of resources are made possible by this strategic approach, which not only maximizes efficiency but also significantly improves the bank's financial performance. This study essentially asks for a reevaluation of priorities and resource allocation since it highlights the importance of crucial elements that impact the operational environment of Indian public sector banks and hence encourage heightened financial resilience.

REFERENCES

1. Al-Homaidi, E., Mosab I. Tabash, Najib H. S. Farhan & Faozi A. Almaqtari. (2018). Bank-specific and macro-economic determinants of profitability of Indian commercial banks: A panel data approach, Cogent Economics & Finance, 6 (1), https://doi.org/10.1080/23322039.2018.1548072
2. Amandeep. (1983). Profits and Profitability in Commercial Banks. Deep & Deep Publications, New Delhi.
3. Barua, R., Roy, M. and Raychaudhuri, A. (2017). Structure, conduct and performance analysis of Indian Commercial Bank. South Asian Journal of Macroeconomics and Public Finance, 5(2), 157–185.
4. Bhayani, S.J. (2006). Performance of the New Indian Private Sector Banks: a comparative study. ICFAI Journal of Management, Research, 5(11), 53–70.
5. Brahmaiah, B. and Ranajee. (2018). Factors influencing profitability of banks in India. Theoretical Economics Letters, 8, 3046–3061. doi: 10.4236/tel.2018.814189.
6. Hausman, J.A. (1978). Specification tests in econometrics. Econometrica, 46(6), 1251–1271.
7. Kuknor, S and Rastogi, S. (2021). Determinants of profitability in Indian banks: a panel data analysis. International Journal of Modern Agriculture, 10(2), 978–986.
8. Mahajan, Poonam. (2018). A Panel Data Analysis of Profitability Determinants: Empirical study of Indian Public and Private Sector Banks. MERC Global's International Journal of Management, 6(3), 47–59.
9. Mishra, M.N. (1992). Analysis of profitability of commercial banks. Indian Journal of Banking and Finance, 5.
10. Pat, K.A. (2009). Why Indian banks are healthy in this global crisis? Economic and Political Weekly, 44(17), 21–22.
11. Satish, D., Sharath, J. and Surender, V. (2005). Indian banking – performance and development 2004–05. Chartered Financial Analyst, 11(10), 6–15.
12. Singla, H.K. (2008). Financial performance of banks in India. The IUP Journal of Bank Management, 1, 50–62, available at: https://ideas.repec.org/a/icf/icfjbm/v7y2008i1p50-62.html

Emerging Horizons: Business and Society in the Post Pandemic Era –
Brig. Dr. Rajiv Divekar et al. (eds)
© *2024 Taylor & Francis Group, London, ISBN 978-1-032-90822-9*

2

Does Virtual Reality Experience Affects Tourists Visit Intentions?

Sudin Bag[1]

Assistant Professor,
Department of Business Administration,
Vidyasagar University,

Kousik Mandal[2]

Research Scholar,
Department of Business Administration,
Vidyasagar University,

ABSTRACT

Virtual Reality (VR) promises to create a new wave of technology in consumer marketing. Virtual reality allows companies to communicate and attract potential consumers. The Travel & Tourism industry also uses virtual reality technology as a collaborative & communication tool to communicate with travelers to select their destination. In the travel and tourism technology domain, the researchers focused on how users adopt technology-oriented services in the tourism industry, especially mobile and e-based services. But this study investigates how VR can provide integrated tourism experiences before they visit the destination and the intention to recommend VR experience. Also, the study will examine the effect of mental imagination and emotional involvement in selecting the destination using virtual reality technology. The path model reveals that the perceived VR interactivity and perceived visual appeal stimuli directly relate to the intention to visit a new destination. Moreover, the study found that stimuli significantly influence the organism's emotional involvement and mental imagery. In addition, the result of the study depicts that the intention to visit significantly influences the intention to recommend VR experiences by VR users.

KEYWORDS: Virtual reality, Mental imagery, Emotional involvement, Intention to visit, Consumer marketing

[1]sudinmba@mail.vidyasagar.ac.in, [2]kousikmandal1997@outlook.com,

DOI: 10.4324/978100355996-2

1. Introduction

In the age of visual information, vision is the most direct and fastest sensitive channel for a person to get information. Lots of feelings are influenced by the initial visual perception. From tourists' point of view, visual information can unconsciously influence their best behaviour. In the tourism industry, informative communication plays an essential role due to its intangibility in nature. Virtual Reality (VR) is mitigating the information required for tourists at this new juncture. Continuous innovations of technologies have an excellent effect on the tourism sector, promoting the tourism industry in the right way. For instance, virtual reality's visual appeal significantly impacts the promotion of the tourism business in the 21st century. Virtual Reality can be described as a most important technological innovation that pulls the consumers to the reality of a particular destination. The tourism market gets a new upward trend in selling different packages. By applying VR technology, the tourism industry is using different three-dimensional (3D) images and 360° videos, which can affect tourists' mind to select a destination to visit.

Moreover, VR leads to tourists' satisfaction, loyalty, desire to revisit and behavioural changes in the form of tourists recommendations. The existence of VR in hotel experience, including adventure activities, destination branding, and cultural heritage places, the applicability of VR has pervaded various travel industries. The relevance of VR in different sectors depends upon the adjuration that technology can renovate experience and ultimately influence tourists' behaviour. Inimitable VR features of vitality and interactivity can deliver new ways to engage and persuade customers (Nah et al., 2011). In 2020, Statista forecasted that the AR and VR market would be growing to a $160 billion market by 2023.

Tourists can experience the destination before they visit with the help of three-dimensional (3D) technology by creating a virtual form of the physical world through Virtual Reality technology. VR milieu can be considered a virtual space where a person's activities or actions are traced, and surrounding environments are digitally formed and exhibited to the individual to stimulate their right mind according to their activities and reactions. Therefore, by enabling consumers in a VR environment to block evidence from the "real" world, consumers should be offered an alternative world so they can be completely engrossed in the virtual ecosystem (Fox et al., 2009). A computer-mediated environment can enable a sagacity of virtual reality existence that refers to a state where a person feels like being there or a state in which a person can feel like being bodily existing in a virtual milieu. Therefore, the individual senses like they have been getting rid of the natural world to becoming engrossed in a substitute simulated world. The details of the present literature propose that the sensitivity of existence experienced through VR could have an optimistic impact on tourists' experience and stimulus tourists' intentions to visit a holiday destination. Communicating sensitive info into VR experiences can stimulate tourists' attitudes toward a holiday destination;

consequently, VR plays a remarkable role in destination branding and promotion. However, with budding curiosity, tourists and travel marketers are trusted with the appearance of a destination over a website that demonstrates primary non-dynamic metaphors of the goal. While basic destination images can only present vibrant non-verbal information to tourists, VR can provide a wide range of verbal and nonverbal sensory information and mental imagination. As VR is sensitive and media-rich content compared to other nonverbal previews, VR offers an essentially different understanding of consuming destination info. But, despite VR's ability to present such sensitive rich report, VR experiences may differ meaningfully in the level of their sensitive information.

Therefore, there is a tremendous curiosity to use VR as a pre-experience destination advertising instrument. Prior studies on the tourism industry have improved our knowledge of how the stimulus of mental metaphors through VR can enhance the experience of a tourism product (Bogicevic et al., 2019). Therefore, the study has dual purposes: the first is to know the role of VR in tourists' emotional involvement and mental imagery about a holiday destination selection, and the second aims is to know the impact of various levels of sensitive information conferred through VR on the advancement of mental imagery, emotional involvement and visit intention towards the destination. The VR experiences allowed tourists to discover visiting attractive spots in the destination and plunge themselves into the holiday destination. Thus, this study develops a theoretical understanding on VR, the importance of intrinsic sensitive information in VR, and its usefulness in tourism sector. This study also has hands-on implications for marketers. This is because tourism marketers are excited to gather more knowledge about VR, which doesn't just help them to elevate the company's brand equity but also be effective for designing more impactful communication strategies.

2. Theoretical Framework & Hypotheses Development Perceived Interactivity

Since interactivity is a significant distinction in marketing communication, tourism advertising interactivity is crucial to fascinate tourist attention towards visit intention a holiday destination. Therefore, tourists' insight into tourism advertisement interactivity is among the most significant features of this medium. Interactivity is specified as the capability of tourists to alter the fabricated content and form of the intermediary environment in actual time (Steuer, 1992). The existing research on e-commerce, interactivity is extensively observed from the viewpoint of intercommunication among customers and products. Perceived Interactivity also relates to tourists' online trust and their higher intent to engage with the media when they trust it.

Moreover, interactivity improves users' experience by enhancing perceived ease of use (PEOU). In the travel industry, perceived interactivity is a critical factor that leads to PEOU of digital marketing and an uplifting system of booking, including making payments (SanMartín et al., 2012; Park &Gretzel, 2007). On the same line, Marrison et al. (2023) suggested that perceived interactivity remarkably benefits the tourists' PEOU of AR technology. So, according to the literature, our subsequent hypotheses are mentioned below:

H1a: Perceived Interactivity positively affects tourists' emotional involvement.

H1b: Perceived Interactivity positively influences tourists' mental imagery.

H2: Perceived Interactivity with an advertisement featured has an optimistic effect on tourists' intention to visit.

3. Perceived Visual Appeal

Due to the rising curiosity in the empirical facets of tourists' sentimentality and technology-mediated use (Carù & Cova, 2007), the inspiration of various quality facets of technology on tourists' feelings has acknowledged the consideration by scholars in the province of human-computer interface. According to Pohlmeyer & Blessing (2011), technology's high standards and tempting presence might be considered a precondition of emotional engagement. The desire to apply technology relies on the amalgamation of purposeful and pragmatic qualities; users are contented with technology because of its intuitive interface, sound quality, gratifying experience and emotional attachment. Concerning VR, the visual component can enhance the mesmeric emotional consequence of VR; subsequently, the eminence of 3D images can enhance the emotional state of tourists in the virtual milieu (Guttentag, 2010). Moreover, Wu et al. (2016) examined the association between visual, acoustic and sensible impetus in VR systems and persuasive emotions among users. It observed that the impact of visual stimulus on emotion is higher than the acoustic and rational facets.

Similarly, Hyun & O'Keefe (2012) argued that virtual cognitive leads to generating users' images of virtual emotion. Furthermore, Reiners et al. (2014) claimed that with the overview of generation-Z Head-Mounted Displays (HMDs), similar to Oculus Rift, huge mesmerizing and trustworthy virtual milieus can be fabricated that stimulate states of real-world emotion and states of mind. Thus, the perceived visual appeal can positively influence tourists' emotional involvement, mental imagery and visit intention. Therefore, the following hypotheses are designed to measure the relationships.

H3a: Perceived visual appeal influences tourists' emotional involvement.

H3b: Perceived visual appeal influences the mental imagery of tourists.

H4: Perceived Visual appeal while watching an advertisement has an optimistic effect on tourists' intention to visit.

4. Mental Imagery

Mental Imagery is considered a critical organism part, an internal imagining procedure that activates in the mind of tourists. Mental Imagery stimulates trust and feeling associated with tourists' experience in a pictographic mode (MacInnis & Price, 1987). In this line, Miller et al. (2000) proposed a scale to estimate mental imagery with three fundamental dimensions vividness, quantity and valence. Vividness is defined as image quality, which includes lucidity, intensity and uniqueness that emerges in individuals. The interpretations of the emotional connotation are associated with concrete reminiscences that represent the meaning of mental imagery, which carries either positive or negative connotations that direct to valence (Lee et al., 2012).

While processing information of mental imagery, the moment the numerous images come into our mind refers to the quantity (McGill & Anand 1989). The mental imagery process involves multiple concepts and constructs, limited to the simple retrieval or innovation of a cognitive image like problem-solving, creative thinking and daydreaming. We develop psychological metaphors based on our experience or existing information when we visualise something. Travel marketing studies recognized mental imagery as the vital driver that explores consumers' positive outcomes (Lee &Gretzel, 2012). Moreover, mental images depend on the vibrancy of the image and interact with substances in the virtual milieu. Virtual Reality facilitates mental imagery processing with the unique technical characteristics of vibrancy and interactivity. Rather than traditional advertising, if the pictures or videos of the destination are presented in VR, it will increase the interest in the destination (i.e., telepresence) and visualizing travel to the destination will develop (i.e., mental imagery). Moreover, telepresence mediates the mental image formation in virtual arena (Hyun & O'Keefe, 2012). The perceived mechanism of construction of the image that is reflected in the developed concept of the mental image has not been examined. Telepresence is an important psychological condition that convinces one to enter the virtual world. But the term mental imagery refers to information processing in users' memory.

Similarly, Bogicevic et al. (2019) argued that telepresence is the supremacy of greater involvement in mental imagery than others. Therefore, when one experiences telepresence and is immersed in the virtual, they are expected to be involved in mental imagery. Therefore, to identify the impact of mental imagery on visit intention of tourists, H5 is proposed.

H5: Tourists' mental imagery while viewing an advertisement has positively influenced tourists' visit intention.

5. Emotional Involvement

Emotion is essential to understand better humans connecting to their destination. Thus, emotional involvement is the mirror image of the mental bond between tourists and destinations, which may stimulate tourists to dedicate their intent to visit the holiday destination (Gross & Brown, 2008). Similarly, Laurent &Kapferer (1985)argued that involvement is an activity or product-related psychological state of interest, motivation and stimulation. Along the same line, Gursoy, D. & E. Gavcar (2003) designated that using the concept of individual involvement in tourism is not so remarkable because of its difficulty. Holsapple and Wu (2007) established a theoretic outline based on elements of imaginary and emotional responses, explaining users' virtual reality experience. They found that dimensions of emotional involvement are more effective in understanding why tourists want to interact to virtual platforms, implying the degree of 'individual emotional engagement in behaviour'. However, McGehee et al. (2003) contend that emotional involvement is important in understanding tourists' behaviour and the decision-making process toward a destination.

Although some research has been done on the emotional involvement of tourists in different travel contexts, there has been some empirical research into the emotional involvement process of engaging in the destination VR experience. Therefore, pursues if the study is to explore the emotional involvement of tourists for its relationship with the tourists' interactivity and visual appeal of VR experience and visit intention to a holiday destination.

H6: Emotional involvement of tourists has positively influenced tourists' intention to visit.

6. Intention to Visit and Recommended to VR Experience

The term 'visit intention' or intention to visit can be defined as a rational choice and a systemic process of decision-making (Hennessey et al. 2010). According to, Kaplanidou et al. (2006), the intent is expected to forecast their actual behaviour precisely. The prior studies on tourists' behavioural intentions show a happy relationship between their attitudes and their purpose or buying behaviours (Armitage et al., 2000). This line of the study confronts the concept that tourists' behavioural intention is elucidated by their intentions to choose a holiday destination. However, factors like travel provocations (advertisement) and outlying variables (image) play a vital role in tourists' intentions to visit a holiday destination (Zhang et al., 2014).

In addition, the term intention to recommend VR experience refers to people with sound knowledge and sweetened experience with VR; they share personal experiences with peers and close mates. The study conducted by Grappi et al. (2011) profound that a tourist recommended their sweetest tourist experiences to others. Therefore, we can hypothesize that:

H7: Tourists who intend to visit are highly optimistic about recommending the VR experience.

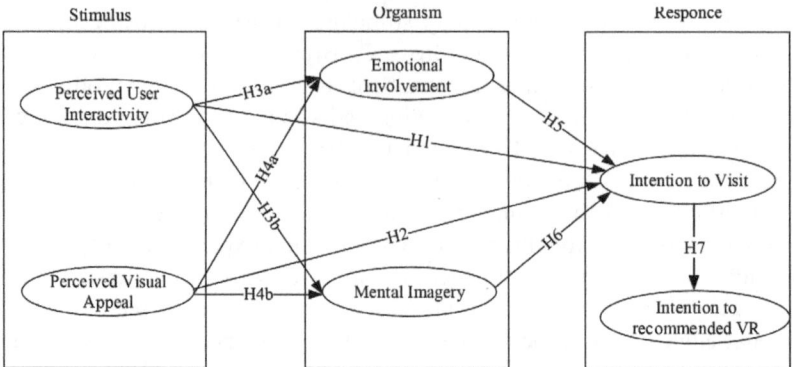

Fig. 2.1 Theoretical framework

Source: Authors' own work

7. Method

7.1 Research Questionnaire and Respondents Profile

The present study's multi-measurement scale was designed to avoid measurement errors. The measurement scales of each construct were taken from present literature to match the objectives of research and purpose. After that, a pilot survey was conducted and based on the pilot survey result questionnaire was revised and improved. Lastly, 33 items for six constructs were considered based on literature review and practical research.

Perceived visual appeal was studied using six scales taken from Chang et al. (2015). After that, the items were slightly modified to make the perfect fit for our study. Perceived Interactivity was evaluated using four items proposed by McMillan et al. (2002) and Liu et al. (2016) and altered to fit our study. The scales of Emotional involvement were taken from Saeed et al. (2009) and modified according to our research. Mental Imagery was assessed by three scales taken from Lee et al. (2012) and revised the items to fit our study. The measurement scale for the visit intention was taken from Kozak et al. (2001) and Tan et al. (2016) and revised to fit our study. The measurement scale of intention to recommend VR experience was adapted from the study of Xu et al. (2018) and Hosnay et al. (2013) and modified the items to fit this study.

7.2 Sample Characteristics

The study's sample size is 265 out of 274, which exceeded the minimum number of samples of 138 according to the G*Power 3.1, with five predictors, 0.05 as the value of λ, 95% power, and an effect size of 0.15.

Regarding the sample structure of the respondent group, 70% of respondents were male, 30% were female, and almost one-third of respondents, i.e. 66%, in the age bracket of 20 – 30 yrs, 21% respondents in the age bracket of 30-40 yrs. The highest qualification of most respondents, 59%, was post-graduate. Regarding marital status, 71% were single, and 29% were married. Regarding the distribution of occupations, 43% of people were private service holders, 22% had specialized jobs or other occupations, and 14% had govt. jobs. Regarding the distribution of travelling in the last couple of years, 67% of people were travelled and 33% of people were not travelling to any places.

7.3 Testing of Common Method Bias (CMB)

Since the researcher uses single cross-section data may cause spurious relations among variables, which could be a severe problem for results and analysis. As the study is rely on a single cross-section and data were collected using a single research instrument, there may be the possibility of CMB. To address the matter of CMB, we have considered the assessment of full collinearity, as suggested by Kock (2015). When the value of VIF is lower the verge value of 3.3, it implies that it is free from CMB. The result reveals that VIF values for all items are lower than the threshold, indicating CMB does not affect our study (Hair et al., 2017, Kock, 2015).

7.4 Reliability and Validity

Before validating the hypotheses, reliability was first tested to confirm the correctness of the research tool. The reliability is performed by smart PLS to check that the questionnaire results have internal consistency. Cronbach's λ was used to estimate the internal consistency. Regarding the acceptance level, Cronbach (1951); Ormane and Bag (2022) proposed that $\lambda < 0.6$ indicates low reliability, while $0.6 < \lambda < 0.8$ indicates the reliability is satisfactory and when λ value is greater than 0.8 reflects higher reliability(Bag et al., 2021). However, Hulin et al. (2001) confront that if λ values lie between 0.6 to 0.7 it indicates a reliability level of acceptance. The λ values of the six constructs range from 0.612 to 0.872. Therefore, the questionnaire of the study has good reliability and is satisfactory. The composite reliability (CR) of all constructs is between 0.793 to 0.919, thus exceeding the recommended value of 0.6 recommended by Fronell and Larcker (1981). In addition, the average variance extracted (AVE) is lies between 0.546 to 0.792; therefore, all the values exceed the threshold of 0.5 Fronell and Larcker (1981); Bag et al., (2020). So, it represents that all six dimensions had adequate convergent validity.

Table 2.1   Results of convergent validity

Construct	λ (Alpha)	CR	AVE
EI	0.872	0.919	0.792
IV	0.796	0.868	0.624
IRE	0.793	0.857	0.546
MI	0.612	0.793	0.564
PI	0.756	0.844	0.577
PVA	0.874	0.906	0.617

Source: Authors' own calculation

7.5 Discriminant Validity

Discriminant validity is used to check the difference among the proposed variables. According to (Fornell & Larcker, 1981), when the square root of the constructs AVE is more than the off-diagonal rudiments in the matching columns and rows, these pointers are more closely related to the construct than other pointers. Table 2.2 presented the value of square roots of the on-diagonal AVE was larger than the off-diagonal values, which proves the discriminant validity.

Table 2.2   Result of fornell–larcker test

Construct	EI	IV	IRE	MI	PI	PVA
EI	**0.890**					
IV	0.554	**0.790**				
IRE	0.389	0.703	**0.739**			
MI	0.371	0.755	0.570	**0.751**		
PI	0.279	0.307	0.262	0.457	**0.760**	
PVA	0.509	0.762	0.496	0.834	0.303	**0.786**

Note: EI = Emotional Involvement; IV = intention to Visit; IRE = Intention to Recommended VR Experience; MI = Mental Imagery; PI = Perceived Interactivity; PVA = Perceived Visual appeal.
Source: Authors' own calculation

To test the discriminant validity, we are applying the HTMT ratio test. The studies of Bagozzi & Fornell (1982) suggested that a value lower than 0.9 implies the vividness of the construct. Table 2.3 depicts the result of HTMT ratio, where all constructs' values are lesser than the threshold. Thus, results indicate that discriminant validity is established.

Table 2.3   Result of heterotrait–monotrait (HTMT) ratio

Constructs	EI	IV	IRE	MI	PI	PVA
EI						
IV	0.648					
IRE	0.430	0.865				
MI	0.495	0.845	0.781			
PI	0.385	0.408	0.506	0.692		
PVA	0.561	0.894	0.568	0.915	0.409	

Note: EI = Emotional Involvement; IV = intention to Visit; IRE = Intention to Recmonded VR Experience; MI = Mental Imagery; PI = Perceived Interactivity; PVA = Perceived Visual appeal.
Source: Authors' own calculation

7.6 Testing of hypothesis

The path analysis has been performed using structural equation modelling, which shows a good model as R^2 value for the endogenous variable (intention to visit) is 0.657 (Chin, 1998). As we anticipated, our hypothesis supported a positive association between perceived user interactivity and visit intention (*H1: β = 0.189, p<0.05*); perceived visual appeal and visit intention (*H2: β = 0.705, p<0.05*) (refer to Fig. 2.2). The result confirmed that perceived user interactivity

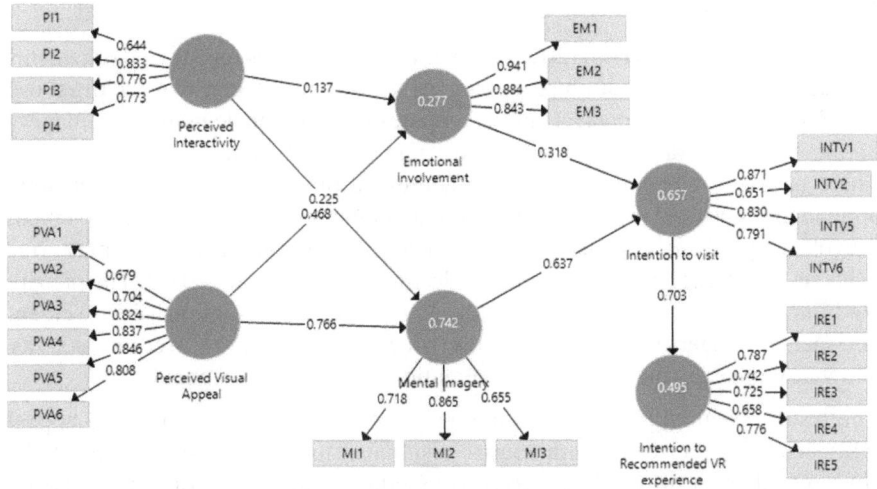

Fig. 2.2 Results of path model

Source: Authors' own work

significantly influences internal tourist state, i.e., emotional involvement $(H_{3a}: \beta = 0.137, p<0.05)$ and mental imagery $(H_{3b}: \beta = 0.225, p<0.05)$ and Perceived Visual Appeal was found a significantly influenced on both emotional involvement *(H4a: $\beta = 0.468$, p<0.05)* and mental imagery *(H4b: $\beta = 0.766$, p< 0.05)*. Emotional involvement was found to have a significant effect on the visit intention of tourists *(H5: $\beta = 0.318$, p<0.05)* and Mental Imagery was found to significantly influences visit intention *(H6: $\beta = 0.637$, p<0.05)*.

Moreover, the association between the Intention to recommend VR experience concerning the intention to visit a holiday destination. Intention to recommended VR experience has a significant relations with visit intention *(H7: $\beta = 0.703$, p<0.005)*, which indicates that tourists are ready to share their best experiences in virtual reality with their peers and others and encourage them to use VR technology to select a holiday destination.

Table 2.4 Structural path analysis

	Structural Path	Path Coefficients	Remarks
H1	Perceived interactivity → Intention to visit	0.189	Supported
H2	Perceived visual appeal → Intention to visit	0.705	Supported
H3a	Perceived Interacitivity → Emotional Involvement	0.137	Supported
H3b	Perceived Interacitivity → Mental Imagery	0.225	Supported
H4a	Perceived Visual Appeal → Emotional Involvement	0.468	Supported
H4b	Perceived Visual Appeal → Mental Imagery	0.766	Supported
H5	Emotional Involvement → Intention to Visit	0.318	Supported
H6	Mental Imagery → Intention to Visit	0.637	Supported
H7	Intention to visit → Intention to recommended VR experience	0.703	Supported

Source: Authors' own calculation

7.7 Discussion

The study of Lee & Gretzel, (2012); Yoo & Kim, (2014) has recognized organisms as a apparatus of information processing of VR stimuli. Because of the often use of VR interactivity, the present study compares the emotional and mental imagery of the VR with traditional interactions, namely, 360^0 tour and static images. There is less number of studies have addressed this issue; they predominately applied the causal relationship in the milieu of emotional and mental involvement provoked by advertisements (Marasco et al., 2018), digital learning platforms (Zhao et al., 2020) and tourists holiday destination (Wei et al., 2019). The present study investigates the underlying process organism (i.e., emotional involvement and mental imagery) that explicates the effects of VR stimuli (user interactivity and visual appeals) on tourists' visit intention to a holiday destination.

The result reveals that perceived interactivity (H1) and perceived visual appeal (H2) positively correlate with tourist visit intention. The results confront the study of Chen et al. (2021), who also assertained sound relationship between interactivity and tourists' intention to visit a holiday destination by analysing the specification of travelogue. Also, Marasco et al. (2018) protrate a significant impact of perceived visual appeal on visit intention towards a destination. This association may indicate that the tourist's selection criteria for a holiday destination are shifting from traditional to modern tech-orientated behaviour. Moreover, in the travel & tourism sector, VR is broadly accepted among tourists to choose a holiday destination. VR is referred to as most imperative technology to improve and influence the tourism experience (Wei et al., 2019).

Furthermore, the result also established a positive relations between emotional involvement and intention to visit a holiday destination. Similarly, the result also reveals that mental imagery strongly correlates with the tourists' visit intention to a destination. The study of Yeh et al. (2017) confronts that emotional involvement is directly associated with the tourists' visit intention and that mental imagery (Bogicevic et al., 2019) leads to travel intention. Thus, to enhance the visit intention, the tourist service providers should utilise the ample scope of VR, which affluence the tourist's emotions and imagination through interactivity and visualization of a destination.

Furthermore, the study reveals that satisfied VR users about the selection and intent to visit a destination are more likely to recommended their VR experience to others. It is an effective way of creating awareness about the usefulness of VR to non-VR users and is valuable to attract new users to facilitate them selecting a holiday destination.

7.8 Implication of the Study

Findings of the study have a momentous connotation with the existing literature and practitioners cum policymakers of the tourism industry to inspire virtual reality applications in their promotional campaigns. The implications of this research are represented in dual like theoretical and managerial aspects.

7.9 Theoretical Implications

The study has some theoretical connotations. First, this study conducted a dynamic analysis of the factors affecting the estimated VR experiences of tourism based on S-O-R model. This study inspected pre-visitor emotional involvement and mental imagery are the critical drivers of the VR tourism experience and confirmed the liaison between the emotional involvement of travellers and mental imagery for travel purposes.

Second, in linking to the notch of perceived interactivity, perceived value is the utmost significant forecaster of emotional involvement and mental imagery. This result depicts that perceived visual appeal is the vital factor affecting the tourists' emotional involvement; mental imagery and the perceived visual appeal is the critical factor directly affecting the intention to visit. Thus, the technique for strengthening the perceived value should be considered while conniving VR tourism content to enhance the tourists' emotional involvement and mental imagery and to elevation the feasibility of visit intention of tourists' to the holiday destination.

7.10 Managerial Implications

This study draws some useful inferences for practitioners and policymakers. Tourists often circuitously experience a destinations over the mass media shorn of visiting the destination. This indirect involvement will have a significant impact on upcoming behavioural intentions. The present study's findings propose that virtual content creators should emphasise creating a visual experience because visual appeal greatly influences mental imagery and emotional involvement. Therefore, tourism marketers' could design VR content with immersive characters by using striking factors so that tourists gain a mental image.

Given that the connection between perceived visual appeal and mental imagery is much more robust than the association between perceived visual appeal and emotional involvement, VR content creators may highlight visual appeal to enhance the fun of the content. Since the impact of mental imagery and emotional involvement was found to be important in the user's visit intention to a holiday destination, it is endorsed that tourism service providers should provide practical presentations to users to visit the site after indulging in VR. As such, it is possible to provide the user with VR content with specific information about the tourist location and a discount coupon for potential tourists.

8. Limitations, Further Research Avenues

This study has few drawbacks like others. For instance, despite carefully studying the stability of factors that affect VR experiences in sightseeing, other factors can affect VR tourism, such as existence and attitude. Thus, future research may include these dimensions to generalise outcomes on tourists' visit intention through VR applications. The study considered interactivity and visual appeal as the VR stumili. The future study may consider the other antecedents like vividness, aesthetic knowledge etc. to find more appropriate effects. Similarly, the future researchers may consider the psychological aspected along with the emotional and mental aspect to explicide the actual intention of tourist to visit a destination. Statistical samples have used convenient sampling methods because there was no public information related to VR users in tourists. Future studies may be conducted to improve these limitations.

REFERENCES

1. Armitage, C. J., & Conner, M. (2000). Attitudinal ambivalence: A test of three key hypotheses. Personality and Social Psychology Bulletin, 26(11), 1421–1432.
2. Bag, S., & Omrane, A. (2020). Corporate social responsibility and its overall effects on financial performance: Empirical evidence from Indian companies. Journal of African Business, 23(1), 264–280.
3. Bag, S., Aich, P., & Islam, M. A. (2020). Behavioral intention of "digital natives" toward adapting the online education system in higher education. Journal of Applied Research in Higher Education, 14(1), 16–40.
4. Bag, S., Ray, N., & Banerjee, B. (2021). Assessing the Effects of Experiential Quality on Behavioural Intention of Customers in Banking Services: The Moderating Role of Experiential Satisfaction. FIIB Business Review, 23197145211052817.
5. Bagozzi, R. P., & Fornell, C. (1982). Theoretical concepts, measurements, and meaning. A second generation of multivariate analysis, 2(2), 5–23.
6. Bogicevic, V., Seo, S., Kandampully, J. A., Liu, S. Q., & Rudd, N. A. (2019). Virtual reality presence as a preamble of tourism experience: The role of mental imagery. Tourism Management, 74, 55–64.
7. Carù, A., & Cova, B. (2007). Consumer immersion in an experiential context. Consuming experience, 34–47.
8. Chang, Y. L., Hou, H. T., Pan, C. Y., Sung, Y. T., & Chang, K. E. (2015). Apply an augmented reality in a mobile guidance to increase sense of place for heritage places. Journal of Educational Technology & Society, 18(2), 166–178.
9. Chen, Y., Guo, Z., & Pan, Q. (2021). Analysis on the Characteristics of Travel Vlog Video and Its Impact on Users' Travel Intention. In Proceedings of the 7th International Conference on Humanities and Social Science Research (ICHSSR 2021).
10. Cronbach, L.J. Coefficient alpha and the internal structure of tests. Psychometrika 1951, 16, 297–334.
11. Fornell, C.; Larcker, D. Evaluating structural equation models with unobservable variables and measurement error. J. Mark. Res. 1981.
12. Fox, J., Arena, D., & Bailenson, J. N. (2009). Virtual reality: A survival guide for the social scientist. Journal of Media Psychology, 21(3), 95–113.
13. Gold, A. H., Malhotra, A., & Segars, A. H. (2001). Knowledge management: An organizational capabilities perspective. Journal of management information systems, 18(1), 185–214.
14. Grappi, Silvia and Fabrizio Montanari (2011). "The Role of Social Identification and Hedonism in Affecting Tourist Re-Patronizing Behaviours: The Case of an Italian Festival." Tourism Management, 32 (5): 1128–1140.

15. Gross, M. J., and G. Brown. (2008). "An Empirical Structure Model of Tourists and Places: Progressing Involvement and Place Attachment into Tourism." Tourism Management, 29 (6):1141–51.
16. Gursoy, D. & E. Gavcar. (2003). International Leisure Tourists" Involvement Profile. Annals of Tourism Research, 30 (4), 906–926.
17. Gutierrez, L., Mauriat, M., Pelloux, J., Bellini, C., & Van Wuytswinkel, O. (2008). Towards a systematic validation of references in real-time RT-PCR. The Plant Cell, 20(7), 1734–1735.
18. Guttentag, D. A. (2010). Virtual reality: Applications and implications for tourism. Tourism management, 31(5), 637–651.
19. Hennessey, S. M., Yun, D., MacDonald, R., & MacEachern, M. (2010). The effects of advertising awareness and media form on travel intentions. Journal of Hospitality Marketing & Management, 19(3), 217–243.
20. Holsapple, C. W., & Wu, J. (2007). User acceptance of virtual worlds: The hedonic framework. ACM SIGMIS Database: The DATABASE for Advances in Information Systems, 38(4), 86–89.
21. Hosany, S., & Prayag, G. (2013). Patterns of tourists' emotional responses, satisfaction, and intention to recommend. Journal of Business Research, 66(6), 730–737.
22. Hulin, C., Netemeyer, R., & Cudeck, R. (2001). Can a reliability coefficient be too high?. Journal of Consumer Psychology, 10(1/2), 55–58.
23. Hyun, M. Y., & O'Keefe, R. M. (2012). Virtual destination image: Testing a telepresence model. Journal of Business Research, 65(1), 29–35.
24. Kaplanidou, K., & Vogt, C. (2006). A structural analysis of destination travel intentions as a function of web site features. Journal of Travel research, 45(2), 204–216.
25. Kozak, M. (2001). Comparative assessment of tourist satisfaction with destinations across two nationalities. Tourism management, 22(4), 391–401.
26. Laurent, G., &Kapferer, J. (1985). Measuring consumer involvement profiles. Journal of Marketing Research, 22(1), 41–53.
27. Lee, W., & Gretzel, U. (2012). Designing persuasive destination websites: A mental imagery processing perspective. Tourism management, 33(5), 1270–1280.
28. Liu, L., Suh, A., & Wagner, C. (2016). Watching online videos interactively: the impact of media capabilities in Chinese Danmaku video sites. Chinese Journal of Communication, 9(3), 283–303
29. MacInnis, D. J., & Price, L. L. (1987). The role of imagery in information processing: Review and extensions. Journal of consumer research, 13(4), 473–491.
30. Marasco, A., Buonincontri, P., van Niekerk, M., Orlowski, M., &Okumus, F. (2018). Exploring the role of next-generation virtual technologies in destination marketing. Journal of Destination Marketing & Management, 9, 138–148.
31. McGehee, N. G., Yoon, Y., & Cárdenas, D. (2003). Involvement and travel for recreational runners in North Carolina. Journal of Sport Management, 17(3), 305–324.
32. McGill, A. L., & Anand, P. (1989). The effect of imagery on information processing strategy in a multi attribute choice task. Marketing Letters, 1(1), 7–16.
33. McMillan, S.J.; Hwang, J.S. Measures of perceived interactivity: An exploration of the role of direction of communication, user control, and time in shaping perceptions of interactivity. J. Advert. 2002, 31, 29–42.
34. Miller, D. W., Hadjimarcou, J., &Miciak, A. (2000). A scale for measuring advertisement-evoked mental imagery. Journal of Marketing Communications, 6(1), 1–20.

35. Morrison, A. M., Bag, S., & Mandal, K. (2023). Virtual reality's impact on destination visit intentions and the moderating role of amateur photography. Tourism Review. https://doi.org/10.1108/TR-12-2022-0621.

36. Nah, F. F. H., Eschenbrenner, B., & DeWester, D. (2011). Enhancing brand equity through flow and telepresence: A comparison of 2D and 3D virtual worlds. MIs Quarterly, 731–747.

37. Omrane, A., & Bag, S. (2022). Determinants of customer buying intention towards residential property in Kolkata (India): an exploratory study using PLS-SEM approach. International Journal of Business Innovation and Research, 28(1), 119–139.

38. Pantano, E., & Vannucci, V. (2019). Who is innovating? An exploratory research of digital technologies diffusion in retail industry. Journal of Retailing and Consumer Services, 49, 297–304.

39. Park, Y. A., Gretzel, U., & Sirakaya-Turk, E. (2007). Measuring web site quality for online travel agencies. Journal of Travel & Tourism Marketing, 23(1), 15–30.

40. Pohlmeyer, A. E., & Blessing, L. (2011, July). A conjoint analysis of attributes affecting the likelihood of technology use. In International Conference of Design, User Experience, and Usability (pp. 303–312). Springer, Berlin, Heidelberg.

41. Reiners, T., Teräs, H., Chang, V., Wood, L. C., Gregory, S., Gibson, D., ... & Teräs, M. Authentic, immersive, and emotional experience in virtual learning environments: The fear of dying as an important learning experience in.

42. Saeed, N., Yang, Y., &Sinnappan, S. (2009). Emerging web technologies in higher education: a case of incorporating blogs, podcasts and social bookmarks in a web programming course based on students' learning styles and technology preferences. Educational Technology & Society, 12(4), 98e109.

43. San Martín, H., & Herrero, Á. (2012). Influence of the user's psychological factors on the online purchase intention in rural tourism: Integrating innovativeness to the UTAUT framework. Tourism management, 33(2), 341–350.

44. Steuer, J. (1992). Defining virtual reality: Dimensions determining telepresence. Journal of communication, 42(4), 73–93.

45. Tan, W.K.; Wu, C.E. An investigation of the relationships among destination familiarity, destination image and future visit intention. J. Destin. Mark. Manag. 2016, 5, 214–226.

46. Wei, W., Qi, R., & Zhang, L. (2019). Effects of virtual reality on theme park visitors' experience and behaviours: A presence perspective. Tourism Management, 71, 282–293.

47. Wu, D., Weng, D., & Xue, S. (2016). Virtual reality system as an affective medium to induce specific emotion: a validation study. Electronic Imaging, 2016(4), 1–6.

48. Xu, J. B., Yan, L. B., & Mak, C. (2018). Visitor experience of Hong Kong trams as an unconventional attraction. International Journal of Tourism Research, 20(5), 605–612.

49. Zhang, H., Fu, X., Cai, L. A., & Lu, L. (2014). Destination image and tourist loyalty: A meta-analysis. Tourism management, 40, 213–223.

Emerging Horizons: Business and Society in the Post Pandemic Era –
Brig. Dr. Rajiv Divekar et al. (eds)
© 2024 Taylor & Francis Group, London, ISBN 978-1-032-90822-9

3

Corporate Social Responsibility and Brand Equity: A Methodological and Thematic Review

Siddhi A Pol[1]

MBA student (Batch 2022-2024), Symbiosis Institute of Management Studies (SIMS),
Constituent of Symbiosis International Deemed University, Pune, India

Smita Mehendale[2]

Assistant Professor, Symbiosis Institute of Management Studies (SIMS),
Constituent of Symbiosis International Deemed University, Pune, India

Brig Rajiv Divekar[3]

Director, SIMS, Symbiosis Institute of Management Studies (SIMS),
Constituent of Symbiosis International Deemed University, Pune, India

ABSTRACT

With increasing consumer consciousness towards the integrity and values a brand stands for, there has been a change in the manner organisations conduct business. They are conducting wide scale CSR initiatives to appeal to consumer sentiment and lead to a societal benefit. In this study, we have used a systematic literature review with the primary aim of highlighting the major methodologies and research themes on the impact of CSR on the Brand Equity (BE). We analysed 63 papers for this review, covering a multitude of research themes such as brand studies, strategic CSR, marketing and communication strategies. In the methodological review we observed that the majority of the existing research is primarily quantitative in nature followed by some qualitative research and mixed methods. Keeping both thematic methodological considerations in mind, recommends have been made for future researchers.

Keywords: Corporate social responsibility, CSR, Brand equity, Brand studies, Consumer behaviour, Thematic review, Methodological review, Systematic literature review

[1]siddhi.pol2024@sims.edu, [2]smita.m@sims.edu, [3]director@sims.edu

DOI: 10.4324/978100355996-3

1. Introduction

Post pandemic, Corporate Social Responsibility (CSR) measures have been taken up which have significantly improved organizations reputation. A company's commitment to society and consumer well-being through independent business decisions and financial contributions is known as (CSR) (Van Doorn et al., 2017). A popular definition of CSR by the EC (European Commission) is "The obligation of businesses to consider their effects on society." The Commission also proposes that a company might adopt a socially responsible stance by ensuring that their strategies for running their business incorporate social issues, ethical issues and human rights issues. (Westin & Parmler, 2020)

Consumer behaviour and perception have an impact on how valuable a brand is. The value of having a recognisable and well-recognized brand and the degree of impact a brand name has over consumers' minds are measured by Brand Equity (BE). A brand is said to achieved high brand equity if its customers are happy with the brand. Negative brand equity is earned when a brand fails to meet its consumer's expectations. A disappointed consumer will ensure that they dissuade others from using that brand whereas a happy customer refers the brand to other.

In the past, an effective way to raise the standard of living of society was by showing responsibility towards pressing matters like our environment, hunger and poverty. (Mahmood & Bashir, 2020) The philanthropic component of CSR encourages businesses to make charitable contributions to improve society. Emel Esen identified four categories of CSR: economic (earn money), legal (adhere to the law), ethical (act morally), and discretionary (be a good corporate citizen) (Esen, 2013). Customers' cognitive views regarding companies' corporate social responsibility programmes have had a positive influence on those customers' behaviour, loyalty, and intention to promote the brand. The literature also supports the impact of CSR communications on consumer-based brand equity. Although there is sufficient literature to support the positive impact of CSR on BE, no systematic literature review has been undertaken in the past to the best knowledge of the researchers. This study aims to fulfil this gap in existing literature.

2. Methods

The objective of this literature review is to analyse the association of CSR with BE with a focus on the positive and negative effects they have on each other. The review also aims to study how CSR activities of various organisations impact consumer perception.

2.1 Scope of the Review

This review is extensive research starting with the accumulation of 103 journal papers out of which 97 were shortlisted and the remaining 6 duplicates eliminated

(Figure 1). This review includes academic journal articles out of which a majority of them were critically reviewed. Additionally, it does not include book chapters, non-academic works, such as quick magazine articles, editorials, articles, interviews, and various non-empirical data like theories and hypotheses. The primary focus of this review is to study the link existing between CSR and BE keeping in mind its effects on consumer perception.

2.2 Identification of Relevant Literature

We recognised an array of keywords for search on databases such as "Corporate Social Responsibility", "Brand Value", "Brand equity", "Customer Satisfaction", "Social Responsibility", "Company perception", "Social Accountability" and "Social Commitment". We extensively searched for these keywords on several databases like: Emerald, Scopus, Jstor, Web of Science and Sage. The databases were selected on the basis of the high quality of content they offer and their applicability to many business-related topics, ranging from management to business research. The first phase of research resulted in a corpus of 103 results (Table 3.1) from which all duplicates were eliminated. Next, 34 articles were disqualified for nonconformance to predefined content and form criteria. A sample of 63 articles was produced as a consequence of the initial screening phase (Figure 3.1). The entire text of these papers was extracted in the following phase, and two of the authors finally reviewed them to include them in this review on the basis of the above-mentioned criteria.

Table 3.1 Database search protocol

Database	Scope of Search	Number of Article Items
Emerald	Search: Journals Abstracts	14
Scopus	Search: All journals Abstract, keywords, and titles Document type: article and review article	77
Jstor	Search: Topic Document type: Journals	8
Web of Science	Search: Topic Document type: Journals	2
Sage	Publication type: Academic journal Document type: Articles	2

Source: Made by authors

2.3 Results of Systematic Literature Review

The 63 journal articles that composed this analysis were published from 2007 to 2022, with a gradual and notable surge over this ten-year period from 2012 to the present (Figure 3.2). This pattern of increased research on CSR and BE is reflected in the increased number of articles in this analysis during 2020-22, when the pandemic occurred and brought the focus on societal progress. CSR was one of the techniques used to assist the underprivileged in coping with the pandemic.

Secondly, The Companies Act of 2013 was amended in April 2014, making CSR mandatory for the first time. This created a scope for topic-related research in the Indian context.

During the pandemic, brands promoted their brand by affiliating it with their CSR activities aimed at aiding affected communities. This gave rise to marketing research by organisations as well as the authors.

3. Results and Discussion

Our literature review covers an array of literature published on the relationship between Brand Equity and CSR. A methodological and thematic review was undertaken for this study.

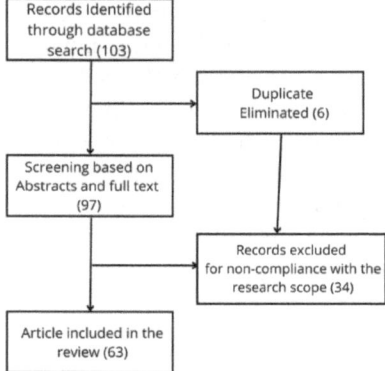

Fig. 3.1 Flowchart of systematic review literature process

Source: Made by authors

3.1 Methodological Review

This methodological review attempts to provide a view of the various approaches utilized by studies on the impact of CSR on brand equity. In terms of methodological approaches, passages from each publication outlining the used methods were taken. After a discussion, the methodologies used in articles were divided into three categories, namely qualitative research, which primarily includes using interviews and focus groups and quantitative research, using mainly statistical tools, regression; mixed methods, that combine both qualitative as well as quantitative methods.

A quantitative approach in 62% of the papers (n = 39), 27% of the papers (n = 17) used qualitative approaches, and mixed methodologies were used in 11% of the total papers (n = 7) (Table 3.2). The multitude of research issues and themes explored in these publications, along with the various degrees of interpretations may be used to explain this methodological fragmentation.

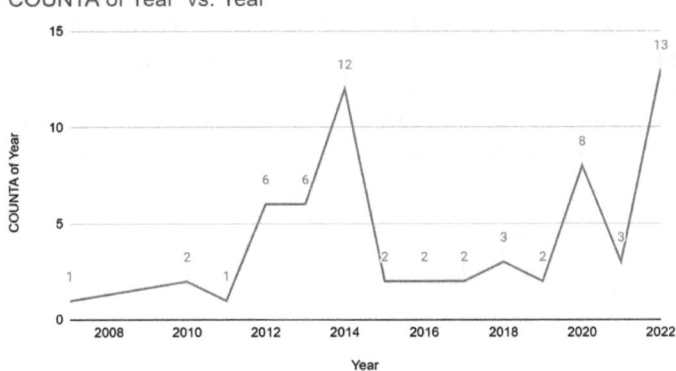

Fig. 3.2 Articles included the review and their year of publication

Source: Made by authors

We observed that there are more quantitative papers (62%) as compared to qualitative papers (27%) and mixed papers (11%). This can be due to the connection of BE to the consumers perception of the brand value and profitability which is measurable through survery and secondary research. A lot of the researchers conducted surveys regarding the impact of CSR on BE in the form of questionnaires, interviews and focus groups, etc which further breaks down the data into the categories of exploratory, descriptive and causal for better understanding. The collected data from structured surveys were quantifiable and were run through statistical tools such as Structural Equation Modelling (SEM) or regression, etc to get the desired results.

Table 3.2 Research methodologies adopted in this review of literature

	Number of Articles	Percentage
Mixed	7	11%
Qualitative	17	27%
Quantitative	39	62%
Total	63	100%

Source: Made by authors

3.2 Thematic Review

To formulate a list of recurrent themes, researcher went through the 63 publications' keywords and abstracts prior to reading the papers in full. The authors reached a consensus on the major theme of each paper. The predominant theme found in 29 out of the 63 journal articles was Brand Studies. Brand Studies encompass several sub-themes such as Brand Reputation, Brand Image, Brand Performance and Brand Loyalty. The second most popular theme identified was Marketing

Strategies with a total of 13 journal articles having this as their main theme. This was followed by Strategic CSR with a total of 12 journal articles which highlighted the ways in which CSR can be used strategically by the organization. Lastly, another recurring theme in 9 articles was Legal Aspects and Ethics that discuss how CSR initiatives differ from county to country based on the prevalent laws of the land. The number of articles with their themes are shown in Figure 3.3.

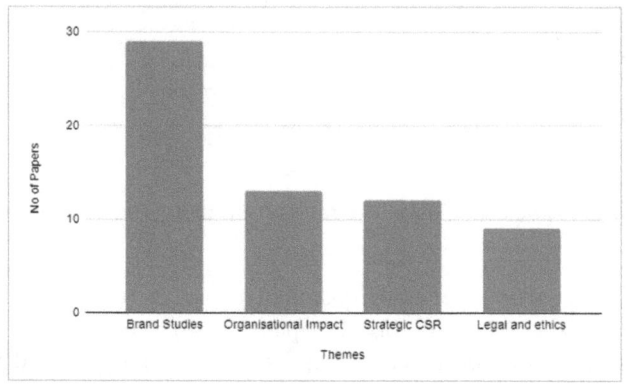

Fig. 3.3 Identification of predominant themes

Source: Made by Authors using Excel

It is not evident why the papers cover such a wide array of topics ranging from Legal Aspects and Ethics to Marketing Strategies. One logical explanation is that these themes are a mere reflection of the prevailing practices carried out by most organisations.

Brand Studies

Brand Studies refers to the understanding of the market and company's position which entails examines multiple elements like image, reputation, value, loyalty, customer experiences and buyer's journey. In the analysis of papers 19 articles talked about how the CSR affects the various elements of brand studies.

Brand Image and Brand Reputation: Brand Image are consumer perceptions of a brand as represented by the brand connections maintained in their memories. Positive brand image enhances customer loyalty and creates favourable word-of-mouth. Building brand equity starts with establishing a strong, positive brand image, which gives businesses a competitive edge. (Blumrodt et al., 2012). Brand image is defined as a visual representation of a company's prior actions and prospective future that conveys the firm's total attractiveness to all of its major stakeholders when compared to other top competitors (Wang, 2010). According to a study, CSR signals for company brands from poorly ranked countries were found to be more effective but as the company's reputation improves over time, customers become more aware of genuine brand initiatives and their expectations change which affects their decision, this may change. (Cowan & Guzman, 2020) Customers' perception of a company's CSR has an impact on their future intentions to buy its brands. (Wang Shu et al., 2021). The push from customers to be more socially responsible is being felt by brands all around the world (Muniz et al., 2019).

Brand Value and Financial Performance: Numerous studies have examined the connections between business success and socially or ecologically responsible behaviour. Although earlier empirical findings have not always been clear-cut (Faller & Zu Knyphausen-Aufse, 2018). More socially conscious businesses are typically seen favourably by consumers who believe they are more credible and value their brands more highly (Hur et al., 2014). Customers are influenced by intangible factors like trust, brand connection, supplier reputation, and image in addition to more obvious factors like price and quality when making purchasing decisions (Lai et al., 2010). Consumers may expect businesses to engage in environmental CSR initiatives and their efforts may be rewarded through purchasing decisions, which may help organisations improve their profitability (Khojastehpour & Johns, 2014). Thus, in any economic setup, corporate governance and social engagement of CSR are always critical prerequisites for enhancing brand equity. (He & Li, 2011; Wang et al., 2021).

Brand Loyalty: Finally, a consumer's commitment to continue buying good products from the same brand in the future is referred to as brand loyalty (Malik, 2015) and different strategies are used to attain the same (Lai et al., 2010). The overall opinion of the public regarding CSR activities will also determine whether CSR is a successful strategic strategy to win customer support. (Xie, 2014) When resources are heterogeneous, constrained, or immobile, it is still possible to gain long-term competitive advantages. (Young & Makhija, 2014) CSR can positively affect brand loyalty through the use of practical and symbolic images, brand identity, customer loyalty, and feeling of contentment (Lin & Chung, 2019). A brand's strength comes from the impressions that consumers have of it over time based on what they have heard, seen, felt, and experienced and CSR can play a role in enhancing customer loyalty (Louis et al., 2019; Muniz et al., 2019).

Organisational Impact

In this literature review, 11 journal articles highlight how CSR can be construed as a powerful organisational impact. CSR plays an imperative role in building a positive image for an organization. Companies advocating change with regard to various social issues and environmental issues are viewed as trailblazers working towards the betterment of the society as a whole (Walsh & Bartikowski, 2013). Numerous studies have examined the connections between a business's success and socially or ecologically responsible behaviour. Although earlier empirical findings have not always been clear-cut. Corporate Social Initiatives have been observed to have a great impact on the BI and Brand Equity of an organization.

(Faller & Zu Knyphausen-Aufseß, 2018). Brand image can be said to be the cornerstone for constructing brand equity, and a concrete, favourable brand image results in a competitive advantage. Most organisations owe their earned Brand Equity to recognition, loyalty and perceived quality (Blumrodt et al., 2012). With regard to Corporate Social Initiatives, businesses have majorly 3 roles: social, economic, and environmental. These roles exist independently of each other but other roles suffer when one of the roles suffers. It is therefore important for organisations to ensure cohesiveness when carrying out these roles (Esen, 2013). Increasingly, empirical data shows that when making purchases, most consumers pay attention to a number of intangible factors, including trust, association, supplier reputation, and BI (Lai et al., 2010).

In this day and age, the majority of customers are concerned about both their own consumer experiences and the effects they have on other stakeholders. Hence, they might deem it simpler to relate to a company's CSR as they convey the avenues in which the brand is trying to make a difference (Martínez & Rodríguez del Bosque, 2013; Hur et al., 2014). Consumers react favourably to CSR that adds value than to CSR which is charitable or promotional in nature. The effectiveness of philanthropic CSR is the same for both types of enterprises (Singh & Verma, 2017). As consumer knowledge and purchase intent are intertwined, consumers will be motivated to pay more for a firm's products, enhancing the reputation and profitability. Customers may demand that businesses participate in CSR programmes and reward them by making purchases, thereby increasing profitability (Khojastehpour & Johns, 2014).

CSR is a powerful tool to enhance a brand's image regardless of the size of its operations. A weak brand presence or insufficient advertising spending can be made up for by perceived CSR, but the same does not apply to poor innovation. The idea that firms with less intense advertising have more to gain by participating in CSR is that intense advertising increases brand awareness and familiarity (Van Doorn et al., 2017). Hence, in the contemporary world, organizations make efforts to indulge in CSR activities. The actual conflict in the realm of CSR currently appears to be fought over how stakeholders view firms' perceived legitimacy, which is carried out via market strategy and communication (Claudia, 2014). Managers are more focused on social responsibility when achieving organisational effectiveness and financial benefits. The challenge lies with the marketers who have to carry on the CSR initiatives in a way that they favour the brand (Dincer & Dincer, 2012).

It is the duty of marketing teams to communicate the advantages of a product, brand, or organisation to the public and CSR is today one of the main paths to success. A dynamic marketing plan will ultimately establish a connection between CSR and brand equity that will be advantageous to all stakeholders (Kang & Hustvedt, 2014).

Strategic CSR

The idea of CSR is constructed on charity and ethical considerations along with law of the land and the economy (Mahmood & Bashir, 2020) and aims to satisfy the demands of the individual as well as society. Strategic CSR focus is evolving from value-supporting to value-driving (Kim et al., 2010). Organisations must make efforts to understand how non-financial assets can be utilised to generate value for their numerous stakeholders (Westin & Parmler, 2020). The four strategic categories of boosting brand equity, creating commercial possibilities, enhancing stakeholder connections, and maximising corporate media and communication strategies are where the most effective CSR actions, which improve corporate performance, fit (Mochales, 2022). Other areas like rural health care are largely neglected. One plausible reason for investors' lack of awareness pertaining to healthcare and rural development programmes could be the fact that they have a considerably low presence in rural areas (Kansal & Joshi, 2014). A managerial finding states that organizations may wish to steer clear of conventional, normal, routine, or mundane processes if they want to use CSR to differentiate their brands. This is an excellent technique to develop a CSR strategy. Instead, they might prefer to create ones that are particularly audacious or radical (Pope & Kim, 2021). In a study performed by Chernev the managers were asked to state whether they thought that an organisation's prosocial activities, like contributing to charitable causes, could affect how customers saw the products ability to perform as intended. According to the findings, there were contradictions as most of the interviewees said that an organisation's socially aligned activities would not have an impact on how well consumers perceived its products to perform, with the rest of them predicted either a positive or negative impact (Chernev & Blair, 2015).

Legal Strategies/ Policy

The study's findings support the idea that businesses ought to have both financial and legal responsibilities (Hanzaee & Sadeghian, 2014). The two primary facets of CSR, legal and ethical duties, enhance brand loyalty by creating favourable functional and symbolic representations. Moreover, distinct roles are played in enhancing brand loyalty by fulfilling legal and ethical obligations (Y. He & Lai, 2014). The genuine ethical commitment of a company might be determined from the way it treats its loosely connected stakeholders who have direct interests in it (Torres et al., 2012). Past research confirms results of a study that show that a customer's expectations for business ethics have an impact on how they evaluate a company's CSR and ethical behaviour when that company exhibits both bad CSR and negative ethical behaviour (Ferrell et al., 2019). Both temporarily and permanently, bad press and bad reputation can affect a firm. There will be clients for their goods and services if the company's commitment to ethics declines, particularly the socially irresponsible behaviour that could do so. It is well understood that ethics is a crucial aspect of CSR. Indian B2B companies could use CSR as a strategic instrument to boost their competitive advantage in addition to adhering to regulatory regulations (Xu, 2014).

4. Limitations

There are two major limitations of the study. First systematic literature review is based on keyword search. It is possible some important keywords were ignored by authors during the search phase which would lead to some relevant papers not being considered. Also, since authors judge the relevance of the manuscript to the context of research based on title and abstract, the biases of authors could lead to rejection of relevant manuscripts.

5. Future Research Agenda

Notwithstanding its numerous contributions, this review presents some limitations which serves as a chance for further research in this highly coveted domain. Since brand equity and CSR are dynamic concepts, this research cannot be considered definitive. In fact, it creates a fresh avenue for investigation, and it is suggested that other variables be examined and tested such as industry specific factors and impact of CSR on BE. Even organization specific factors like country of origin, geographic location, size of the organization and scale of operations can also be considered. Many studies used convenience sampling which leads to only limited generalisation of the results. Advance sampling methods should be used too. Future research should identify the effects of various CSR components such as economic, legal, ethical, and philanthropic, on marketing outcomes in order to determine whether the dimensions have comparable or dissimilar effects on outcomes of the brand.

The substantial of CSR studies reported in management literature were found to be qualitative in nature. There is no precise hypothesis topic in several management journal papers. These papers, on the other hand, develop various hypotheses based on extensive normative descriptions. CSR research in accounting literature, on the other hand, analyses specific research issues and shows causal relationships using empirical data. Hence more mixed method studies are suggested. Therefore, the study implies that the implementation of universal CSR initiatives can be aided by deliberate, steady managerial efforts, lending credence to the existing but relatively limited content on CSR design and development.

6. Conclusion

In the latest trend, it can be observed that organisations are constantly pumping money into CSR activities to strengthen unique, positive and concrete brand equity. The results of the study have significant ramifications for the body of existing CSR and branding expertise. They offer new perceptions of CSR in the corporate world. The assessment of the literature on the effect of CSR on BE revealed that the outcomes of the investigations varied. Despite the fact that several research came to the same conclusion, brand equity and corporate social responsibility are not closely related. Five categories that affect how consumers perceive brand equity and CSRy have been identified. The first step in clarifying the discrepancy among the current literature is our investigation. In our theoretical model, we have identified the areas in which CSR has a positive, neutral or negative effect on BE, Brand Loyalty, Brand Image, Brand Value, and CSR, Customer Satisfaction, Company Perception, Social Accountability and Social Commitment are just a few of the independent variables that are interconnected in the theoretical framework. BE increases as a result of the influence of these variables, demonstrating that both of these mutually exclusive variables have an impact on BE and CSR.

REFERENCES

1. al, W. S. (2021). Hypothesis the role of corporate social responsibility perceptions in brand equity, brand credibility, brand reputation, and purchase intentions.
2. Wang Shu et al. (2021). Hypothesis the role of corporate social responsibility perceptions in brand equity, brand credibility, brand reputation, and purchase intentions. *Scopus*.
3. Mochales, G. (2022). Hypothesis the role of corporate social responsibility perceptions in brand equity, brand credibility, brand reputation, and purchase intentions. *Scopus*.
4. Kansal, M., & Joshi, M. (2014). Perceptions of Investors and Stockbrokers on Corporate Social Responsibility: A Stakeholder Perspective from India. *Scopus*.
5. Claudia, O. (2014). Perceptions on the strategic value of corporate social responsibility – some insights from global rankings.
6. Blumrodt, J., Bryson, D., & Flanagan, J. (2012). European football teams' CSR engagement impacts on customer-based brand equity. *Journal of Consumer Marketing*, 29(7), 482–493. https://doi.org/10.1108/07363761211274992
7. Chen, X., Huang, R., Yang, Z., & Dube, L. (2018). CSR types and the moderating role of corporate competence. *European Journal of Marketing*, 52(7–8), 1358–1386. https://doi.org/10.1108/EJM-12-2016-0702
8. Chernev, A., & Blair, S. (2015). Doing well by doing good: The benevolent halo of corporate social responsibility. *Journal of Consumer Research*, 41(6), 1412–1425. https://doi.org/10.1086/680089
9. Cowan, K., & Guzman, F. (2020). How CSR reputation, sustainability signals, and country-of-origin sustainability reputation contribute to corporate brand performance: An exploratory study. *Journal of Business Research*, 117, 683–693. https://doi.org/10.1016/j.jbusres.2018.11.017
10. Dincer, B., & Dincer, C. (2012). Measuring brand social responsibility: A new scale. *Social Responsibility Journal*, 8(4), 484–494. https://doi.org/10.1108/17471111211272075
11. Esen, E. (2013). The influence of corporate social responsibility (CSR) activities on building corporate reputation. *Advances in Sustainability and Environmental Justice*, 11, 133–150. https://doi.org/10.1108/S2051-5030(2013)0000011010

12. Faller, C. M., & Zu Knyphausen-Aufseß, D. (2018). Does Equity Ownership Matter for Corporate Social Responsibility? A Literature Review of Theories and Recent Empirical Findings Author(s). *Source: Journal of Business Ethics, 150*(1), 15–40. https://doi.org/10.1007/sl0551-016-3122-x

13. Ferrell, O. C., Harrison, D. E., Ferrell, L., & Hair, J. F. (2019). Business ethics, corporate social responsibility, and brand attitudes: An exploratory study. *Journal of Business Research, 95*, 491–501. https://doi.org/10.1016/j.jbusres.2018.07.039

14. Hanzaee, K. H., & Sadeghian, M. (2014). The impact of corporate social responsibility on customer satisfaction and corporate reputation in automotive industry: Evidence from Iran. *Journal of Islamic Marketing, 5*(1), 125–143. https://doi.org/10.1108/JIMA-05-2013-0033

15. He, H., & Li, Y. (2011). CSR and Service Brand: The Mediating Effect of Brand Identification and Moderating Effect of Service Quality. *Source: Journal of Business Ethics, 100*(4), 673–688. https://doi.org/10.1007/sl0551-010-0703-y

16. He, Y., & Lai, K. K. (2014). The effect of corporate social responsibility on brand loyalty: The mediating role of brand image. *Total Quality Management and Business Excellence, 25*(3–4), 249–263. https://doi.org/10.1080/14783363.2012.661138

17. Hur, W. M., Kim, H., & Woo, J. (2014). How CSR Leads to Corporate Brand Equity: Mediating Mechanisms of Corporate Brand Credibility and Reputation. *Journal of Business Ethics, 125*(1), 75–86. https://doi.org/10.1007/s10551-013-1910-0

18. Hur, W.-M., Kim, H., & Woo, J. (2014). How CSR Leads to Corporate Brand Equity: Mediating Mechanisms of Corporate Brand Credibility and Reputation. *Source: Journal of Business Ethics, 125*(1), 75–86. https://doi.org/10.1007/s

19. Kang, J., & Hustvedt, G. (2014). The Contribution of Perceived Labor Transparency and Perceived Corporate Giving to Brand Equity in the Footwear Industry. *Clothing and Textiles Research Journal, 32*(4), 296–311. https://doi.org/10.1177/0887302X14546186

20. Khojastehpour, M., & Johns, R. (2014). The effect of environmental CSR issues on corporate/brand reputation and corporate profitability. *European Business Review, 26*(4), 330–339. https://doi.org/10.1108/EBR-03-2014-0029

21. Kim, J. B., Kwak, G., & Koo, Y. R. (2010). A note on corporate social responsibility (CSR) in city branding and design. *Asian Journal on Quality, 11*(3), 251–265. https://doi.org/10.1108/15982681011094005

22. Lai, C. S., Chiu, C. J., Yang, C. F., & Pai, D. C. (2010). The effects of corporate social responsibility on brand performance: The mediating effect of industrial brand equity and corporate reputation. *Journal of Business Ethics, 95*(3), 457–469. https://doi.org/10.1007/s10551-010-0433-1

23. Lin, M. S., & Chung, Y. K. (2019). Understanding the impacts of corporate social responsibility and brand attributes on brand equity in the restaurant industry. *Tourism Economics, 25*(4), 639–658. https://doi.org/10.1177/1354816618813619

24. Lindgreen, A., Xu, Y., Maon, F., & Wilcock, J. (2012). Corporate social responsibility brand leadership: A multiple case study. *European Journal of Marketing, 46*(7), 965–993. https://doi.org/10.1108/03090561211230142

25. Louis, D., Lombart, C., & Durif, F. (2019). Impact of a retailer's CSR activities on consumers' loyalty. *International Journal of Retail and Distribution Management, 47*(8), 793–816. https://doi.org/10.1108/IJRDM-12-2018-0262

26. Mahmood, A., & Bashir, J. (2020). How does corporate social responsibility transform brand reputation into brand equity? Economic and noneconomic perspectives of CSR. *International Journal of Engineering Business Management, 12*. https://doi.org/10.1177/1847979020927547

27. Malik, M. (2015). Value-Enhancing Capabilities of CSR: A Brief Review of Contemporary Literature. *Source: Journal of Business Ethics, 127*(2), 419–438. https://doi.org/10.1007/sl

28. Martínez, P., & Rodríguez del Bosque, I. (2013). CSR and customer loyalty: The roles of trust, customer identification with the company and satisfaction. *International Journal of Hospitality Management, 35*, 89–99. https://doi.org/10.1016/j.ijhm.2013.05.009

29. Muniz, F., Guzmán, F., Paswan, A. K., & Crawford, H. J. (2019). The immediate effect of corporate social responsibility on consumer-based brand equity. *Journal of Product and Brand Management, 28*(7), 864–879. https://doi.org/10.1108/JPBM-09-2018-2016

30. Pope, S., & Kim, J. (2021). Where, When, and Who: Corporate Social Responsibility and Brand Value—A Global Panel Study. *Business & Society*, 000765032110193. https://doi.org/10.1177/00076503211019315

31. Singh, A., & Verma, P. (2017). How CSR Affects Brand Equity of Indian Firms? *Global Business Review, 18*(3_suppl), S52–S69. https://doi.org/10.1177/0972150917693149

32. Torres, A., Bijmolt, T. H. A., Tribó, J. A., & Verhoef, P. (2012). Generating global brand equity through corporate social responsibility to key stakeholders. *International Journal of Research in Marketing, 29*(1), 13–24. https://doi.org/10.1016/j.ijresmar.2011.10.002

33. van Doorn, J., Onrust, M., Verhoef, P. C., & Bügel, M. S. (2017). The impact of corporate social responsibility on customer attitudes and retention—the moderating role of brand success indicators. *Marketing Letters, 28*(4), 607–619. https://doi.org/10.1007/s11002-017-9433-6

34. Walsh, G., & Bartikowski, B. (2013). Exploring corporate ability and social responsibility associations as antecedents of customer satisfaction cross-culturally. *Journal of Business Research, 66*(8), 989–995. https://doi.org/10.1016/j.jbusres.2011.12.022

35. Wang, H. M. D. (2010). Corporate social performance and financial-based brand equity. *Journal of Product and Brand Management, 19*(5), 335–345. https://doi.org/10.1108/10610421011068577

36. Wang, H. M., Yu, T. H. K., & Hsiao, C. Y. (2021). The Causal Effect of Corporate Social Responsibility and Corporate Reputation on Brand Equity: A Fuzzy-Set Qualitative Comparative Analysis. *Journal of Promotion Management, 27*(5), 630–641. https://doi.org/10.1080/10496491.2020.1851851

37. Westin, L., & Parmler, J. (2020). Inclusion of CSR in the extended performance satisfaction index–new development. *Total Quality Management and Business Excellence*. https://doi.org/10.1080/14783363.2020.1856651

38. Xie, Y. (2014). The Effects of Corporate Ability and Corporate Social Responsibility on Winning Customer Support: An Integrative Examination of the Roles of Satisfaction, Trust and Identification. *Global Economic Review, 43*(1), 73–92. https://doi.org/10.1080/1226508X.2014.884050

39. Xu, Y. (2014). Understanding CSR from the perspective of Chinese diners: The case of McDonald's. *International Journal of Contemporary Hospitality Management*, *26*(6), 1002–1020. https://doi.org/10.1108/IJCHM-01-2013-0051

40. Young, S. L., & Makhija, M. v. (2014). Firms' corporate social responsibility behavior: An integration of institutional and profit maximization approaches. *Journal of International Business Studies*, *45*(6), 670–698. https://doi.org/10.1057/jibs.2014.29

Emerging Horizons: Business and Society in the Post Pandemic Era –
Brig. Dr. Rajiv Divekar et al. (eds)
© *2024 Taylor & Francis Group, London, ISBN 978-1-032-90822-9*

4

Anemia and Health—Study of Population Health

Kamlesh Yagnik[1]
President, Shree Ramkrishna Knowledge Foundation,
Surat, India

Nirav A. Mandir[2]
Chief Human Capital Officer, Shree Ramkrishna Exports Pvt. Ltd,
Surat, India

Mita Mehta[3]
Professor, Symbiosis Institute of Health Sciences,
Symbiosis International (Deemed University),
Pune, Maharashtra, India

Shruti Verma[4]
Independent Researcher, India

ABSTRACT

The present research focuses on the population study of three districts of Amreli named Lathi, Liliya, and Babra, Gujarat, India. The present research aims to recognize the impact of demographic factors on health, especially Anemia, among rural people of the selected district. The study includes fieldwork health data of more than 1,10,339 populations, which has been statistically analyzed with the help of statistical software.

This study contributes to the branch of knowledge in terms of population health study, which is one of its kind in India. This study has used extensive data from the rural population through the SRK-Health Kalam project, a unique SRK foundation step. This research intends to give visibility to such a project and bring an in-depth analysis of the population data collected. The present study confirms the frequency of Anemia and its association with the factors that are part of demographic strata, namely, the age and gender of the population. This study will guide and motivate more such population studies in other parts of India.

KEYWORDS: Anemia, Demographic, Health, Population, India

[1]kamlesh.yagnik@srkkf.in, [2]nirav.am@srk.me, [3]tnrcms.mita@gmail.com, [4]shrutiverrma1993@rediffmail.com

DOI: 10.4324/978100355996-4

1. Introduction

India has been independent for so many years now. India has witnessed tremendous growth in many sectors post-independence, yet this is only across some industries. Some sectors have been showing a consistent growth trend, while others are yet to reach the level of potential to grow. Regardless of India's growth and development, one cannot claim that the country can take the global leadership position with remarkable health and health-related factors development. India has to have similar growth in the health sector as it has achieved in other sectors like infrastructure, rural, banking, and others. India's present performance in these sectors also needs attention (Zodpey & Negandhi, 2018). Healthy does not mean only the absence of disease; instead, it means attaining a state of a human's mental and physical well-being. Changes in demographic factors had an incidental effect on life expectancy via healthcare resources (Chan & Taylor, 2013), which reveals that social class is the prime factor when deciding about health. This shows that there is a significant gap in terms of health benefits experienced in different social classes.In India, anemia affects a significant percentage of the population and is a serious public health concern. Given that anemia is more common in women and children, it is a primary target of research and treatment initiatives. Here are some important details about anemia research and population health in India.

India has an alarming prevalence of anemia; as numerous studies have repeatedly shown. For present study one of th main source of incident of anemia in India is the National Family Health Survey (NFHS). According to the NFHS-4 (2015–16), 58.4% of children under the age of five and almost 53% of women aged 15–49 were anemic. To battle anemia, the Indian government has thrown numerous initiatives. Efforts to prevent and treat anemia, especially in women and children, include the National Iron+ Initiative (NIPI) and the Weekly Iron and Folic Acid Supplementation (WIFS) program. Since it is distressing the majority of the population, particularly children this remains a major health concern. To get more insight about this health issue, this study gives further insights.

2. Literature Review

Anemia is a sickness where the volume of red blood cells is inadequate to meet the body's efficient requirements (Johnson-Wimbley & Graham, 2011; Gautam et al., 2019). Anemia is an illness where the red cells of the body are in a reduced number, or the cells or the hemoglobin absorption is relatively low as compared to normal (Anaemia, n.d.). The initial signals of change in the nutritional status of iron can be observed through erythrocyte factors, for example, ferritin, and later changes in hemoglobin level (Guyatt et al., 1992). Examining micronutrient deficiency is essential to measure the parameters related to health, including iron-related assessments, and such studies are focused worldwide. The studies on iron and its deficiencies were done during the 1990s when authors found that iron deficiency does not always cause Anemia. However, the main reason for Anemia is a deficiency in the iron level (Kassebaum and GBD 2013 Anemia Collaborators, 2016). Thus, the valuation of these parameters is essential for the investigation of possible factors that culminate in reduced iron levels(Lopes et al., 2022), mainly because Anemia is characterized by disorders during hemoglobinization (Chinudomwong et al., 2020), which may be caused by iron deficiency. It is observed in many research papers across the globe that hemoglobin is essential to transmit oxygen (Rhodes et al., 2021). This might result in reduced capacity of the blood to transmit oxygen to the body's tissues. World Health Organization (WHO), Anemia is a serious worldwide public health issue (Chaparro & Suchdev, 2019).

Anemia is a severe issue that primarily affects the health of pregnant women and young children (Stephen et al., 2018). Word Health Organization estimates that around 42 percent of children who are less than the age of five years and around 40 percent of pregnant women across the world are anemic ("Anaemia"). Anemia is extensively spread in public health, and it is considered one of the more significant risk factors for health issues as well as death among children going to preschool, women in their reproductive stage, and older population (André et al., 2018). As Anemia has comparatively high pervasiveness, the World Health Organization has targeted at least a 50 percent reduction in the cases among women of reproductive age and the old population (WHO, 2017). Though, condensed investments in public policies aimed at fighting in direct or indirect form for micronutrient absences/hidden hunger coupled (Lopes et al., 2022) with the health crisis posed by the COVID-19 pandemic has made it more challenging to achieve this goal (Globally, malnutrition in all its forms remains a considerable challenge)

Currently, WHO mentioned that Anemia will impact more than 20 percent of the world's population, and it will impact women and school-going children (McLean et al., 2009). Deficiency of Iron in the body is considered the most known cause of Anemia across the globe and is majorly observed in developing nations in Africa and Asia (Miller, 2013). Multiple factors can be responsible for Anemia, for example, dietary deficiency, obesity, the presence or absence of some infection, irregular menstruation cycle, etc. (Machado et al., 2019). However, demographic factors leading to Anemia should be studied more logically than the availability of health services (Mehrotra et al., 2018). In India, such population studies have yet to be done, especially in rural areas, and data on more than 1 lakh people has yet to be collected. The SRK Knowledge Foundation assumed the role of the integrator and identified population in Lathi Taluka of Amreli district, Gujarat, with the PSM Department, Civil Hospital, Surat, and Care Foundation providing academic inputs like conceptual framework and methodology, analytics and technology support, particularly Internet of things (IoT) devices. The project was named SRK Kalam Health Project (SRK-KHP) in memory of Dr. APJ Abdul Kalam, who departed in July 2015. In a country like India, a high occurrence of Anemia was observed among people in lower school rather than those in higher secondary school (Tesfaye et al., 2015). Research done worldwide reveals that people who live in rural areas are more at risk of developing Anemia than those in urban areas, which may be more than fifty percent (Ismail et al., 2016; Zaytoun & Khan, 2016). Anemia is also causing deaths in many countries, especially in children. Anemia not only results in limiting physical activities among the growing kids and restricting their growth but also impacts other populations and those in the middle age group (Vindhya et al., 2019). Anemia in adulthood might cause poor economic results since it results in poor productivity and, thereby, poor economic outcomes (Subramaniam & Girish, 2015); with this objective, this study has been placed as a form of research based on the data collected from that.

3. Objectives

The present study has the following cited objectives

- To evaluate the population study in terms of the health parameters
- To suggest medical treatment and facility based on the revelation of the study of population
- To create and develop technology-based health benefits where the point of care will be triggered based on the health initiatives

4. Research Methodology

Before collecting data from 1,10,339 populations, the pilot study was initiated at the Sanktoba Medical Center at a public event held in the Lathi Taluka Headquarters before gathering approximately 2000 people and district health officials and workers. This was followed by village-level meetings to build local community awareness for the project. The SRK-KHP Health Committee, consisting of five members, would work with two volunteers from the village to sensitize the local community leaders about the project. The public meetings were held along with the leaders at the village level. The people were informed about the days of screening, the time when screening was open, and where the screening would be conducted. The number of days that screening was held in a village depended on the size of the population and the expected number of participants. Alongside, arrangements for food, water, electricity, space, and other amenities were made in consultation with the villagers. The help of the Internet of Things (IoT) has been taken for this research. IoT was used to create a cloud-based database. This would be further used for analyzing and derivation of indicators about health. Also, this can be used as actual feeds using point-of-care-related machinery for future care and expansion.

Even with noteworthy growth within the intensive care device industry, the extensive incorporation of this technology into medical practice remains limited (Appelboom et al., 2014). All participants were advised to rest for at least 15 minutes before blood collection. Blood collection was done using a blood collection needle and holder. All samples were centrifuged at the screening site using a REMI centrifuge. The separated serum was stored in a head-insulated box with an ice pack to preserve it. Reports were prepared with the help of customized software for data entry, and they were double-checked before the conclusion. As mentioned in objective number 2, village volunteers were contacted by phone or in person by the participants whose samples had abnormal values. They were given the lab reports, counseled, and referred to the Government or specialty hospital for treatment, depending on the context. Exploratory Data Analysis was carried out initially. Basic statistics like frequencies for categorical variables or summary measures like mean and median for continuous variables were computed.

For Ethical considerations; Careful attention was taken to the personal information of every respondent who participated in the survey. Personal information of any kind was not shared with any other company or organization in any form. In addition, the population, rather than the individual, has been represented in our survey report. All the data was managed and stored at the SRK Kalam Health Project Lab, Surat.

5. Data Analysis

As mentioned in the methodology section, researchers used SPSS software to analyze data. For the presented study, the population of three talukas was studied: Lathi (40.73 %), Liliya (20.03 %), and

Table 4.1 Between-subjects factors

		N
SMEAN(sex)	1.0	53679
	2.0	56660

Babra (39.24%). The total number of participants was 110,339. Among the total sample studied, 48.6% is male and 51.4% is female. 72.8% of the sample was suffering from Anemia. 52.9% of the sample was below 35 years of age. The sample was analyzed using a general linear model (GLM) analysis. After adjusting for sex and age, anthropometrical grade pointers are significantly associated with Anemia ($p<=0.05$).

Table 4.2 Tests of between-subjects effects

The dependent variables: SMEAN(Anemia)					
Source	Type III Sum of square	df	Mean Square	F	Sig.
Corrected Model	979.003[a]	2	489.502	2584.944	.000
Intercept	50363.008	1	50363.008	265955.341	.000
age_1	380.306	1	380.306	2008.307	.000
sex_1	608.497	1	608.497	3213.331	.000
Error	20893.932	110336	.189		
Total	200534.000	110339			
Corrected Total	21872.935	110338			

a. R Squared = .045 (Adjusted R Square = .045)

Table 4.3 Estimates

SMEAN(sex)	Mean	Std Error	95% Confidence level	
			Lower Bound	Upper Bound
1.0	1.196[a]	.002	1.192	1.200
2.0	1.345[a]	.002	1.341	1.348

Dependent Variable : SMEAN(Anemia)

a. Covariates appearing in the model are evaluated at the following values: SMEAN (age) = 35.126.

Pairwise comparison

Table 4.4 Pairwise comparisons

(I) SMEAN (sex)	(J) SMEAN (sex)	Mean Difference (I-J)	Std. Error	Sig. [b]	95% Confidence Interval for Difference	
					Lower Bound	Upper Bound
1.0	2.0	-.149*	.003	.000	-.154	-.143
2.0	1.0	.149*	.003	.000	.143	.154

Dependent Variable: SMEAN(Anemia)

Univariate Tests: Based on the marginal means that are estimated
The mean difference is significant at a 0.05 level

Table 4.5 Univariate tests

	Sum of Squares	df	Mean Square	F	Sig.
Contrast	608.497	1	608.497	3213.331	.000
Error	20893.932	110336	.189		

Dependent Variable: SMEAN(Anemia)

The F test is the consequence of SMEAN; this test is based on the linearly independent pairwise comparison among the estimated marginal means.

6. Discussion

The authors have presented the study about the primary concern among politicians, academicians, and the general public nowadays. Post the pandemic, it has become evident that the general public has started looking into the preventive healthcare aspects a lot. The general occurrence of Anemia in this community was 27.24%, with a vast variance between the genders of Males and Females (34.41% vs. 19.67%, respectively). Moreover, among subjects with Anemia, the degree was worse in females than in males (Orellana et al., 2011), with moderate and severe

Anemia being 41.09% and 21.98%, respectively. While submitting the discussion of this study, since it is related to the rural population, it is to be noted that rural populations have some existing risks in their food consumption having the highest nutrient availability. Compared to the urban population, people residing in small towns or villages are at risk of not having access to fruits and vegetables. There have been myths among the Indian population that the consumption of fruits and vegetables would be higher than that of the urban population.

However, due to financial and educational factors (Fernandes et al., 2018), these people need help to afford, access, or even prefer to get nutritious food. Cultural factors (da Silva Lopes et al., 2017) even observed during the study that some people also relied heavily on the self-consumption of farm produce. The COVID-19 pandemic has taught lifestyle focus and even food habits. Indian population residing in small towns and villages needs to be educated about monotonous food habits and how to overcome them (Fao, 2021). There was even an observation related to a lack of awareness and encouragement practices to adopt a healthy lifestyle, including eating food and a balanced diet among productive women. The authors have strongly suggested here to mark timely interventions from the Government and non-government organizations spreading such awareness among the educators and socially impactful personalities among these residents who can timely inform and remind them about the health-related issues if the nutrition is inadequate in their diet. Social and Government policy decisions should be made for people residing in small-town areas where access to such health facilities is also limited (Stoltzfus, 2003). The results of this study stress the significance of promoting public health actions (Lopes et al., 2022), especially with people residing in villages and rural areas.

This study focuses on large populations that have not been studied previously, supporting the findings of earlier studies that focus on rather than pool factor push factors that play a significant role in speeding knowledge related to public health.

Female Anemia was expressively more significant (Abdo et al., 2019). As shown in the line chart in Fig. 4.1, as age increases, the prevalence of Anemia increases in females and decreases in males. Further, Anemia is worse in adult females older than 15 years. This unsurprising contrast may be partly attributed to the failure to address the satisfaction and stress of pregnancy and childbirth (Mahamoud et al., 2020). This chart shows a significant impact of gender and age on the prevalence of Anemia. It continues to be the most serious health issue facing the community, which can be attributed to a lack of attention towards nutritional food intake among children and hormonal imbalances among women. The present study validates the frequency of Anemia and its relationship with factors about the demographic environment, namely, the age and gender of the population. This study has also been conducted in parallel with earlier studies. Earlier research quantified that the occurrence of Anemia in women was almost double as compared to men in India (Kerala) (Ismail et al., 2016) and also found that the rate of Anemia in men

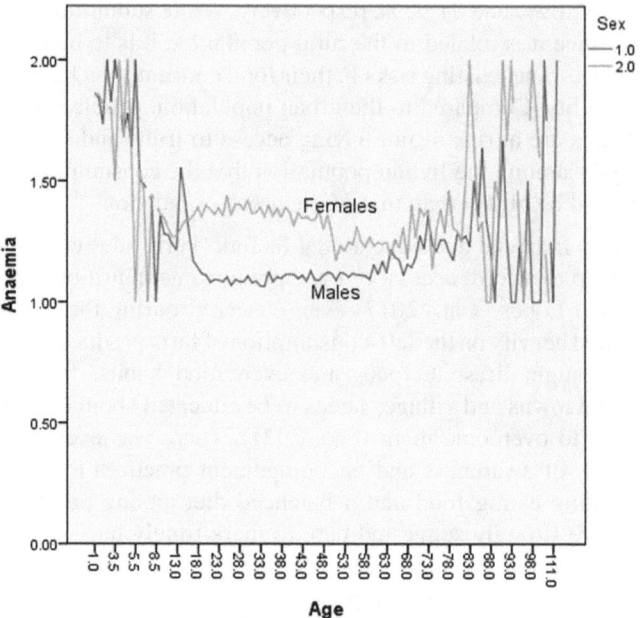

Fig. 4.1   Line chart showing trends of prevalence of Anemia based on Age and Gender (In this figure, Sex:1=Male; 2=Female)

corresponds to age, but it in women increases double with mountains in the age group 40–49 years and 80–85 years. (Zaytoun & Khan, 2016). Anemia remains a public health issue in rural areas (Hoang et al., 2019), and this study has been conducted in rural areas where it was found that in this population study, Anemia remained a factor of concern.

7. Conclusion

This study focuses only on Gujarat, India, and is therefore geographically limited. Other demographic factors, such as education level, socio-economic status, etc., have yet to be considered in this study. Other factors leading to an increase in the prevalence of Anemia, like diet, lifestyle, health, genetics, etc., have not been considered here. Some of the earlier research discovered that education and the occurrence of Anemia have a direct association. Some of the influences like economic and social factors, including demographic factors (Balarajan et al., 2011) like level of education, have a direct or high correlation with the level of Anemia among women (Mahamoud et al., 2020); researchers suggest that such type of association can be further investigated to understand the level of education among female participants and the prevailing rate of Anemia. This study can eventually lead to the development of a nationwide Population Health Model covering one in every six humans living on the planet. The present study validates the idea that the symbol of the field of population health is an essential consideration to the multiple determinants of such health outcomes, irrespective of how they are measured. Despite continuous endeavors, certain obstacles endure, such as insufficient cognizance, insufficient healthcare facilities, and socioeconomic elements impacting eating patterns. An all-encompassing strategy that includes community involvement, education, and healthcare is needed to address anemia.

REFERENCES

1. Abdo, N., Douglas, S., Batieha, A., Khader, Y., Jaddou, H., Al-Khatib, S., El-Khatib, M., AbuZaid, H., & Ajlouni, K. (2019). The prevalence and determinants of anaemia in Jordan. *La Revue de Sante de La Mediterranee Orientale [Eastern Mediterranean Health Journal]*, *25*(5), 341–349. https://doi.org/10.26719/emhj.18.047
2. *Anaemia.* (n.d.). Who.int. Retrieved November 30, 2023, from https://www.who.int/health-topics/anaemia
3. André, H. P. (2018). Food and nutrition insecurity indicators associated with iron deficiency anemia in Brazilian children: a systematic review. *Ciencia & Saude Coletiva, 23*, 1159–1167.
4. Appelboom, G., Camacho, E., Abraham, M. E., Bruce, S. S., Dumont, E. L. P., Zacharia, B. E., D'Amico, R., Slomian, J., Reginster, J. Y., Bruyère, O., & Connolly, E. S., Jr. (2014). Smart wearable body sensors for patient self-assessment and monitoring. *Archives Belges de Sante Publique [Archives of Public Health], 72*(1). https://doi.org/10.1186/2049-3258-72-28
5. Aziz Ali, S., Abbasi, Z., Feroz, A., Hambidge, K. M., Krebs, N. F., Westcott, J. E., & Saleem, S. (2019). Factors associated with anemia among women of the reproductive age group in Thatta district: study protocol. *Reproductive Health, 16*(1). https://doi.org/10.1186/s12978-019-0688-7
6. Balarajan, Y., Ramakrishnan, U., Özaltin, E., Shankar, A. H., & Subramanian, S. V. (2011). Anaemia in low-income and middle-income countries. *Lancet, 378*(9809), 2123–2135. https://doi.org/10.1016/s0140-6736(10)62304-5
7. Chan, M. F., & Taylor, B. J. (2013). Impact of demographic change, socioeconomics, and health care resources on life expectancy in Cambodia, Laos, and Myanmar. *Public Health Nursing (Boston, Mass.), 30*(3), 183–192. https://doi.org/10.1111/phn.12005
8. Chaparro, C. M., & Suchdev, P. S. (2019). Anemia epidemiology, pathophysiology, and etiology in low- and middle-income countries. *Annals of the New York Academy of Sciences, 1450*(1), 15–31. https://doi.org/10.1111/nyas.14092
9. Chinudomwong, P., Binyasing, A., Trongsakul, R., & Paisooksantivatana, K. (2020). Diagnostic performance of reticulocyte hemoglobin equivalent in assessing the iron status. *Journal of Clinical Laboratory Analysis, 34*(6). https://doi.org/10.1002/jcla.23225
10. da Silva Lopes, K., Ota, E., Shakya, P., Dagvadorj, A., Balogun, O. O., Peña-Rosas, J. P., De-Regil, L. M., & Mori, R. (2017). Effects of nutrition interventions during pregnancy on low birth weight: an overview of systematic reviews. *BMJ Global Health, 2*(3), e000389. https://doi.org/10.1136/bmjgh-2017-000389
11. Fao, I. (2021). *WFP and WHO. The State of Food Security and Nutrition in the World 2021. Transforming food systems for food security, improved nutrition, and affordable healthy diets.*

12. Fernandes, M. P., Bielemann, R. M., & Fassa, A. G. (2018). Factors associated with the quality of the diet of residents of a rural area in Southern Brazil. *Revista de Saude Publica, 52*, 6s. https://doi.org/10.11606/s1518-8787.2018052000267

13. Gautam, S., Min, H., Kim, H., & Jeong, H.-S. (2019). Determining factors for the prevalence of anemia in women of reproductive age in Nepal: Evidence from recent national survey data. *PloS One, 14*(6), e0218288. https://doi.org/10.1371/journal.pone.0218288

14. Gedefaw, L., Tesfaye, M., Yemane, T., Adisu, W., & Asres, Y. (2015). Anemia and iron deficiency among school adolescents: burden, severity, and determinant factors in southwest Ethiopia. *Adolescent Health, Medicine and Therapeutics*, 189. https://doi.org/10.2147/ahmt.s94865

15. Hoang, Orellana, Le, Gibson, Worsley, Sinclair, Hoang, & Szymlek-Gay. (2019). Anaemia and its relation to demographic, Socio-economic and anthropometric factors in rural primary school children in Hai Phong City, Vietnam. *Nutrients, 11*(7), 1478. https://doi.org/10.3390/nu11071478

16. Ismail, I., Kahkashan, A., Antony, A., & Sobhith. (2016). Role of socio-demographic and cultural factors on anemia in a tribal population of North Kerala, India. *International Journal of Community Medicine and Public Health*, 1183–1188. https://doi.org/10.18203/2394-6040.ijcmph20161381

17. Johnson-Wimbley, T. D., & Graham, D. Y. (2011). Diagnosis and management of iron deficiency anemia in the 21st century. *Therapeutic Advances in Gastroenterology, 4*(3), 177–184. https://doi.org/10.1177/1756283x11398736

18. Kassebaum, N. J. (2016). The global burden of anemia. *Hematology/Oncology Clinics of North America, 30*(2), 247–308. https://doi.org/10.1016/j.hoc.2015.11.002

19. Lopes, S. O., Ribeiro, S. A. V., Morais, D. de C., Miguel, E. da S., Gusmão, L. S., Franceschini, S. do C. C., & Priore, S. E. (2022). Factors associated with anemia among adults and the elderly family farmers. *International Journal of Environmental Research and Public Health, 19*(12), 7371. https://doi.org/10.3390/ijerph19127371

20. Machado, Í. E., Malta, D. C., Bacal, N. S., & Rosenfeld, L. G. M. (2019). Prevalência de anemia em adultos e idosos brasileiros. *Revista Brasileira de Epidemiologia [Brazilian Journal of Epidemiology], 22*(suppl 2). https://doi.org/10.1590/1980-549720190008.supl.2

21. Mahamoud, N. K., Mwambi, B., Oyet, C., Segujja, F., Webbo, F., Okiria, J. C., & Taremwa, I. M. (2020). Prevalence of anemia and its associated Socio-demographic factors among pregnant women attending an antenatal care clinic at kisugu health center IV, makindye division, Kampala, Uganda. *Journal of Blood Medicine, 11*, 13–18. https://doi.org/10.2147/jbm.s231262

22. McLean, E., Cogswell, M., Egli, I., Wojdyla, D., & de Benoist, B. (2009). Worldwide prevalence of anaemia, WHO Vitamin and Mineral Nutrition Information System, 1993–2005. *Public Health Nutrition, 12*(04), 444. https://doi.org/10.1017/s1368980008002401

23. Miller, J. L. (2013). Iron deficiency anemia: A common and curable disease. *Cold Spring Harbor Perspectives in Medicine, 3*(7), a011866–a011866. https://doi.org/10.1101/cshperspect.a011866

24. Nath, A., Vindhya, J., Murthy, G. V. S., Metgud, C., Sheeba, B., Shubhashree, V., & Srinivas, P. (2019). Prevalence and risk factors of anemia among pregnant women attending a public-sector hospital in Bangalore, South India. *Journal of Family Medicine and Primary Care, 8*(1), 37. https://doi.org/10.4103/jfmpc.jfmpc_265_18

25. Orellana, J. D. Y., Cunha, G. M., Santos, R. V., Coimbra, C. E. A., Jr, & Leite, M. S. (2011). Prevalência e fatores associados à anemia em mulheres indígenas Suruí com idade entre 15 e 49 anos, Amazônia, Brasil. *Revista Brasileira de Saúde Materno Infantil*, *11*(2), 153–161. https://doi.org/10.1590/s1519-38292011000200006

26. Rhodes, C. E., Denault, D., & Varacallo, M. (2021). *StatPearls [Internet. StatPearls Publishing.*

27. Stephen, G., Mgongo, M., Hussein Hashim, T., Katanga, J., Stray-Pedersen, B., & Msuya, S. E. (2018). Anaemia in pregnancy: Prevalence, risk factors, and adverse perinatal outcomes in Northern Tanzania. *Anemia*, *2018*, 1–9. https://doi.org/10.1155/2018/1846280

28. Stoltzfus, R. J. (2003). Iron deficiency: Global prevalence and consequences. *Food and Nutrition Bulletin*, 24(4_suppl2), S99–S103. https://doi.org/10.1177/15648265030244s206

29. Subramaniam, G., & Girish, M. (2015). Iron deficiency anemia in children. *Indian Journal of Pediatrics*, 82(6), 558–564. https://doi.org/10.1007/s12098-014-1643-9

30. Yadav, S., Mehrotra, M., Deshpande, A., & Mehrotra, H. (2018). A study of the prevalence of anemia and associated sociodemographic factors in pregnant women in Port Blair, Andaman and Nicobar Islands. *Journal of Family Medicine and Primary Care*, 7(6), 1288. https://doi.org/10.4103/jfmpc.jfmpc_139_18

31. Zaytoun, S., & Khan, E. A. (2016). SOCIODEMOGRAPHIC RISK FACTORS OF IRON DEFICIENCY ANEMIA IN YOUNG ADULT MALES OF UPPER EGYPT. *Khyber Medical University Journal*, 8, 123–123.

32. Zodpey, S., & Negandhi, P. (2018). Tracking India's progress in health sector after 70 years of independence. *Indian Journal of Public Health*, 62(1), 1. https://doi.org/10.4103/ijph.ijph_391_17

Note: All the figures and tables in this chapter were made by the authors.

Emerging Horizons: Business and Society in the Post Pandemic Era –
Brig. Dr. Rajiv Divekar et al. (eds)
© *2024 Taylor & Francis Group, London, ISBN 978-1-032-90822-9*

Social Entrepreneurship through Sustainable Business Model: A Case Study

5

Sriparna Guha[1]
Amity Business School, Amity University, Kolkata

Anirban Mandal[2]
ICFAI Business School, Kolkata

ABSTRACT

This article examines social innovation in the context of community-based entrepreneurial activity of a section of the artisans to aid in the preservation of local waste while also providing social inclusion to the members of the "South Asian Forum for Environment (SAFE)". Our findings are based on a thorough investigation of the work of SAFE, which trains men and women how to turn local waste into crafts and assists them in selling them to earn money. This qualitative study is based on interviews with people who are members of SAFE. According to the data, trainees are fully supported by the SAFE, whether in terms of activity, planning, technical and financial investment, or product sales. Furthermore, those who work in this enterprise feel useful and proud that they are helping to protect the environment. The objective of this article is to review SAFE's innovative business strategy and determine how well and efficiently it has been put into practise. The information that has been analysed is also being used to establish a strategy for improving community-based development's efficacy and efficiency.

KEYWORDS: Social entrepreneurship, Social innovation, Waste management, Sustainability, Business model

1. Introduction

Traditional business theories are built on the idea of maximising economic profit, which forces businesses to concentrate on enhancing their competence to better

[1]sriparna.pink@gmail.com, [2]anirban3009@gmail.com

DOI: 10.4324/978100355996-5

meet customer expectations (Nager, 2007; Cao, 2014). Business is currently undergoing a paradigm transition. Old beliefs and a singular concentration on economic gain are said to be ineffective as they create a barrier to sustainable community-based development in a particular society (Ramadani et al., 2020). The traditional idea of business is fading away as more and more people and organisations realise that addressing and fixing the challenges faced by society is profitable. A firm may improve people's lives and make money at the same time by solving urgent challenges (Thorsen, 2015). Finding efficient and long-lasting solutions to new societal issues, however, is a significant task (Guha et al., 2024). These might necessitate taking actions linked to effective company innovation. Reformation and innovation are being used simultaneously to satisfy the market and society.

The main economic challenges now are biodiversity loss, the economic slump, and unequal wealth distribution. They are a direct result of broken global economic markets and unsustainable, short-term economic gain-oriented development patterns (Nagler, 2007). Locally, in many developing nations, environmental degradation is heavily influenced by persistent poverty connected to rapid population growth (Li, 2014). To meet short-term livelihood needs, rural populations are compelled to overuse the environment, which limits prospects for long-term development. This results in the creation of a "poverty trap," a vicious cycle of growing poverty and environmental destruction. Environmental protection must be a key component of any strategy for inclusive, sustainable growth (Ramadani et al., 2020). The state of the economy is what policymakers are most concerned with; the environment is a secondary topic at the top.

Rapid industrialization, urbanisation, and economic growth have all contributed to an increase in waste production. Any item that has not been directly used as a result of human activity is considered waste. There are two types of waste: biological and mineral waste, which are further subdivided into domestic and non-domestic waste (Harun et al., 2021). Every nation has focused on finding solutions for waste management problems. The main problem that is associated with solid waste management is mainly related to a lack of understanding and awareness about the source of creation of waste (Ilo et al., 2020).

Since 2004, the SAFE, a recognised civil society group, has worked to reduce poverty and promote sustainable environmental development in the South Asian Indian ecoregion. Through community involvement, partnerships, and reciprocity, the SAFE is dedicated to working toward ecological restoration and conservation to promote sustainable environmental development in the South Asian ecoregion of India. To preserve human habitation and ensure the livelihood of peripheral communities, SAFE has fostered stakeholder participation and community partnerships. In urban cities, SAFE collaborates with local communities to develop creative, entrepreneurial waste management solutions that foster microbusinesses rooted in the neighbourhood and reduce landfill emissions. "Resolve Trash2Cash," a SAFE initiative that won many prestigious awards at the United Nations, is currently being expanded in Bangladesh, Bhutan, and India. They convert the dried water hyacinth into different decorative items for households (SAFE, 2017).

Eichhornia crassipes, a weed, is a popular and common sight in lakes, rivers, and other bodies of water all round the world (Segbefia et al., 2019). Water forms with water hyacinth invasions are typically stimulating to clean up due to their high rates of rebirth, survival, and evolution (Ilo et al., 2020). These characteristics of water hyacinth can be viewed as positive traits nonetheless. Hyacinth has been tested as an absorber for heavy metals, water pollution, and other contaminants (Ilo et al., 2020). This water-born plant is ranked among the 10 worst weeds in the world, yet it is also regarded as a very productive plant (Ajieh et al., 2020; Aboul-Enein et al., 2011).

Turning an apparent disadvantage into an opportunity is one way to be innovative in resource management. The practice of water hyacinth in the production of handicrafts is an important method of managing the weed problem in fresh waters, as well as creating employment and income (Ramadani et al., 2020). Despite the growing number of successful social community-based entrepreneurs and their growing businesses in recent years, their growth momentum and market acceptability are still relatively new (Haugh & Talwar, 2016). It is interesting to explore why this sort of business endeavour emerged and developed globally, as well as how its concept and operation could be described and explained, especially for many nations that are confronting rural poverty and looking for solutions to cope with economic and societal challenges. This article's goal is to evaluate SAFE's creative business strategy and assess the degree to which it has been implemented effectively and efficiently. Additionally, a strategy for enhancing the effectiveness and efficiency of community-based development is developed using the data that has been analysed.

We shall address a review of significant theories about socially enabled entrepreneurial activities and business model innovation in the following section of this paper. In the methodology section, we will discuss a brief description of the case study. Following that, it will gain insight, focusing primarily on the selection of SAFE and its social impacts. In the next section, problems and constraints will be discussed. Results and discussions will be in the next section. Finally, conclusions and recommendations for social entrepreneurship will be discussed based on the research.

2. Literature Review

Every entrepreneurial effort begins with a vision of a compelling possibility. An "attractive" break has a high enough budding growth trajectory for a good socio-economic impact on the life of the people belonging to that society. This is required to justify the time, energy, and money spent on it. Social entrepreneurship (SE) has emerged as an important domain of entrepreneurship study that is "increasingly maturing" (Sassmannshausen and Volkmann, 2018). Accountability for social consequences and the triple bottom line—economic, societal, and environmental sustainability—a term coined by John Elkington—are essential components of social entrepreneurship (Savitz, 2013). Social entrepreneurs have dual objectives in mind. On the one hand, they want to contribute to society economically on the other hand they want to do something unique that can alter the world. Entrepreneurs are increasingly creating enterprises because they see a chance to further a cause that is dear to them (Garcia et al., 2021). The rise of a hybrid business model sometimes called a "social business," that is neither entirely for-profit nor entirely non-profit (Zimmerer & Scarborough, 2005; Gupta et al., 2020), has been called social enterprise (Elkington & Hartigan, 2008).

The initial mission and commercial impacts are the primary alterations between social and traditional entrepreneurship. Social entrepreneurs are concerned with social issues; thus, they concentrate on finding ways to reduce or get rid of social constraints and provide beneficial externalities or public goods (García-Jurado et al., 2021). SE has been considered innovative as well as market-oriented. The term "innovative" describes a change in operating philosophy and company style. Social enterprises that are "market-oriented" engage in commercial activity. They pay their workers, try to make money to stay self-sufficient, and put the money they make back into their social goal (Li, 2014).

In the past 20 years, SE has grown significantly (Yunus et al., 2010; Grassl, 2012; Mair & Ganly, 2015). The rise of SE not just among practitioners but also in academia and policy-making was sparked by a number of occasions and worldwide shifts. SE has been pushed by welfare issues, environmental concerns, rising economic inequality, and a chronic lack of access to clean electricity, water, and basic healthcare in some regions of the world (Nicholls, 2012). SE steps in and tries to discover new ways to meet these demands because markets can seldom address these problems. This is due to the fact that market failure offers both social and commercial entrepreneurs' unique chances (Austin et al., 2006). However, in order to take advantage of these opportunities and fulfil their social mission, these businesses must develop, organise, and innovate their business model (Seelos & Mair, 2007; Seelos et al., 2011; Wilson & Post, 2013).

Social innovation (SI) is an essential component of any discussion about SE. SE and SI are interconnected (Spiess-Knafl et al. 2015). In that regard, it is frequently used as a standard to categorise a business as a social enterprise (Dees, 1998; Zahra et al., 2009; Alexandre-Leclair, 2017). Business innovations, in contrast to social advances, typically aim to maximise profits. To put it another way, the goal of business innovation is to make money from the idea by generating economic value (Weis, 2017). These innovations are typically categorised as either technological innovations, like new goods and services, or organisational innovations, such as enhancing a business's systems and structures (Pol & Ville, 2009; Zainea et al., 2020). In terms of innovation spill overs like knowledge spill overs, these inventions might also be advantageous for society; nonetheless, innovators and customers are the main beneficiaries of business innovations (Alexandre-Leclair, 2017).

Academics have expanded on SE and how value creation and capture are structured at the corporate and societal scales to provide a foundation for social business models (Seelos & Mair, 2007; Seelos et al., 2011; Kusumasari, 2016). According to Wilson and Post (2013), this can be accomplished by concurrently aiming for both turnover and non-profit outcomes. A value proposition is the first component of a social business model. It defines the firm's customers and beneficiaries, as well as the products and services that it provides to social target groups and customers. Second, social business models demonstrate a value constellation that mirrors a firm's value chain and consumer interface, just like traditional business models do. It describes the networks of partners and suppliers who are tangled in the company's processes in addition to the internal value chain (Agrawal & Gugnani, 2014). Third, the social profit calculation stipulates the type of worth shaped to address societal issues positively. This can result in the manufacture of either social or commercial worth (Kusumasari, 2016). Fourth, the economic profit equation defines the economic model, or how the venture financially supports its social mission. However, social businesses seek only to recover costs and capitalised capital, not to maximise financial profit (Dhewanto et al., 2018).

In order to gain a competitive edge, firms rely on business models to help with data collection, analysis, and decision-making. (Cao, 2014; Weis, 2017). With new social challenges and increased social pressure, many firms are becoming concerned about CSR and philanthropy. Business model innovation has become their trend. Through its work at the intersection of science and society, SAFE has been working to alleviate poverty and promote sustainable environmental development in the Indian ecoregion of South Asia since 2004. In the face of climate change, SAFE was formed to pursue sustainable environmental development goals for poverty alleviation through empowerment, equity, and reciprocity. There has been a substantial increase in emissions worldwide, and one major contributor is the lack of proper waste management. After energy and transportation, waste is the third most major contributor to global climate change. SAFE has set up a number of climate initiatives to improve waste management in order to deal with this growing problem.

This is still a new idea, even if more and more social companies and businesses are finding success in recent years. It's worth looking into how and why this type of business started and spread around the world, as well as how to describe and explain how it works, especially since many countries are facing problems and looking for ways to deal with the stresses of the economy and society. After going over important literatures about social entrepreneurship and business model innovation, the goal of this study is to look at SAFE as a practical example of social entrepreneurship that has been successful.

3. Methodology

A case study methodology and qualitative approaches were used to perform this study. Since the problems highlighted here are specific to this particular organisation, a case study methodology is appropriate. In research questions like "how" or "why," when the researcher has limited influence over the events under investigation, and when the emphasis is on current happenings in the actual world, a case study is the method of choice (Yin, 2012). This article is a case study to furnish a thorough evaluation and analysis of facts pertaining to a community empowerment programme that employs a social orientation approach in processing water hyacinth and garbage. Qualitative methods of description and purposive sampling are employed in this investigation. This study included fifteen persons from SAFE. Thorough interviews and careful observation are used to gather data, which can be used as a reliable source of triangulation data. Interview guides, observation sheets, documentation, and note-taking on interview and observation outcomes were some of the methods used to collect data for this study.

3.1 Selection of Case

Country: In Kolkata, India, an urban climate initiative called "Resolve Trash to Cash" (SAFE) is working to convert the city's municipal solid wastes into an alternative livelihood for the city's ragpickers and slum dwelling women, who are stigmatised as "people of dirt" and left as victims of social abuse. For equitable respray and social well-being, SAFE equips them to accomplish inclusive growth objectives through community governance and participatory "change management" in protecting natural capital. The main workshop is in Purulia, and they opened a branch in Chingirighata, Kolkata. There are 15 female members in the group. Each member is from a different location, and they come together at the organisation and work unitedly by helping each other. Every year between October and December, this project assists in the removal of water hyacinth, a weed that chokes aquatic bodies. De-weeding not only keeps the pond alive with fish and clean water, but it also generates revenue.

Product/Industry: The South Asian Forum for Environment's "Resolve Trash2Cash" is an urban climate initiative aimed at converting the city's municipal solid wastes into an alternative source of income for waste workers and slum dwellers, who are stigmatised as "dirt citizens" and left behind as victims of flesh trade and social abuse. The project's goal is to create a women-led microenterprise focused on waste recycling, and they produce handicraft products.

3.2 Firm's Dynamic Capabilities to Respond to Changes in the Business Ecosystem

Environmental challenges are among the most serious social issues that the world faces today; environmental entrepreneurship is portrayed as a subset of sustainable entrepreneurship, which is a subset of SE. The objective of SAFE is to engage in environmental activities in climate-vulnerable ecosystems of global importance through community interventions aimed at habitat restoration and biodiversity conservation. It also encourages smallholder farmers to adopt climate-smart agro-farming practices in order to commit to less water and less chemical-intensive sustainable production. In addition, the organisation strives to develop rural capacity for innovation and green technology transfer as well as encourage environmental stewardship for health and sanitation (Bhattacharyya, 2021).

In Kolkata, India, around 5,000 metric tonnes of solid trash are created daily (Roy-Basu et al., 2020). This waste's disposal pollutes groundwater and generates significant quantities of methane gas, which traps heat 25 times more efficiently than carbon dioxide. The firm aspires to recycle 70.85 percent of commercial and residential garbage in urban Kolkata. More than half of the urban poor are employed as trash collectors, sorters, or suppliers. Additionally, the organisation recycles composted organic waste, such as hyacinth. They began by recycling paper waste into useful goods or materials. They then began utilising the hyacinth plant's stems from ponds and lakes to create ornamental items for homes.

They dry the hyacinth stems, then use a machine to flatten the fibre, and then use it to weave environmentally beneficial products like baskets, containers, vases, table mats, coasters, purses, and other items that have found a market across the world. They go through a cleaning process, during which the roots and leaves are taken off. The stems are exposed to sunshine for five to seven days in order to dry. The dried stems are kept in plastic bags to prevent moisture damage. If properly packaged, they can be used for years. Following coloration, hyacinth stems are let dry for further processing. Over 85 percent of the craftspeople participating in hyacinth weaving are women, generating sustainable livelihoods in rural communities and revitalising water bodies.

Since most women work from home, it provides them with an additional income. They earn between INR 8,000 and INR 10,000 per month by selling products to wholesalers. The only motive behind constituting a group of female members was to provide them with the financial independence that all women strive for. This helps them balance their personal and professional lives. They recycled thrown paper into productive diaries and various types of recycled products through paper, such as small diaries, notebooks, pen stands, photo stands, small decorative boxes, etc. Their price ranges from INR 20 to INR 300. They used to go to various fairs in different places, such as Mumbai, Jharkhand, Tripura, Jharkhand, and Kolkata, organised by the National Bank for Agriculture and Rural Development (NABARD). SAFE provides employment, promotes women's empowerment, and also helps the environment grow. In this way, it can solve the financial problem while also increasing the value of the company and making its products much better for society.

3.3 The Social Impact

Through empowerment, equality, and reciprocity, SAFE has worked for a decade to accomplish sustainable environmental development goals for poverty reduction in the Indian ecoregion. In rural areas, SAFE worked with local marginal farmers and fisher communities, who are vulnerable to the effects of climate change, to promote climate-smart agro-environmental practises like farming that uses less water and fewer chemicals, agro-waste management, agrobiodiversity conservation, and so on. In cities, they have mostly focused on water, sanitation, equal rights for men and women, and protecting habitats. SAFE has worked on a national level to create business solutions for managing municipal solid waste and reducing emissions from landfills. They have also worked to use renewable energy sources in the water and sanitation sectors to help the urban poor. Wetland conservation, which is one of SAFE's most important programmes, has been put in place at the regional level. Trash2Cash gives low-income people in cities, especially women and young people who are out of work, long-term jobs. So far, the project has taught more than 300 women how to make crafts from used paper. This gives women more power and gives them financial security. Trash2Cash is not only able to grow, but it can also be used in other cities with low incomes around the world.

4. Problems and Constraints

Some technical and social problems need to be solved. According to the external and internal analyses, the public's lack of knowledge about the waste bank programme is one of the internal factors (strengths and weaknesses). Culture, motivation, openness to new things, and administrative growth are all things that can make it hard to understand things in society. Secondly, not many professionals are interested in waste management because they don't understand the economic benefits of getting rid of trash. The external factor can also be affected by budgeting and regional coordination among stakeholders (opportunity-threat).

5. Results and Discussions

The "value proposition" is the worth of a group of products or services that are offered to meet customer needs and wants. Murphy and Narkiewiez (2010) say that this value includes what a company promises to its customers. In this study, the value proposition is examined through the organization's history, its goals, the social problems it wants to solve, its customers, and what it offers to them. The value proposition that is used in this study is stated in the following table.

Table 5.1   Value proposition of social entrepreneurship

Indicators	Findings
Organisation's purposes	Do everything you can to put an end to global poverty.
	We must prioritise the eradication of hunger, the attainment of food security, the improvement of nutrition, and the promotion of sustainable agriculture.
	Encourage healthy living and overall wellness among people of all ages.
	Promote lasting, broad-based economic expansion, full-and productive employment, and a living wage for everybody.
	Create human communities and cities that are more welcoming, secure, robust, and sustainable.
	Preserve, restore, and promote the responsible utilisation of terrestrial ecosystems. Preserve forest areas through responsible management. Stop the spread of deserts. Reverse land degradation and put a stop to it.
Social Issues to be focused on	Environment, Health, Energy, Education, Skill enhancement
Customers	Community, Marginal and Vulnerable Communities

This organisation is focused on environmental, educational, and health challenges, as well as the empowerment of underserved communities and skill development. The users are given access to protection, efficient technology, support with trash management, and health care. The organisation offers training in environmental protection, health, and education, as well as waste management. It also assists in the production of products generated from trash.

In a nutshell, SAFE makes and sells products that are good for the environment to people in the market. In the long run, it helps solve one of the most important problems in the world—waste—in order to save resources and protect the environment. It makes everyone's lives better in the long run. The services that SAFE offers are the source of the value it brings to its customers. That is, using things and recycling them at the same time, so there is no "waste."

Value creation necessitates a precise understanding of the client segments that a business targets, the current value proposition, and the organization's process for creating value for consumers of its goods and services (Kohler & Chesbrough, 2019). In this study, this includes the organization's value-adding activities, job performance, sustainability, collaborative partners, and activity funding (Borquist and de Burin, 2019). An organisation engaged in social entrepreneurship should aim to create value in a way that more people can benefit from the executed initiatives. The following table shows the value creation of social entrepreneurship at SAFE.

Table 5.2 Value creation of social entrepreneurship

Indicators	Findings
Activities Conducted	Sustainable Consumption and Production a. Resolve T2C b. UNEP 10FYP c. Vermin-composting
	Climate Smart Agriculture a. Organic farming b. Agro-waste management
	Renewable Energy a. Solar Power b. Bio-gas Energy
	Water & Sanitation a. Rain Water Harvesting b. Trans-boundary Water issues Biorights & Ecosystem Services a. EKW & Biorights project b. Ramsar Wetlands of India & Ecosystem services c. ESs Mapping (IWMI & Earthwatch)
	Corporate Social Responsibility a. Urban Forestry b. Water sanitation c. Renewable Energy d. Waste management
How SAFE works	By putting into practise, the maximisation of recycling, minimization of waste, reduction of consumption, and making sure that things manufactured may be reused, enhanced, or recycled, it makes products that are environmentally friendly.
	By experimenting, creating, educating, and mentoring the neighbourhood about innovative, relevant technology-based programmes.
	Utilizing the financial and economic system and building networks with government and non-government agencies, it is possible to market the product both domestically and internationally.
	People and other community members were helped by the many events that took place, and volunteers and people from poor communities made friends with each other.
With whom the organisation works	Local Government, Funding Organisations, NGOs
How the organisation raises funds	Government assistance, funding, donations, and profits from company activities

Value capture is crucial since the financial profit obtained will be a wheel for an organization's sustainability. A business must be able to give value to its consumers in order to attain value capture (Bhushan, 2020). A social entrepreneurial organization's value capture is realised through a variety of actions, such as conducting a humanism-based program, building capacitys consumers in order to attain value capture (Bhushan, 2020). A social entrepreneurial organization's value capture is realised through a variety of actions, such as conducting a humanism-based program, building capacity, and teaching and training on environmental issues (Bhushan, 2020).

Table 5.3   Value capture for social entrepreneurship

Indicators	Findings
How does this organisation make profit?	By selling the product in different Government sponsored fair.
	When buyers purchase products based on environmental concerns
	improvement of the biological, psychological, social, and spiritual well-being of the marginalised community
Obstacles	Minimum support from Government
	Financial and Human resources
	Strong political issues in waste management
	Quality control on product sales
How the organisation measures the work performance?	Financial gain from waste management services and the selling of recycled products
	Quality Assurance
	Monitoring and evaluation

In light of the foregoing, it is possible to evaluate the effects of waste management by considering both internal and external factors related to SAFE waste management. Here is a table that outlines the main SWOT analysis of the organisation: strengths, weaknesses, opportunities, and threats. The organisation will be more effective and efficient with the help of both internal and external supporters. Both internal and external factors have an effect on the establishment's structure; the former determines the regulatory framework while the latter determines the community services offered.

Table 5.4   SWOT analysis

Internal Business Analysis	
Strength	**Weakness**
1. Beneficial for earning additional income	1. Socialisation is not optimal
2. Adaptable to the environmental condition	2. Difficult to accept new things
3. Well-organised system	3. A limited number of professionals
4. Good Service from the workers	4. Only a handful of trash removal services
External Business Analysis	
Opportunity	**Threat**
1. This is not the best possible market	1. The disapproval of the community
2. Improvements in technology	2. Expensive machinery
3. Support from the government	3. Vulnerable to corruption
4. Increase the creativity and skill enhancement	

Source: Authors' compilation after qualitative study

6. Conclusion

The growth of social enterprise, which is a new kind of business, shows and helps the progress of society. Many non-profit organisations are changing into social enterprises, and some active entrepreneurs with strong corporate social responsibility are repositioning themselves as social entrepreneurs. The business model will tell how well this transformation and repositioning can be done. By looking at the business models of existing social enterprises and enterprises that are similar to social enterprises, it is clear that business models are important for the survival and growth of social enterprises, which still have a long way to go. Knowing the business models of different organisations that deal with environmental, educational, and health problems is helpful in a number of ways. SAFE is a typical social enterprise. It has a unique business model and way of doing things that other businesses can learn from. SAFE is an organisation where people care a lot about the environment and support it. A social enterprise can achieve its social mission and keep a balance between its economic profits and social values if it runs in the right way. But there is always a risk. So, other social enterprises or businesses with a social mission must find their own ways to create new business models that work for them and try to achieve their social missions with as little help from the government and social donations as possible. Trash2Cash creates long-term work options for the urban poor, notably women and young unemployed people. To date, the project has taught over 300 women to create paper-recycled crafts. This empowers women and provides them with economic stability. Not only is Trash2Cash scalable, but it is also replicable in other urban impoverished regions throughout the world. In order to attract the attention of young entrepreneurs and build corporate actions in this new field of chance, this area of study requires more research with many more comparable cases. In the same way, similar studies will help academics show that social entrepreneurship is an important topic to study.

7. Recommendation

Studying the community's waste habits and changing the waste management programme accordingly is one unique method each firm planning to adopt it. This sets the stage for an intriguing setting where the two parties can innovate their business models. The effectiveness and efficiency of waste banks can be improved with the help of both internal and external sources of support. According to the Indonesian trash bank's SWOT analysis, the community has paid close attention to the bank's programme and functioning, which have been adjusted to meet their needs. Reasonable and affordable pricing is essential for reused products. New initiatives need to be created and existing ones need to be diversified. The usage of e-commerce and internet banking, as well as promotional activities, learning, sales, and advertisements, in addition to the acquisition of financial aid, can be achieved through partnerships with both state and federal governments.

8. Declaration of Competing Interest

The authors of this study affirm that they are free from any ties or financial conflicts of interest that might seem to have affected the results presented here.

9. Acknowledgements

The authors would like to thank SAFE and its members for sharing all of the information and documents with us. We also appreciate their assistance in facilitating the interviews with the artisans.

REFERENCES

1. Aboul-Enein, A. M., Al-Abd, A. M., Shalaby, E., Abul-Ela, F., Nasr-Allah, A. A., Mahmoud, A. M., & El-Shemy, H. A. (2011). Eichhornia crassipes (Mart) solms: from water parasite to potential medicinal remedy. *Plant Signaling & Behavior, 6*(6), 834–836.

2. Agrawal, S., & Gugnani, R. (2014). Creating successful business model: Lessons for social entrepreneurship. *International Journal of Entrepreneurship and Innovation Management, 18*(5-6), 438–445.

3. Ajieh, M. U., Ogbomida, T. E., Onochie, U. P., Akingba, O., Kubeyinje, B. F., Orerome, O. R., & Ogbonmwan, S. M. (2020). Design and construction of fixed dome digester for biogas production using cow dung and water hyacinth. *African Journal of Environmental Science and Technology, 14*(1), 15–25.

4. Alexandre-Leclair, L. (2017). Social entrepreneurship and social innovation as a tool of women social inclusion and sustainable heritage preservation: The case of the Sougha Establishment in UAE. *International Journal of Entrepreneurship and Small Business, 31*(3), 345–362.

5. Bhattacharyya, S. (2021, September). Revisiting East Kolkata Wetlands–Management Options with Holistic Approach. In *Conference GSI* (pp. 129–138).

6. Bhushan, B. (2020). Motivational model of social entrepreneurship: exploring the shaping of engagement of social entrepreneur. In *Methodological Issues in Social Entrepreneurship Knowledge and Practice* (pp. 111–136). Springer, Singapore.

7. Borquist, B. R., & de Bruin, A. (2019). Values and women-led social entrepreneurship. *International Journal of Gender and Entrepreneurship*.

8. Cao, L. (2014). Business model transformation in moving to a cross-channel retail strategy: a case study. *International Journal of Electronic Commerce, 18*(4), 69–96.

9. Dhewanto, W., Lestari, Y. D., Herliana, S., & Lawiyah, N. (2018). Analysis of the business model of Waste Bank in Indonesia: a preliminary study. *International Journal of Business, 23*(1), 73–88.

10. García-Jurado, A., Pérez-Barea, J. J., & Nova, R. J. (2021). A new approach to social entrepreneurship: A systematic review and meta-analysis. *Sustainability, 13*(5), 2754.

11. Guha, S., Mandal, A., Kujur, F., Chakrabarti, S., & Chattaraj, D. (2024). Entrepreneurial Ability of Rural Women Artisans: A Case of Birbhum District of West Bengal. In Perspectives in Human Resources (pp. 155–162). Routledge India.

12. Gupta, P., Chauhan, S., Paul, J., & Jaiswal, M. P. (2020). Social entrepreneurship research: A review and future research agenda. *Journal of Business Research, 113,* 209–229.
13. Harun, I., Pushiri, H., Amirul-Aiman, A. J., & Zulkeflee, Z. (2021). Invasive water hyacinth: ecology, impacts and prospects for the rural economy. *Plants, 10*(8), 1613.
14. Haugh, H. M., & Talwar, A. (2016). Linking social entrepreneurship and social change: The mediating role of empowerment. *Journal of Business Ethics, 133*(4), 643–658.
15. Ilo, O. P., Simatele, M. D., Nkomo, S. P. L., Mkhize, N. M., & Prabhu, N. G. (2020). The benefits of water hyacinth (Eichhornia crassipes) for Southern Africa: A review. Sustainability, 12(21), 9222.
16. Kohler, T., & Chesbrough, H. (2019). From collaborative community to competitive market: The quest to build a crowdsourcing platform for social innovation. *R&d Management, 49*(3), 356–368.
17. Kusumasari, B. (2016). The Business Model of Social Entrepreneurship in Indonesia. *BISNIS & BIROKRASI: Jurnal Ilmu Administrasi dan Organisasi, 22*(3), 156–168.
18. Li, Y. (2014, August). Business model innovation of social entrepreneurship firm: A case study of TerraCycle. In *2014 International Conference on Management Science & Engineering 21th Annual Conference Proceedings* (pp. 507–514). IEEE.
19. Nagler, J. (2007). *The Importance of Social Entrepreneurship for Economic Development Policies.* Univeristy of New South Wales. Sydney: UNSW.
20. Ramadani, R. F., Heryanto, N., Komar, O., & Hasanah, V. R. (2020). Community empowerment through social compass strategy: Case study of empowerment in processing waste and water hyacinth. *Journal of Nonformal Education, 6*(2), 139–147.
21. Roy-Basu, A., Bharat, G. K., Chakraborty, P., & Sarkar, S. K. (2020). Adaptive co-management model for the East Kolkata wetlands: A sustainable solution to manage the rapid ecological transformation of a peri-urban landscape. *Science of the Total Environment, 698,* 134203.
22. SAFE (2017), https://www.safeinch.org/current-projects
23. Segbefia, A. Y., Honlah, E., & Appiah, D. O. (2019). Effects of water hyacinth invasion on sustainability of fishing livelihoods along the River Tano and Abby-Tano Lagoon, Ghana. *Cogent Food & Agriculture, 5*(1), 1654649.
24. Thorsen, E. (2015). *Food waste reduction in the retail sector: a feasibility study in social entrepreneurship* (Doctoral dissertation).
25. Weis, M. (2017). Business Models and Business Model Innovation in Social Entrepreneurship.
26. Zainea, N. L., Toma, S. G., Grădinaru, C., & Catană, S. (2020). Social entrepreneurship, a key driver to improve the quality of life: The case of TOMS Company. *Business Ethics and Leadership, 4*(3), 65–72.

Note: All the tables in this chapter were authors' compilation after qualitative study.

Emerging Horizons: Business and Society in the Post Pandemic Era –
Brig. Dr. Rajiv Divekar et al. (eds)
© 2024 Taylor & Francis Group, London, ISBN 978-1-032-90822-9

6

The Role of Internal Communication Leadership on Brand Perceptions and Employee Experience during Crisis

G. Nikita[1]

Assistant Professor,
Symbiosis School of Media and Communication,
Symbiosis International (Deemed University)

Sayak Pal[2]

Research Scholar,
Symbiosis Institute of Media and Communication,
Symbiosis International (Deemed University)

Aniisu K Verghese[3]

Communication Leader and Independent Researcher

ABSTRACT

Crises like COVID-19 create unprecedented scenarios that leaders need to help employees and other stakeholders to cope with. Through active roles related to discussions on social, political, and environmental related issues to their organization, the industry and society, leaders influence internal and external perceptions. Communication aimed at employees often finds their way into the public domain which paints a picture of the brand identity and leadership engagement. Through a review of in-depth interviews with CEO to analyse the content and context of the message and their influence on stakeholder perceptions of the brand and employee's experiences. Hinging on the leadership framework, we offer a perspective of how internal communications content is perceived and aligned with the organization's core values and performance. The paper provides insights and practical advice for leaders and communicators to frame their messaging while communicating during crises. A qualitative study through in-depth interviews with nine corporate leaders from different industries was used to help uncover perspectives from the point of view of those considered as brands. This data collected for content analysis is used to recommend approaches communicators and leaders can take while framing their messages during crises.

KEYWORDS: Brand perception, Crisis, Leadership, Internal communication, Employee experience

[1]nikita1913@gmail.com, [2]palsayak01@gmail.com, [3]aniisu3@gmail.com

DOI: 10.4324/978100355996-6

The understanding of how leaders' internal communication influences brand's external perceptions has been sparsely studied. By acknowledging and creating communication that works for both internal and external audiences can result in improved brand perceptions and supportive employee behaviour. No study has looked at the relationship between leaders' internal communication and how they are perceived by brand's stakeholders externally during crises. Also, the value of internal communications on employees' experiences needs to me studied further. This study aims to broaden discussions on boundary spanning ability of internal communications in the context of brand perceptions.

1. Introduction

Internal communication is one of the crucial aspects of managing communication at workplace during a crisis. Corporate leaders adopt various strategies to implement an effective communication strategy to minimize further damage to the organization. An employee plays a major role in portraying positive image of their company to the outside world and hence, an overall employee experience is important to create better image of the company. As the coronavirus spread worldwide, Apple's CEO Tim Cook, in an internal memo told all his employees in all the company's offices to work from home if required. Further, Tim told employees that Apple is trying to minimize contact in the office and therefore investing in cleaning the premises. Space and continuing enhanced deep cleanings inside the company. This is obviously to help avoid the spread of coronavirus in the workplace. The CEO of Amazon Jeff Bezos had written an open letter to his employees thanking them for their hard work during the pandemic on the company blog. He also added that it was not just him but also customers across the world thanking on social media for the work done. He mentioned that 1,00,000 new roles and rising wages will be offered to hourly workers who had fulfilled orders by delivering to customers during this time of stress and turmoil. Amazon has also been purchasing and placing orders for millions of face masks for their contractors and employees who were unable to work from home during the period.

Similarly, Microsoft CEO Satya Nadella wrote a lengthy email to more than 140000 of his employees worldwide applauding them for their response to coronavirus pandemic and urging them to do the best they can do to help others on a personal level and professional level. He wrote in the email "We are in uncharted territory. He knows much is unknown and I know how uncertain it feels. Like many of you there have been times over the past few weeks when it has felt overwhelming and all encompassing for me. I worry about the health and safety of my co-workers and friends. There is no playbook for this coronavirus. We need to take care of us and others in this situation". Apart from emails, another message on social media from Ex Goldman Sachs CEO took to his Twitter account to suggest to the employees that afterall social distance is not that much important and the struggles to flatten the virus curve is crushing the economy, jobs and morale also a major issue.

This decision by the former CEO struck a chord with the US president Donald Trump and less than two hours of Lloyd Blankfein's controversial tweet, Trump tweeted saying we cannot let the cure be worse than the problem and at the end of fifteen days period we can decision on which way to go. As far as information is concerned, it is important to balance the communication between internal and external stakeholders are most internal stakeholders and shareholders expect information well in advanced compared to external stakeholders who consume information about the organization through media. It is important to understand that unless communication within the organization is not clear and strong, communication outside the company cannot be strategies well. There is definitely an overlap between the two forms of communication, whereas it is observed that most organizational studies are directed towards external communication and focus towards internal communication is rarely addressed.

Hence, the study focussed on understand how leadership within company plays a major role during crisis and identity the channels and mediums used by corporate leaders to share messages to their employees during a crisis. The study also attempts to recognize the position of a corporate leader during a global crisis towards their employees using the leadership framework directed towards leading the business, people and yourself as a leader.

1.1 Leadership in Internal Communication

Internal communication allows employees to convey information, construct relationship while upholding organizational culture and values and make meaning (Berger, 2008). The popularity of internal communication is ever-growing since 1990 from the US and spared across to Europe and other nations restructuring organizational communication. The concept has grown to be popular in Asian market where employers often struggle to engage the employees emotionally. There has been a series of initiatives to understand the potentiality and usage of internal communication and its applications, while looking at the importance of the filed practitioners of internal communication, United Kingdom has established 'Institute of Internal Communication' in 2010 to deal with the specific discipline (Ana Tkalac Verčič, 2012). The application of leadership has been thoroughly witnessed in many areas of management; however, the public relation domain is yet to explore much of its support in the field. A good leadership benefits the organization in multiples ways like strengthening the organization's structure, develop a healthy culture, nurture and manage excellent public relation practices, facilitating greater communisation to internal and external audiences and many more. While organization is supported by employees of different levels and from different domains, a stronger communication channel needs to be established and facilitated among them, in order to maintain the standard of information flow within and surrounding the organization. One of the most important responsibilities of a leader is to ensure the free flow of unbiased information without any obstruction. Researchers have found that the immediate supervisors manage to get more credibility with the employees than the other levels which prove the leader's efficiency of that level (Linjuan Rita Men, 2014).

The field of leadership has been studied by various leaders while there was an ongoing debate on measuring the impact of leadership based on the abilities, skills or style. Among various styles of leaderships, there are few which have prominent usage in the industry like 'Transactional leadership', often called 'authoritative leadership' promotes personal oversight, certainty, clear direction and 'just' treatment among the employees of an organization. Although the 'authoritative leadership' satisfies psychic needs and lower ordering material, many believe this style of leadership alone is not very effective for an organization. Another style of leadership called 'Transformational leadership' or 'charismatic leadership' has strong inclinations towards articulation of goals, self-assertion, emphasizing collective identity, higher expectations, risk taking and vision of the organization. The motto of 'charismatic leadership' is to fabricate a symbol or meaning for his followers. The 'pluralistic leadership' on the other hand encourages participative decision making process while providing recognition to other people's values and opinions, fulfilling the goals of the organization. While researchers often argue on the application of different leadership styles, the leaders are often fond of changing their leadership style according to the situation or circumstances (Linda Aldoory, 2004).

1.2 Leaders in Crisis Communication

Leadership is found to be extremely crucial support during a crisis and often prove to be effective in manging those crisis for the organization (Wooten, 2008) . It is also expected from a leader to communicate the crisis, the nature and the possible solution among the stakeholders to ensure a successful recovery (Burnett, 2002) . Crisis can be tricky and a seasoned leader may fall into biasness and exclusion at the moment of desperation which might create confusion and distrust among the employees. This in extension can worsen the situation and may discourage the employees to work towards the solution to prevent the forthcoming damages (Tulshyan, 2020) . Therefore, the leaders who welcome diversity and inclusion may seem to be more appropriate to manage crisis. Another benefit of hosting a diversity-oriented or rational leader is that the leader would invite and welcome the sharing of opinion and ideas in favour of the growth of the organization. They also set the goals according to the flavour of the organization including the diversity of the employees, which would uphold a fair as well as free of prejudices culture for the organization (Abraham Carmeli, 2010).

Crises are common phenomena in organization and it is often described as the techniques though which management responses to the crisis (Matthew W. Seeger, 1998). The management decision during crisis helps in setting up the image of the organization for the stakeholder, however, based on how the information is received and the crisis is addressed, the crisis communication can be divided into two distinct categories, once being the 'public crisis communication' and another is the 'private crisis communication'. When 'public crisis communication' addresses the information to the stakeholders outside of the organization, 'private crisis communication' concerns the internal employees and crisis team to act in response. 'Public crisis communication' stretches to the three broader traditions, namely 'practitioner lessons', 'rhetorical' and 'social-psychological' which focus particularly on decision-making and information processing. These two factors also play a significant part in 'private crisis communication' where information and knowledge are represented as the raw materials and output in the process. The traditional mediums are overcome by internet which became a faster medium of information discrimination through the mediums like blogs, videos social media and similar (Coombs, 2008).

Leaders are expected to act fast in the time of crisis in order to reduce the level of damage for the organization, employees and its stakeholders. Connecting with the stakeholder during the time of crisis has to be learned over a period of time and required greater leadership skills. The same applies to the internal public at the time of emergency and the speed and skills of leaders also ensure faster recovery and less damage to the organization (Yeunjae Lee, 2020). The leader is expected to deliver competent and effective responses to the crisis with a full proof plan including 'honest message', 'multiple channels to receive information from consumers' concerning the crisis along with its suggestion and the implementation of best possible solutions. While social media helps to increase the phase of information dissemination, it also makes it complex and challenging for the leaders to face the situation. An able leader needs to be aware of the different media channels to transmit the message while keeping the reputation of the firm in check. The media in the time of crisis for both the cases of delivering and receiving the message needs to be chosen carefully by the leader to get maximum benefits out of them. Although the management institutes are trying to incorporate numerous training related to leadership and crisis communication, the best way to learn the role of a leader in crisis communication is to go beyond the conventional ways and learn from the real life situation handling (Foote, 2013).

1.3 Employee Experience During Crisis

The crisis for an organization is often considered as a high-level ambiguity which is also associated with higher level of uncertainty. An organization in such situation is expected to communicate about the crisis accurately with uttermost transparency and truthfulness, especially to their internal stakeholders. (Winni Johansen, 2012). The crisis also identifies the responsibility of the leaders towards their subjects. In an instance at Northern Italy, a worker was reported to death by accidental at a manufacture plant and the employee surprisingly refrained from blaming the organization and vouched for the attention paid by the company towards the employees. This was an example where the organization managed the situation and also abled to pull in the support of the employee during the crisis. During the crisis, people in an organization releases three primary types of reactions affective, cognitive and behavioural. While affective reactions like rumours bring damages to the loyalty, cognitive reactions bring changes in the decision making protocol and also influences company's goals. Behavioural reactions impact organizational effectiveness through altering the agendas and distorting responsibility distribution (Alessandra Mazzei, 2012). Pandemic is one of the major crisis situations where the management has to come up with a 'strategic communication plan' to deliver plans on continuing business further. Leaders are expected to manage the situation empathetically rather than suffering from fear of wrong decision making. This is the very reason the leaders need to make the communication compassionate, clear and empathetic during crisis by answering 'how' and 'what' of the situation. The 'British multinational investment bank' has followed the 'soft model of HRM' to focus on the market in Asia while reducing their business in other countries, putting emphasis on re-skilling upskilling their employees during the COVID crisis. The bank allowed ninety percent of their employees to continue their works from home while the crucial ten percent employees were provided safer environment to maintain the essential functions of the bank's day to day activities (Garima Prajapati, 2020).

In the organizational setup, not all the facts carry equal importance like the behavioural differences. Similarly, the perception of leadership varies across the employees and their statures. Based on the perception of the subordinates and their perception about the leader, leadership can broadly be categorised into 'task oriented leadership' and social emotional leadership' (Mauk Mulder, 1971). Researchers often consider external communication to evaluate the impact of crisis communication however the studies revealed that the effective internal communication often becomes instrumental in preventing crisis for an organization as it impacts upon the culture, climate and relationship of an organization. The stakeholders' management should also be an important agenda for leaders as the stakeholders carries expectation from the organization and the crisis can perceived to be a violation in their expectation, causing further misunderstandings. According to Kim and Rhee, employees communication behaviour can be conceptualized and measured though three aspects, 'megaphoning', 'scouting' and 'micro boundary spanning'. Studies also shows that the employees can either advertise or advocate the organization they work for while being vocal about the crisis among their social, familial and professional circle, therefore an organization needs to take utmost care during a crisis situation (Alessandra Mazzei, 2012). Another research on South Korean manufacturing organizations shows the changing paradigm of employment practices of the nation after the East Asian Economic crisis in 1997. Prior to the crisis the employment practise was under massive pressure because of the nation's labour practices, where employees were expected to be loyal towards their employer and enjoyed excellent job security in return. The crisis forced the organization to downsize their employees and also encouraged practices like low wages and long working hours. On the other hand, the study also stresses on the relationship between the government and private organizations that are found to limit the amount of downsizing due to the support received from the government (Ekin Alakent, 2010).

2. Theoretical Framework

This research uses the leadership framework that set principles on what a manager must know in order to practise essential practises of a leader at all level i.e. three basic levels: individual, team and organizational level. The framework defines the requirements of a leader, its practical sets and standards that needs to be maintained. It also acts as a toolkit for managers to access their challenges. The three levels of leadership framework are: leading yourself, leading people and leading organization. Each level has its own set of principles such as, leading people including providing safe working place, creating effective roles and evaluative measure for employees, enabling improvement and rewarding them. Whereas, leading yourself is very important for a leader as he or she must first understand their own role to manage others and develop skillset for themselves to create a better relationship with others.

A manager employee relation is a two-way trusting, productive working relationship focussed on achieving business goals by making people work towards their full potential. Leading people deals with managing people based on: safe working environment, creating effective roles, assigning and assessing work, developing team capability, reporting and recognizing work, lead change and continuous improvement. The role as a manager in an organization deals with leading yourself by: understand self-role, respect others roles, managing relationships, develop skills and behaviours. After leading yourself and your people, leading an organization deals with additional requirements of designing and implementing workplace conditions, business strategy, productive system of work, systematic trust and fairness, understand workforce capability and manage strategic relations. The level of leading organizations arrives from strategy building for better trust, relationship, employee capability and productivity. Hence, this framework is apt to apply for understanding leadership as a part of internal communication on brand perception and employee experience during a crisis.

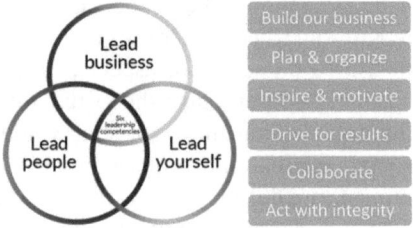

Fig. 6.1 Leadership framework
Pty Limited by Peter Mills

2.1 Objectives of Study

The study attempts to understand role of leadership in internal communications with employee during a global crisis. Since brand perception and employee experience can vary during crisis it is important to understand how a leader must communicate with his or her stakeholders within the company. The objectives of this research are to:

1. Understand how leadership within company plays a major role during crisis
2. Identity the channels and mediums used by corporate leaders to share messages to their employees during a crisis
3. Recognize the position of a corporate leader during a global crisis towards their employees.

2.2 Research Questions

The attempt to understand the role of leadership in internal communication during crisis can be observed globally and seeking this opportunity, the researcher aims to answer the following questions:

1. How leadership messages shared internally help address crisis?
2. What approaches do corporate leaders adopt to share messages with employees during a crisis?
3. What are best practices for corporate leaders to communicate crisis messages that also help improve brand perceptions?

3. Research Methodology

As internal communication is an integral part of corporate communication, it is majorly linked to the messages flowing from the leader who acts as a source for communicating with their stakeholders. As a part of this study a structured interview was conducted with nine corporate leaders across different sectors educational, personal care services, travel and tourism, media that includes public relations. A thematic content analysis was done for the transcripts extracted from the interviews of these corporate leaders.

A thematic content analysis was done for surveys, interview transcripts and semi structured interviews that follow a particular thematic pattern with open ended questions. There are two types of thematic content analysis such as, inductive, and deductive thematic approach. The inductive approach is done when the data helps in determining the themes that can be used for the analysis driven down through similarity and patterns that is observed in the data. A deductive approach is deduced from the theory or frameworks that exist in literature which are used as themes to analyse the data. It usually follows the 6 major steps in analysis:

1. Familiarization

The first step involves understanding data and transcribing the interviews if there are any audio recordings taken while conducting interviews. Even the initial notes are quite helpful in this case to make notes and draw familiarization from the data collected.

2. Coding

The second step involves coding the data and highlighting texts that are helpful for analysis. It also includes labelling, creating short codes to describe context based on the patterns observed in the data.

3. Generating themes

Once the codes are made the researcher must look at the codes and identify patterns and combine codes into themes to classify them and make the process of analysis must more simpler.

4. Reviewing themes

The themes must miss out on certain codes or identification of certain patterns and hence a review is important to check the accuracy by returning to the dataset and check the appropriateness of the themes generated.

5. Defining themes

The themes must be named and formulated by giving it a meaning. This helps to figure out how it helps in understanding the dataset.

6. Naming themes

Succinct is a term used to describe briefly something that is spoken of writer with a easy name and this is important while naming a particular theme to make it easily understood and decoded.

7. Writing up

The final stage of summarizing and presenting the dataset in writing up analysing through tabulation expressing the aims and approaches of the study.

4. Data Analysis and Interpretation

This study used the deductive approach to thematic content analysis based on the leadership framework identifies three basic themes: leading yourself, leading people and leading the organization. Some of the major aspects of the study revolved around understanding of crisis by these organizations and it was noted that most of them had never expected a pandemic at this scale and with such a huge impact into the lives of people. "They were never prepared for something like this" as quoted by one of the CEO of a leading HR consultant he added "initially everyone thought it was for three to four days and then this turned into months." The impact of this pandemic was massive yet the work continued from home and the sounds of children, pets and parents seen on screen started to normalize after a certain period of time. The corporate communications head of internal communication at a multinational retail corporate spoke about this impact as "women faced a lot of challenges at home." It is true that domestic violence had also risen during this time through news reports, yet there are very few discussions about this issue.

Most of the companies made sure to involve employees in every decision making and kept the employee well being at the top priority. Most leaders i.e., 7 out of 9 chose to communicate on a weekly basis using platforms such as, Emails, WhatsApp, and other social media platforms. Two out of the nine leaders chose townhalls are channels to seek employee feedbacks for effective communication. Zoom was used as a regular platform for work and other meetings on a weekly basis. In case of leadership messages and approach of leadership, most leaders (8 out of 9) believe that having an upfront of even transparent communication is the most important position during a crisis whereas, one leader believes that a low-key approach is softer and can be a better choice during certain situations. The following codes were generated as a result of repetitive patterns observed in the interview transcripts under the three themes identified from the leadership framework:

The Table 6.1 depicts some key characteristics of a leader that is required during a crisis for the organization to overcome crisis such as, being calm and sure of the information shared as it is important to not convey any misinformation that

Table 6.1   Thematic content analysis

Managing yourself	Managing people	Managing organization
Stay calm	Empathy	Gradual trust with stands crisis
Be sure of yourself	Experience	Do not compare
Slightly diplomatic	Communicate	Be selfish
Open	Well-being	Solid brand amplified by leader
Transparent	Encourage/ motivate	Mould for millennials
Approachable	Awareness	Shareholder communication
Fake it if you cannot make it	Weekly messages	Values
Be upfront	Feedback	Policy implementation
Less concern more influence	Rewards and recognition	Communication
Awareness and speed	Profit showcasing	Flexibility to adapt change
Leading	Security and job stability	
Show vulnerability	Treat as partners with frankness	
Address issues	Convey problems	
Honest	No overcommunication	
Credible	Medium- Emails, WhatsApp, LinkedIn, Twitter, Townhalls and Zoom	
Listen	70% positive and 30% negative information	
Invest time	Motherhood	

Source: made by author

could lead to further damage. It is observed that being diplomatic is also a trait to be carried on as sometimes being so can help buying time and better clarity to respond. The CEO of beauty salon brand quotes "Fake it till you make it" can also be a mantra for a few leaders in this case. After this, one must be able to be 'aware with speed' which means, to be open to quickly learn and adapt the change to respond honestly and truthfully to the public. Being transparent with both internal and external stakeholders is a trait that most leaders are expected to be. Addressing issues and taking time in understanding by listening is yet another trait of a good leader. Although showing vulnerability to people is alright, it is important to note that this is only for giving out 70 percent of positivity and only 30 percent of negative vulnerabilities. This also helps in being more approachable and help in leading with 'less concern but more influence' that is the sole mantra of a success leader.

Managing people has been bought down to overall employee experience and employee well-being. This could entail empathy and motivation at workplace. As a part of motivation, rewards and recognitions plays a major role in building the motives. Most leaders manage their people through regular weekly communication through emails, social media platforms and townhalls. Today, leaders treat the employees as partners and are expected to give them information showcasing profits as well as communicating problems. Treating the employees with empathy and giving them a sense of employee job security is crucial during a crisis. The jargon of "motherhood" was highlighted in one of the interviews with head of a leading newspaper that support the former statement. She added "internal campaign during crisis and giving them a sense of togetherness during crisis is important." Taking regular feedbacks from employees is the key to build up a better management system for the workforce.

Organizational management in the leadership framework identified through the interviews were based on building a gradual trust over a period of time. This helps in overcoming a crisis during difficult times as there are people who will support the company. Building values right from the beginning can help in establishing a good position in the society. Once the brand is built the leader must act as a amplifier to further bring out the strong presence of the company. For an organization during crisis, the utmost priority is not just external communication but also internal stakeholder and shareholder communication. Bringing the policy implementation in practice and communicating regularly is essential. Being selfish and not comparing with others, adaptability to change for younger workforce keeps business alive.

5. Conclusion

This study is a clear emphasised on understanding the role of leadership during a crisis. Since, it is very important for a corporate leader to communicate in an apt manner using appropriate modes of communication to manage a crisis, the research delves deep into the leadership framework to list down the ways to manage oneself as a leader, people, and the organization. As nine corporate leaders were interviewed as a part of this research most leaders choose to use the social media platforms such as, LinkedIn and Twitter, emails and townhalls mostly in Zoom or MS teams as mediums or channels of communication. It was observed that most leaders believe in being upfront, honest, transparent and credible in their position, whereas, it is also important to note that despite all these traits having a slightly diplomatic front is also acceptable during a crisis to buy time and come back to the audience with fully aware information to address the public. Managing an organization is not easy, satisfying all the aspects to internal and external communication as well as adapting to change is the only way ahead for organizations today. This research focusses on the importance of leadership, its message and channels during a crisis that is important for organizations today to prepare ahead of time to bring out the best effective mode of internal communication for the future.

6. Limitations

The study is limited to CEOs from different organizations and is purely qualitative in nature that reflects on the generalization of this research as a major limitation to the study. This research can be spread across globally for future research to understand the global crisis scenario through other leaders located in different parts of the world. Although, the participants for this research were part of global corporate giants, it has not been able to capture the reflections from leaders of other nations and is restricted solely to India.

As the **error in sampling** can be observed in the size of sample being small, this can also be supported by observing that the study is qualitative in nature and this research delves deeper into understanding leadership with respect to internal communication and its role in understanding brand perception through employee experience. Since, the sample was purposive that included respondents from expertise in leadership positions, it helped in also getting connects from various leaders from the domain.

This research study was done using no research grant and was purely done keeping the information of interviewees caveat to avoid any conflicts.

REFERENCES

1. Abraham Carmeli, R. R.-P. (2010). Inclusive Leadership and Employee Involvement in Creative Tasks in the Workplace: The Mediating Role of Psychological Safety. *Creativity Research Journal, 22*(3), 250–260. doi:doi.org/10.1080/10400419.2010.5 04654
2. Alessandra Mazzei, J.-N. K. (2012). Strategic Value of Employee Relationships and Communicative Actions: Overcoming Corporate Crisis with Quality Internal

Communication. *International Journal of Strategic Communication, 6*(1), 31-44. doi:https://doi.org/10.1080/1553118X.2011.634869

3. Ana Tkalac Verčič, D. V. (2012). Internal communication: Definition, parameters, and the future. *Public relations review, 38(2), 223-230., 38*(2), 223–230.

4. Berger, B. (2008, November 17). Employee/ organizational communications. Retrieved from http://www.instituteforpr.org/topics/employee-organizational-communications/

5. Burnett, J. (2002). The Flow of Business Communication. In J. Burnett, *Managing Business Crises* (pp. 145–148). Quorum Books.

6. Coombs, W. T. (2008). Crisis Communication. *The international encyclopedia of communication*, 1–7. doi: https://doi.org/10.1002/9781405186407.wbiecc156

7. Ekin Alakent, S.-H. L. (2010). Do institutionalized traditions matter during crisis? Employee downsizing in Korean manufacturing organizations. *Journal of Management Studies, 47*(3), 509–532. doi: https://doi.org/10.1111/j.1467-6486.2009.00863.x

8. Foote, L. M. (2013). Honing Crisis Communication Skills: Using Interactive Media and Student-Centered Learning to Develop Agile Leaders. *Journal of Management Education, 37*(1), 79–114. doi:https://doi.org/10.1177/1052562912455419

9. Garima Prajapati, S. P. (2020). Enhancing Employee Experience during Covid-19: A Qualitative Study on Investment Banks. *International Journal of Modern Agriculture, 9*(3), 1711–1734. Retrieved from http://www.modern-journals.com/index.php/ijma/article/view/354

10. Linda Aldoory, E. T. (2004). Leadership and Gender in Public Relations: Perceived Effectiveness of Transformational and Transactional Leadership Styles. *Journal of Public Relations Research, 16*(2), 157–183. doi:doi.org/10.1207/s1532754xjprr1602_2

11. Linjuan Rita Men, D. S. (2014). The Effects of Authentic Leadership on Strategic Internal Communication and Employee-Organization Relationships. *Journal of Public Relations Research, 26*(4), 301–324. doi:10.1080/1062726X.2014.908720

12. Matthew W. Seeger, T. L. (1998). Communication, Organization, and Crisis. *Annals of the International Communication Association, 22*(1), 231–233. doi:doi.org/10.108 0/23808985.1998.11678952

13. Mauk Mulder, J. R. (1971). An Organization in Crisis and Non-crisis Situations. *Human Relations, 24*(1), 19–41. doi:doi.org/10.1177/001872677102400102

14. Tulshyan, R. (2020, April 10). How to Be an Inclusive Leader Through a Crisis. Boston, MA 02163, United States. Retrieved from https://hbr.org/2020/04/how-to-be-an-inclusive-leader-through-a-crisis

15. Winni Johansen, H. K. (2012). Entering new territory: A study of internal crisis management and crisis communication in organizations. *Public Relations Review, 38*(2), 270–279. doi:doi.org/10.1016/j.pubrev.2011.11.008

16. Wooten, L. a. (2008). "Linking crisis management and leadership competencies: the role of human resource development. *Advances in Developing Human Resources, 10*(3), 352–379. doi:doi.org/10.1177/1523422308316450

17. Yeunjae Lee, W. T.-Y. (2020). Enhancing employees' knowledge sharing through diversity-oriented leadership and strategic internal communication during the COVID-19 outbreak. *Journal of Knowledge Management*, 1526-1530. doi:10.1108/JKM-06-2020-0483

Emerging Horizons: Business and Society in the Post Pandemic Era –
Brig. Dr. Rajiv Divekar et al. (eds)
© 2024 Taylor & Francis Group, London, ISBN 978-1-032-90822-9

Readiness of Manufacturing Organizations to Concord with Global Aims of Fighting Climate Change and Sustainability—An Exploratory Study

7

Sanjay K Deshpande[1]
Associate Professor
KLS, Gogte Institute of Technology
Udyambag, Belagavi, Karnataka, India

Vanishri R Hundekar[2]
Associate Professor
KLS, Gogte Institute of Technology
Udyambag, Belagavi, Karnataka, India

M M Munshi[3]
Professor and Chairman
Dept of Management Studies
Visvesvaraya Technological University (VTU)
Macche, Belagavi, Karnataka

ABSTRACT

Frequent occurrences of climate disasters and catastrophes are the harbingers of the deteriorating health of ecology and disequilibrium caused by the environmental balance, albeit growing GDP and the rising economy is a tale of acute and latent irony. This research study aims to ascertain the level of awareness of changing climate and its risks amongst manufacturing firms, the study further also aims to find out the state of organizational readiness to be able to shift to sustainable ways of production to concur with the global aims to mitigate the damage caused. This particular research study is exploratory and is conducted on three variables namely Awareness about Climate Change is the independent variable, Eco-Innovation is the Moderating variable, and Sustainability is the Dependent variable. It is administered to 166 respondents comprising MDs, CEOs, Factory Managers, Department Managers working for various manufacturing firms. SPSS 25.0 is deployed for this research study. Results reveal that the awareness level of climate change is mediocre and the correlation between existing practices and future goals is not significant.

KEYWORDS: Climate change, Sustainable production, Organisational readiness, Climate risks

[1]sanjaydeshpande@git.edu, [2]vrhundekar@git.edu, [4]mmmunshi@rediffmail.com

DOI: 10.4324/978100355996-7

1. Introduction

Business processes, Operations, and products are driven by certain inevitable externalities beyond internal resources. Although customers' needs and demands are the propelling forces for organizations to decide on their products, processes, and services, overdoing any business activity proves to be detrimental to the health of the ecology and environment. The anthropogenic influence exerted by rampant commercialization is pernicious and has spelled disaster for environmental health, there is a dire need for the business ecosystem to welcome the rays of sustainability to ensure a secure future.

Regulatory scaffolding and compliance promulgated as Sustainable Development Goals (SDG) by the United Nations (UN) are for the betterment of sheltering global citizens from the unexpected hazards of global warming. Climate change is the most deliberated and discussed topic the world over, amongst policymakers, business heads and firms, conference dignitaries, and global ambassadors almost every responsible private or public body is concerned about reducing the unsavory impact of climate change. Paris Agreement in December 2015 defines climate change as the increase in global average temperature and resolves to limit the rise by 1.5 degrees when compared to pre-industrial times of the late 1800s. Climate change is depriving people of co-existence with nature and is snatching away basic rights, should the global average temperature rise by 2 degrees, the consequence will be unbearable and extremely hard-cutting (UN SDG 2030).

The manufacturing sector is a laborious, people and process-oriented, employment-generating activity and plays a vital role in social and economic development, however, it comes at a cost of tampering with and degrading the ecological state and environmental balance if done in a rampant manner. Despite substantial advancement in deciphering the factors influencing sustainability and consequent explanations proposed to address them, currently deployed production and consumption processes are principally not sustainable per se. To move towards better , advanced ,safer and scientific methods that respect the planet's vulnerabilities collaborative actions, caution driven wotkrforce and management, solution based and tailor made intervention is the need ,This research study proposes a novel approach for practicing managers across the echeleons in the hierarchy of manufacturing companies to assess their organizational sustainability readiness to further build capabilities to make manufacturing processes sustainable. Despite massive efforts invested in comprehending the sustainability issues certain degree of enigma still lurks around.

Sustainability is a multifaceted concept that encompasses Institutional, social, environmental, and financial, economic dimensions however its applicability is far and wide with no exclusions in any sphere of life (IlariaBarlett, 2021).

1.1 Objectives

1. To know the state of awareness amongst manufacturing firms on global warming and climate change
2. To ascertain the anticipatory state of Organisational Sustainable Readiness (OSR) of manufacturing firms to combat climate change
3. To develop a sustainability model to be used by manufacturing organizations to track and assess their impact on the environment

1.2 Prominent Reasons for Expediting the Climate Change Process

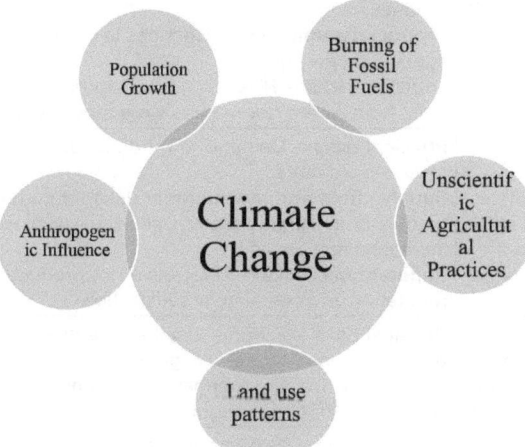

Fig. 7.1 Prominent reasons for expediting the climate change

Source: Self developed concept (UNO further delineates the prominent reasons for climate change as mentioned above in the figure)

1.3 Theoretical Framework for the Study

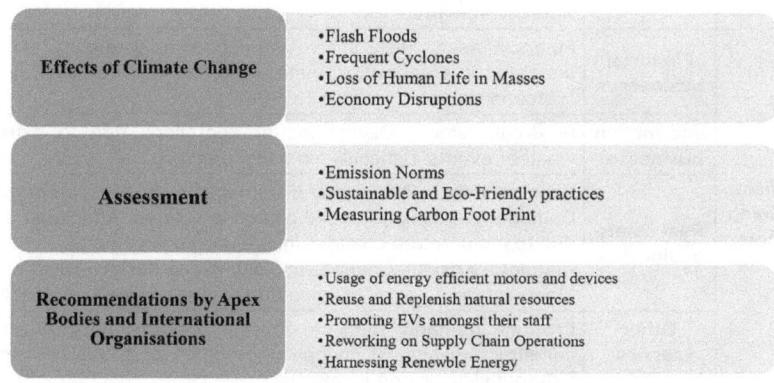

Fig. 7.2 Theoretical framework

Source: Self-developed model

1.4 Impact of Climate Change on Prominent Sectors

Table 7.1   Impact of climate change on prominent sectors

Goods producing sectors	**Manufac-turers**	**Physical risks** – Disruption to operations due to extreme weather events, Damage to infrastructure; Restrictions to production due to rising temperature, variations in water quality and in water availability
	Agriculture and mining businesses	**Physical risks** – Extreme weather events increase physical nsks to business operations; Risk of overflow of storage due to increased rainfall; Resource extraction could be limited by sea level and water availability **Supply chain and raw material risks** – Water scarcity affects production **Product demand risks** – Changes in quality, quantity and type of agricultural products **Logistics risks** – Risks to the transport corridors and transport hubs from where raw materials are processed and exported
Goods and services providing sectors	**Retailers and distrib-utors**	**Physical risks** – Damage to products during transportation due to extreme events **Supply chain and raw material risks** – Interruption, inefficiency or delays in supply chain; Difficulties with water scarcity and increased fuel prices **Reputational risks** – Decrease in product quality affecting reputation and consumers' satisfaction
	Trans-portation	**Physical risks** – Extreme weather events causing delays, supply disruptions and losses of goods; Access to transport routes affected by flooding, permafrost thawing and mass movements, subsidence due to drought
	Utilities	**Physical risks** – Disruptions of supply due to flooding or extreme events; Business interruption due to extreme weather **Supply chain and raw materials risks** – Reduced output due to water scarcity impacting hydropower and power plants using a thermal plant cooling system **Product demand risks** – Demand effects due to temperature changes **Regulatory risks** – Increasing pressure to conserve water in water scarce areas
Services providing sectors	**Financial businesses**	**Financial risks** – Risks in investment portfolio where investments are made in areas with climate vulnerabilities; Increased risk of customer default
	Information businesses	**Physical risks** – Disruptions of operations due to extreme weather events; Difficulties in transportation
	Real estate businesses	**Physical risks** – Delays and disruptions in construction projects; Damage to buildings and drainage problems; Additional costs due to temperature changes increasing cooling loads **Regulatory risks** – Changes in building and design requirements **Financial risks** – Loss of value due to climate change impacts
	Other service businesses	**Product demand risks** – Tourism industry affected in its infrastructure and by changes in tourism demands caused by different climatic conditions

Source: Illustrative framework developed by Agrawala, S. et al. (2011) OECD working paper

1.5 Constraint Model

Fig. 7.3 Constraint model

Source: Self-developed Model

2. Scope of the Study

This study is focused partially on the 7th and intensely on the 12th and 13th Goals of SDG 2030 and is conducted with specific reference to manufacturing firms of Tier II cities. A gist of 17 SDG goals published by UNO is represented below

Fig. 7.4 UN SDG 2030

Source: UN SDG 2030

3. Literature Review

3.1 Sustainability and Climate Change

To support the sustainability of the industrial sector in the green transition, the energy-saving and emission-reduction (ESER) plan is a critical step. There are commonalities between the drivers of adaptive capacity, mitigate ability, and the elements that support sustainable development, but there is currently little knowledge on how to identify and take advantage of them. (Qazi K. Ahmad Nigel Arnell et al., 2020)

Academics, corporate executives, and public servants all agree that innovation plays a significant role in sustainability. This is due to the fact that organizations, governments, and the general public must all move quickly to address the pressing issue of sustainable development. (Silvestre & Țîrcă, 2019)

By 2030, chemical manufacturing is anticipated to overtake all other factors as the leading cause of world oil consumption. Carbon dioxide from stacks or the air can be used as an alternate carbon source for chemicals, reducing the need for oil and the resultant greenhouse gas (GHG) emissions. (Kätelhön et al., 2019)

The combination of some factors such as unskilled labor, high obsolescence, high consumer demand, and low eco-efficiency will hurt environmental performance (Bonilla et al., 2018)

Additionally, it is predicted that a company's ability to innovate sustainably will become even more crucial as a source of competitive advantage, and that the sustainability-related features of its product offerings will serve as the basis for positioning, target marketing, market segmentation, and differentiation. (Varadarajan, 2017)

Climate change is the greatest hazard facing humanity. During the course of two centuries of industrial progress, human civilization has drastically changed the chemistry of the atmosphere and seas. (Wright & Nyberg, 2017)

(Rajeev et al., 2017) observed that studies addressing social issues are scarce, and more focus is required on the measurement of social impacts along the supply chain Governments in OECD nations have developed a wide range of environmental policies during the past 20 years

Financial obstacles, including difficulty obtaining capital from outside sources, seriously limit the ability to manufacture SMEs' eco-innovative capacity (Ghisetti et al., 2017) to enhance environmental conditions. These regulations inevitably have an impact on labor intensity, capital investment, resource reallocation, manufacturing processes, and innovation incentives. As a result, the continued tightening of environmental regulations is expected to have an impact on both economic performance and environmental consequences. (Albrizio et al., 2017)

Changes in weather patterns, including the frequency and intensity of severe events, as well as indirect effects on biodiversity, ecosystem services, and infrastructure, will pose challenges to the sustainability of the region's industry(admin, n.d.) Compared to less-intensive businesses, industrial sectors that use a lot of energy are more likely to see production decline and net imports rise. (Aldy & Pizer, 2015).

3.2 Awareness of Climate Change

Implementing eco-innovation demands more formal sources of information and awareness of enterprises than mainstream innovations do (Sanni, 2018) buyer-driven knowledge activities have a stronger favorable effect on the development of green products (Awan et al.,2021)

Eco-innovation will improve sustainable company performance, support the development of service innovation skills, and make it more challenging for rivals to enter the same market. These encouraging outcomes ought to allay any concerns businesses may have regarding the significance of implementing eco-innovation and strengthening their capacity for service innovation (Fernando et al, 2019)

Governments must support businesses in conducting autonomous innovation activities. Additionally, more public efforts in R&D are required (Fernández Fernández et al., 2018).

Firm value is consistently reduced by carbon emissions. The market constantly "penalizes" a firm's poor environmental performance more than its strong performance (Lee et al., 2015).

3.3 Impact of Climate Change

Climate Change harms the health of the cities and human health as well. The incidence of chronic diseases owing to toxic air and excess heat caused by climate change has crippled the health index of citizens of big cities in developing countries Wang and Xiang (2018)

Climate Change is evident and occurring, and the impact of the same is in developing and less developed vulnerable countries. Underdeveloped countries are more prone to the ill effects of extreme climate events (IPCC 2018).

Heavy precipitation events have increased the risk of flooding and damage to human settlements in most areas. Climate change brings uncertainty and causes loss of property and abysmal consequences to humankind like flash floods, logistics disarray, and severing communication lines and electricity connections (IPCC report 2014).

It calls upon the players in this sector to embark on new ways of business, and resort to mitigate the ill effects of climate change, Cities with tourism activities are likely to be significantly impacted by climate change due to changes in peak seasons and natural conditions (Himanshu Grover (2010)

The most Direct Implications of Climate Change are on the Agriculture Sector with diabolic effects like the temperate zones which are too cold will open up for agricultural production and tropical zones will be hit by scanty rainfall or floods. Food security status will be affected thereby resulting threatening the world to be deprived of food, and the right to live. SDG goals of reducing world hunger continue to move distant if climate change is not addressed (Stephen Devereux and Jenny Edwards 2003)

3.4 Readiness of Manufacturing Firms

OSR—Organisational Sustainable Readiness is a nuanced concept that helps assess the state of readiness of manufacturing organizations for sustainable ways of operations Barletta, Ilaria Despeisse, Mélanie, Hoffenson, Steven Johansson, Björn (2020)

Climate Change adaptability (CCA)—It is considered a modification of anthropogenic systems and socio-economic activities to reduce the negative implications of climate change (Yiming Wang and Pengcheng Xiang (2018)

Sustainable Index—A tool consisting of sustainable indicators that helps organizations track and measure their corporate sustainability to achieve a common global problem of climate change Susana Azevedo, João Matias, Radu Godina (2017)

4. Research Gap

From past studies and statistical figures, it is quite evident that Global Warming is on the rise, and the manufacturing sector is contributing a great deal to this. However, past studies have indicated the importance of having green and eco-friendly practices to help organizations reduce emissions and further damage the health of Mother Earth.

4.1 Problem Statement

It is interesting and inquisitive to understand if the manufacturing companies in Tier II cities like Belagavi are ready to concur with the global objectives promulgated by the UN as Sustainable Development Goals (2030), hence this study is taken up to understand the state of readiness of organizations and sustainable practices adopted by them to mitigate the ill effects of climate change.

4.2 Research Questions

RQ1—Why should manufacturing organizations be motivated to shift to sustainable production platforms?

RQ2—What are the challenges likely to be encountered by manufacturing organizations for the transformation toward sustainable production

4.3 Hypothesis

Awareness of the importance of environmental conservation and the impending danger if ignored is a critical component for the wellness of future generations.

Eco-innovationis and has been in practice to assist companies in deploying environmentally friendly processes, and rawmaterials, to produce eco-friendly products and services. Environmental and operational information should be integrated for eco-innovation to be implemented successfully. Businesses that engage in such a learning process get exclusivity that is challenging for rivals to imitate. Thus, the use of eco-innovation will facilitate the well-being of society.

4.4 Research Gap

Previous works centered on how to achieve Sustainable business; However, little is understood in the Indian Context as to how to achieve sustainability in the backdrop of climate change considering the dimensions, viz. efficient use of renewable energies, adopted devices to track energy consumption, Basic training for employees, and involvement in learning programs about climate change impact sustainability. This is an essential area to research, as the previous research studies explore sustainability as a compound concept; missing the necessity to consider which of the components have a larger effect on sustainability. A fresh perspective is expected to reshape policies, strategies, and practices of sustainability

H1 – There is an association between challenges faced in shifting to a sustainable platform to combat climate change and the degree of readiness for the implementation of sustainability using eco-friendly processes and initiatives (Eco-Innovation)

H2 – Eco -Innovation depends on Awareness of Sustainable Practices

(Eco-innovation is a new concept and practice of promoting sustainability throughout the life cycle of the product and helps organizations to expand markets with eco-friendly and environmentally sensitive practices thereby helping reduce damaging consequences on the ecology Machiba, T. (2009) and Sanni, M. (2018).

4.5 Conceptual Framework

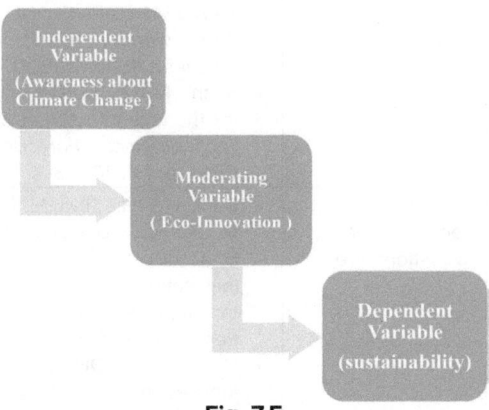

Fig. 7.5

Source: Self-Developed Model based on Literature Review

Independent Dependent variable (Climate Change)—For this research study, Climate change is considered an independent variable as it may trigger off many events, and processes. Although climate change, in reality, is an outcome of unabated anthropogenic influence on the environment, the Extent of awareness of climate change and climate risks may or may not influence or stimulate concern for environmental health. Upon influence, it makes way for organizational readiness for sustainability, albeit it is to be ascertained.

Moderating Variable—Readiness of the organizations to bring about eco-innovation by adopting eco-friendly methods and practices of production.

The Dependent variable (Readiness of firms) is the ability to accept, adopt, and shift to sustainable ways of manufacturing to be able to concur with global SDG 30. It involves measures such as ways and means to reduce the detriment to the environment.

- Incorporating recycling and reuse
- Adopting smart technology
- Reducing the emission of greenhouse gases
- Waste reduction and waste treatment
- Harnessing green, cleaning, and renewable energy

4.6 Construct Validity

Table 7.2

Variable	Application in the instrument	Source
Independent Variable (Awareness about Climate Change)	Used in the Second Section of the Data Collection Instrument (Questionnaire)	• **UN SDG 2030 Goals** UN. (n.d.). *The 2030 Agenda for Sustainable Development*, https://sdgs.un.org/goals.
Moderating Variable (Eco-Innovation)	Used in the Third Section of the (Questionnaire)	• Machiba, T. (2009). (rep.). *SUSTAINABLE MANUFACTURING AND ECO-INNOVATION -Framework, Practices, and Measurement Synthesis Report*. OECD. • Sanni, M. (2018). Drivers of eco-innovation in the manufacturing sector of Nigeria. *Technological Forecasting and Social Change*, 131, 303–314.
Dependent Variable (Sustainability)	Used in the Third Section of the (Questionnaire)	• Bonilla, S. H., Silva, H. R. O., Terra da Silva, M., Franco Gonçalves, R., & Sacomano, J. B. (2018). Industry 4.0 and Sustainability Implications: A Scenario-Based Analysis of the Impacts and Challenges. *Sustainability* Fernández Fernández, Y., Fernández López. • M. A., & Olmedillas Blanco, B.2018) Innovation for sustainability: Theimpact of R&D spending on CO2 emissions. *Journal of Cleaner Production*, 172,

Source: Self-developed for construct validity

4.7 Research Methodology

Data collection: The data collection instrument was circulated online (Google form online Survey) and responses were recorded based on the filled Google forms.

Data: Primary Data was collected through a self-structured questionnaire through the Internet platform

Data Collection Instrument/Questionnaire: The questionnaire structure is designed to collect the necessary data with 16 items relating to the objectives. The instrument has three sections, the first section pertains to respondents' profiles and second section pertains to awareness of climate and global warming, and the third section is earmarked for the implementation of green practices.

Secondary: OECD reports, McKinsey Reports, Research articles, and Papers

Sampling Frame: Manufacturing Units located within the city limits of Belagavi

Sampling Units: Foundries and Engineering Units within the city limits of Belagavi

Sample Size: 166

Respondents Profile: MDs, CEOs, Factory Managers, Department Managers

(MDs – 64, CEOs - 40, Factory Managers – 40, Department Managers – 22, Total - 166)

Sampling Method: Convenient sampling from a finite Population

Research tools used: Cronbach Alpha, Chi-Square Test, Correlation Analysis (Bivariate)

Confidence Level: 95%

Determination of sample size: Out of 285 Manufacturing firms / Production units in Belagavi Taluka (DIC report) the chosen sample size is 166

The formula for sample size calculation as recommended by Yamane (1967)

$$n = \frac{N}{1 + N(e)^2}$$

$$n = 285/ 1 + 285 \ (0.05) \ ^\wedge 2 = 166$$

Table 7.3

n = Sample Size
N = Population (285)
e = margin of error (0.05)

Source: dimensions explained

5. Data Analysis

5.1 Descriptive Statistics

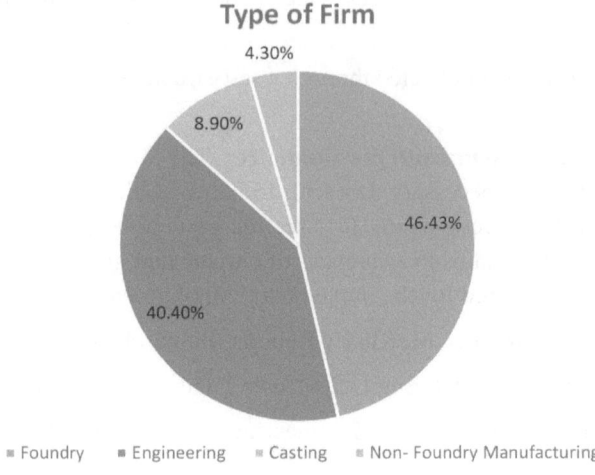

Type of Firm

Foundry • Engineering • Casting • Non- Foundry Manufacturing

Fig. 7.6

Interpretation: Figure 7.6 represents population proportion with 46.43% for foundries, 40.4% for engineering units, 8.9% for casting, and 4.3% for non-manufacturing.

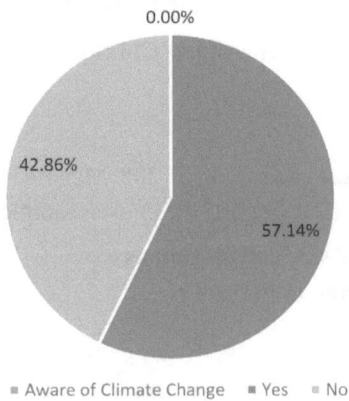

Aware of Climate Change and Global Warming

Aware of Climate Change • Yes • No

Fig. 7.7

Interpretation: 57.14% of the respondents and 42.86% are aware of and oblivious to climate change and global warming respectively

How did you come to know about Climate Change and Global Warming

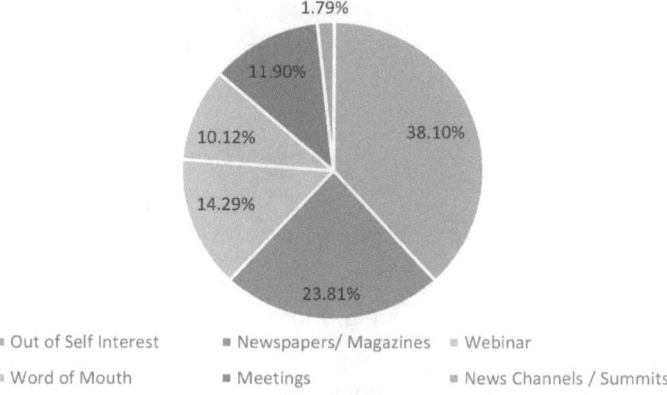

■ Out of Self Interest ■ Newspapers/ Magazines ■ Webinar

■ Word of Mouth ■ Meetings ■ News Channels / Summits

Fig. 7.8

Interpretation: 38% of the respondents say they got to know about climate change and global warming, followed by 23.8% opining that they learnedabout climate change and global warming through newspapers.

Challenges faced to shift to sustainable platform to combat the climate change

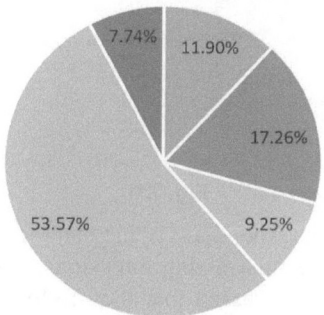

■ Investment on Transition Cost ■ Lack of Supporting Law and Regulatory Framework

■ Lack of Financial Back up and Mobility ■ Changing the mindset

■ Lack of Clarity and Incentives

Fig. 7.9

Interpretation: 53.5% of the respondents opined that changing the mindset is the biggest challenge faced in shifting to a sustainable platform to combat climate change

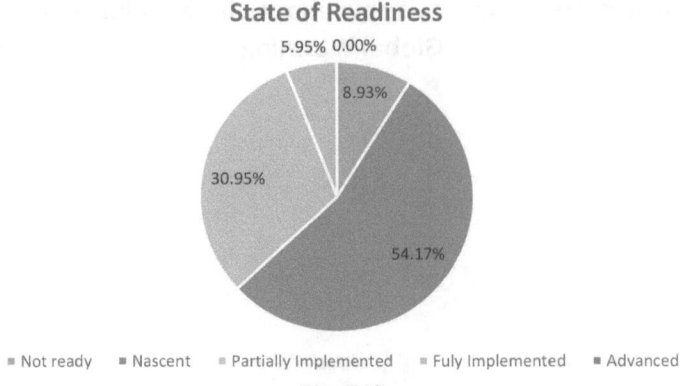

Fig. 7.10

Interpretation: 54 % of the respondents opine that they are in a nascent stage of readiness to achieve sustainability through eco–friendly processes and initiatives

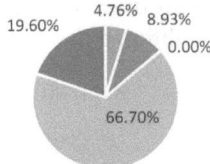

Fig. 7.11

Interpretation: 68 % of the respondents opine that they do not follow sustainable practices and initiatives like minimizing emissions, and decarbonizing. 17.8 % percent of the respondents expressed that they follow wastewater management techniques to prevent environmental degradation.

5.2 Inferential Statistics

Table 7.4

Cronbach's Alph[a]	N of Items
.070	3

Source: made by author

Reliability for internal consistency was checked through the Cronbach Alpha Test on the items having continuous measurement scales for the dimensions mentioned in construct validity namely awareness, eco-innovation, and sustainability. Test values for the same are 0.70 which is above the acceptable range of 0.60.

H1 – *There is an association between challenges faced in shifting to a sustainable platform to combat climate change and the degree of readiness for the implementation of sustainability using eco-friendly processes and initiatives (Eco-Innovation).*

Interpretation: Tables 7.5 and 7.6 represent that there exists an association between *Challenges faced and state of readiness as a P value (0.001 < 0.005),* Hence alternate hypothesis (H1) is accepted

H2 – Eco -Innovation depends on Employee awareness of Sustainable Practices

Table 7.5 Summary Table

	Cases					
	Valid		Missing		Total	
	N	Percent	N	Percent	N	Percent
State your degree of readiness for the implementation of sustainability using eco-friendly processes and initiatives * Challenges faced to shift to the sustainable platform to combat climate change	168	100.0%	0	0.0%	168	100.0%

Source: made by author

Table 7.6 Chi-square table

	Value	df	Asymptotic significance (2-sided)
Pearson Chi-Square	32.931[a]	12	.001
Likelihood Ratio	41.917	12	.000
Linear-by-Linear Association	2.908	1	.088
N of Valid Cases	168		

Source: made by author

Interpretation: Test results from Table 7.7 indicate that Pearson's chi-square statistic is 12 and the p-value = 0.000. The likelihood chi-square statistics is 12 and the p-value = 0.000. Therefore, at a significant value of 0.05, it can be concluded that there is an association between Eco-Innovation and Employee awareness of Sustainable Practices.

Table 7.7 Chi-sqaure table

	Value	df	Asymptotic significance (2-sided)
Pearson Chi-Square	146.844[a]	12	.000
Likelihood Ratio	100.283	12	.000
Linear-by-Linear Association	5.585	1	.018
N of Valid Cases	168		

Source: made by author

Interpretation: Test results from Table 7.8 indicate that the coefficient of Spearman's correlation is very weak with r as 0.002 and the p-value = 0.975 (P 0.975 > 0.005). Therefore, it is to be concluded that although there exists an association between Eco-Innovation and Employee awareness of Sustainable Practices., the degree of association is very weak.

    a. Not assuming the null hypothesis.

    b. Using the asymptotic standard error assuming the null hypothesis.

    c. Based on normal approximation.

Table 7.8 Correlation table

			Employees are trained on the following aspects	Which of the below-mentioned strategies have you implemented in your business process?
Spearman's rho	Employees are trained on the following aspects	Correlation Coefficient	1.000	.002
		Sig. (2-tailed)	–	.975
		N	168	168
	Which of the below-mentioned strategies have you implemented in your business process	Correlation Coefficient	.002	1.000
		Sig. (2-tailed)	.975	–
		N	168	168

Source: made by author

5.3 Findings Results and Discussions

This study indicates that the level of awareness of global warming and climate change in Tier II cities is discouraging. Although it is found that, awareness of the same can usher in Eco-innovation. Unwillingness, Changing the mindset of stakeholders, and lack of legal framework incentives for the sustainable shift are the biggest impediments affecting the said sustainable revolution. Implementation of sustainable practices and accomplishingeco-innovation is a distant journey, Eco-innovation when practiced meticulously can provide rich dividends, and many successful business cases at the Individual level could together create global sustainability (OECD 2009). Our study contradicts the findings of the OECD as the intensity and seriousness of eco-innovation in Tier –II is meek and needs to be reinforced to bring about Macro-level changes.

6. Contribution to the Body of Knowledge

This research was configured as an exploratory study that opens the way for new vistas of research for Industries, Government officials, Research bodies, and Universities to adapt their business practices, policies, studies, and programs to achieve sustainable development goals for the betterment and benefit of the entire Globe.

6.1 Expected Outcome and Scope for Further Research

This study will provide insights into the awareness level of manufacturing firms on the common global problem of climate change, thus also reflecting the state of readiness to concur with guidelines issued by SDG 2030 to mitigate and prevent extreme climate events in the year to come. It will also help understand if local governing bodies under the aegis of nodal bodies are to be established to attain synergy with national &international bodies. Local Governing bodies shall act as change agents to educate and train the stakeholders on imminent dangers if climate change goes unabated. What are the possible initiatives to be taken to create a larger group of climate activists to act as ambassadors at making the local levels begin a revolution to save the ill effects of climate change?

6.2 Scope for Further Research

Based on the findings of this research study, interested research scholars can study the role and importance scope of (ULBs) Urban Local Bodies in promotional sustainability through sustainable practices and eco-innovation. The role of ULBs is critical to achieving Global Sustainability.

6.3 Suggested Model for Organizations

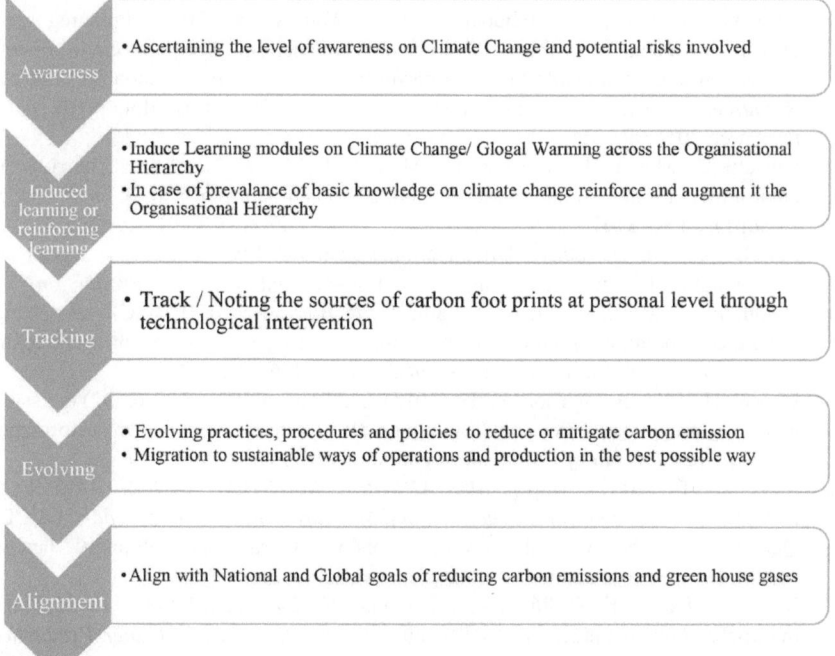

Awareness
• Ascertaining the level of awareness on Climate Change and potential risks involved

Induced learning or reinforcing learning
• Induce Learning modules on Climate Change/ Glogal Warming across the Organisational Hierarchy
• In case of prevalance of basic knowledge on climate change reinforce and augment it the Organisational Hierarchy

Tracking
• Track / Noting the sources of carbon foot prints at personal level through technological intervention

Evolving
• Evolving practices, procedures and policies to reduce or mitigate carbon emission
• Migration to sustainable ways of operations and production in the best possible way

Alignment
• Align with National and Global goals of reducing carbon emissions and green house gases

Fig. 7.12

Source: This is a self-proposed model developed by the authors based on the literature review and research findings

REFERENCES

1. Albrizio, S., Kozluk, T., & Zipperer, V. (2017). Environmental policies and productivity growth: Evidence across industries and firms. *Journal of Environmental Economics and Management, 81*, 209–226. https://doi.org/10.1016/j.jeem.2016.06.002

2. Aldy, J. E., & Pizer, W. A. (2015). The Competitiveness Impacts of Climate Change Mitigation Policies. *Journal of the Association of Environmental and Resource Economists, 2*(4), 565–595. https://doi.org/10.1086/683305

3. Awan, U., Arnold, M. G., & Gölgeci, I. (2021). Enhancing green product and process innovation: Towards an integrative framework of knowledge acquisition and environmental investment. *Business Strategy and the Environment, 30*(2), 1283–1295. https://doi.org/10.1002/bse.2684

4. Bonilla, S. H., Silva, H. R. O., Terra da Silva, M., Franco Gonçalves, R., & Sacomano, J. B. (2018). Industry 4.0 and Sustainability Implications: A Scenario-Based Analysis of the Impacts and Challenges. *Sustainability, 10*(10), 3740. https://doi.org/10.3390/su10103740

5. Effects Of Climate Change On Industries In The Wet Tropics. *Wet Tropics Plan.* Retrieved July 19, 2022, from https://www.wettropicsplan.org.au/regional-themes/sustainable-industries/climate-and-sustainable-industries/

6. Fernández, Y., Fernández López, M. A., & Olmedillas Blanco, B. (2018). Innovation for sustainability: The impact of R&D spending on CO2 emissions. *Journal of Cleaner Production, 172*, 3459–3467. https://doi.org/10.1016/j.jclepro.2017.11.001

7. Fernando, Y., Chiappetta Jabbour, C. J., & Wah, W.-X. (2019). Pursuing green growth in technology firms through the connections between environmental innovation and sustainable business performance: Does service capability matter? *Resources, Conservation and Recycling, 141*, 8–20. https://doi.org/10.1016/j.resconrec.2018.09.031

8. Ghisetti, C., Mancinelli, S., Mazzanti, M., & Zoli, M. (2017). Financial barriers and environmental innovations: Evidence from EU manufacturing firms. *Climate Policy, 17*(sup1), S131–S147.

9. IlariaBarlett, M. D. (2021). Organizational sustainability readiness: A model and assessment tool for manufacturing companies—Journal *of Cleaner Production*.

10. Kätelhön, A., Meys, R., Deutz, S., Suh, S., & Bardow, A. (2019). Climate change mitigation potential of carbon capture and utilization in the chemical industry. *Proceedings of the National Academy of Sciences, 116*(23),

11. Lee, K.-H., Min, B., & Yook, K.-H. (2015). The impacts of carbon (CO2) emissions and environmental research and development (R&D) investment on firm performance. *International Journal of Production Economics, 167*, 1–11.

12. Machiba, T. (2009). (rep.). *SUSTAINABLE MANUFACTURING AND ECO-INNOVATION -Framework, Practices, and Measurement Synthesis Report.* OECD.

13. Qazi K. Ahmad Nigel Arnell, Stewart J. Cohen, & Chris Hope Anthony C. Janetos. (2020). Perspectives on climate change and sustainability. *IPCC*.

14. Rajeev, A., Pati, R. K., Padhi, S. S., & Govindan, K. (2017). Evolution of sustainability in supply chain management: A literature review. *Journal of Cleaner Production, 162*, 299–314. https://doi.org/10.1016/j.jclepro.2017.05.02

15. Sanni, M. (2018). Drivers of eco-innovation in the manufacturing sector of Nigeria. *Technological Forecasting and Social Change, 131*, 303–314. https://doi.org/10.1016/j.techfore.2017.11.007

16. Silvestre, B. S., & Ţîrcă, D. M. (2019). Innovations for sustainable development: Moving toward a sustainable future. *Journal of Cleaner Production*, *208*, 325–332. https://doi.org/10.1016/j.jclepro.2018.09.244
17. UN. (n.d.). *The 2030 Agenda for Sustainable Development,* https://sdgs.un.org/goals.
18. Varadarajan, R. (2017). Innovating for sustainability: A framework for sustainable innovations and a model of sustainable innovations orientation. *Journal of the Academy of Marketing Science*, *45*(1), 14–36. https://doi.org/10.1007/s11747-015-0461-6
19. Wright, C., & Nyberg, D. (2017). An Inconvenient Truth: How Organizations Translate Climate Change into Business as Usual. *Academy of Management Journal*, *60*(5), 1633–1661. https://doi.org/10.5465/amj.2015.0718
20. Yamane, Taro. 1967. Statistics, An Introductory Analysis, 2nd Ed., New York: Harper and Row.

Emerging Horizons: Business and Society in the Post Pandemic Era –
Brig. Dr. Rajiv Divekar et al. (eds)
© *2024 Taylor & Francis Group, London, ISBN 978-1-032-90822-9*

8

Cast and Crew Wellbeing in the Entertainment Industry and the Impact of Covid-19 Pandemic: A Conceptual Framework

Lekshmi Geetha[1]
Symbiosis International Deemed University,
Pune, India

Jaya Chitranshi[2]
Symbiosis Institute of Management Studies
Symbiosis International Deemed University, Pune, India

ABSTRACT

This paper seeks to uncover the well-being concerns of the cast and crew in the India Entertainment Industry. Literature reviews from e-journals, books, research papers, and online news on well-being and the entertainment industry were considered for the conceptual framework. For employees working in any industry, lack of job security, a disrespectful work environment, and challenging job demands create stress and anxiety resulting in poor mental and physical well-being. As the entertainment industry works on atypical working hours, engages people in freelancing, and is prone to bullying and harassment, there is an urgent and significant need to understand the state of well-being of people in this industry. Across developed markets, especially in Australia and Europe, several studies were conducted to understand the welling of cast and crew, which led to establishing support mechanisms for their welfare. However, in India, there have yet to be any relevant studies done in this area. As the industry was severely affected by the pandemic by paused/ delayed productions, canceled shows, and economic crises, it is imperative to research the impact on the well-being of people. At the same time, Entertainment in India is poised for explosive growth through the next decade or more. With a scientific investigation, such an aspiring industry must identify and acknowledge the challenges in working conditions and plan for adequate support for its talent.

KEYWORDS: Wellbeing, Cast & crew, Entertainment industry, Covid-19 impact, Stress, Protean career, Covid-19 impact

[1]lekshmigita@gmail.com, [2]jaya.chitranshi@sims.edu

DOI: 10.4324/978100355996-8

1. Introduction

The entertainment industry in India has always been in the limelight. There has been a strong Indian presence in major entertainment events of national and international fame (Barat, Somjit. (2017). The Indian media and entertainment industry is projected to grow 13.5% from 2019 to 2024 and is estimated to reach $100 billion by 2030. Films, Television, and OTT industries are estimated to touch $22.3 billion in 2022. The country is the largest producer of movies and the fourth-largest theatrical box office market globally. Today, the industry employs 7.4 lakh people while generating indirect employment of 23.6 lakhs (https://www.mpa-apac.org/). While the movies, TV, and Over-the-top (OTT) industries worldwide have been generating exceptional works of art and entertainment, cast and crew experience in their respective jobs has been only subjective, if not regressive. Though this sector has gained never-before attention with the foray of internet-streaming companies, any scientific attempts to comprehend these "workplace practices" of these sectors remain negligible. Off late, however, in an effort to understand the workplace challenges of their respective workforces, Australian and UK film industries have collaborated with academic investigators, which has shed light on underwhelming facts concerning the psychological health of the cast and crew. This later led to policy creation to address specific critical issues in the respective countries. The industry, in general, has been having a considerably greater quantity of depressed professionals than any other (Melanie Wikes et al., 2020). This might be due to the prevailing work conditions, the industry's culture, the question of capability, and its repetitive public scrutiny. The lives of cast and crew are characterized by exceptionally long hours, decreased work-life balance and higher stress, episodes of bullying or intimidating behaviors, alcohol or drug abuse, manic competitiveness, absence of trust/professional relationships, and no assistance for capability enhancement. And any work environment with difficult working conditions and a poor support system creates work stress (Bhui K et al., 2016)

While the Covid 19 global pandemic has adversely impacted several industries in the country, its impact on the entertainment industry was enormous. Theatres were shut down, and several television and OTT projects were paused or even canceled by the impact of the pandemic. This, in turn, led to job loss and put the people through a financial crisis. The industry also lost several individual talents during this period, including those who committed suicide due to the anxiety and depression caused by the slowdown in production (Mamun MA et al., 2020.). This research paper is to explore the support extended to the cast/crew community of the Indian entertainment industry during the Pandemic period and to understand their general well-being concerns.

2. Literature Review

Historically, while the Indian entertainment space was pivoted around a creative cast and crew passionate about their work, the industry has remained hierarchical, extremely competitive, and prone to bullying. From a cultural perspective, thus, the industry confines individuals and their whole selves to follow an order defined at work. As a result, Individual creativity declines with consequent stress in people. Most of the time, this environment does not offer individuals an optimal psychological experience and functioning. In the work of cast and crew, most of these aspects of actualization are placed in an external locus where an individual has little control over their situations. The work that they are passionate about thus may become one of the factors contributing to depression and physical symptoms.

The work of cast and crew can be defined by the construct protean careers (Douglas T Hall, 1996). A protean career is navigated by individuals and not their employers. (Paul DeBettignies, 2009). Unlike that in Corporations, a career in the entertainment industry is primarily characterized by personal ownership, challenging work, more learning-how than knowing-how, and employability. The cast and crew mostly enjoy protean careers except for the fact that it is muddled by the sporadic nature of work, variations in pay, a sense of inequity, and hierarchical relationships. The growth-fostering relational interactions are negligible in the industry owing to extreme competitiveness. Any room for interdependence, mutuality, and/or reciprocity was, thus, eliminated to form a culture of toxicity. While leading a protean career, individuals often take ownership of their careers. As this working style gives a lot of freedom in what they do, they also have to take the sole responsibility for the success and failure of their careers. Some tend to enjoy this freedom, but this can also create anxiety for many thinking about career growth and success. A developmental or learning process is required to adapt. Most cast and crew may find it uncomfortable to operate independently in a complex environment (Robert Kegan, 1996). The industry needs to build a professional, developmental, and caring support system for its participants to leverage the beneficial traits (such as autonomy) of a career in entertainment. Compared to the general population, people working in the entertainment industry experience more mental health problems, depression, and anxiety, as per the studies carried out in developed markets. A recent study in the industry (e.g., Eynde et al. (2016) in the Australian entertainment and creative industries revealed well-being concerns like long working hours and issues with work-life balance, and toxic work culture induced by workplace bullying. There is little awareness of mental health, little social support, and insufficient tools and resources to help deal with mental health issues.

In the past, several studies have tried to understand the well-being of employees working in the film and TV industry by bringing light on the industry's troubles due to odd working hours, destructive coping skills, lack of social support, etc.(eg: Wilkes et al., 2020). This has called for immediate help for the people working in this industry as there are elevated mental health sufferings. This points to a detailed study of the cast crew requirements in the Indian entertainment industry, especially after the increase in suicidal rates in the industry during the pandemic. (Mamun MA, et al., 2020).

Besides the stress related to the work environment, performance anxiety is also prevalent among artists, based on research done in the entertainment industry. A study by Furuya S et al. (2021) established the relationship between performance anxiety and distraction theory in performers. Performance anxiety reduces the connectivity between the motor and prefrontal cortex, which supports the distraction theory. While this study tried to understand the well-being of people behind the camera, further research may be carried out to understand if the cast members face similar or aggravated challenges. Also, the recent development in the industry indicates support mechanisms should differ for people from different backgrounds, like women, the LGBTQI community, the disabled, etc., and research can shed light on the needs of a diverse set of people. Additionally, the well-being needs of new entrants in the industry can be quite different from that of the successful. These parameters, in total or based on priority, can be chosen to do more research in India.

While studies conducted among the creative population in some countries in Europe (Shorter, G. W. et al., (2018) have thrown light on Mental health issues, substance use, and suicidality, it also gives hope that the people are passionate about their work and are expecting that their living conditions will improve over time. However, this passion for delivering creative output ignoring the sufferings due to lack of recognition and absence of support mechanisms, needs to be studied as there is evidence of destructive coping skills among people impacted. As this study was done on people in their late thirties with 15+ years of experience, the results may vary for those in their early careers. Further research can help understand the stigma related to mental health and whether it has affected the survey response of this study. A way to balance this should help understand the results better if carried out in a country like India, where the industry is booming with the entry of OTT platforms and have no significant evidence for cast crew support.

In addition, The COVID-19 pandemic that started in late 2019 created worldwide problems that affected people's mental health and well-being. (Wang C et.al., 2020). The financial crisis that came along with the lockdowns has impacted the entertainment industry and affected vulnerable populations, and even pushed them to suicide (Bhuiyan et al., 2020). The industry that already needed increasing attention to the well-being of its employees due to work culture and environment might have been adversely affected by the loss of jobs, financial crisis, and lack of social support brought in by the pandemic. This research paper focuses on the current well-being of cast and crew in the Indian entertainment industry. It attempts to understand if the Covid 19 has further impacted their well-being. It also intends to understand the current supporting mechanisms available for the well-being of people and explore the opportunities for creating more avenues to support them.

3. Research Questions

1. What is the well-being status of the employees working in the Indian entertainment industry?
2. How did Covid 19 impact their well-being during the last three years?
3. Were they supported during the Covid 19 Pandemic by the industry and other social systems?

4. Research Methodology

An In-Depth Survey - This research proposes an in-depth survey to investigate factors affecting the well-being of cast and crew during the COVID-19 pandemic.

- Entertainment Industry - OTT, Films, and TV industry of India
- Population - Cast and crew of the Indian entertainment industry
- Articles Reviewed: The research framework is proposed after referring to 30+ research articles published in several databases, including Scopus and Web of Science, on psychological well-being, protean careers, the entertainment industry, and coping skills.
- Variables under study:
    a. Dependent Variable - Psychological Well-being
    b. Independent Variable - Work (Job Demands, Job Resources), Covid-19 Impact, Protean Career

The proposed framework for the research explores the relationship between work and well-being moderated by protean careers in the entertainment industry. JDR theory and a specific adaptation of Carol Ryff's Psychological Well-being Scale are used. Job demands and resources (JDR) theory studies the relationship between work stress and psychological well-being. This concept is developed from several primary and secondary data collected from studies on well-being in general, the impact of well-being during the covid 19 pandemic specific to the entertainment industry, and the workforce in general.

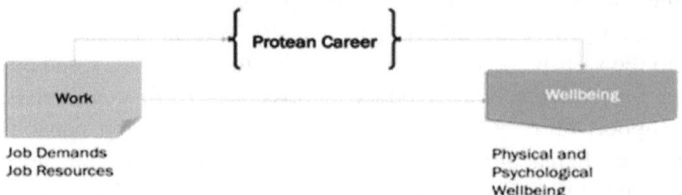

Fig. 8.1   Conceptual model - researcher's conceptualization

Source: Made by authors

It is proposed to use a purposive sample for this study. This will ensure enough samples representing the OTT, Film, and TV industries. Also, considering we need to take samples from different demographics, a purposive sample is proposed.

Also, it will ensure a broad representation of types of work, age groups, gender, and organizations impacted during the pandemic.

The proposed data collection tool for this research is given below:

5. Data Interpretation

Fig. 8.2   Adapted from Melanie wilkes, heather carey and rebecca florisson february 2020. Mental health in the UK film, TV and cinema industry

Rapid Evidence Assessment: Secondary data analysis was done by reviewing the literature on the Indian entertainment industry and its personnel. This was supported by an analysis of the available data on mental health issues. This has assisted in identifying any escalation of mental health problems during the pandemic.

Mental Health/Mental Well-being Survey: An investigation was conducted on the relationship between the well-being and working conditions of Indian entertainment industry personnel, utilizing a particular modification of Ryff's Psychological Well-Being Scale. Which components need to be improved in order to improve working conditions in this industry are shown by the survey questions based on JDR theory.

Direct Interviews: Conversations with experts in the field, included scheduled online conversations as well as in-person interviews.

Provision research and case studies: An analysis of the support networks for the sector in industrialized countries such as India was also done. It was recommended to give Indian creative workers access, to tried-and-true strategies that have been successful outside of the industry as well.

6. Results

Table 8.1 presents the critical findings collected from the review of papers done as part of this conceptual paper. This covers the investigation of the work environment of the entertainment industry, aspects that have been measured through data collection, critical measures used to measure psychological well-being, and suggested and available support mechanisms for cast and crew in the industry.

Table 8.1   Findings from literature review

Distressing work environment	Destructive coping skills	Measuring psychological well being	Support mechanisms/ interventions
• Long Working Hours • Lack of Autonomy • Prone to Bullying • Job demands • Job Insecurity	Alcohol Use Drug Use Poor eating habits Anger Denial Aggressive Behavior	Self-acceptance Positive relations Personal growth Autonomy Environmental mastery Purpose in life	Social Support Cultural changes in the industry Support programs to recover from addictions Early Intervention and preventive programs

Source: Made by authors

7. Conclusion

This conceptual paper has found that when the job demands and job resources are not favorable in creating a good working environment, the employees in the entertainment industry could experience work stress. As the work in the entertainment industry is professional and artistic, passionate individuals in the entertainment industry continue to produce work of quality irrespective of whether their working environment is supportive. While this allows the industry to keep the well-being concerns aside, it may not be sustainable for the industry not to address the challenges at work. This research has further revealed that the life of the cast and crew are prone to mental health issues, including suicidal thoughts and self-harm. Long working hours, challenges associated with a protean career, and episodes of bullying at work affect their well-being. The impact of the Covid 19 pandemic on the industry calls for more research to investigate the reasons behind increased stress and depression and related destructive coping skills of the cast and crew in the Indian entertainment industry. The extent of damage from this work stress on employees' physical and psychological well-being also calls for immediate support from policymakers and industry leaders.

8. Implications of the Study

Good work helps in good mental and physical work (Waddell G, Burton A, 2006). At the same time, a poor work environment can contribute to well-being concerns. Despite its economic contribution and its ever-growing size and quality of output, the Entertainment industry in India has never been formally researched for its practices concerning careers or the well-being of cast and crew. The work environment in the entertainment industry is distressing with the challenges in the job demands and job resources. This often leads to destructive coping skills and affects the cast and crew's physical and psychological well-being. With Covid induced job insecurity, their conditions have worsened due to a lack of support mechanisms in the industry. It is time for industry experts to make deliberate efforts to understand the real challenges of this population and initiate support mechanisms like awareness-building workshops, training, helplines to report grievances, and employee assistance programs that include counseling and therapy. However, before that, the need of the hour is to conduct a comprehensive study among the cast and crew of this industry to understand their current state of well-being and, in turn, develop practices to support them in the long run. The increased suicidal cases from the industry during the pandemic period have made clear that the cast and crew support needs immediate attention.

9. Limitations

Opportunities for further investigating vulnerable populations in the industry, like women, the disabled, and members of LGBTQI, can reveal if their well-being concerns differ from other populations. The findings of this research paper can benefit the policymakers to design support mechanisms exclusive to the industry that can be replicated in industries with similar challenges in job demands and resources. This can also have implications for the entertainment business if further research can be done to measure their motivation to continue working in this industry. There are also opportunities to research how a stable support system can be established for a freelancing population on which the industry gets its work done.

Références

1. Adams, J. S. (1963). Towards an understanding of inequity. Journal of Abnormal and Social Psychology, 67, 422–436
2. Andi Stein, Beth Bingham Evans, An introduction to the entertainment industry (2009)
3. Barat, Somjit. (2017). The entertainment industry and India, Inc.. Asian Cinema. 28. 219–234. 10.1386/ac.28.2.219_1.
4. Bhui K, Dinos S, Galant-Miecznikowska M, de Jongh B, Stansfeld S. Perceptions of work stress causes and effective interventions in employees working in public,

private and non-governmental organisations: a qualitative study. *BJPsych Bull.* 2016;40(6):318–325. doi:10.1192/pb.bp.115.050823

5. Blustein, D. L. (2008). The role of work in psychological health and well-being: A conceptual, historical, and public policy perspective. American Psychologist, 63, 228–240. doi:10.1037/0003-066X.63.4.228

6. Bridgstock, Ruth (2007), Success in the protean career: A predictive study of professional artists and tertiary arts graduates

7. Cabrera, Elizabeth F, Protean organizations Reshaping work and careers to retain female talent

8. Connie, H.L. & Fujimoto, Z.Y. (2016). Inclusion, organisational justice and employee wellbeing.International Journal of Manpower, 37(6), 1–24.

9. Dagenais-Desmarais, V. & Savoie, A. (2012). What is Psychological Well-Being, Really? A Grassroots Approach from the Organizational Sciences. Journal of Happiness Studies. DOI:10.1007/s10902-011-9285-3

10. Diener, E. (1984). Subjective well-being. Psychological Bulletin, 95, 542–575

11. Dodge, R., Daly, A. P., Huyton, J., & Sanders, L. D. (2012). The challenge of defining wellbeing. International Journal of Wellbeing, 2(3).

12. Dor sher, B., and Klei ner, B. 1997. "Practices of excellent companies in the entertainment industry". Man ag ing Service Quality, Vol. 7 (3), pp.127–131.

13. Duffy, R. D., Blustein, D. L., Diemer, M. A., & Autin, K. L. (2016). The psychology of working theory. Journal of Counseling Psychology, 63, 127. Doi.10.1037/cou0000140

14. Ed ward E. Lawler III and Su san A. Mohr man. 2000. "Beyond the Vision", What Makes HR Effective? December, Vol. 23 (4) p.10.

15. Eynde, Julie van den, Fisher, Adrian (2016). Working in the Australian Entertainment Industry: A research project by Entertainment Assist in association with College of Arts, Victoria University.

16. Fujishiro, K. & Heaney, C.A. (2009), "Justice at work, job stress, and employee health", Health Education & Behavior, 36(3), 487–504.

17. Goff L. 1999. "What it's like to work at...Uni ver sal Studios". Com puter - world, Apr. 26, Vol. 33 (17), p.63.

18. Hall T, Douglas (1996). Protean Careers of the 21st Century, The Academy of Management Executive (1993-2005), Nov., 1996, Vol. 10, No. 4, P-8, 12

19. Indian Brand Equity Foundation, Media and Entertainment Industry Snapshot (2021). www.ibef.org.

20. Jennifer Leff (2021), What's Going On Behind the Scenes? Mental Health and the Entertainment Industry, GoodTherapy.org

21. Mark R. W. Williams (2018), Falling Through the Gaps: Our Artists' Health and Welfare, Issue 56 of Platform papers.

22. Mayer, K. J. 2002. "Human resource practices and service quality in theme parks". The International Journal of Contemporary Hospitality Management, Vol. 14 (4), p.169.

23. Muanya, C. & Ezea, S. (2017). Worrisome rising cases of suicides in Nigeria. The Guardian Saturday Magazine.

24. Nguyen Hoai Anh, Brian H. Kleiner (2005), Effective human resource management in the entertainment industry, Management Research News, Vol. 28 No. 2/3, pp. 100–107

25. Obobanyi Momohjimoh Ahmed, Bidayatul Akmal Mustafa Kamil, and Awanis Ku Ishak (2018). Influence of Perceived Stress and Organizational Justice on Employee Wellbeing amongst Academia: A Conceptual Paper.
26. R. Kegan, In Over Our Heads: The Mental Demands of Modern Life. Cambridge, MA: Harvard University Press, 1994
27. Ryff D, Carol (2013), Psychological Wellbeing Revisited: Advances in the Science and Practice of Eudaimonia, Journal of Psychotherapy and Psychosomatics, P-16
28. Samuel B Harvey, Matthew Modini et al. 1 (2017). Can work make you mentally ill? A systematic meta-review of work-related risk factors for common mental health problems, Occupational and Environmental Medicine, (April 2017), pp. 301–310
29. Sarriera, Jorge Castellá, Abs, Daniel, Casas, Ferran, Bedin, Lívia Maria (2011), Relations Between Media, Perceived Social Support and Personal Well-Being in Adolescence, Vol 106, No 3, P 545–56.
30. Thomson, Paula, Jaque, Victoria S. (2017), Creativity and the Performing Artist | ScienceDirect
31. Volmer, Judith, Spurk, Daniel, Volmer, J, Spurk, · D (2005), Protean and boundaryless career attitudes: relationships with subjective and objective career success, Doi.10.1007/s12651-010-0037-3
32. Waddell G, Burton A. *Is work good for your health and well-being?* London: The Stationery Office, 2006
33. Wilkes, Melanie, Carey, Heather and Florisson, Rebecca (2020). Mental health in the UK film, TV and cinema industry, The Work Foundation with Lancaster University Management School.

Emerging Horizons: Business and Society in the Post Pandemic Era –
Brig. Dr. Rajiv Divekar et al. (eds)
© 2024 Taylor & Francis Group, London, ISBN 978-1-032-90822-9

9

Impact of Service Quality on Customer Satisfaction of Delhi Metro Rail Commuters

Vijit Tyagi[1]
Indian Institute of Management Lucknow, India
Anita Goyal[2]
Indian Institute of Management Lucknow, India

ABSTRACT

This research focuses to understand the impact of service quality parameters in creating customer satisfaction with implications to provide delighting journey experience for its continual usage. The responses were received through a close-ended questionnaire from Delhi metro commuters. Total 630 valid responses were examined to assess customer satisfaction based on ten service quality factors. The respondents had indicated high satisfaction with cleanliness and security factors of service quality with further improvement possibilities. On the other side, there is a need for improvement in physical conditions, comfort, connectivity, information, availability and accessibility, price, and reliability dimensions of service quality for creating customer satisfaction. The understanding from this study can help the metro service providers to offer a better satisfying service.

KEYWORDS: Service quality, Customer satisfaction, Metro services, India

1. Introduction

The urbanization of Indian cities results in an increase of vehicular traffic (at an annual growth rate of 9.5-11% to meet the urban travel requirement, which leads to slower mobility and high emissions (Jain et al., 2012). In this context, with the recent technological and economic development across the world, each country tries to increase the quality of life of its population implementing affordable and sustainable intercity mobility solutions. A Mass Rapid Transit (MRT) System

[1]efpm06013@iiml.ac.in, [2]anita.g@iiml.ac.in

DOI: 10.4324/978100355996-9

is seeming to be an affordable and effective solution for improving the travel quality of city dwellers. It can offer a fast and environmentally-friendly means of transport. Increased private vehicle usage tends to increase vehicular traffic, which further results in a raised air pollution level, noise pollution level, increased fuel consumption. More public transport usage will ease the vehicular traffic issue and causes reduction in public vehicle usage (Xia et. al., 2013).

Thus, to decrease the increasing traffic congestion across existing road infrastructure has been developed by the local transport agency. To facilitate the travel, need of urban commuters, a Metro Rail Transport System seems the most suitable and successful mode of transport solution among the available transportation modes for urban mobility requirements with its high passenger carrying ability. Being a capital-intensive urban transport solution, the adoption of this mobility system majorly depends upon its financial viability and self-sustainability so that a system can work effectively and efficiently in the long run without any financial support from Government and City transport agencies.

Due to the continuously growing travel need of city residents and the unavailability of a safe, reliable, energy-efficient mode of the public transport system, Delhi Government has decided to introduce a rail-based transport system known as Delhi Metro. It was observed that public transport use in India is reducing, despite increasing travel demand (Ranganathan, 1995). The main contributors were deficient infrastructure, inferior service quality, and an imperfect image associated with public transport organizations.

The metro transit system is an improvised version of light rail and suburban railways. It can carry a high volume of passengers from one place to another while running at-grade, elevated, and underground sections. Delhi Metro has changed and revolutionized the concept of travel in Delhi and given a new dimension to the Public Transport system. It is a safe, reliable, well-connected, comfortable, cost-effective, and eco-friendly mode of travel. Delhi Metro is impacting the social, economic, and environmental factors, thereby creating a path and direction for future Metro expansion in India. Delhi Metro, the largest and busiest metro network in India considered for this research to understand the role of service quality parameters in creating customer satisfaction and thereby delivering delighting journey experience for its usage in the future.

Service quality dimensions play a vital role in enhancing the passenger journey experience, as variability in transport service quality is affected by people's perception of the service based on their experiences. It is well-known that maintaining uniform service quality to generate a similar experience for everyone is difficult. A Service provider needs to establish trust and confidence among passengers regarding service quality. The existing studies indicate that besides five service quality dimensions as stated in the SERVQUAL framework, additional dimensions such as connectivity and convenience will also exist that affect the satisfaction, loyalty, and behavior intentions of commuters for choosing the metro as traveling mode. Service quality in the service industry has been explored and studied in a different context by many researchers in the past and is a vital component for creating customer satisfaction. It helps to understand the factors responsible for enhancing customer satisfaction and developing differentiation in today's competitive world.

The impact of railway station accessibility on customer satisfaction levels is studied and evaluated by Givoni and Rietveld (2006). The different aspect of customer satisfaction, such as punctuality, comfort, overcrowding, attitude, cleanliness, and catering in the railway system of the United Kingdom was studied and analyzed by Disney (1999). Steyn et al. (2011) have also studied and observed the customer satisfaction impact on continual relationships in the case of domestic travelers of South African airlines for sustainable growth. In the Indian context, researchers (Shainesh & Mathur, 2000; Sreedhar, 2012) have assessed the relationship between the quality of service and satisfaction of the customer in the public transit system based on Parasuraman et al. (1988) SERVQUAL scale.

Detailed studies and extant literature show that most of the studies undertaken to analyze the impact of service quality dimensions are done on buses, airlines, and passenger trains usually for long distances. Although few studies were done on the metro network using SERVQUAL in India /abroad. some new dimensions like connectivity, and convenience has not been studied in the Metro rail framework. Based on the existing literature gap, there is a need to examine the impact of these quality dimensions on customer satisfaction in the framework of metro rail services considering the Delhi Metro as the base of this study. The current study will help to improve the metro services to its commuters. It will contribute to developing satisfying services which will have an impact on better life through less pollution, controlled traffic, and comfortable travel modes to meet the requirement of the masses in countries like India.

In light of the above research gap and the motivation of current research, the research objectives are:

- To understand the impact of service quality dimension on the satisfaction level of Delhi Metro Commuters.
- To identify the service quality dimensions that has greatest impact on commuter's satisfaction and of high priorities for improvement in order to enhance the travelling experience of Delhi Metro commuters.

2. Review of Literature

In the transport sector, service quality dimensions play a significant and vital role in enhancing the passenger journey experience. Service quality creates a differential advantage and is also responsible for the profitability and productivity of the firm. The Literature review suggests that there were five different streams of research, such as the nature and concept of service quality, measurement of service quality dimension, measures to improve service quality, strategic implication of quality of service, and service quality impact on consumer behaviour.

The nature and concept of service quality is a comparison of the expectation of the customer with the actual service delivered. The presence of the customer mostly observed in all the service delivery. Service quality is considered to be affected by the emotional and behavioural aspects of consumers, and the same need to be taken into account while assessment of service quality (Brady et al., 2001). Service quality intangibility makes it more difficult to manage quality delivery than tangible products (Friman & Fellesson, 2009). Crosby (1979) considered service quality as Conformance to requirements. Juran's (1992) definition of quality is "fitness to use".

There are two thought processes to define service quality; as per European tradition, Gronroos (1982) ned the service quality dimensions as technical quality (What is received by the customers) and functional quality (How the service is delivered to the customer). Again, Gronroos (1991) has further indicated service quality as physical quality (service quality tangible aspect), interactive quality (interaction between a service provider and consumer), and corporate quality (Image of the firm in the eyes of the consume. Parasuraman et al. (1988), as per the North American tradition, defined the quality of service as a measurement of difference among customer's expectations and customer service performance perceptions using the SERVQUAL scale having total of 22 items, which were measured using a questionnaire in Likert scales on the five dimensions such as Tangibility (i.e. physical appearance, four items), Reliability (i.e. dependable, accurate performance, five items), Responsiveness (i.e. Promptness and helpfulness, four items), Assurance (i.e. competence, courtesy, credibility, and security, four items), and Empathy (i.e. easy access, good communications, and customer understanding, five items). Service quality is considered a multidimensional construct (Parasuraman et al., 1988; Gronroos, 1990; Cronin & Taylor, 1992; Cronin et al., 2000).

Carman (1990) has elaborated that service quality affects the satisfaction level of consumers, and thus subjective nature i.e., perceived quality becomes more important as compared to the objective aspect i.e., technical quality. Gronroos (1984) clearly states that the image of the firm plays an imperative role in making the expectation of the consumers.

The third service quality research dimension has studied how an organization can improve service quality. It is well-known that quality improvement has a determinantal effect on customer retention, market share, and profitability because of increased sales, lower prices, and decreased costs (Deming, 1982). Harvey et al. (2014) have studied the perception of commuters of the high-speed railway system in the United Kingdom and found that factors like security, company's prestige, comfort, and traveling time seems essential factor for the users and commuters are willing to pay more for the reduction in travel time. The study also showed that women passengers consider security a vital criterion compared to men.

Better service offerings in public transport systems, such as information provisions and on-board communication, helps in better scheduling, which results in the enhanced commuter's experience and makes the journey comfortable and pleasurable studied by Foth and Schroeder (2010); Camacho et al. (2012). Comfort and Convenience seems reasonable and inexpensive quality parameters in improvement of service quality for public transport resulting in increased ridership as studied by Litman (2008).

Litman (2023) has studied the preference of consumers for choosing a mode of travel and concluded that commuters prefer qualitative factors such as comfort, convenience, and reliability in the selection of mode of travel as compared to quantitative factors such as cost and speed in order enhance their traveling experiences. So, firms should improve qualitative factors to provide a better traveling experience.

The fourth research stream explains the strategic consequences of quality for differential competitive advantage for sustainability in the long run. Service quality has been considered a vital feature and an essential medium for developing a leading competitive edge (Parasuraman et al., 1988; Gronroos, 2001). Improvement of quality of service has a positive influence on the customer retention, better market dominance, and desirability as a consequence of improved sales, lower prices, and reduced costs (Deming, 1982; Juran, 1998). Service quality acts as a differentiator in the service industry for creating a positive correlation between customer satisfaction and customer behavioural intentions (Tam, 2008).

The quality-of-service dimension has a favourable effect on consumer behaviour, and strategic decision-making for sustainable growth in the competitive market (Boulding et al., 1993; Friman & Garling, 2001; Friman & Fellesson, 2009; Rust et al., 1995) have established the positive influence of quality of service on the customer's satisfaction level and the firm's profitability. Yilmaz and Ari (2017) analysed the factors responsible for creating loyalty for the high-speed public transport railway system running between Eskisehir and Ankara in Turkey and observed that improvement of service quality and image of the firm positively affects customer satisfaction and loyalty. Redman et al. (2013) have explained that to motivate the continual usage of public transport and to enhance customer's journey experience, an affordable and attractive offering must be developed for commuters.

Improvement in Service quality factors like cleanliness, ticket price, employee attention, and ticketing services increases customer satisfaction and finally results in increased ridership (Weinstein, 2000; Chou & Kim, 2009; Lee et al., 2009; Kao et al., 2009; Kim & Lee, 2011; Stuart, et al., 2000).

There is specific research literature on mass rail transport systems. It includes high-speed rail, metro, light rail, etc. wherein the influence of various construct of service quality on customer satisfaction and loyalty was studied. Silcock (1981) has concluded the measurement of accessibility, reliability, comfort, convenience, and safety parameters are effective for assessing service quality for the public transport industry. Winsted (1997) stated that the service quality dimensions are affected by country of origin and it varies from country to country. Disney (1999) has studied the Spanish rail commuter satisfaction using the parameters like punctuality, cleanliness, attitude, overcrowding, comfort, and catering and observed that the service recovery process has a deep impact on customer satisfaction and in case personalized attention is given, commuter becomes more satisfied.

Prasad et al. (2010) have introduced a management model of quality of service to analyse and evaluate the quality of services of Indian Railways at Secunderabad station based on SERVQUAL scale and developed three new dimensions namely "service product, social responsibility, and service delivery" for increasing passenger satisfaction. Service delivery, reliability, and empathy got the lowest mark among the dimensions.

Randheer et al. (2011) have examined passengers' perception of public bus transport services in Hyderabad and Secunderabad (India) using culture as the sixth dimension of service quality and found that the SERVQUAL framework needs to be changed to suit the actual study situation.

3. Methodology

A survey with a convenience sample was conducted with Delhi metro commuters to analyse the impact of service quality dimensions on the satisfaction of Delhi metro commuters. The survey was run for four weeks at Rajiv Chowk, Noida City Centre, Huda City Centre, Botanical Garden, Sarita Vihar, Dwarka, Kashmiri Gate (07 busiest) metro stations of the DMRC network. A total of 750 responses were received. However, only 630 respondents filled out the questionnaire and are considered for this study.

A questionnaire was developed in consideration of the service quality dimensions indicated in the literature (primarily for the transport system), and EN13816 (Standard for evaluating and analysing the quality of services provided by public transport authorities). The questionnaire was implemented to measure the quality of service in the Metro Rail Mass Rapid Transport system (MRTS) based on the dimensions of physical conditions, cleanliness, comfort, safety, connectivity, information availability and accessibility, security, price, and reliability. Responses were collected from the passengers based on a closed-ended questionnaire using the Likert scale, wherein the highest service quality perception rating corresponding to strongly agree is +5 and vice versa.

3.1 Drivers of Measurement (EN-13816)

Accessibility – It determines the accessibility to public passenger transport arrangement along with the interface with other transport mediums.

Information – It deals with the systematic sharing of knowledge for planning and execution of journey in public transport network.

Time – It determines the actual /predicted time related to planning and execution of journey.

Customer care – It deals with requirement of customer to enhance their travelling experience.

Comfort – It is an important service element for making traveling in public transport system   pleasurable.

Security – It is basically an experience gained by commuters while travelling in public transport system from the actual safety measures applied and from the activity designed to ensure that commuters are aware of from those measures.

Environmental impact – It deals with the impact of public transport system on the ecosystem for its sustainable operation.

4. Data Analysis

The data of 630 respondents (actual commuters) was considered and analysed to identify their demographic profile and satisfaction with service quality factors. A total of ten factors were considered. Table 9.1 shows the commuter's demographic profile.

Sample data shows that Delhi metro commuters were from all age groups. However, nearly 80% of commuters are below the age of 40 years. 65% of metro commuters were males, and 35% were females. There were a nearly equal number of married and unmarried travellers. Most of the metro commuters were salaried people. Around 98% of commuters had a monthly salary of less than or equal to 50,000.

Sample data shows that commuters of the Delhi metro come from every part of the capital with the majority of commuters from North Delhi (31%) followed by South Delhi (21%), Central Delhi (18%), East Delhi (16%), and West Delhi (14%). The majority of daily metro commuters were literate and more than 60% of them have a graduation degree. Commuters come from all walks of life. Nearly 43% were working professionals followed by students (34%) and business personnel (17%). Sample data shows that the majority of commuters are daily passengers and data clearly shows that there is a possibility available to increase ridership and create a modal shift for sustainable growth. Further, 59% of commuters spend more than INR 2000 on travelling expenditures. However, only 10% of them spend nearly INR 2000 on metro expenses.

Table 9.2 presents responses towards commuters' satisfaction in terms of quality perceptions for various service factors of the Delhi metro. With Concerning

Table 9.1 Commuter's demographic profile (Total 630 responses)

Demographic profile of commuter's		No. of commuters	Percentage
Age (in years)	10-20	73	12
	20-30	287	45
	30-40	155	24
	40-50	85	13
	>50	30	6
Gender	Male	410	65
	Female	220	35
Marital Status	Unmarried	265	42
	Married	350	56
	Separated	15	2
Monthly Income (in Indian Rupees)	<10000	162	26
	10000-30000	245	38
	30000-50000	210	33
	50000-100000	10	2
	>100000	3	1
Location	North Delhi	198	31
	South Delhi	133	21
	East Delhi	102	16
	West Delhi	85	14
	Central Delhi	112	18
Education	Under Graduate	177	28
	Graduate	329	52
	Post-Graduation	92	15
	None	32	5
Occupation	Student	216	34
	Service	270	43
	Business	111	17
	Retired	12	2
	Unemployed	21	4
Frequency of Travel	Occasional	151	24
	First time User	31	5
	Daily	337	53
	Weekly	111	18
Monthly Travel Expenditure	<Rs1000	29	5
	Rs1000-Rs2000	225	36
	>Rs2000	376	59
Metro Expense	<Rs1000	179	28
	Rs1000-Rs2000	386	62
	>Rs2000	65	10

Source: Made by Authors

Table 9.2 Customer satisfaction response towards service quality factors (in percentages)

Factor	Sub Factors	Strongly agree	Agree	Neutral	Disagree	Strongly disagree
Physical Conditions	Air conditioning	45	20	18	13	4
	Lightening in train and station	54	29	2	13	2
	Space inside coach	41	21	7	28	3
Cleanliness	Ticket Counter	47	31	5	17	0
	Station/Platform Premises	59	31	6	4	0
	Train Coaches	52	44	4	0	0
Comfort	Ambience inside metro	48	23	5	24	0
	Comfortable boarding & de-boarding of train	18	16	4	59	3
	Ease of entry/ exit	17	23	5	48	7
Safety	Feel safe at platform	42	53	5	0	0
	Feel safe inside train coach	34	61	5	0	0
	Feel safe in parking area	7	17	2	56	18
Connectivity	Last mile connectivity	3	18	4	51	24
	Connectivity with bus stand, station and airport	19	73	6	2	0
	Feeder bus service	0	8	5	79	8
Information	Travel timetables /route map	33	50	7	10	0
	Announcement at station and in train	20	67	4	9	0
	Website	30	63	5	2	0
Availability and Accessibility	Frequency of service	18	35	4	38	5
	Lift & escalator at station	19	57	5	19	0
	Infrastructure facility at station	7	19	5	61	8
Security	Entrance frisking system	33	60	5	3	0
	CCTV at station and inside coaches	42	52	6	0	0
	Separate coach for woman	18	68	6	8	0
Price	Method of ticket buying	37	51	7	5	0
	Value for money	30	50	6	14	0
	Economical (peak/off peak hours)	19	51	5	21	3
Reliability	On time departure	33	37	10	20	0
	Travel time	35	33	8	21	3
	Train failure	22	42	6	28	2

Source: Made by Authors

physical conditions (the first quality factor), commuters are found satisfied with the available services i.e., air conditioning system, lighting system, and space availability inside metro coaches and at the platform area. However, there is a scope for improvement in each of these infrastructures for enhancing travelling experience especially space inside coaches. The majority of commuters are satisfied with the cleanliness (second quality factor) at the station counter, inside coaches, and at the platform area, but this indicates the improvement in cleanliness at ticket counters. Considering the comfort levels (third quality factor), commuters are found not satisfied with the facility of boarding and de-boarding facility, ease of entry/exit at the station, and ambience inside coaches. There is a need to improve comfort parameters for a comfortable travelling experience.

Metro commuters feel safe (fourth quality factor) while travelling in metro network due to the close surveillance through CCTV at station and inside coaches. This can be due to the availability of dedicated CISF for security check at entry side. But there is a need of improvement in outside parking area security. Commuters are found not at all satisfied with the last mile connectivity and feeder bus service available for connectivity (fifth quality factor). Normally, it is considered important for reaching to a destination timely and economically. However, connectivity of metro network to major bus stand and airport was perceived with satisfaction. Commuters seem satisfied with information (sixth quality factor) of journey planner and train arrival/departure timetable, announcement system installed at station and inside train. Respondents also found satisfied with the information on website which indicates that mostly commuters prefer to use website for getting required information about travelling. Regarding availability and accessibility (seventh quality factor), commuters were not satisfied with the train availability, lift and escalator and other infrastructure facility at station. It indicates that there is a room of improvement to make their journey experience more comfortable.

Commuters have indicated their satisfaction with entry security frisking, CCTV monitoring inside coaches and at stations and prefer separate coach for woman passengers. Thus, there is a high satisfaction perception for security (eighth quality factor) in metro services. Further, responses show a mixed opinion regarding the fares and value for money. This indicates that price (ninth quality factor) for metro services is perceived high by some and they may not prefer increase in fare for travelling.

Respondents indicate satisfaction with method of ticket buying which indicates that various modes of ticket availability are convenient to commuters. Data presents that commuters are not fully satisfied with the reliability (tenth quality factor) of metro services based on scheduled departure, travel time and train failures during its operation. Thus, there is scope of improvement for enhancing their traveling experience.

5. Discussion

Demographic data of respondents (Table I) indicates that people from all walks of life travel in Delhi Metro irrespective of age, gender, occupation, location, and other factors. However, older people travel less in the metro, considering the respondents above 50 years of age profile and the percentage of retired respondents. The people with a high-income group, above INR 50000 per month, travel less in the metro.

This study has identified customer satisfaction for metro commuters on ten quality factors, which are not studied earlier in metro travel services. Existing studies have considered the different combinations of service quality parameters in other transport services like buses, railways, and others (Disney, 1999; Prasad et al., 2010). The majority of existing studies have primarily considered the public transport system in general rather than the metro services context in particular (Rahman et al., 2017). Further studies have also not considered all ten service quality factors together to analyse the role of these factors in commuters' satisfaction.

The respondents' (actual commuters) have indicated high satisfaction with cleanliness, security, information, and safety factors of service quality. Among the safety factor, responses showed a high satisfaction level except for safety perception in the parking area (74% not satisfied). Improvement in cleanliness with other service quality factors like ticket price, employee attention, and ticketing services seems to increase customer satisfaction and ridership (Chou & Kim, 2009; Lee et al., 2009; Kim & Lee, 2011). Studies by Camacho et al., 2012; Foth & Schroeder, 2010), and Rahman et al., 2017) support the impact of information available on positive consumer experience and satisfaction. It is identified that information access results in satisfaction in terms of ease of planning the travel. Harvey et al. (2014) have indicated the importance of security along with the factors of company's prestige, comfort, and traveling time towards commuters' satisfaction and experience. Thus, existing studies explains the importance of cleanliness, security, information and safety factors of service quality towards high customer satisfaction. These four factors (cleanliness, security, information, and safety) are identified as one of the factors among other service quality factors in different studies. The current study in Indian context for metro services emphasizes these four service quality factors of high importance for customer satisfaction in Delhi metro services. The results are in line with the understanding shared by Winsted (1997) that the service quality dimensions are affected by country of origin and varies from country to country.

Extant literature indicates that comfort and convenience seem reasonable quality parameters in improvement of service quality for public transport for increased ridership (Litman, 2008, 2023). This study results show that there is a need of improvement in comfort, physical conditions, connectivity, availability and accessibility along with price and reliability dimensions of service quality for creating customer satisfaction. There are responses where respondents disagree to have satisfaction. At the same time, there are a smaller number of respondents who have indicated for strongly disagree option to indicate dissatisfaction except for safety in parking area and last mile connectivity. These two dimensions need to be addressed because indicated high level of dissatisfaction.

According to the existing studies in different countries' contexts all factors are important; there is a need to give priority to reliability dimension of service quality, which is considered a very important basic service quality factor (Parasuraman et al., 1988). Thus, there is a scope for improvement in the service quality dimension resulting in customer satisfaction, which may help to create a modal shift and result in increased ridership for sustainable growth in the future.

6. Future Research Implications and Limitations

Existing literature indicates that there exists a linkage between dimensions of service quality and customer satisfaction. The current research findings indicate the areas of improvement in quality factors to provide better-satisfied services to metro commuters. This study is limited to understanding customer satisfaction's relationship with service quality factors. There is a possibility to explore how the service quality perception led to customer satisfaction and loyalty in the metro transport system for increased ridership and sustainable growth in the long run. This study may help the metro authority devise a more attractive value offering for commuters for a self-sustainable mobility solution.

REFERENCES

1. Boulding, W., Kalra, A., Staelin, R., & Zeithaml, V.A. (1993). A dynamic process model of service quality: From expectations to behavioural intentions. *Journal of Marketing Research*, 30(1), 7–27.
2. Brady, M. K., & Cronin, J. J. (2001). Some new thoughts on conceptualising perceived service quality: A hierarchical approach. *Journal of Marketing*, 65(3), 34–49.
3. Crosby, P. B. (1979). *Quality is free: The Art of Making Quality Certain*. New American Library.
4. Carman, J. M. (1990). Consumer Perceptions of Service Quality: An Assessment of the SERVQUAL Dimensions. *Journal of Retailing*, 66 (1), 33–55.
5. Cronin, J.J., & Taylor, S.A. (1992). Measuring service quality: A re-examination and extension. *Journal of Marketing*, 56(3), 55–68.
6. Cronin, J.J., Brady, M.K., & Hult, G.T.M. (2000). Assessing the effects of quality, value, and customer satisfaction on consumer behavioural intentions in service environments. *Journal of Retailing*, 76(2), 193–218.
7. Chou, J.-S., & Kim, C. (2009). A structural equation analysis of the QSL relationship with passenger riding experience on high-speed rail: An empirical study of Taiwan and Korea. *Expert Systems with Applications*, 36(3), 6945–6955.
8. Camacho, T.D., Foth, M., & Rakotonirainy, A. (2012). Pervasive technology and public transport: Opportunities beyond telematics. *IEEE Pervasive Computing*, 12(1), 18–25.

9. Deming, E.W. (1982). *Quality, productivity and competitive position.* Centre for advanced engineering study. Cambridge, MA.
10. Disney, J. (1999). Customer satisfaction and loyalty: The critical elements of service quality. *Total Quality Management*, 10(4–5), 491–497.
11. Friman, M., & Garling, T. (2001). Frequency of negative critical incidents and satisfaction with public transport services. *Journal of Retailing and Consumer Services*, 8(2), 105–114.
12. Foth, M., & Schroeder, R. (2010). Enhancing the experience of public transport users with urban screens and mobile applications. In Proceedings of the 14th International Academic Mind Trek Conference: Envisioning Future Media Environments, 33–40.
13. Friman, M., & Fellesson, M. (2009). Service supply and customer satisfaction in public transportation: The quality paradox. *Journal of Public Transportation*, 12(4), 57–69.
14. Redman, L., Friman, M., Garling, T., & Hartig, T. (2013). Quality attributes of public transport that attract car users: A research review. *Transport Policy*, 25, 119–127.
15. Gronroos, C. (1982). An applied service marketing theory. *European Journal of Marketing*, 16(7), 30–41.
16. Gronroos, C. (1984). A service quality model and its marketing implications. *European Journal of Marketing*, 18(4), 36–44.
17. Gronroos, C. (1990). *Service management and marketing: Managing the moment of truth in service competition.* Lexington Books.
18. Gronroos, C. (1991). Scandinavian management and the Nordic school of services – Contributions to service management and quality. *International Journal of Service Industry Management*, 2(3), 17–26.
19. Gronroos, C. (2001). *Service management and marketing* (2nd ed). Wiley.
20. Givoni, M., & Rietveld, P. (2006). Access to railway stations in the Netherlands, 46th Congress of the European Regional Science Association: "Enlargement, Southern Europe and the Mediterranean," August 30th - September 3, 2006, Volos, Greece. European Regional Science Association (ERSA). Louvain-la-Neuve, France.
21. Harvey, J., Thorpe, N., Caygill, M., & Namdeo, A. (2014). Public attitudes to and perceptions of high-speed rail in the UK. *Transport Policy*, 36, 70–78.
22. Juran, J. M. (1992). *Juran on quality by design: The new steps for planning quality into goods and services.* Free Press.
23. Juran, J. M. (1998). *Juran's quality handbook* (5th ed). McGraw-Hill Professional.
24. Jain, V., Sharma, A., & Subramanian, L. (2012). Road traffic congestion in the developing world. In Proceedings of the 2nd ACM Symposium on Computing for Development (1–10).
25. Kao, L. H., Stewart, M., & Lee, K-H. (2009). Using structural equation modelling to predict cabin safety outcomes among Taiwanese airlines. *Transportation Research Part E: Logistics and Transportation Review*, 45(2), 357–365.
26. Litman, T. (2008). Valuing Transit Service Quality Improvements. *Journal of Public Transportation*, 11(2), 43–64.
27. Lee, J. H., Jin, B. S., & Ji, Y. (2009). Development of a Structural Equation Model for ride comfort of the Korean high-speed railway. *International Journal of Industrial Ergonomics*, 39(1), 7–14.
28. Litman, T. (2023). Evaluating accessibility for transportation planning. *Victoria Transport Policy Institute*, 1–65.
29. Kim, Y.K., & Lee, H.R. (2011). Customer satisfaction using low-cost carriers. *Tourism Management*, 32(2), 235–243.

30. Meyer, C.F., & Mostert, P.G. (2011). The influence of passenger satisfaction on relationship formation in the South African domestic airline industry. *South African Journal of Business Management*, 42(4), 79–88.
31. Rahman, F., Chowdhury, T.D., Haque, T., Rahman, R., & Islam, A. (2017). Identifying existing bus service condition and analysing customer satisfaction of bus service in Dhaka city. *Journal of Transportation Technologies*, 7(2), 107–122.
32. Randheer, K., Al-Motawa, A.A., & Vijay, J.P. (2011). Measuring Commuters' Perception on Service Quality Using SERVQUAL in Public Transportation. *International Journal of Marketing Studies*, 3(1), 21–34.
33. Parasuraman, A., Zeithaml, V.A., & Berry, L.L. (1988). SERVQUAL: A multiple-item scale for measuring consumer perceptions of service quality. *Journal of Retailing*, 64(1), 12–40.
34. Prasad, M.D., & Shekhar, B.R. (2010). Impact of service quality management (SQM) practices on Indian railways-a study of South-Central railways. *International Journal of Business and Management*, 5(9), 139–146.
35. Rust, R.T., Zahorik, A.J., & Keiningham, T.L. (1995). Return on quality (ROQ): Making service quality financially accountable. *Journal of Marketing*, 59(2), 58–70.
36. Ranganathan, N. (1995). National urban transport policy – A framework. *Indian Journal of Transport Management*, 19(2), 85–98.
37. Silcock, D. T. (1981). Measure of operational satisfaction in public transport sector of Pakistan: A performance for urban bus services. Traffic empirical study. *International Journal of Economics and Engineering and Control*, 22(12), 645–648.
38. Stuart, K. R., Mednick, M., & Bockman, J. (2000). Structural equation model of customer satisfaction for the New York City subway system. *Transportation Research Record*, 1735(1), 133–137.
39. Shainesh, G., & Mathur, M. (2000). Service quality measurement: The case of railway freight services. *Vikalpa: The Journal for Decision Makers*, 25(3), 15–22.
40. Steyn, T.F.J., Mostert, P.G., De Meyer, C.F., & Van Ransburg, L.R.J. (2011). The effect of service failure and recovery on airline-passenger relationships: A comparison between South African and United States airline passengers. *Journal of Management Policy and Practice*, 12(5).
41. Sreedhar, R. (2012). Service Quality and passenger Satisfaction: An empirical analysis. *BVIMR Management Edge*, 5(2), 45–62.
42. Tam, J.L.M. (2008). The effects of service quality, perceived value and customer satisfaction on behavioural intentions. *Journal of Hospitality and Leisure Marketing*, 6(4), 31–43.
43. Xia, T., Zhang, Y., Crab, S., & Shah, P. (2013). Co-benefits of replacing car trip with alternative transportation: A review of evidence and methodological issues. *Journal of Environmental and Public Health*, 797312.
44. Yilmaz, V., & Ari, E. (2017). The effects of service quality, image and customer satisfaction on customer complain and loyalty in high-speed rail service in Turkey: A proposal of the structural equation model. *Transportmetrica A: Transport Science*, 13(1), 67–90.
45. Weinstein, A. (2000). Customer satisfaction among transit riders: How customers rank the relative importance of various service attributes. *Transportation Research Record*, 1735(1), 123–132.
46. Winsted, K. F. (1997). The service experience in two cultures: A behavioural perspective. *Journal of Retailing*, 73(3), 337–360.

Emerging Horizons: Business and Society in the Post Pandemic Era –
Brig. Dr. Rajiv Divekar et al. (eds)
© *2024 Taylor & Francis Group, London, ISBN 978-1-032-90822-9*

10 ⟩ Exploring The Perception of Management Students Regarding Online Learning during COVID-19 in India

Mitashree Tripathy[1]
Assistant Professor, Birla Global University

Nibedita Das[2]
HR Executive, SMS India Pvt. Ltd.

Abhijeet Sharma[3]
Research Analyst Tech, ABM Business Solution LL P

ABSTRACT

The coronavirus pandemic has undoubtedly become a test of resilience, which implies not just having the immunity to fight the virus but also the 'mental immunity', or resilience to see one through. India, after already being labeled as the world's 'most depressing country' by WHO, has yet, not made any concrete efforts to safeguard its citizens' mental well-being especially, with the beginning of the COVID-19 pandemic and the numerous challenges it has brought along on the lines of an imminent economic recession, death anxiety due to the virus itself, badly hit job prospects, and residual effects of the lockdown and social distancing norms amongst others. This has led to an even heavier burden upon its already insufficient medical framework for mental health.

The current study aims to be a frontrunner in quantitatively exploring anxiety-causing factors leading to psychological distress among Indian adults. Thereby aiding researchers, scholars, psychologists, the government, and any other stakeholder interested in studying and obtaining data-backed factors to formulate further the course of action to be taken for combating them through integrative and holistic psychological intervention strategies.

KEYWORDS: E-learning, Online learning, Management students' perception, Technology acceptance model (TAM).

[1]mitashreetripathy84@gmail.com, [2]nibedita.das@sms-group.com, [3]abhijeetsharma2708@gmail.com

DOI: 10.4324/978100355996-10

1. Introduction

UNESCO supported countries worldwide in their endeavors to alleviate the direct impact of the pandemic on the closers of educational institutions to smooth the progress of the stability of education through remote learning. Most of the universities in India were in the middle of the academic year when the lockdown was executed. Students were seen as anxious during this period, which further promoted timely initiatives in response to the difficulty. Several arrangements, like online portals and educational channels, were made for students to continue learning. Many universities made quick arrangements to offer learning by continuing with the classes through virtual modes to keep the students engaged and core educational processes going through the lockdown. Reports on the Chairman of UGC stated that to make education progressive and to maintain social distancing, at the same time, the Universities ought to opt for online learning and e-education and that "it was the need of the hour for students, teachers, and the education system as a whole" (Menon, 2020)—further, many initiatives of Swadeshi Sankalp: Made in India. Made for India, like the Zoho app for online classes, it was also made accessible to the students where teachers uploaded courses and assignments, set deadlines took live classes, clarified doubts, and allowed students to study at their own pace. Other apps like Zoom, WhatsApp, Skype, and Google Classroom also surged in conducting e-learning. Education, as a result, has shifted mainly to virtual modes. The difference in the way the educational system worked before and during the COVID-19 lockdown showed apparent disruption. Indeed, in India, there never existed a curriculum format that focused on E-learning for regular impart of education. Such an evolution in the education system incorporated the full potential of technology in the wake of this pandemic. Different stakeholders and management of various educational institutions approved E-learning, keeping in mind the academic concern and the need to grow in learning and not withdraw from it.

2. Literature Study

Somewhere close to the 1980s, the concept of learning through television was introduced by Doerken, who believed that due to the enormous flow of information that television offers and also due to the lot of time that it consumes, very shortly, "the small screen will be used as an educator/communicator in the decades to come. The skirmish for the audience will expand tremendously in the not-too-distant future and we should be prepared for a new kind of learning" (Doerken, 1983). Education and learning as an alternative way of accomplishing education is built on to digital platform that includes developments like "radio and TV courses, videotaped lessons, computer-aided instruction and a host of others (...) are examples of various applications of different learning strategies and adoption of new technologies of communication to suit educational needs" (Sharma, 1993).

The relationship between education and learning is a vital one because there is always a tension between didactic techniques, methods, and contents used in imparting education and learning situations. The analysis between the two extremes should not be done through independent techniques and processes as they may not be sufficient for a liberating pedagogy. While it is important to pay attention to the critical content, it is equally important that the content must have roots in teaching and learning situations, otherwise, "it can become isolated and isolating" (Tennant, 1997). Hence, the concern for quality education is of prime importance when offering flexible learning modes. Hence, learning should satisfy and be relevant to the basic needs of students.

In India, numerous open and distance learning institutions were established somewhere close to the 1960s. However, it was introduced as an experiment open and distance learning had envisaged three main objectives: "to provide an efficient and less expensive method of educational instruction at the higher educational level, to provide facilities to willing persons who had failed to join regular university courses due to personal and economic reasons and to improve the standard of knowledge and learning without disturbing their present employment" (Rathore, 1993). Acquisition of knowledge imparted informatively by a teacher or a given syllabus comprises a tiny section of the curriculum. However, the deconstruction of the shared knowledge is typically done through a group process. One may wonder if any similar form of learning exists through the online system. With the advent of information technology, teaching and learning have become significantly multifaceted and pervasive. The use of the latest technology symbolizes that a learner may not need to sit in a traditional classroom to accomplish education through online mode.

However, the terms open distance learning and online learning are frequently used interchangeably. Existing literature argues that, unlike open and distance learning, online learning is a method of distance learning that allows different types of learners to experience connectivity, convenience, and interaction. Some authors even recognize online learning as a more contemporary restatement of distance learning that enhances access to "educational opportunities for learners described as both non-traditional and disenfranchised" (Moore, Dicksen-Deane, Galyen, 2010). Similarly, e-learning is also a form of "internet-based learning which utilizes web-based communication, collaboration, knowledge transfer, and training to add value to individuals and to organizations they work within" (Kelly & Bauer, 2004). Other studies indicate that e-learning "is a type of system of learning which utilizes electronic technologies to access educational curriculum outside traditional classrooms" (Jama, Mapesela, & Beylefeld, 2009).

Further, studies defined E-learning as an instructional approach incorporating electronic media and devices to improve access to education encircling all or part of the educational model applied to facilitate "training and communication" (Sangrà, Vlachopoulos, & Cabrera, 2012).

Hence, E-learning is explicitly delivered through the internet to some locations apart from the traditional classroom to support learning. This further signifies that learners need not come to the classroom or receive lectures and so with the lectures. Still, both of them are connected through information and communication technology to promote learning. Hence, "the aspect of information and communication technology that has brought about this revolution in students' learning is e-learning" (Oye, Salleh, & Iahad, 2010).

Many authors understand e-learning as a comprehensive and universal channel of hybrid or blended learning. Studies claim that the concept of hybrid learning denotes the blend of "an online learning environment by gaining the flexibility of distance or outside-of-classroom learning, and face-to-face classroom instruction" (Alnajdi, 2014). Hybrid learning offers benefits to the learners by facilitating them with teachers, mentors, and instructors to meet the students face to face whenever necessary and provide instructions, debate, discuss, clarify doubts, and receive instant feedback.

Understanding the concept of all three forms of learning and knowledge acquisition, one fact is that these forms are not similar to the traditional classroom that has been considered an old pattern of imparting education. While many authors are quite positive in envisaging the future of e-learning, especially in higher education, Farrelly is quite skeptical of the predictions of e-learning in elevating higher education. He asserts given the swift evolution of both society and technology, exploring the precision of the impact of e-learning's revolutionary approach appears challenging at this predisposition. Farrelly claims it is very difficult to "talk about e-learning in higher education without referring to specific software platforms and delivery mechanisms" (Farrelly, 2014). In a similar context, sources claim that "this abrupt transition to online hardly compensates for the absence of the classroom experience" (Sudevan, 2020). There have been several studies comparing online vs. traditional courses. One such finding was given by Stack where the findings suggested "neither any notable variances observed in the results of the examinations between students who appeared online classes and traditional classes, nor any significant differences found in the perceptions of instructional methods" (Stack, 2015). Further studies indicate that "most institutions have extended the array of online courses offerings with an increasing proportion of students favoring online courses over traditional face-to-face courses "due to flexibility, convenience and a host of other factors" (Alsaaty, et.al, 2016). Still further studies signify that the "impact of e-learning significantly improved academic performance and learning process" (Elfaki, Abdulraheem, & Abdulrahim, 2019).

Considering e-learning as the only possible, convenient, and effective way of imparting education, considering the recent conditions that the pandemic has brought, is still a matter of debate. Believing that the education system in India has undergone immense disruption due to the unavoidable situation is also not completely incorrect. Arguably, this paper focuses only on management students and their experience; management because it is not simply a degree but also a skill, and the acquisition of both, opens the doors to the world of business. Management is a blend of theoretical and practical learning that involves analytical, creativity, and additional knowledge skills to disseminate knowledge to form new connections besides syntheses critically. Evaluating whether the same experience is possible through e-learning is a question. Hence, this paper assesses perceptions of e-learning experience among management students at the university level during the COVID-19 lockdown in India using the Technology Acceptance Model (Davis, 1989) so that the same can be implemented to determine further the method of learning in times of contingencies.

2.1 Theoretical Framework

Proposed by Davis (1989), the Technology Acceptance Model (TAM) serves as the main concept for this paper that evaluates the effectiveness and efficiency of E-learning. Davis explains although information technology substantially improved professional performance, users' hesitance to accept and further use information systems often restricts performance gains (Davis, 1989). This explains and validates should a user accepts or rejects information technology. Further studies elaborate on why TAM is a valuable framework to comprehend and clarify use behavior in IS implementation. The model introduces two determinants inclined by external factors validating the intention to use a technology that is perceived usefulness (PU), which delineates "the degree to which a person believes that using a particular system would enhance his or her job performance" (p. 320) and perceived ease of use (PEU) that defines "the degree to which a person believes that using a particular system would be free of effort" (p. 320). The model further suggests that these two determinants additionally influence the person's attitude (AT) towards accepting technology, which further affects the person's behavioral intention (IU) to use the technology, resulting in the decision to use the technology. Further studies suggest that TAM "has been tested in many empirical types of research and the tools used with the model have proven to be of quality and to yield statistically reliable results" (Legris, Ingham, & Collerette, 2003).

Applying PU to this paper, the model facilitates deducing perceptions of management students towards e-learning during COVID-19 and evaluating their intention to use the same as a substitute to traditional classroom learning in similar or worse situations. Therefore, here, perceived usefulness can be understood as to what level management students understand using an e-learning platform will enhance their learning. However, it must be noted here that respondents of this study were management students studying fully on-campus before mid-week of March, and due to the outbreak of COVID-19, they had to vacant their on-campus residential hostel rooms and travel back to their respective homes. In contrast, the localities were restricted from coming to the campus. Hence, they stayed back at home and entirely depended on e-learning, through links, that the universities provided them through emails, to resume their semesters. Therefore, this makes them appropriate respondents to derive their perceptions on e-learning.

Further, since the use of technology is one of the most essential features of e-learning, one necessitates a firm level of ease and convenience to participate entirely in e-learning via the net, technology, and computers. Hence, it's evident that students must have essential knowledge of the various forms of hardware and software applications. Studies also indicate that "when students have more experience with online technologies; they feel more confident in using online technologies, and their self-efficacy increases, accordingly" (Lee & Witta, 2001). On the other hand, a lack of essential technical skills may lead to a barrier to e-learning and may further impact the perception of e-learning. Hence, the application of PEU to this study helps to infer the ease at which the management students perceive e-learning. Furthermore, the external factors that have influenced the perceived usefulness and perceived ease of use estimation include research papers, news reports, and the influences of families and friends on the significance of e-learning. Studies claim that "to many an extent, these external variables also create an impact on the student's attitude towards the use of technology" (Davis, Bagozzi & Warshaw, 1989).

Attitude (AT) in TAM "refers to a person's evaluation of a specified behavior involving the object (Davis, 1993). Studies signify that attitude is an "evaluation of an object, concept, or behavior along a dimension of favor or disfavor, good or bad, like or dislike" (Ajzen & Fishbein, 2000). Thus, in a nutshell, attitude springs from the results of the evaluation as to what degree of perception or experience, whether a positive or negative feeling, an individual has about the use of technology. In the present study, the model signifies that attitude towards the use of technology is either a constructive or an undesirable reciprocation of a student towards e-learning that leads to their behavioral intention towards e-learning. The model proposes that users' attitudes towards technology and information systems largely impact the behavioral intention toward e-learning. Studies ascertain that "attitude is more than a substitute for satisfaction and that satisfaction should be used as a complement to usage when evaluating end-users acceptance of computer technologies" (Gahtani & King, 1999). If perceived usefulness and perceived ease of use towards e-learning are either constructive or undesirable, the attitude towards using it will also be the same.

Hence, if e-learning as a learning platform is found not easy to use, there is a high chance that it would not be accepted as valid and vice-versa. On a similar note, the usefulness and ease of use of e-learning may lead to the formation of an attitude towards it, thereby further deducing behavioral intention towards the use of e-learning. Keeping in mind the primary objective of the paper is to assess the e-learning experience among management students during the COVID-19 lockdown and their behavioral intention toward e-learning in the future, research questions like the perceived usefulness of e-learning, the perceived ease of use of e-learning, attitude towards e-learning and finally the behavior intention to use e-learning in the future, were asked to fulfill the aim of the research. Hence, TAM was found to be the most appropriate model to study the objective of receiving students' perception of technology and, particularly in this paper, e-learning.

2.2 Hypotheses

The main objective of the paper is to evaluate the perceptions of the management students about e-learning at the university level during COVID-19 and to determine behavior intention or the intention to use e-learn post-COVID-19D-19 or in times of contingencies. The study primarily focused on one significant aspect, considering the correlation of four variables. The study evaluates the perception-learning among management students during the COVID-19 lockdown through TAM. Secondly, the study attempted to determine the behavior intention of e-learning in the future post-COVID-19, mostly during times of uncertainty. The current research takes PU, PEU, and AT as independent variables and IU as the dependent variable. Based on theoretical argumentation, the following hypotheses may be propositioned.

H1 E-learning is perceived as efficient and effective among management students during the COVID-19 lockdown and can be employed as a long-term strategy during contingencies.

H2 E-learning is not perceived as efficient and effective among management students during the COVID-19 lockdown and cannot be employed as a long-term strategy during contingencies.

3. Research Methodology

The current study employs a methodology that includes context explanation, questionnaire preparation, data collection, and analysis. To receive students' perception of e-learning, the research was conducted across universities that offer Masters and Bachelors in Business Administration. Although these universities also offer other programs like arts, science, and commerce, this study typically focused on students pursuing management programs. The main reason for choosing the management domain as a field of research for this paper is because recent sources convince us that management is one of the most flexible domains that complements research work and that "management research, by nature, is interdisciplinary, drawing from multiple fields in humanities and social sciences and often amalgamating them to produce innovative research contribution" (Bothello & Roulet, 2020). Further, management programs offer practical skill sets to help students explore, inquire, and seek solutions to multi-diversified problems through direct human engagement that requires teamwork, effective decision-making, interpersonal relationships among peers, both formal and informal ones, emotional management, and other intellectual abilities. Before the pandemic outbreak, management students were exposed to several practical knowledge-based platforms offered by the universities through industrial visits, seminars, and conferences. Although theoretical knowledge has a predisposition to adjust its timelines through the mode of teaching and evaluation, what is being argued here is how far the practical aspects are a part of this extensive digitalization of education in this current situation.

3.1 Materials

The participants were introduced to the research topic and instructed to fill out the questionnaire that was included. There were a total number of 19 questions divided into five segments. The first segment consisted of questions on gender, age groups, and academic year in BBA and MBA were asked first. Questions on their acquaintance with e-learning before the pandemic outbreak were also requested. Further, whether their respective universities conducted online classes and their frequencies before COVID-19 was also asked.

The rest of the sections in the questionnaire were on research questions, and the TAM is the main component of this study. The remaining segments carried four units: perceived usefulness (PU) of e-learning, perceived ease of use (PEU) of e-learning, attitude (AT) using e-learning, and finally, intention to use (IU) e-learning in the future. Most of the questions had options like Agree, Disagree, and Undecided.

3.2 Participants

Participants in the study were selected from various universities in India through a simple random sampling method to reach out to students from the business administration domain, both masters and undergraduates, who underwent e-learning after their institutions shut down during the pandemic break. Students were sent an email with the link describing a brief about the study. There was a total of 309 participants.

3.3 Procedure

The study used SPSS for data analysis and interpretation to check reliability. Questions in the questionnaire were drafted in simple language to certify a determined comprehension from the student's point of view. A random selection of questionnaires was fed and verified with its corresponding data to ensure accuracy. The analysis was done based on four criteria: perceived usefulness (PU), perceived ease of use (PEU), attitude towards using e-learning (AT), and finally, intention to use (IU) under the TAM that guided the theory of this research.

3.4 Findings

Table 10.1 shows the reliability test done through SPSS in the study.

Table 10.1 Reliability statistics

Cronbach's alpha	Cronbach's alpha based on standardized items	N of items
0.765	0.812	12

Table 10.2 exhibits the mean, median, mode, and standard deviation of the variables taken from all four criteria, which are Perceived Use, Perceived Ease of Use, Attitude, and Intention to use in the future.

Table 10.2

		Convenient time	Convenient place	Technologies/Apps convenience in submission	Enabled interactive communication	Doubts/clarifications were cleared	Internet connectivity issue	E-learning platforms are convenient & user friendly	Convenience for quantitative & theoretical subjects	Improved satisfaction Level & efficiency	Costlier than classroom teaching	Use E-learning in future	Preference post-COVID-19
N	Valid	309	309	309	309	309	309	309	309	309	309	309	309
	Missing	0	0	0	0	0	0	0	0	0	0	0	1
Mean		1.77	1.57	1.64	1.79	1.53	1.74	1.49	1.59	1.94	2.61	1.87	2.08
Median		2	1	1	2	2	2	1	2	2	2	2	2
Mode		2	1	1	1	2	2	1	2	2	2	1	2
Std. deviation		0.727	0.692	0.758	0.772	0.5	0.439	0.501	0.492	0.721	1.355	0.806	0.567
Sum		547	486	508	553	472	538	459	493	601	807	579	643

Table 10.3 exhibits the correlation analysis of the study.

Table 10.3

Control variables		Con venient_ time	Con venient_ place_	s_Apps_ con venience_ in_sub mission_	Enabled_ interactive_ communi cation	Doubts clari fications _were_ cleared	Internet_ con nectivity issue	Elearning_ plat forms_are_ convenient_ user_friendly	Convenience_ for_ quantitative_ theoretical_ subjects	Improved_ satis faction_ level_ efficiency	Costlier_ than_ classroom_ teaching	Using e-lear ning in future	Pre ference_ post COVID19
Convenient_	Correlation	1	0.45	0.358	0.244	0.308	0.139	0.29	0.218	0.186	0.206	0.216	0.077
	Significance (2-tailed)		0	0	0	0	0.015	0	0	0.001	0	0	0.176
	N	309	309	309	309	309	309	309	309	309	309	309	309
Convenient_p	Correlation	0.45	1	0.495	0.403	0.419	0.158	0.413	0.364	0.161	0.093	0.165	0.105
	Significance (2-tailed)	0		0	0	0	0.005	0	0	0.005	0.104	0.004	0.066
	N	309	309	309	309	309	309	309	309	309	309	309	309
Apps_convenience _in_submission_	Correlation	0.358	0.495	1	0.382	0.394	0.22	0.389	0.358	0.107	0.083	0.16	0.082
	Significance (2-tailed)	0	0		0	0	0	0	0	0.061	0.145	0.005	0.149
	N	309	309	309	309	309	309	309	309	309	309	309	309
Enabled_interactive_ communication	Correlation	0.244	0.403	0.382	1	0.423	0.174	0.316	0.423	0.248	0.133	0.223	0.113
	Significance (2-tailed)	0	0	0		0	0.002	0	0	0	0.02	0	0.047
	N	309	309	309	309	309	309	309	309	309	309	309	309
Doubtsclarifi cations_were	Correlation	0.308	0.419	0.394	0.423	1	0.358	0.478	0.534	0.324	0.27	0.295	0.158
	Significance (2-tailed)	0.003	0	0	0		0	0	0	0	0	0	0
	N	309	309	309	309	309	309	309	309	309	309	309	309
Internet_con nectivity_2t_i	Correlation	0.139	0.158	0.22	0.174	0.358	1	0.441	0.412	0.294	0.06	0.247	0.163
	Significance (2-tailed)	0.015	0.005	0	0.002	0		0	0	0	0.295	0	0.004
	N	309	309	309	309	309	309	309	309	309	309	309	309
_platforms_are_conve nient_user_friendly	Correlation	0.29	0.413	0.389	0.316	0.478	0.441	1	0.503	0.281	0.288	0.249	0.17
	Significance (2-tailed)	0	0	0	0	0	0		0	0	0	0	0.003

Control variables		Con venient_ time	Con venient_ place_	s_Apps_ con venience_ in_sub mission_	Enabled_ interactive_ communi cation	Doubts clari fications _were_ cleared	Internet_ con nectivity issue	Elearning_ plat forms_are_ convenient_ user_friendly	Convenience_ for_ quantitative_ theoretical_ subjects	Improved_ satis faction_ level_ efficiency	Costlier_ than_ classroom_ teaching	Using e-lear ning in future	Pre ference_ post COVID19
for_quantitative _theoretical_subjects	N	309	309	309	309	309	309	309	309	309	309	309	309
	Correlation	0.218	0.364	0.358	0.423	0.534	0.412	0.503	1	0.376	0.176	0.385	0.223
	Significance (2-tailed)	0	0	0	0	0	0	0.001	.	0	0.002	0	0
tisfaction_level_efficiency	N	309	309	309	309	309	309	309	309	309	309	309	309
	Correlation	0.186	0.161	0.107	0.248	0.324	0.294	0.281	0.376	1	0.178	0.346	0.178
	Significance (2-tailed)	0.001	0.005	0.061	0	0	0	0	0	.	0.002	0	0.002
Costlier_than_ classroom_teaching_	N	309	309	309	309	309	309	309	309	309	309	309	309
	Correlation	0.206	0.093	0.083	0.133	0.27	0.06	0.288	0.176	0.178	1	0.092	0.054
	Significance (2-tailed)	0	0.104	0.145	0.02	0	0.295	0	0.002	0.002	.	0.108	0.347
Use E-learning in	N	309	309	309	309	309	309	309	309	309	309	309	309
	Correlation	0.216	0.165	0.16	0.223	0.295	0.247	0.249	0.385	0.346	0.092	1	0.264
	Significance (2-tailed)	0	0.004	0.005	0	0	0	0	0	0	0.092	.	0
Preference_postCOVID19	Correlation	0.077	0.105	0.082	0.113	0.158	0.163	0.17	0.223	0.178	0.054	0.264	1
	Significance (2-tailed)	0.178	0.066	0.149	0.047	0.005	0.004	0.003	0	0.002	0.347	0	.
	N	309	309	309	309	309	309	309	309	309	309	309	309

Table 10.4 indicates the regression analysis of the study.

Table 10.4

Model		Sum of squares	df	Mean square	F	Sig.
1	Regression	43.224	10	4.322	8.212	.000b
	Residual	156.854	298	0.526		
	Total	200.078	308			

4. Data Analysis

Considering the hypotheses, the findings indicate that e-learning is neither perceived as a suitable mode of learning during the COVID-19 lockdown nor can be regarded as a unified platform for education in times of uncertainty. Thus, the alternative hypothesis for the study stands correct. The study showcased that although e-learning was quite flexible in terms of time and place, internet connectivity was a primary issue. Apart from this factor, other essential factors like students' lack of knowledge of specific subjects and clarification of doubts about the same due to lack of face-to-face interaction were also issues. Students also have doubts that their suitability to be employable can be a significant problem. Students also believe that faculties are biased towards a few students, which directly or indirectly impacts students' motivation. As teaching through the online mode requires experience with novel teaching techniques, lack of training towards the same makes the teachers incompetent, and the students are hampered with their learning process. On the other hand, students also had positive perceptions towards e-learning as many of them could avail of class recordings, access to library databases, and e-books if they missed any of the classes. Further, many of them could benefit from digital internships and webinars and attend conferences, both national and international, which in physical mode could not have been possible given the time constraints.

Findings also indicate that the correlation between the technology apps' convenience in submission to convenient places is positively correlated (r=0.495). This shows there was ease in e-learning as there was no barrier to commuting from different areas, and technology made learning more accessible. Further, findings also indicate that e-learning is costlier than classroom learning as the entire semester was taken via electronic mode; a lot of data got consumed, overall, not being cost-effective towards the learning process. Although e-learning was convenient with regards to distance, at the same time, it was not cost-effective, which is why the figure analyzed was (r=0.082).

Additionally, findings discovered that hybrid learning could serve as a promising solution for the future of higher education. Hybrid learning, integrates both online and face-to-face instructional methods, with a significant proportion of traditional classroom time substituted with internet-based activities. Despite hybrid learning not being a novel concept in education and widely adopted, the recommendation to implement it regularly or during contingencies remains uncertain. Furthermore, this also prompts about the suitability of exposure that the management students received during industry visits, paper presentations during conferences, internships, and research projects, which may be an effective determination during such a contingency because learning in higher education means much more than this.

4.1 Limitations

Despite the implementation of the quantitative methodology for the study, there remained a few limitations. For example, the sample size was limited to 309 participants. Had there been a more significant number of participants, the results could have varied. Further, the respondents were strictly from the management discipline. Should the data have been collected from other fields as well, the study could be more extensive. Also, the data collected were only from a few cities like Bhubaneswar, Kolkata, Bangalore, Noida, Delhi, and Mumbai, thus excluding still a more significant proportion of the country.

Furthermore, if the psychological mindset of the respondents towards the study is considered a critical component of the study, then it would be another limitation as the survey conducted was through virtual mode due to the pandemic restrictions. Another end of the study was that the sample selection was mainly from private universities across the country. Only a few government universities were taken into account. The reason is that most of the government universities were completely shut down due to the pandemic. The research was conducted during the stage when reaching most of the government universities was a challenge since the lack of resources restricted education. There were no open communication doors to connect with the management students of these universities. However, later, when the government universities gradually started gelling up with the prevailing conditions, most of our research work was almost complete.

Furthermore, government universities lack a well-thought-out curriculum in comparison to the curriculum of private universities. Unlike the curriculum of the private universities, the curriculum of the government universities lacks rigorous study. Besides, they could not be resilient to the given situation and took a lot of time to modify the syllabus and accept the new pedagogical approaches towards teaching and learning. Hence, there is a vast skill gap among the students of government universities. Further, government universities lack academic-industry connections, depriving students of the insights of industry participation.

4.2 Implications of the Study

The current study could encourage more interactive sessions among the students to provide them with a feel of physical classrooms. Similarly, the curriculum must also involve less theoretical approach and focus more on discussions, research, activities, and practical and game-based learning. Unlike the physical mode of teaching and learning, online classrooms must have a time limit to reduce lengthy exposure to devices' screens. Classroom management should be promoted through regular mentoring that would include doubt-clearing sessions and encourage creative thinking among the students and the like. Students would feel more comfortable if there were more informal classes like chit-chat sessions with every student individually to have personal interactions regarding subjects, classes, or guidance towards complex subjects. Most importantly, data concession/data packs should be provided by educational institutions for ease of free learning. Lastly, collaboration with tech firms to develop ERP systems to have a user-friendly interface website for live class interactions with students, attendance, assignments, and online examinations should be conducted transparently to make the management students career-ready and prepare them for a better career.

The methodology applied in the current study may be implied to assess the perception of students belonging to technical, medical, social sciences, law, statistics, and economics backgrounds. Further, the same tool IBM-SPSS that is used in this study can also be carried out in further studies using different methodologies like experimental research, cause and effect research, and relational and correlational research analysis to assess behavioral and psychological changes among students during the period. Besides, the methodology may also be used to determine the emotional well-being of employees from various organizations.

5. Conclusion

It is essential to have a thorough understanding and gather further research on the extent to which e-learning should be deployed in higher education. This paper evaluated the perceptions of e-learning of management students during the COVID-19 lockdown in India. While e-learning has made it crucial to realize the significant issues behind learning strategies to support a digitally enhanced learning system, concerns like to what extent this learning system will help support greater access and success are still unstated claims. Although the findings revealed that hybrid learning could be an option in higher education, this blended form may be suggestive and not prescriptive as India should make more efforts, investing in tools and training for students, teachers, and the concerned universities to become more technology savvy to meet the demands of the situation.

REFERENCES

1. Ajzen, I. & Fishbein, M. (2000). Attitudes and the Attitude-Behaviour relation: Reasoned and Automatic Processes. European Review of Social Psychology, 11(1), 1-33. http:// doi: 10.1080/14792779943000116

2. Al-Gahtani, S., & King, M. (1999). Attitudes, satisfaction, and usage: Factors contributing to each in the acceptance of information technology. Behavior and Information Technology, 18(4), pp. 277–297.
3. Alnajdi, S. M. (2014). Hybrid Learning In Higher Education. Conference: Society For Information Technology & Teacher Education International Conference, pp. 214–220.
4. Alsaaty, F. M., Carter, E., Abrahams, D., & Alshameri, F. (2016). Traditional Versus Online Learning in Institutions of Higher Education: Minority Business Students' Perceptions. Business and Management Research, 5(2), 31–41. doi: 10.5430/bmr.v5n2p31
5. Bothello, J., & Roulet, T. (2020). Why management academics matter. Retrieved May 27, 2020, from https://theconversation.com/why-management-academics-matter-97232
6. Cashion, J., & Palmieri, P. (2002). The Secret Is The Teacher: The Learners View Of Online Learning. Leabrook, S. Aust.: NCVER.
7. Davis, F. D. (1989). Perceived Usefulness, Perceived Ease of Use, and User Acceptance of Information Technology. MIS Quarterly, 13(3), 319. doi: 10.2307/249008
8. Davis, F. D. (1993). User acceptance of information technology: System Characteristics, User Perceptions and Behavioural Impacts. International Journal of Man-Machine Studies, 38(3), 475-487. http://dx.doi.org/10.1006/imms.1993.1022
9. Davis, F. D., Bagozzi, R. P. & Warshaw, P. R. (1989). User acceptance of computer technology: A comparison of two theoretical models. Management Science, 35(8), 9821003. http://www.jstor.org/pss/2632151
10. Doerken, M. (1983). Classroom combat: Teaching and television. Englewood Cliffs: Educational Technology Publications.
11. Elfaki, N. K., Abdulraheem, I., & Abdulrahim, R. (2019). Impact of E-Learning vs Traditional Learning on Student's Performance and Attitude. International Journal of Medical Research & Health Sciences, 8(10), pp. 76–82.
12. Farrelly, T. (2014). E-Learning and Higher Education—Hyperbole and Reality. In Higher Education in Ireland, pp. 198-215. Palgrave Macmillan, London.
13. Harry, K. (1999). Higher Education through Open and Distance Learning: World Review of Distance Education and Open Learning. London: Routledge.
14. Jama, M., Mapesela, M., & Beylefeld, A. (2009). Theoretical Perspectives on Factors Affecting the Academic Performance of Students. South African Journal of Higher Education, 22(5), pp. 992–1005. doi: 10.4314/sajhe.v22i5.42919
15. Kelly, T., & Bauer, D. (2004). Managing intellectual capital via e-learning at Cisco. In C. Holsapple (Ed.), Handbook on knowledge management 2: Knowledge directions, pp. 511–532. Berlin, Germany: Springer
16. Lee, C.Y., & Witta, E.L. (2001). Online Students' Perceived Self-Efficacy: Does It Change? Annual Proceedings of Selected Research and Development, 1(2), pp. 228-233.
17. Legris, P., Ingham, J., & Collerette, P. (2003). Why do people use information technology? A Critical Review of The Technology Acceptance Model. Information & Management, 40(3), pp. 191–204. doi: 10.1016/s0378-7206(01)00143-4
18. Menon, S. (2020, April 30). Limitations of Online Learning. Retrieved May 20, 2020, from https://www.thehindu.com/opinion/op-ed/limitations-of-online-learning/article31466511.ece

19. Moore, J. L., Dickson-Deane, C., & Galyen, K. (2011). E-learning, online learning, and distance learning environments: Are they the same? The Internet and Higher Education, 14(2), pp. 129–135. doi: 10.1016/j.iheduc.2010.10.001

20. Mukama, E. (2014). Bringing Technology to Students' Proximity: A Sociocultural Account of Technology-Based Learning Projects. International Journal for Research in Vocational Education and Training, 1(2), 125-142. doi:10.13152/ijrvet.1.2.3

21. Oye, N. D., Salleh, M., & Iahad, N. A. (2010). Holistic E-learning in Nigerian Higher Education Institutions. Journal of Computing, 2(11), pp. 20–26

22. Rathore, H. C. S. (1993). Management of Distance Education in India. New Delhi: Ashish Pub. House.

23. Sangrà, A., Vlachopoulos, D., & Cabrera, N. (2012). Building an Inclusive Definition of E-learning: An Approach to the Conceptual Framework. The International Review of Research in Open and Distributed Learning, 13(2), pp. 145–59. doi: 10.19173/irrodl.v13i2.1161

24. Sharma, K. D. (1993). Open Learning System in India with Special Reference to School Education. New Delhi: Allied Publ.

25. Sudevan, P. (2020). Why E-learning isn't a sustainable solution to the COVID ... Retrieved May 23, 2020, from https://www.thehindu.com/sci-tech/technology/why-elearning-is-not-a-sustainable-solution-to-the-covid19-education-crisis-in-india/article31560007.ece

26. Tennant, M. (1997). Psychology and Adult Learning. London: Routledge.

Source: All the tables in this chapter were made by the author.

Emerging Horizons: Business and Society in the Post Pandemic Era –
Brig. Dr. Rajiv Divekar et al. (eds)
© *2024 Taylor & Francis Group, London, ISBN 978-1-032-90822-9*

11

The Curious Case of Intellectual Property Rights, Foreign Direct Investments and Economic Growth of Countries Affiliated with Regional Trade Agreements

Soumit Datta[1]

Department of Social Sciences,
CHRIST (Deemed to be University),
Bannerghata Road Campus, Bangalore, Karnataka, India

Melba Judieth Fernandes[2],
Sunil Kumar Ambrammal[3]

Department of Humanities & Social Sciences,
National Institute of Technology Goa,
Goa, India

ABSTRACT

Intellectual Property Rights (IPR) & Foreign Direct Investments (FDI) usually go hand in hand in designing the growth story of a country. This paper is a humble attempt to understand the countries bound by Regional Trade Agreements (RTA) and how do Intellectual Property Rights (Patents, Trademarks, and Industrial Designs) along with Foreign Direct Investments affect the Growth of member countries. The data has been collected from World Trade Centre Website and World Intellectual Property Organization after 64 Regional Trade Agreements were identified from a total of 334 agreements for a decade i.e from 2011 to 2020. A simple regression model was run that indicated the curious case of IPR, FDI and Economic Growth of member countries affiliated with RTA. The results were in sharp contrast to the available existing literature. The paper faced a couple of limitations mainly due to incomplete data for several countries and territories belonging to a RTA either due to geographical jurisdiction or non-availability of data. This paper could give meaningful insights about the future of RTAs in a global dynamic world. The paper has included only RTA and excluded bilateral trade agreements.

KEYWORDS: Intellectual property rights, Foreign direct investments, Economic growth, Regional trade agreements, Member countries

[1]soumit.datta05@gmail.com, [2]melbafernandes5@gmail.com, [3]sunilkumar@nitgoa.ac.in

DOI: 10.4324/978100355996-11

1. Introduction

Intellectual property rights have come a long way from being first recognized on a global platform. The Patents Act of 1970 is being utilized in stimulating research and development (R&D) and the creation of cutting-edge technology across various fields in an economy. For many years, Intellectual property rights (IPR) were left untouched and their significance on an economy was far from being studied. In the 20st century, economists recognised the scope of intellectual property rights and how their establishment can facilitate and assist international trade and thereby in development of economic growth. In the current economic scenario profit and welfare are the two main drivers for economic development fuelled by innovations resulting in Intellectual Property Rights. Thus, it is seen through numerous studies that a long run relationship exists between IPR, international trade, & economic development (Amassoma, Ogbuagu, & Niniola, 2020). Development creates a path to license innovation through patents and employ them to have an unbeatable advantage through trade thus eliminating competition or by reducing it to a larger extent. For every business in a country, protected processes and innovations are the key assets entitled to them, to spur more economic inflow and trade with other countries (Anulekha, 2020).

Seyoum (1996) concluded his study by stating that Foreign Direct Investment (FDI) is dependent on Intellectual Property Rights within a country. Usually, low-income countries tend to have a low protection over their Intellectual Property Rights, making it very tough to attract Foreign Direct Investment from high income countries to flourish. Thus, studying Foreign Direct Investment would be essential to benefit backward countries within a trade agreement since there would be no tariff or barriers for trade. Studies show that IPRs is a favorite to have an increased flow in trade and capital between low, middle, high-income countries around all seven continents.

The objective is to analyse the influence IPR has over the FDI inflows within the trade agreements. The analysis of the trading blocs and regional trade agreements are as per listings of the WTO. By studying them, we could help determine an association between IPR, FDI and GDP of a nation and give instances on the trade situation of a country. The inclusion of FDI could provide concrete evidence on the economic atmosphere of such countries and their further scope of development with the help of investments. The comparison of trading blocs proves another useful advantage, highlighting the blocs that have many intellectual property rights with a large volume of GDP signifying their development status. Providing such evidence is critical for less developed and primitive bloc/ countries on their path to achieving a higher and increasing growth rate and indulge in trade agreements with developed countries to initiate exports and imports of knowledge and capital. This paper is one comprehensive study trying to analyse the 64 multilateral trade agreements (excluding bilateral agreements).

2. Review of Literature

One of the renowned papers that extensively contributed to the field of IPR & economic growth was by Park & Ginarte (1997). They primarily wanted to study the association between IPR and economic growth for 60 countries from 1960 to 1990. Furthermore, Park & Ginarte wanted to ascertain whether a stronger and stricter intellectual protection would result in an increased economic welfare and development in a country, along with an influx of foreign investment. To assist their research, they developed an IPR index for the 60 countries considered for the study thus, providing a pathway to understand whether factor accumulation was directly impacted by the intellectual property rights existing in a country. By running a Seemingly Unrelated Regression (SUR) with the help of a modified MRW function (Mankiw, Romer and Weil), the results were in accordance to the stated objectives. The analysis indicated that countries with a strong intellectual property protection had the probability to significantly improve economic growth. However, it was also evident that stronger IPRs do not contribute to growth merely by just being collated into laws. Instead, they will do so by generating more investment activities, particularly research and development activities. While R&D is an important determinant for a country's growth rates, IPRs play a significant role for the R&D undertakings that take place in developed economies but is absent in that of less developed economies.

In succession to the study done by Park & Ginarte, Aricioglu & Ucan (2013) investigated the relationship and the after-effects IPRs have on the economic growth of a country. By studying developed countries of Turkey & Europe during 1995 till 2005, it became easy to analyse on whether IPRs affect various economic variables pertaining to each country. For the analysis, seven variables namely GDP per worker, physical capital investment, human capital stock, index measuring market freedom, expenditure into research and development, and the index to measure intellectual property right was taken to assess the impact on the economic growth. By running an OLS (Ordinary Least Square) and SUR (Seemingly Unrelated regression) on the variables, the empirical results depicted that investment and market freedom variables affect economic growth positively. On the other hand, the results convey that the investment and market freedom variables are statistically significant but there ceases to exist a negative covariance among growth and the two variables. This leads to an interference between the economic variables in the long run, leading them to affect one another. Thus, from the empirical results, it can be concluded that IPRs are a crucial factor when it comes to the growth rates of a country.

Lesser (2017) analysed the state of developing nations and how the TRIPS agreement mandated them to follow suite. To throw more light on how IPRs in these nations affected the domestic growth as well as the interaction with international trade, Lesser was focused on empirically studying the relation between the robustness of the IPR and Foreign Direct Investment (FDI) and imports of the nations. A vast selection of variables was taken into consideration which were categorised based on riskiness, agglomeration benefits and classical gravity types of variables. Along with this, Lesser created an IPR score for each country involved in the study. Using a data set of 44 countries with a limitation to 38 countries for data on imports, the analysis implied that few of the variables were insignificant and were not affect by IPR nor FDI. The results concluded that stronger IPR leads to an increase in both imports & FDI. Again, the model outputs indicate that a point increase in the IPR score would significantly intensify a country's FDI by $1.5 billion and facilitate import by 8.9 billion dollars. The strengthening of IPRs can be considered as an effective policy measure when it comes to countries who are on the look out to open the economy to the global trade sector. Lesser (2017) concluded his paper by stating that strong IPR leads to an increase in both FDI and imports. Stronger IPR protection would attract the flow of FDI into the country, resulting in a spillover effect of technology and knowledge among the levels of society in that country.

Kumar, Yadav & Verma (2018) took BRICS as their centre of study to check whether an inflow of FDI - dependent on the strength of IPR protection, has promoted economic growth among the developing countries in the BRICS trading bloc. The study constructed an econometric panel data model over the 2000-2015 period, taking 2000 as the base year of comparison to provide consistency with the study's prediction. The findings were consistent and in agreement with the studies done in the past few years. The model concluded two main findings: first, IPR protection in the developing countries belonging to BRICS had a positive influence over the amount of FDI flowing into the country. Second, by increasing IPR protection within the country, the process of market expansion and its resulting effect, market power increases. But the authors suggested that strengthening of IPR is not the way to attract FDI due to the size of the economic markets in the developing countries in the BRICS bloc.

Lisi & Xiangdong (2008) argued on the objectives of many international innovation policies that promote innovation followed by a spurt in economic growth. To test whether the Western economic policies can be adapted by certain cities in China, they opted to conduct their analysis in Guangxi, a backward area in China. With certain criteria laid down, their main intention was to find the linkage between growth & innovation in the backward area of China, to support their study of clearly analysing the Western economic growth. The analysis conducted took into consideration two proxy variables, GDP for regional economy and patent application for innovation. After running an augmented Dickey-Fuller test on the variables, their study revealed that increasing the level of patent protection in Guangxi would cause equivalent increase in economic growth. The results also provided a substantial view on western economic though and their growth measures, making it suitable to be adapted by China. Another striking result showcased that a less aged economy like Guangxi in China could improve the degree of IPR protection to create a well-defined legal framework, which would help in stimulating innovation among the industries. Technological process is closely connected to a firm's growth and profitability, indicating that economic growth that is highly dependent on technological progress would be boosted by a stronger IPR protection. While there are very few papers that cease to analyse this state of affairs, Liu (2015) decided to investigate the triangular relation between IPRs, R&D & FDI and their overall impact on the economic growth of a country. Using a larger panel data set covering 92 countries, which were categorised based on income levels (high, middle, and low) in each country, over a period of 38 years with more than 7 explanatory variables, Liu could provide concrete evidence to support his results. The analysis proposed two critical findings; first, the results depicted that R&D was the major engine for economic growth in high-income countries, while middle & low-income countries saw FDI as their major force in stimulating positive economic growth. Second, in high-income and low-income countries, a positive impact on economic growth was realized by the level of IPRs protection in these countries. Unfortunately, in middle-income countries, there was an absence of in the cause and effect of IPRs protection on economic growth. The onset of the TRIPS agreement initiated multiple changes in the legal framework for numerous countries around the globe. A significant part of the globe has adopted the agreement with many developing and under-developed countries opting in to abide by the TRIPS agreement as it provides a uniform platform to innovate and bring stability to their economies. With the same perspective, Yang & Zhang (2015) analysed whether the TRIPS agreement stimulated an increase in FDI in developing countries over the period of 1985-2012. The gravity model which is commonly used to elaborate international trade and FDI inflow patterns was used to draw conclusions. The analysis concluded that countries that adopted the TRIPS agreement had a positive correlation with the influx of FDI in host developing countries. The chosen time saw many different political and economic issues taking place in each country, thus the distinct drivers of FDI had divergent effects in different countries. Further on, variables like GDP, R&D, country risk, trade and investment safety showed a positive impact on inflow of FDI while, the openness to trade variables had contradictory effects on the inflow of FDI. A by-product of the global financial account liberalisation which took place in the early 1980s and late 1990s was the Foreign Direct Investment (FDI). As Yang & Zhang (2016) concluded that the TRIPS agreement played a major role in the inflow of FDI into the host countries. Chan & Tang (2017) ventured into analysing the impact of IPRs had on FDI inflows by categorizing countries into three income groups: - high-, middle- and low-income groups. After successfully running the ad-hoc test, Augmented Dickey-Fuller test and a cointegration analysis, their study provided evidence on the existence of a cointegration relationship between IPRs and FDI inflow in the global framework. In the long run, factors like IPRs, per capita GDP and real exchange rate prove to be crucial for the FDI inflow for high-income countries. While on the other hand, the short run provided emphasis on the past patterns of FDI inflow and joining the TRIPS agreement were vital influences in determining the short run entrance of FDI into the host countries. Another implication deduced from the analysis was from the foreign investor's point of view. They were more interested in the IPR protection in countries before they provide any form of investment into that country, thus highlighting the importance of IPR protection and how it could be using a policy measure to boost the influx of FDI into a nation. Over many years, economists have recognised the role of intellectual property rights and its influence on creating trade opportunities. But as low IPR protection discourages a country from initiating R&D, resulting in a diminishing growth rate of that respective country. Taylor (1994) threw light on this argument by connecting the IPR protection to trade, growth and technology transfer in a two-country model, an extension from the model state in Taylor(1993a). By the means of a theoretical methodology to study these linkages, the two- country endogenous model concluded that the offering of a partial IPR protection system would fail to provide factor price equalisation, which would improve the allocation and efficiency of technological resources, stimulating growth in a country. Another drawback of offering an asymmetric IPR protection system is the deviation from the best practise R&D methods, which would lower innovation and influence the economy to grow at a stagnant rate. Many trade agreements between developing and developed nations fell apart mainly due to the presence of weak Intellectual Property regimes in the developing nations. In response to these drawbacks, the past few years saw developing nations provide great emphasis on creating stringent Intellectual property regimes. As a result, developed nations could come into agreements with developing nations to receive the fruits of their extensive R&D activities. On this basis, Lee, Alba & Park (2018) took a step further by subsuming the size of the host country's informal economy into their study between IPR protection and FDI inflows. By means of a gravity FDI specification, a standard panel regression model was developed using data from 13 OECD countries & 48 developing host nations. The evidence provided as per the regression model threw light on two main findings: first, the effect of IPR protection on FDI inflows was significantly weak in countries residing with a larger informal economy; second, there was a threshold limit on the size of the informal economy, wherein the effect of IPR in attracting FDI was stronger in countries whose informal economy size was below the threshold level.

3. Research Objectives

- To understand if Intellectual property rights, Foreign Direct Investments affect the Gross Domestic Product of countries belonging to the various multilateral trading agreements as listed by World Trade Organization.
- To examine the relationship between the number of members countries in a group (Regional Trade Agreement) and the GDP performance.

4. Research Methodology

4.1 Variables, Measurement and Data Sources

This study consists of a panel data set for 64 multilateral regional trading agreements for a duration of 10 years from 2011-2020. The secondary data was collected from the databases of the World Intellectual Property Organisation and World Trade Organisation. The identification of the Trading Blocs was obtained from the World Trade Organisation categorized under the Regional Trade Agreements (RTA). The description of each variable is mentioned in the corresponding table.

Table 11.1   Variable definition and sources

Variables	Definition	Measurement	Source
GDPC	GDP per capita	Positive	World Intellectual Property Organization (WIPO)
PATENT	Total patent application	Positive or Null	WIPO
TM	Total trademark application	Positive or Null	WIPO
DESIGN	Total industrial design application	Positive or Null	WIPO
FDI	Amount of Foreign Direct Investment	Positive/Negative or Null	World Bank

5. Results and Discussion

To gauge the relationship between IPR, Foreign Direct Investments and Gross Domestic Product of countries belonging to 64 multilateral trade agreements and to test the first objective we ran through a regression test with Fixed Effect and Random Effect. The Log Values were taken to counter the missing variables. The component of IPR are represented by Patents, Trademarks and Industrial Designs. Due to high multicollinearity the variable of Industrial Designs was omitted from the analysis. Table 11.2 highlights the results as under:

The results point out that patents trademarks and foreign direct investments significantly contribute to the GDP of a country. The results could also be due to the other factors that affect the GDP of respective countries. While examining the second objective i.e., Table 11.3 the results show that patents and trademarks significantly affect GDP but the other variables namely group do not significantly contribute to growth. Also, evidently FDI significantly contributes to GDP. Also, there is faint evidence that the greater number of countries in a group significantly does not positively impact GDP count in any country. Thus, we can infer that a group of countries working in RTA do not significantly impact GDP in a positive way.

Table 11.2   The association between IPR, FDI, and GDP of countries belonging to the various trading agreements

Variables	Fixed effect	Random effect
Lagged GDP	0.634*** (0.0101)	0.99*** (0.0009)
LogPatent	0.007*** (0.0019)	-0.006*** (0.0009)
LogTradeMarks	0.0278*** (0.0027)	0.0058*** (0.0012)
LogFDI	0.0036*** (0.0007)	0.0036*** (0.0007)
Year Dummy	Yes	Yes
_cons	1.746*** (0.0588)	-0.0144** (0.007)
R^2	0.86	0.82
F-Test	5.14***	
Wald Test		31.8***
No. of Observations	4399	4399
No. of Groups	642	642
Hausman Test	1063.70***	

Note: *** $p<.01$, ** $p<.05$, * $p<.1$

Table 11.3   The relationship between the number of members countries in a group

Dependent variable: loggdp	Coefficient
LogPatent	0.051*** (0.003)
logtm	0.097*** (0.004)
logfdi	0.006*** (0.001)
group	0.167*** (0.057)
Year Dummy	Yes
Overall R^2	0.446
Chi-square	8106.638
R^2 within	0.695
Number of obs	4816
Prob > chi2	0.000
R^2 between	0.508

Note: *** $p<.01$, ** $p<.05$, * $p<.1$

The outcomes also show faintly that countries experience negative GDP if in more than one Regional Trade Agreement, compared to countries who are not a part of or just a part of one regional trade agreements. FDI is significant in the growth of the GDP of countries whereas the IPR variables also have do contribute to GDP in a positive way.

6. Limitations

The limitations of this study can be summed up as below: First, the information collected for the study is limited from 2011 to 2020. This was mainly done to incorporate and study the changes in Intellectual Property due to the introduction of the National Intellectual Property Rights Law, 2016 and the Companies Law of 2013 in India which were major changes to the Indian Economy. Second limitation was that multiple agreements listed by the World Trade Organization include territories and islands that are under the jurisdiction of another country, thus making it incredibly difficult to obtain data pertinent to those places. Third, Bilateral trade agreements were not considered for the purpose of this study. Fourth, several countries participating in various agreements have not updated nor provided complete information on the World Intellectual Property Organization (WIPO) and World Bank, proving to be another limitation to our study.

7. Conclusion and Further Scope of Study

The results obtained are in sync with available literature that Foreign Direct Investments do contribute to the GDP of a country. Also, Intellectual Property Rights that include Patents, Trademarks and Industrial Designs also have a contribution towards GDP of a country. The study can be extended to study regional trade and economic dynamics along with the growing influence of IPR's. Also, this paper could be extended to various sectors and industries for a more in-depth view.

REFERENCES

1. Amassoma, D., Ogbuagu, M., & Niniola, F. (2020). International Trade, Intellectual Property Right and Economic Development in Nigeria: Is There Any Link? *Journal Of Business and Entrepreneurship*, 1–25.
2. Anulekha, M. (2020). Role of IPR in Economic Development. Retrieved from ipleaders: https://blog.ipleaders.in/role-of-ipr-in-economic development/#Economic_Benefits_of_Intellectual_Property_Rights
3. Aricioglu, E., & Ucan, O. (2013). Intellectual Property Rights and Economic Growth in Europe. *International OFEL Conference on Corporate Governance*, (pp. 123–136).
4. Chan , S. M., & Tang, T. C. (2017). Foreign Direct Investment Inflows and Intellectual Property Rights: Empirical Evidence from Different Income Groups. *Global Economic Review*, 1–30.

5. Ginarte, J. C., & Park, W. B. (1997). Intellectual Property Rights and Economic Growth. *Contemporary Economic Policy*, 51–61.
6. Kumar, R., Verma, S., & Yadav, S. K. (2018). Intellectual property rights protection and foreign direct investment: a study of BRICS countries. *World Review of Entrepreneurship, Management and Sustainable Development*, 694–704.
7. Lee, M., Alba, J. D., & Park, D. (2018). Intellectual Property Rights, Informal Economy, and FDI into Developing Countries. *Journal of Policy Modeling*.
8. Lesser, W. (2017). The Effects of TRIPS-Mandated Intellectual Property Rights on Economic Activities in Developing countries.
9. Lisi, S., & Xiangdong, C. (2008). Technology-based Relationship between Innovation and Growth. *International Seminar on Business and Information Management*, (pp. 257–259).
10. Liu, W.-H. (2015). Intellectual Property Rights, FDI, R&D and Economic Growth: A Cross-country Empirical Analysis. *The World Economy*, 1–22.
11. Seyoum, B. (1996). The Impact of Intellectual Property Rights on Foreign Direct Investment. *The Columbia Journal of World Business*, 50–59.
12. Taylor, M. S. (1994). Trips, Trade, and Growth. *International Economic Review*, 361–381.
13. Zhang, H., & Yang, X. (2015). Trade-related aspects of intellectual property rights agreements and the upsurge in foreign direct investment in developing countries. *Economic Analysis and Policy*, 1–14.

Note: All the tables in this chapter were author's compilation.

Emerging Horizons: Business and Society in the Post Pandemic Era –
Brig. Dr. Rajiv Divekar et al. (eds)
© 2024 Taylor & Francis Group, London, ISBN 978-1-032-90822-9

12

Drivers of Value of P2P Lending Segment: A Doughnut Economics Perspective

Aneeta Elsa Simon[1]
Latha Ramesh[2], Surekha Nayak[3]
Rameesha Kalra[4]
School of Business and Management,
CHRIST (Deemed to be University),
Bangalore, India

ABSTRACT

Peer-to-peer lending or P2P Lending is a segment within the ambit of Fintech, showcasing immense potential for growth globally, especially in India. Widely explored and adopted especially during the pandemic, the advantages associated with the P2P lending business model draw a variety of stakeholders from lenders, borrowers, institutions and others and is here to stay as the pandemic moves to an endemic stage. Simultaneously, the possible risks posed to the financial system are also critical for consideration, especially for investors during their valuation efforts and regulators across economies. Thus, this conceptual paper adopts an exploratory approach wherein the value drivers of P2P lending have been analysed using the Doughnut Economics perspective and by reviewing existing literature. Subsequently, a list of risk factors and cash inflows and outflows have been listed to provide vital inputs relevant to building a valuation model suited for ventures in the P2P lending space. Thus, this study aims to synthesise thoughts on value creation by the P2P lending segment, as present in a pool of literature obtained from databases such as Proquest and Google Scholar, government and company websites. Ultimately, the paper aims to provide critical inputs for analysing ventures in the P2P lending ecosystem and also reach at their valuations as diverse stakeholders make critical financial decisions with long- and short-term impacts. Hence, the paper is one of the first attempts to synthesize literature available on P2P lending, especially concerning drivers for value creation by the segment and with a more sustainable Doughnut Economics approach. The work can be further expanded by including interactions with relevant practitioners by

[1]aneeta.simon@res.christuniversity.in, [2]latha.ramesh@christuniversity.in, [3]surekha.nayak@
christuniversity.in, [4]rameesha.kalra@christuniversity.in

DOI: 10.4324/978100355996-12

adopting more rigorous methodologies such as case studies, interviews, and focus group discussions and further substantiated with authentic quantitative data on the different financial parameters.

KEYWORDS: Financial inclusion, Intrinsic valuation, Value creation, Doughnut economics, Sustainable development goals

1. Introduction

Peer-to-peer lending or P2P Lending is a segment within the ambit of Fintech, showcasing immense potential for growth globally. It aims to provide more transparency in financial processes and better access to capital to the unserved segments of society. Such platforms cater to the needs of individuals who are new to the credit system and hence, do not have strong credit scoring or small-scale enterprises which do not have adequate collateral to support their loan application. Therefore, P2P lending in turn aims to address crucial dimensions of economic development such as equality, financial inclusion, sustainable development and several others. Furthermore, during the pandemic, we witnessed several forms and levels of restrictions being imposed which posed challenges to the livelihoods and sustenance of businesses worldwide. This eventually led to the widespread adoption of Fintech products in payment, credit including P2P lending, personal finance management and many more. Thus, in an economy like that of India, even though the adoption of technology-backed services is usually slow, the pandemic triggered a fast-paced trying and adoption of Fintech services, which is bound to continue even as the pandemic comes to an end. All this can be attributable to the changes in the consumer attitude and behaviour, in turn shaping their preferences in favour of the ramifications in the area of financial services, information technology, networking, etc. which have brought about a phygital mode of conducting businesses and digitisation of most services.

Based on crowdsourcing concepts, P2P lending is a source of alternative finance wherein smaller portions of money can be raised from larger groups of persons to finance a financial goal. Thus, the model aims to disintermediate banks or the unorganised money lending sector to facilitate more secure, faster, and more convenient access to funds. Initially started in the UK and parts of Europe and being an enormous success in China, P2P lending is gaining traction in India and other Asian countries among stakeholders ranging from customers, investors, employees, regulators, and governments. Investors are especially viewing this as an alternative finance avenue and actively looking out for ventures to fund. However, being nascent and involving complexities such as lack of clearer definitions, blurred distinction between being a technology company or a financial services company, dynamics of the ecosystem in which it operates, and many more, P2P lending requires prudent consideration. Thus, understanding the factors driving its popularity and how it is placed differently from traditional banks can enable one to be well-informed about this investment option. Additionally, the regulations drafted to avoid or mitigate critical risks associated with P2P lending are worth assessing. Hence, an overall understanding of a business model facilitating better access to credit which is termed to be more authentic and secure enables individuals and businesses in the ecosystem to collaborate and co-create value.

Given the backdrop, a synthesis of literature obtained from databases such as Proquest and Google Scholar and official and company websites, based on the theme of value creation of the P2P lending segment is presented. The paper thus aims to provide critical inputs for analysing ventures and companies in the P2P lending ecosystem and arrive at valuations, as diverse stakeholders make critical financial decisions with long- and short-term impacts. Hence, the paper is one of the first attempts to synthesise literature available on P2P lending, especially in listing out the drivers for value creation by adopting the Doughnut Economics approach. Given today's scenario where there is growing impetus given to socially responsible enterprises and concerns around the business environment, sustainability and governance (ESG), a more comprehensive mind set is deemed necessary to ensure a better future. Therefore, the entire business model and the ecosystem in which P2P lending works are explored from a Doughnut Economics perspective; which drastically rethinks from the perspective of 20th-century economics to one where human prosperity is defined as meeting the needs of all people within the means of the living planet (Doughnut Economics Action Lab, 2022). The branch of economics which instigates nations and societies to rethink was first presented by Kate Raworth in a report in 2012 and thereafter, in a book in 2017. The doughnut acts as a compass to ensure human progress is well within the safe haven between social and planetary boundaries, which for a very long time mankind have exploited.

The paper presents its idea in the following flow: initially, an overview of the P2P lending landscape is given by citing instances from across the globe. Subsequently, based on an extensive review of the existing literature, comprehensive lists of value drivers and risk factors have been arrived at. Financial parameters such as revenue (inflows) and cost (outflows) are also listed, with the conclusion of the paper providing vital inputs relevant to building a valuation model suited for ventures in the P2P lending space.

2. Literature Study

2.1 Evolution of P2P Lending

Initiated back in the 1700s, community-based initiatives to provide loans to low-income families through the Irish Loan Funds is the first instance of well-documented crowdfunding, which had immense success by the 1800s, too (Hollis & Sweetman, 1996). Fast forward to 1976, when Nobel laureate Dr Mohammad

Yunus popularised the concept of microfinance by founding Grameen Bank in Bangladesh, which backed sustainable credit/lending (Organisation for Economic Co-operation and Development, 2019) wherein credit was extended to poor women especially to overcome poverty by generating self-employment or income generating opportunities instead of focusing on consumption (Grameen Bank, 2020). These innovations aided in the evolution of crowdfunding with the first successful modern and online crowdsourcing of funds for the US tour of Marillion, a British rock band by its fans registered in 1997 (Trautman & Aho, 2018). By the 2000s, multiple ventures and crowdfunding platforms emerged (Iman, 2020) with the industry's revenue reaching exponential growth within a decade. Owing to easier access to a wider pool of funds, convenience in terms of fewer processes and better responsiveness, lesser processing time (Wang et al., 2015), and better access for the 'credit unworthy' (Setiawan et al., 2021), crowdfunding emerged as a recognised funding source (Candy et al., 2022)with numerous ventures set up based on the business model and its multiple variations. Subsequently, in 2011, much in line with the efforts to overcome the Great Financial Crisis, the Jumpstart Our Business Startups (JOBS) Act brought about a framework legalising crowdfunding. Thus, today crowdfunding exists in various forms and shapes such as reward-based (including against security, be it debt or digital (ICO) or litigation), equity crowdfunding and donation-based crowdfunding. (Securities Exchange Board of India (SEBI), 2014)

2.2 Recent Developments in P2P Lending

The crowd-investing market which includes P2P lending is attributed to a total of 974 platforms from across the globe with the US, UK, Italy, Indonesia and Germany being at the forefront in terms of count while 133 platforms are based out from Asia, with 13 platforms operating from India (P2PMarketData, 2022). The majority of platforms cater to businesses, followed by consumers and property in the Indian market while globally, the order goes business, property and consumer. The business model followed, ranges from direct marketplace lending, equity crowdfunding, invoice financing, investment fund marketplace, crypto marketplace lending, balance sheet lending, resale marketplace lending, donation crowdfunding and reward crowdfunding with the count of platforms operating under each model. An interesting observation from the statistics is that regions with more developed economies i.e. the European and North American regions have the highest proportion of crowd investing platforms. Also, Asian platforms tend to focus their funding on consumers over properties unlike other markets while businesses take the topmost priority across markets. The operational business model of platforms incorporated in India includes that they are mainly registered as tech companies under the Companies Act with a recent trend of addressing a few of them as non-banking financial companies (NBFCs) provided they adhere to the guidelines drawn out by RBI.

P2P lending or direct marketplace lending happens over an online platform which brings together individuals or legal persons who have excess money and those who require money, without the need for collateral. Thus, such platforms act as an aggregator aiming to match lenders and borrowers (Klein et al., 2021), wherein initial due diligence of both parties is carried out by the platform during on boarding. There can be a set of criteria that needs to be met by the borrower. For instance, the individual should be salaried, self-employed or retired with sufficient backup to repay the amount borrowed. Other parameters considered in the decision-making process include ownership of the individual's house, average income, the purpose of the loan and several more. Subsequently, a reverse auction model is followed wherein lenders bid for a loan proposal post which the borrower chooses the course of action. There can be either complete or partial fulfilment of the loan amount by the lender, in which case there can be pooling of funds from multiple lenders. On acceptance of the bid, the loan agreement is signed between the parties, post which the money is transferred from the lender's bank account to the borrower's bank account. While the borrower is extended funds at a timely pace without undergoing much excruciating process for their needs ranging from financing their small-scale businesses to supporting their aspirations, the lender/retail investor is vested in this alternative investment avenue due to the higher returns earned on the invested amount primarily in terms of the interest paid by the borrower. Such loans are characterised by lower interest rates (on average ranging from 6.5% to 15%) and shorter tenure (minimum of 3 months to a maximum of 36 months) for loan amounts from ₹10,000 to ₹10,00,000 (BankBazaar, 2018). Such critical parameters are discussed, negotiated and arrived at as terms of the agreement entered into by both the parties with the portal taking the position of mere facilitator. Furthermore, the lenders enjoy returns much higher than the interest earned on their fixed deposits with banks which usually range from 2.50% to 6.65% in the Indian market, as the savings in terms of not setting up brick and mortar branches across the countries of operations, reduced person-hours and effort for processing and other statutory requirements, are passed to both the customers. However, classified more appropriate as debt or fixed return instrument, the risks associated with P2P lending are relatively on a higher side within the category, since the exposure is risk associated with a pool of individuals who have lower credit scores in spite of a level of diversification. The rate of default is around 6-7% in India while globally it is 20% and hence the product is more appealing to individuals with a high-risk appetite and sufficient capital pool. Furthermore, the platform facilitates the collection of post-dated cheques from the borrower in the lender's name as a proxy for repayment of the loan. The P2P forum, in general, also helps in the recovery process and as part of this, follows up for repayments and if need be, employs recovery agents too.

Subsequently, the primary source of earnings for the platform is through fees paid by the borrower on the receipt of the sanctioned loan amount (origination fee) and in certain instances the application fee (LendingClub, 2022) while the processing fee and administration fees for value-added services such as initial credit assessment, legal services in terms of drafting the loan agreement; paid by the lenders also add to the pool. All these sources are utilised to meet the cost of getting new customers onboard, providing services such as credit scoring, meeting the regulatory requirements, and running and maintaining the IT infrastructure which is critical to the whole fintech process, among others (Suryono et al., 2019). Thus, being a mere facilitator and not a counter-party to the loan, the profit for such P2P lending platforms is basically from the various fees charged to facilitate a seamless lending process than the spread between lending and deposit rates (Reserve Bank of India (RBI), 2016) while the entire process comes under the radar of RBI, in India while associations such as P2PFA act as a representative and self-regulatory body in the UK.

2.3 Regulating P2P Lending in India

Given the backdrop and the issues in P2P lending (Suryono et al., 2021), the regulatory position adopted in India is not clearly defined with guidelines and regulations continuously evolving to protect the interests of all stakeholders and facilitate orderly growth of the sector as an alternative credit source. Subsequently, such platforms which are incorporated as companies or cooperative societies, are defined as NBFCs by RBI. The ventures register themselves for the licensing, post which set prudential norms and requirements have to be adhered to which brings about a lot of goodwill in the eyes of the intended market. The regulatory framework specified by the apcx bank of India encompasses the definition of permitted activity for NBFCs, the prudential norms regarding capital to be adhered to, and critical guidelines regarding governance, business continuity plan, and customer interface and reporting (Reserve Bank of India (RBI), 2016). However, P2P platforms adopting an organisational structure other than the above-mentioned are deemed illegal within RBI purview or are subject to the supervision of the concerned state government.

Since the segment is in its nascent stages, wherein lending is primarily from one individual to another, the know your customer or KYC and recovery practices are concern areas subject to careful surveillance. Since all payments are through accounts set up at recognised banks, the KYC exercise can be deemed to have been carried out by the concerned banks. However, though these platforms claim to follow soft recovery practices, the possibility of the use of coercive methods cannot be ruled out and hence needs to be carefully considered.

The growth potential of the entire digital lending and fundraising space within Fintech has been a key attraction for all stakeholders with several of them taking proactive steps to participate in and regulate the ecosystem. This has been evident in the growth trajectory achieved during the last decade across the globe with digital lending and fundraising volume growing from 5.09 million USD in 2013 to 1.52 billion USD in 2020 (Cambridge Centre for Alternative Finance, 2022). However, the pandemic and the strict crackdown on Chinese P2P platforms have brought about repercussions in the lending activity as well as funding of such ventures. In terms of funding, the entire alternative investment market has witnessed a downfall in 2022 with a decline in funding volume of 12% in July 2022 compared to June 2022 with the funding at around 383 million euros in July 2022. Meanwhile, consumer, business and property lending has also shown a decline owing predominantly to the aftermath of the pandemic. However, the sector is viewed positively in terms of growth prospects and the ability to address macroeconomic concerns such as filling the credit gaps, given the continuous efforts to regulate and monitor its entire functioning.

3. Conceptual Framework

3.1 P2P Lending: A Doughnut Economics Perspective

Being an emerging area with huge prospects to grow, it is worth understanding and analysing alternative finance as an area and consequently, P2P lending using the economic mind-set, much suited for the 21st century. Thus, we see that start-ups/ventures involved in P2P lending, being at the initial stages of their growth, aim more in thriving than initially meeting the goal of endless GDP growth. Such ventures view the bigger picture by creating an ecosystem for themselves and thus arriving at an embedded economy rather than constraining themselves with a self-contained market (like traditional banks). Furthermore, the ecosystem ensures a sense of co-opetition wherein increasingly companies cooperate with a competitor to achieve a common goal or to get ahead (Brandenburger & Nalebuff, 2021). Owing to the complexities and interdependence of the economies, and societies that they operate in, systems thinking is adopted wherein dynamic complexities are addressed rather than arriving at a mechanical equilibrium and work on the principles of regenerative and distributive economics. Thus, in turn, such ventures help achieve the sustainable development goals (SDGs) by reducing inequalities, driving innovation and ultimately economic growth.

For the purpose of evaluating a venture from the doughnut economics point of view, the deep design of the organisation is to be investigated since it shapes what organizations can be and do. With this regard, Majorie Kelly (Miller, 2012) attributes five layers of design which attribute to the Design of the Enterprise such as Purpose, Networks, Governance, Ownership and Finance which together aid in bringing the entire humanity into the doughnut. Each of the multiple layers has been detailed in Table 12.1 with an illustration from the area of P2P lending within fintech.

3.2 P2P Lending Landscape

Having analysed as to how P2P lending can facilitate the promotion of doughnut economics, which is the need of the hour during current critical times, an understanding of the different stakeholders addressed and their intermingling, the value drivers and key sources of revenue and cost is much needed. For this

Table 12.1 Doughnut economics: Layers of design and P2P lending

Layer of deep design	What does it intend? (As derived from Doughnut Economics.org)	How is it met? (Taking an instance of a P2P lending company)
Purpose	Why does this organisation exist? What end does it serve in the world - and is that vision shared by all involved?	Aims to address the credit gap and hence primacy of a pressing social concern of financial inclusion
Networks	What relationships does local government hold, and how does it bring its purpose and values to life through them?	Provides a facilitative platform to both borrowers and lenders for the sharing of funds and renders services and other value adds through a collaborative network partnering with ecosystem business partners
Governance	Who has voice in decision making? What are the hard rules, and the unwritten culture, of how things get done? What are the metrics of success?	Active interest and interaction with the community for deliberative decision-making. Further, the board has adequate representation enabling ease of communication and sharing power with those who represent the interests of the community
Ownership	What are the sources of wealth creation in this place, and who benefits from how they are owned?	Community ownership of funding and responsibility, to facilitate regeneration of capital by distributing capital to achieve sustainable livelihood
Finance	What are the sources of finance here, and what does that finance expect and demand? What is extracted, what is reinvested and who does it serve?	Funding is pooled to serve the unmet credit needs of the society wherein amounts are reinvested for impact and to expand the set of beneficiaries to ensure community wealth building.

Source: Compiled by authors

process, instances of P2P lending ventures or enterprises from the Indian and global contexts are used to substantiate.

P2P lending companies, through their platform, facilitate the interaction between borrowers and lenders for the exchange of funds, as illustrated in Fig. 12.1. To ensure the conduct of operations, the human capital vested in the company and its operations form part of the inner circle since they are indispensable for the existence of the venture. Further, to facilitate the seamless functioning of the platform which deals with crucial assets (both identity and monetary) of the individuals participating in the system and in turn are part of the overall economy, trusted parties in terms of partner banks to hold the corpus fund, credit agencies such as Transunion (CIBIL in India), Equifax, Experian to provide with crucial credit scoring reports and other partners across specialities such as Paypal, Billdesk, Stripe, AWS, Microsoft Azure, Google Cloud, and several others providing strong information technology infrastructure and the guaranteed data storage and backup, privacy and data protection form the intermediate circle among others. Overall, all

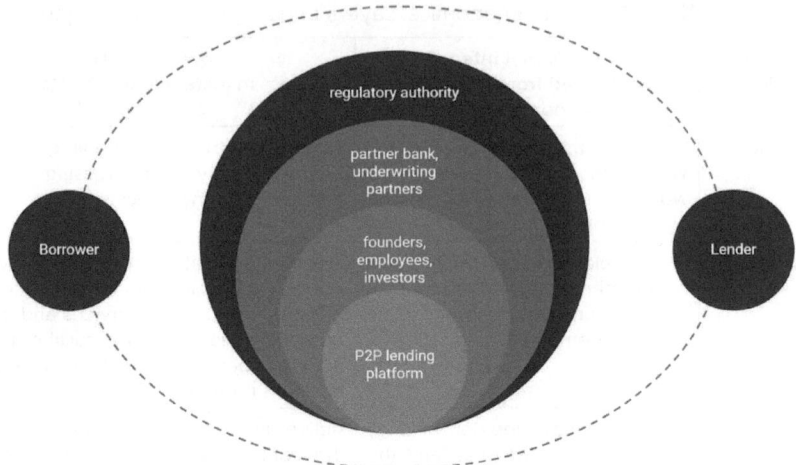

Fig. 12.1   Stakeholders in the P2P lending scenario

Source: Authors' work

the players and factors work well within the regulatory framework and guidelines laid down by the regulatory authority(es) of the respective countries. It is vital that all the stakeholders work in tandem for efficient business processes.

Subsequently, the value drivers for the growing adoption and success of P2P lending are explored and listed in Fig. 12.2. Enhanced value of an enterprise (Corporate Finance Institute (CFI), 2022) helps it to earn higher cashflows and reduce its risk exposure. For enterprises operating in the Fintech space, including

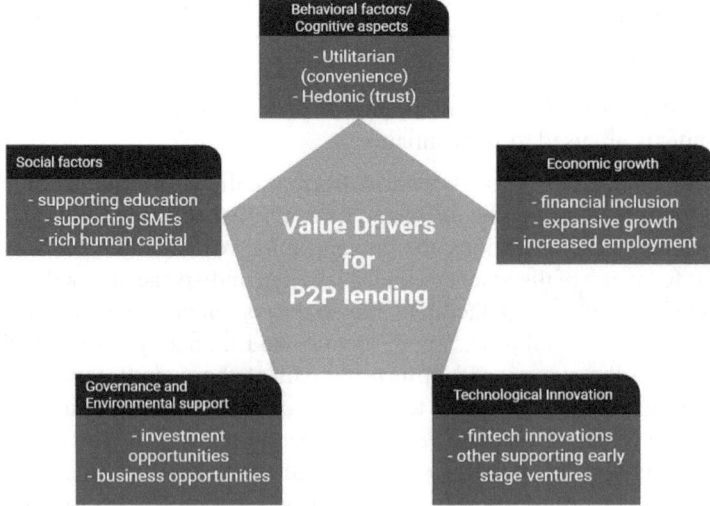

Fig. 12.2   Value drivers for P2P lending

Source: Authors' work

P2P lending, value is driven by political and legal factors broadly put together as governance, the economic impetus received and facilitative environment, social attributes and cognitive aspects, all supported by strong technological innovations. The political and legal framework surrounding P2P lending is varied across economies, with many countries recognising such platforms as intermediaries while others as banks. Meanwhile, certain economies have outright prohibited P2P lending while others have termed it as an exempt market due to a lack of definition (Reserve Bank of India (RBI), 2016). In India, such ventures are termed as NBFCs in an effort not to curb innovation and promote the best side put forward by the segment. Therefore, recognition and the licensing granted to P2P lending enterprises facilitate business and enhance promote to the value of the firm. Encouraging and conducive environment in terms of investment and business opportunities to facilitate expansive economic growth and its by-products such as increased employment and better financial inclusion aid in improving the value of the segment. Furthermore, factors pertaining to the society such as enhanced education and rich human capital, along with increased demand from small and medium enterprises, technological innovations in the space of fintech and the support from peers are also important value drivers. All this works well provided the basic user is satisfied which is through meeting his/her cognitive or behavioural needs ranging from the satisfactory usage of the product in terms of convenience and reduced turnaround time to trust which can ensure the prolonged usage of the services.

Alternatively, the cost and revenue aspects which can be quantified in an attempt to arrive at the valuations of P2P lending companies are listed in Fig. 12.3. Expenses to build and maintain the technology to run the platform and the supporting infrastructure form a crucial component. Further, customer acquisition and retention costs are critical to ensure the segment's expansion. Additionally,

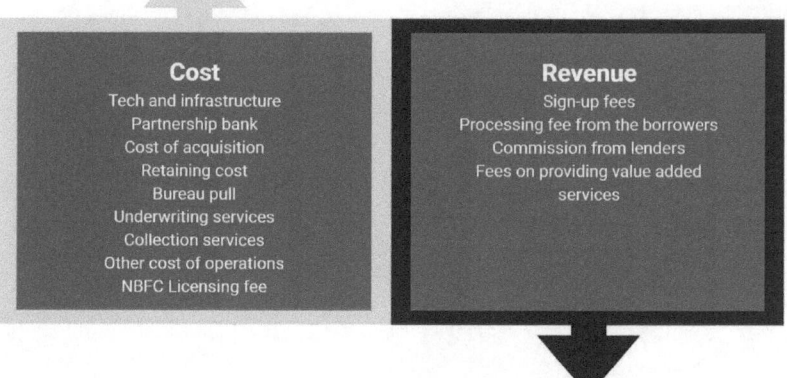

Fig. 12.3 Revenue and cost factors for P2P lending platforms

Source: Authors' work

costs pertaining to partnering with banks who would be custodians of the money dealt with, for bureau pull to obtain the credit scoring and critical information pertaining to one's credit history, underwriting services which form the foundation while processing applications and collection services ensure seamless functioning. Other costs pertain to the day-to-day operations and NBFC licensing, which are also important. Incomes are from sources such as sign-up fees, processing fees from the borrowers, commissions from lenders and the fees for providing value-added services aid in generating cashflows for firms operating within the P2P lending space apart from the investment funds.

For a comprehensive analysis of the P2P lending landscape, the systematic and unsystematic risks involved in running P2P lending businesses are worth evaluating. Downtime, compromise in the competence of the technology infrastructure and data protection and privacy concerns form part of the crucial technology-related risk of running any fintech enterprise. Social risk can stem from the changes in social norms such as changing perceptions among the users and prospective users and also the gaps in the capability and competence in the usage of the platforms while operational risks can arise during interactions with crucial partners and within the network, due to errors in underwriting and problems in the collection process. Management risks can be attributable to the managerial board composition and networks, the goodwill of the members and more importantly due to untimely and miscalculated decisions of management. Evolving complexities associated with regulations and guidelines and changing definitions in law cause legal and regulatory risks while continuous competition faced from similar competitors as well as attempts made by incumbents and well-established enterprises to venture into allied areas are also risky. (Corporate Finance Institute (CFI), 2022)

Fig. 12.4 Risks associated with P2P lending platforms

Source: Authors' work

4. Conclusion

With the increased inaccessibility to the banking sector coupled with the convenience in the usage and access to funds promised by alternative financing modes, P2P lending has gained immense popularity across economies and sections of society. Thus, analysing the factors promoting the adoption of P2P lending platforms and their functioning across nations helps individuals, businesses, competitors and regulators to arrive at well-informed decisions and perform their responsibilities diligently. Furthermore, investors, partners and other participants in the financial support system can better evaluate and judge ventures basis their value drivers, sources of inflows and outflows and associated risks in running the business. Therefore, this article has drawn an understanding of the broad P2P lending landscape, right from its inception to the current times based on official reports and existing literature. Furthermore, since economies and business models are increasingly recognising the importance of sustainable operations, evaluating the emerging area in the light of Doughnut economics has thrown a great deal of light on the current operations and how future endeavours have to be shaped to ensure sustainable growth over the long term. P2P lending enables regenerative and distributive development by having distinct value drivers supporting sustained valuations over the years, which have the potential to grow by leaps and bounds. However, during the process getting adequate funds is crucial for which valuations depend on the growth potential of the ventures that are brought about by the value drivers and the revenue stream and costs and risks involved in arriving at the same.

However, the nascency of the fields, both P2P lending and doughnut economics, has resulted in the limited extent of reporting or literature in the field to support the analysis of the area from the doughnut economics perspective. Furthermore, the limited publicly available financial and operational information can imply that the list of value drivers, cash inflows and outflows and risks can have scope for more inclusions, in spite of efforts to come up with comprehensive lists on the part of the authors. Thus, the directions for future work pertaining to this article can aim at extending the lists of drivers resulting in the overall valuations of the segment by considering specific economies and demographics in depth. Furthermore, research using multifarious perspectives such as legal, policy-related, and several more, along with diverse quantitative and qualitative methods of data collection and eventual appropriate analyses can help substantiate this initial compilation of the different facets relating to valuing P2P lending ventures

5. Implications of the Study

Peer-to-peer lending or P2P Lending is a segment within the ambit of Fintech, showcasing immense potential for growth globally, especially in India. Widely explored and adopted especially during the pandemic, the advantages associated with the P2P lending business model draw a variety of stakeholders from lenders, borrowers, institutions and others and is here to stay as the pandemic moves to an endemic stage. Simultaneously, the possible risks posed to the financial system are also critical for consideration, especially for investors during their valuation efforts and regulators across economies. This paper is one of the first attempts to synthesize literature available on P2P lending, especially concerning drivers for value creation by the segment and with a more sustainable Doughnut Economics approach.

6. Limitations

The work can be further expanded by including interactions with relevant practitioners by adopting more rigorous methodologies such as case studies, interviews, and focus group discussions and further substantiated with authentic quantitative data on the different financial parameters. This helps to strengthen the external validity of applying the approach to analyse the segment.The results of the study cannot be generalized since it needs to be tested in different business environments and across different companies in the same space.

REFERENCES

1. BankBazaar. (2018). *Peer to Peer Lending Interest rates, Eligibility and Benefits.* BankBazaar. Retrieved August 3, 2022, from https://www.bankbazaar.com/personal-loan/peer-to-peer-lending.html
2. Brandenburger, A., & Nalebuff, B. (2021). *The Rules of Co-opetition.* Harvard Business Review. Retrieved August 20, 2022, from https://hbr.org/2021/01/the-rules-of-co-opetition
3. Cambridge Centre for Alternative Finance. (2022). *Cambridge Alternative Finance Benchmarks.* Cambridge Centre for Alternative Finance (CCAF.io). Retrieved August 17, 2022, from https://ccaf.io/cafb/digital_lending/region_comparison
4. Candy, C., Venessa, Zakhariah, C., & Vincent. (2022). The Utilization of Fintech to Increase Financial Inclusion in Indonesia: A Conceptual Paper. *SEIKO Journal of Management & Business*, 5(1), 261–280.
5. Corporate Finance Institute (CFI). (2022, March 28). *Valuation Drivers - Definition, Examples, and Key Takeaways.* Corporate Finance Institute. Retrieved August 10, 2022, from https://corporatefinanceinstitute.com/resources/knowledge/valuation/valuation-drivers/
6. Corporate Finance Institute (CFI). (2022, April 22). *Risk - Definition, Types, Adjustment and Measurement.* Corporate Finance Institute. Retrieved August 23, 2022, from https://corporatefinanceinstitute.com/resources/knowledge/finance/risk/
7. Doughnut Economics Action Lab. (2022). *About Doughnut Economics.* Doughnut Economics Action Lab. Retrieved August 25, 2022, from https://doughnuteconomics.org/about-doughnut-economics
8. Grameen Bank. (2020, April 15). *What is Microcredit? – Grameen Bank.* Grameen Bank. Retrieved August 3, 2022, from https://grameenbank.org/what-is-microcredit/\
9. Hollis, A., & Sweetman, A. (1996, January 2). *The Evolution Of A Microcredit Institution: The Irish Loan Funds, 1720 – 1920* [Working Paper Number UT-ECIPA-

ECPAP-96-01]. Department of Economics and Institute for Policy Analysis. : http://www.epas.utoronto.ca:8080/wpa/wpa.html

10. Iman, N. (2020, January). The rise and rise of financial technology: The good, the bad, and the verdict. Cogent Business & Management, 7. https://doi.org/10.1080/23311975.2020.1725309

11. Klein, G., Shtudiner, Z., & Zwilling, M. (2021, June 17). Why do peer-to-peer (P2P) lending platforms fail? The gap between P2P lenders' preferences and the platforms' intentions. Electronic Commerce Research. https://doi.org/10.1007/s10660-021-09489-6

12. LendingClub. (2022). *Personal Loans Rates & Fees*. Lending Club. Retrieved June 29, 2022, from https://www.lendingclub.com/loans/personal-loans/rates-fees#

13. Miller, K. (2012, April 2). Marjorie Kelly: Saving Capitalism From Itself. *The Nation*. https://www.thenation.com/article/archive/marjorie-kelly-saving-capitalism-itself/

14. Organisation for Economic Co-operation and Development. (2019, March). *OECD export credits and sustainable lending*. Sustainable lending. Retrieved July 23, 2022, from https://www.oecd.org/trade/topics/export-credits/sustainable-lending/

15. P2PMarketData. (2022). *P2P Finance Statistics of the World*. P2PMarketData. Retrieved August 30, 2022, from https://p2pmarketdata.com/p2p-finance-worldwide-statistics/

16. Raworth, K. (2017). *Doughnut Economics: Seven Ways to Think Like a 21st Century Economist*. Chelsea Green Publishing. https://www.kateraworth.com/

17. Reserve Bank of India (RBI). (2016, April). *Consultation Paper on Peer to Peer Lending*. Consultation Paper on Peer to Peer Lending. Retrieved June 22, 2022, from https://rbi.org.in/scripts/Bs_viewcontent.aspx?Id=3164

18. Securities Exchange Board of India (SEBI). (2014, June 17). *Consultation Paper on Crowdfunding in India*. Retrieved July 18, 2022, from https://www.sebi.gov.in/sebi_data/attachdocs/1403005615257.pdf

19. Setiawan, B., Nugraha, D. P., Irawan, A., Nathan, R. J., & Zoltan, Z. (2021, August 12). User Innovativeness and Fintech Adoption in Indonesia. *Journal of Open Innovation: Technology, Market and Complexity*, 7(3), 1–18. MDPI. https://doi.org/10.3390/joitmc7030188

20. startups.com. (2022). *The History of Crowdfunding*. Fundable. Retrieved July 12, 2022, from https://www.fundable.com/crowdfunding101/history-of-crowdfunding

21. Suryono, R. R., Budi, I., & Purwandari, B. (2021, April 8). Detection of fintech P2P lending issues in Indonesia. *Heliyon*, 7. https://doi.org/10.1016/j.heliyon.2021.e06782

22. Suryono, R. R., Purwandari, B., & Budi, I. (2019). Peer to Peer (P2P) Lending Problems and Potential Solutions: A Systematic Literature Review. Procedia Computer Science, 161, 204–214. https://doi.org/10.1016/j.procs.2019.11.116

23. Trautman, L. J., & Aho, O. W. (2018, September 18). Crowdfunding, Entrepreneurship, and Start-Up. SSRN, 1–32. http://dx.doi.org/10.2139/ssrn.3251538

24. Wang, H., Chen, K., Zhu, W., & Song, Z. (2015, June 9). A process model on P2P lending. Financial Innovation, 1(3), 1–8. https://doi.org/10.1186/s40854-015-0002-9

Emerging Horizons: Business and Society in the Post Pandemic Era –
Brig. Dr. Rajiv Divekar et al. (eds)
© 2024 Taylor & Francis Group, London, ISBN 978-1-032-90822-9

Impact of Screen Time and Other Factors on Sleep Time

Surya Rashmi Rawat[1]
Professor, HPKV Business School,
Central University of Himachal Pradesh,
Dharamshala, HP, India

Raghav Singh Rawat[2]
Symbiosis Law School, Pune,
Symbiosis International (Deemed University)
Pune, India

ABSTRACT

Screen time (ScT) is the time spent by a person on the screen of an electronic device such as television, smartphone, computer or a game console. There has been a sudden spurt in the use of electronic devices by the youth. A lot has been researched in the field of screen time and its impact on sleep time (ST) but interestingly people belonging to different socio-demographic backgrounds have exhibited different responses. A survey called "Sleep in the Modern Family(SMF)", conducted by National Sleep Foundation in the year 2014 found that three out of four teens and 96% of sample between 15 to 17 years of age admitted of using electronic gadgets in their bedrooms. The study in hand was conducted to look into the requirements in an area which touches the lives of the majority of the population across the globe today. The basic objective behind the research was to study the impact of various factors on the quality (waking up fresh / soundness of sleep) as well as the quantity (number of hours) of sleep. The research is based on both primary as well as secondary sources of information. Secondary sources of information were drawn from research papers published in the journals. The primary data was collected through a questionnaire circulated amongst 300 people belonging to three different age groups, 12 to 18 years, 18 to 25 years, and 25 to 45 years. The survey was conducted in the city of Pune (Maharashtra). The findings were then analyzed using ANOVA, correlation, and regression tests with the help of SPSS 21. The result revealed that screen timing

[1]rawatsuryarashmi@gmail.com, [2]rawatraghavsingh@gmail.com

DOI: 10.4324/978100355996-13

has no relationship with the quality and quantity of sleep but there are other factors that affect the soundness of sleep.

KEYWORDS: Sleep, Screen time, Insomnia, Sleeplessness, Health science students, Electronic device

1. Introduction

Sleep is an unconscious condition necessary to maintain the healthy physiology and psychology of an individual. It restores normal neural activity and prevents irritating and unusual behavior. During Covid Pandemic, there has been a rise in exposure to blue light due to the sudden shift from offline to online modes of working and studying. This shift in the mode resulted in various health implications. Before Covid Pandemic, a study conducted in the US in the year 2014 on families with children between 6 and 17 years of age concluded that screen timing affected the quality as well as the quantity of sleep. However, various authors observed that in addition to screen time, other factors too have influenced sleep quality and quantity. Through the present research, the authors are making an attempt to study the impact of various factors on the quality (waking up fresh / soundness of sleep) as well as the quantity of sleep (Number of hours of sleep).

2. Literature Study

On the basis of review of literature, the authors came up with a list of consequences of longer screen timings. Majority of these studies have been conducted outside India and mainly in Europe, the US, and Australia.

2.1 Effects of Screen Time

After a detailed review of more than 18 articles, Drumheller and Fan (2022) found that during COVID-19 pandemic, ScT adversely affected the sleep in terms of duration(Sd), quality(Sq), onset latency(Sol), and wake-up time(Wot). But at the same time there was ample evidence contradicting this finding and thus clearly hinting at the presence of other factors too affecting the relationship between ScT and the ST. Arshad et al. (2021) observed that ScT is negatively correlated with sleep quality leading to various adverse physical and psychological manifestations. Gupta et al.(2022) while studying the college girls aged 18 to 21 years of age, found a significant association of ScT and Sleep Time with the dry eye. The sample also experienced severe waking up difficulty. In a study conducted on European children, Guzmán et al.(2022) observed that the increase in ScT and decrease in ST leads to weight gain or obesity by 13–20%. Emond et al.(2021) found that amongst infants (3 - 12 months), ScT was inversely associated with nighttime sleep duration. Sun et al.(2022) studied the Association between Average Evening Screen Time(AEST) and sleep quality among sample belonging to different age groups and found that the response was different for people belonging to different age groups. Amongst the sample belonging to 18 to 34 years of age and 65 years and above, AEST has no relationship with sleep quality(Sq). However, for people between 35 to 64 years of age, AEST was harmful to the quality of sleep. Hjetland et al. (2021) observed that evening ScT is more strongly related with ST than the total ScT in a day. Nakshine et al. (2022) found that excessive ScT has a damaging effect on the sperm viability and motility. Social media addiction is one of the major reasons behind screen time and has become a necessary evil today, therefore; it is advisable to use smartphones and other sources of blue light in a disciplined manner.

According to Christakis et al. (2018), audio-visual media exposure during early childhood can lead to attention deficit hyperactivity disorder (ADHD) and according to the emerging literature; it may also cause other psychiatric disorders amongst teens. Young children spending more than 8 hours a week on home computers with very less to barely no time on outdoor sports have considerably higher body mass index (BMI) than others who are active in outdoor sports (Attewell et al., 2003). Children who were exposed to cell phones both prenatal and postnatal showcased higher behavioural problems in comparison to the ones who had exposure during either or neither of the time periods (Divan et al., 2012). Beyens et al., (2018) observed that a very insignificant relationship exists between Screen usage & attention deficit hyperactivity disorder among kids and teenagers does exist but the relationship is quite small. Use of electronics at least 1 hour before bedtime has been observed to have affected the quality and duration of sleep among Americans casting an adverse effect on the health of users (Chang A. M., et al., 2015). Most the teens get less than nine hours (a mandatory requirement for their age group) of sleep per night. This lack of appropriate sleep affects academic performance, physical and mental health. It may also lead to cardiovascular and metabolic diseases (George & Davis, 2013).

Lerner (2015) observed both positive and negative implications of screen exposure. According to the researcher on one hand umpteen studies support that excessive watching of television in childhood may affect attention, learning, sleep, and even weight contrary to this if content, context, and the personality of the child is monitored properly then the same may serve as an amazing learning tool. Paper reading is better than screens as the latter utilizes more mental resources and helps us retain relatively less than what is achieved by reading a paper (Jabr, 2013).

A child's bedroom with more displays was linked to increased adiposity, greater overall screen time and lesser effective sleep. The form of screen presence that seems to be connected to a greater level of adiposity is having a TV in the bedroom. These results are increasingly relevant to health promotion measures given the prevalence of screens amongst youngsters (Chaput J.P., et al., (2014). Limiting certain forms of ScT still makes sense since excessive sedentary and passive ScT have been linked to detrimental effects on a young child's development. To clarify the specific kinds of technology usage that should be restricted, the 1999 two-hour recommendation may need to be revised. Guidelines on time allocation may be helpful as technology usage must be balanced with other activities (Daugherty, et al., 2014). Lacy et al., (2012) found that lower physical activity(PA), and high screen usage adversely affects health-related quality of life(HRQoL). According to Margarita et al., (2017), body obesity serves as a very important predictor of HRQoL, the games enhance, and television (TV) and video games worsen it. Guardians and physicians must know that all screen and exercise-based behaviours may not have clear associations with the child's HRQoL.

2.2 Alternatives to Screen Time

More homework hours has a favorable impact on Secondary Education results however, there is virtually little association between test results and screen use (Hawkes, 2015). Children who live in neighborhoods with adequate services, sidewalks, and neighborhood satisfaction are considerably more likely to participate in screen time of not more than two hours and engage more in physical activity. They are also more likely to use active transportation to go 'to and from' school in neighborhoods with nice parks and sidewalks. However, the perceived safety of the neighborhood did not affect activities. The installation of sidewalks is also suggested so that people may use bikes or walk to school (Carson et al., 2010).

2.3 Effects of Caffeine

Drake et al., (2013) recommended refraining caffeine consumption (tea/coffee) at least 6 hours prior to bedtime to have a sound sleep. According to Burke et al., (2015), caffeine if consumed immediately before bedtime delays the triggering of sleep. Orbeta et al., (2006), conducted cross-sectional studies over more than 15,000 American adolescents and found that students consuming high caffeine daily comparatively wake up more tired in the morning than ones with less consumption.

2.4 Effects of Sleep Schedule

McMahon et al., (2020) found that a proper sleep schedule gives relatively better sleep than having an unstructured sleep schedule. Kang and Chen (2009) observed that students without a proper routine of bedtime generally experience a bad quality of sleep. LeBourgeois et al. (2005) addressed the role of Sleep hygiene in imparting better quality of sleep among teenagers from Italy and America. They recommended that the good sleep hygiene practices should be made the part of course curriculum.

3. Objective

Through the present research, authors made an attempt to study the impact of following over the quality (waking up fresh / soundness of sleep) as well as the quantity (number of hours of sleep) of the sleep.

- Screen timing including exposure to blue light in any form and media
- Drinking coffee/tea before sleep time
- Regular sleep-wake routines

3.1 Null Hypothesis

H^01: Exposure to blue light in any form and media has no significant impact on sleep time

H^02: Drinking coffee/tea before sleeping has no significant impact on the number of hours of sleep

H^03: Regular bedtime has no significant impact on the quality of sleep (freshness whenever one wakes up)

4. Research Methodology

Data was collected from secondary as well as primary sources of information through stratified random sampling. The sample size was 300 belonging to three different age groups including, 12 to 18 years, 18 to 25 years, and 25 to 45 years. The data was collected through online as well as offline questionnaire surveys conducted in the city of Pune (Maharashtra). Students with a history of sleep disorders and on other medications were excluded from the study. Quality and pattern of sleep were assessed by using the Pittsburgh Sleep Quality Index(PSQI) questionnaire under seven components – subjective sleep quality, sleep latency, sleep duration, sleep disturbances, habitual sleep efficiency, use of sleeping medications, and daytime dysfunction over the past month. The findings were analysed through ANOVA, correlation, and regression tests with the help of SPSS 21.

5. Data Analysis and Interpretation

Figures 13.1 and 13.2 below depict the demographic distribution of our study in terms of age and gender. The sample collected was homogeneous with equal representation from all three age groups of school-going students, college students, and professionals / other employees to correctly record the responses of the population that has no choice but to use screens for their academic and professional work. The advent of covid has further added to the miseries.

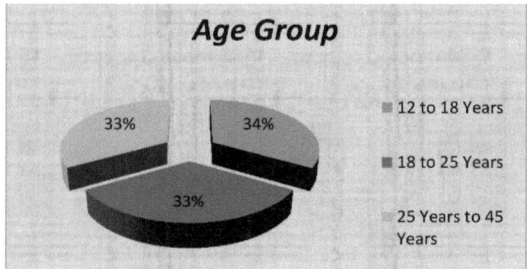

Fig. 13.1 Age group

Source: Made by author based on data analysis

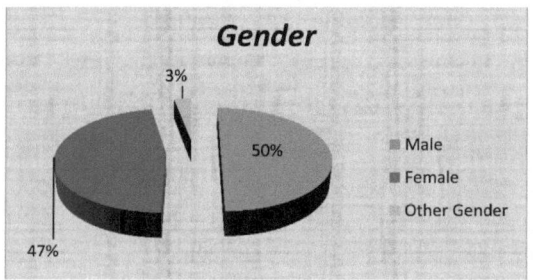

Fig. 13.2 Gender

Source: Made by author based on data analysis

The sample had a representation of 47 percent of females, 50 percent of males, and 3 percent of other gender. It is interesting to note that the responses of all three genders did not exhibit much of a difference.

The data collected through a questionnaire survey was run through SPSS 21 and gave the following results.

5.1 Impact of Exposure to Blue Light in Any Form and Media over Sleep Time

Table 13.1 (T1): Regression

Variables Entered/Removed(VarEnt/Rem)

M	VarEnt	VarRem	Meth
1	Frequency of exposure to blue light in any form and media[b]	.	Enter

a. Dependent Variable: Generally I sleep for   b. All variables entered.
Source: Made by author based on data analysis through SPSS21

Table 13,.2 T2: Sum of Model(M)

M	R	R Square(Sq.)	Adj R Sq.	Std. Error of Est
1	01.000[a]	01.000	01.000	0.0000

a. Predictors : (Constant), Frequency of exposure to blue light in any form and media
Source: Made by author based on data analysis through SPSS21

Table 13.3 ANOVA[a]

M		Sum of Squares	df	Mean Sq.	F	Sig.
1	Reg (Reg.)	565.490	1	565.490	.	.b
	Residual (Res.)	0.000	147	0.000		
	Tot.	565.490	148			

a. Dep.Var.: Generally I sleep for
b. Predictors: (Constant), Frequency of exposure to blue light in any form and media
Source: Made by author based on data analysis through SPSS21

Table 13.4 Coeff.[a]

M		Unstandardized (U S) Coeff.		Standardized (S) Coeff.	t	Sig.
		B	Std. Err.	β		
1	(Const.)	0.000	0.000		.	.
	Frequency of exposure to blue light in any form and media	1.000	0.000	1.000	.	.

a. Dependent Variable: Generally I sleep for longer hours
Source: Made by author based on data analysis through SPSS21

The ANOVA table above clearly shows that exposure to blue light in any form & and media and the sleep time has no significant relationship. Hence the First null hypothesis i.e., $H^0 1$: Exposure to blue light in any form and media has no significant impact over sleep time, gets accepted.

5.2 Impact of Drinking Coffee/Tea Before Sleeping Over Quantity of Sleep

Table 13.5 T5: Reg

Var Ent/Rem[a]

M	VarEnt	VarRem	Method
1	I take tea/coffee before going to bed[b]	.	Ent.

a. Dep. Var.: My sleep is disturbed   b. All var. ent.
Source: Made by author based on data analysis through SPSS21

Table 13.6 Summary of Model(M)

M	R	R Sq	Adj R Sq	Std Err of the Est
1	.60[a]	0.36	.001	1.25527

a. Predictors: (Constant), I take tea/coffee before going to bed
Source: Made by author based on data analysis through SPSS21

Table 13.7 T7: ANOVA[a]

M		Sum Sq.	Df	Mean Sq	F	Sig
1	Reg.	03.494	01	03.494	.914	.000[b]
	Res.	561.995	147	3.823		
	Total	565.490	148			

a. Dependent Variable: My sleep is disturbed
b. Predictors: (Constant), I take tea/coffee before going to bed

Source: Made by author based on data analysis through SPSS21

The ANOVA table above clearly reveals that Drinking coffee/tea before sleeping and quantity of sleep has a significant relationship, as the significance value is less than .05. Hence the Second null hypothesis i.e. H^02: Drinking coffee/tea before sleeping has no significant impact over my sleeping hours, stands rejected and the alternate hypothesis stating Drinking coffee/tea before sleeping has significant impact over my sleeping hours, gets accepted.

Table 13.8 Coefficients

M		UN Coeff.		S Coeff.	t	Sig.
		B	Std. Err.	β		
1	(Const.)	5.318	.467		011.395	0.000
	I take tea/coffee before going to bed	.164	.087	.179	1.056	.05

a. Dependent Variable: My sleep is disturbed
Source: Made by author based on data analysis through SPSS21

T8 reflects that significance value is less than 0.05, t-value is positive, and the Beta value too is positive. All indicate that drinking Tea or coffee is positively related to the disturbance in sleeping i.e., if I drink tea/coffee before sleeping, my sleep is disturbed and I don't get a sound sleep.

5.3 Impact of Regular Bedtime on Quality of Sleep (Freshness Whenever One Wakes Up)

Table 13.9 Regression

Variables Entered(Ent.)/Removed(Rem,)[a]

M	Var. Ent.	Var. Rem.	Method
1	I have regular bedtime	.	Ent.

a. Dep. Var.: I wake up fresher
b. All var. ent.
Source: Made by author based on data analysis through SPSS21

Table 13.10 Summary of model (M)

M	R	R Sq	Adj R Sq	StdErr of the Est.
1	.70[a]	0.49	.001	1.51664

a. Predictors: (Constant), I have a regular bedtime
R square value indicates that it explains 49% of data.
Source: Made by author based on data analysis through SPSS21

Table 13.11 ANOVA[a]

M		Sum Sq	Df	MeanSq	F	Sig
1	Reg.	2.677	1	02.677	01.164	.000[b]
	Resi.	335.829	146	02.300		
	Tot.	338.507	147			

a. Dep. Var.: I wake up fresher   b. Predictors: (Constant), I have a regular bedtime
Source: Made by author based on data analysis through SPSS21

The ANOVA table above clearly shows that regular bedtime and waking up fresh in the morning have a significant relationship as; the significance value is less than .05. Hence the third null hypothesis, H^{03}: Regular bedtime has no significant impact over my freshness whenever I wake up, gets rejected and the alternate hypothesis stating "Regular bedtime has significant impact over my freshness whenever I wake up" gets accepted. Therefore, waking up early in the morning and sleeping on time is still a panacea for good health.

Table 13.12 Coeff.

M		US Coeff.		S Coeff.	t	Sig.
		B	Std. Err.	β		
1	(Const.)	05.135	.343		14.973	.000
	I have a regularbedtime	.170	.065	.189	1.079	.05

a. Dependent Variable: I wake up fresher
Source: Made by author based on data analysis through SPSS21

We see that the significance value is less than .05, the t-value is positive, and the Beta value too is positive. All indicate that regular bedtime is positively related to waking up fresh i.e., if I sleep early, I wake up fresh.

5.4 Measures to Reduce the Impact of Screen Time(ScT)

Figure 13.3 above has been drawn on the basis of the results obtained through the questionnaire survey. The findings reveal that there are various ways to minimize the impact of blue light (screen time) such as having access to parks and gyms in nearby vicinity; sleep health and hygiene as a compulsory subject in schools; active involvement of students in physical activities; and teaching screen

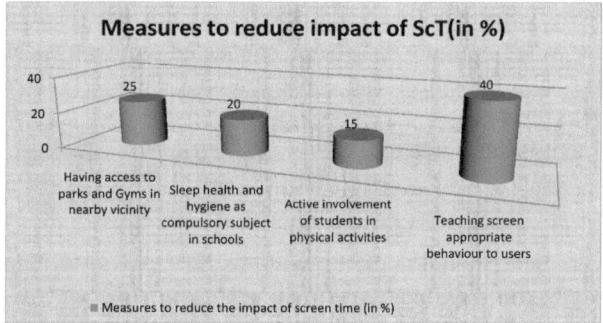

Fig. 13.3 Measures to reduce impact of ScT(in%)
Source: Made by author based on data analysis

appropriate behaviour to users. The support garnered from the sample for each of these options was 25, 15, 20 and 40 % respectively. Let us understand the meaning of "Teaching screen-appropriate behaviour to users". Teaching screen-appropriate behaviour to users includes, encouraging people to use Kindle and prefer printed papers over its digital version for reading, having proper light in the room; adjusting the contrast & and brightness of the screens, and most importantly using a blue light filter for PCs.

6. Conclusion

On the basis of findings, data analysis and interpretation the authors conclude that:

- The study revealed that inappropriate sleep is related to inattention and lack of concentration in the classroom among the teenagers.
- Drinking tea /coffee before going to bed makes kids take less sleep than recommended.
- The ones who have a schedule of sleeping on time get longer sleep.
- Proper and consistent sleep-wake rules at home impart better age-appropriate sleep. It was observed that adequate sleep quantity & and quality had a direct relationship with sleep hygiene rules (limited caffeine and regular bedtime).
- Insufficient sleep was found to have no relationship with exposure to blue light or screen timing. But the blue light is surely causing physical and mental ailments as supported by the review of literature too.

7. Recommendations

In view of the research it is recommended that the:

(a) Quality and quantity of sleep have very little impact over screen time. Rather other factors such as sleep hygiene principles are more significant and thus should be strictly followed.

(b) The caffeine consumption should be reduced or avoided before bedtime.

(c) Excessive screen timing has been connected with physical and mental ailments (lack of attention and concentration), especially during childhood and adolescence.

(d) Therefore, it is advisable to:

- Reduce the exposure to screen time
- Give up a sedentary lifestyle
- Government should come up with a strong policy to reduce sedentary lifestyles the way it has a policy for reducing tobacco (McAnally H.M., & Hancox R.J., 2014)
- Best way to handle the impact of blue light is to practice screen-appropriate behavior

8. Future Scope

As the present research was conducted in Pune, the future research may be carried out in rural India and other metros of the country so as to compare and verify the results of this research. The research may further be conducted among people with age beyond 45 years of age as nowadays, specifically during covid this age group has also learned to aggressively use screens for various activities ranging from work to entertainment.

REFERENCES

1. Arshad, D., Joyia, U. M., Fatima, S., Khalid, N., Rishi, A. I., Rahim, N. U. A., Bukhari, S. F., Shairwani, G. K. and Salmaan, A. (2021). The adverse impact of excessive smartphone screen time on sleep quality among young adults. *Sleep Science*, Vol. 14 No. 4, pp.337–341.

2. Attewell, P., Garcia, B. S., and Battle, J. (2003). Computers and Young Children: Social Benefit or Social Problem. *Social Forces*, Vol. 82 No. 1, pp. 277–296.

3. Beyens, I., Valkenburg, P. M., and Piotrowski, J.T. (2018). Screen media use and ADHD-related behaviors. *Proceedings of the National Academy of Sciences of the United States of America*, Vol. 115 No.40, pp. 9875–9881.

4. Burke, T. M., Markwald, R. R., McHill, A. W., Chinoy, E. D., Snider, J. A., Bessman, S. C., Jung, C. M., O'Neill, J. S., and Wright, K. P., Jr. (2015). Effects of caffeine on the human circadian clock in vivo and in vitro. *Science translational medicine*, Vol. 7 No. 305, pp. 305–346.

5. Carson, V., Kuhle S., Spence, J. C. and Veugelers, P.J. (2010). Parents' Perception of Neighbourhood Environment as a Determinant of Screen Time, Physical Activity and Active Transport. *Canadian Journal of Public Health / Revue Canadienne de Santé Publique* , Vol. 101 No. 2, pp. 124–127.

6. Chang, A. M., Aeschbach, D., Duffy, F. J., and Czeisler, C. A. (2015). Evening use of light-emitting eReaders negatively affects sleep, circadian timing, and next-morning alertness. *Proceedings of the National Academy of Sciences of the United States of America*, Vol.112 No. 4, pp. 1232–1237.

7. Chaput, J.P., Leduc, G., Boyer, C., Bélanger, P., LeBlanc, A. G., Borghese, M. M. and Tremblay, M.S. (2014). Electronic screens in children's bedrooms and adiposity, physical activity and sleep: Do the number and type of electronic devices matter? *Canadian Journal of Public Health / Revue Canadienne de Santé Publique* , Vol. 105 No. 4, pp. 273–279.

8. Christakis, D. A., Ramirez, J. S. B., Ferguson, S.M., Ravinder, S. and Ramirez, J. M. (2018), How early media exposure may affect cognitive function. *Proceedings of the National Academy of Sciences of the United States of America*, Vol. 115 No. 40, pp. 9851–9858.

9. Claire, L. (2015). Screen Sense: Making Smart Decisions about Media Use for Young Children. *YC Young Children*, Vol. 70 No. 1, pp. 102–103.

10. Daugherty, L., Dossani, R., Johnson, E. E. and Wright, C.(2014). Moving Beyond Screen Time Redefining Developmentally Appropriate Technology Use in Early Childhood Education. *Moving Beyond Screen Time*, RAND Corporation.

11. Divan, H. A., Kheifets, L., Obel, C. and Olsen, J. (2012). Cell phone use and behavioural problems in young children. *Journal of Epidemiology and Community Health*, Vol. 66 No. 6, pp. 524–529.

12. Drake, C., Roehrs, T., Shambroom, J., Roth, T. (2013). Caffeine effects on sleep taken 0, 3, or 6 hours before going to bed. *J Clin Sleep Med*, Vol. 9 No. 11, pp. 1195–1200.

13. Emond, J. A., O'Malley, A. J., Neelon, B., Kravitz, R. M., Ostbye, T., Neelon, S. E. B. (2021). Associations between daily screen time and sleep in a racially and socioeconomically diverse sample of US infants: a prospective cohort study. *BMJ Open*, Vol. 11 No. 6, e044525.

14. George, N.M., and Davis, J.E. (2013). Assessing Sleep in Adolescents through a Better Understanding of Sleep Physiology. *American Journal of Nursing*, Vol. 113 No. 6, pp. 26–32.

15. Gupta, P. C., Rana, M., Ratti, M., Duggal, M., Agarwal, A., Khurana, S., Jugran, D., Bhargava, N., Ram, J. (2022). Association of screen time, quality of sleep and dry eye in college going women of Northern India. *Indian J Ophthalmol*, Vol. 70, pp. 51–58.

16. Guzmán, V., Lissner, L., Arvidsson, L., Hebestreit, A., Solea, A., Lauria, F., Kaprio, J., Reisch, L. A., Hawkes, N. (2015). Every hour of daily screen time knocks two grades off teenagers' exam scores, study shows. *BMJ: British Medical Journal*, Vol. 351, pp. 231–41.

17. Hjetland, G. J., Skogen, J. C., Hysing, M. and Sivertsen, B. (2021). The Association between Self-Reported Screen Time, Social Media Addiction, and Sleep among Norwegian University Students. *Front Public Health* Vol. 9:794307.

18. Jabr, F.(2013). Why the Brain Prefers Paper? *Scientific American*, Vol. 309 No. 5, pp. 48–53.

19. Drumheller, K. and Fan, C. W., (2022). Unprecedented times and uncertain connections: A systematic review examining sleep problems and screen time during the COVID-19 pandemic. *Sleep Epidemiology*; Vol. 2,100029.

20. Kang, J. H. and Chen, S. C. (2009). Effects of an irregular bedtime schedule on sleep quality, daytime sleepiness, and fatigue among university students in Taiwan. *BMC Public Health*; Vol. 9: 248. https://10.1186/1471-2458-9-248

21. Lacy, K.E., Allender, S. E., Kremer, P. J., Sanigorski, A.M.D.S., Millar, L.M., Moodie, M.L., Mathews, L.B., Malakellis, M. and Swinburn, B. A. (2012). Screen time and physical activity behaviours are associated with health-related quality of life in Australian adolescents. *Quality of Life Research*, Vol. 21 No. 6, pp. 1085–1099.

22. LeBourgeois, M. K., Giannotti, F., Cortesi, F., Wolfson, A. R., Harsh, J. (2005). The Relationship between Reported Sleep Quality and Sleep Hygiene in Italian and American Adolescents. *Pediatrics* Vol. 115 No. 1, pp. 257–265.

23. Tsiros, M. D., Samaras, M. G., Coates, A. M., and Olds, T. (2017). Use-of-time and health-related quality of life in 10- to 13-year-old children: not all screen time or physical activity minutes are same. *Quality of Life Research*, Vol. 26 No. 11, pp. 3119–3129.

24. McAnally, H. M. and Hancox, R. J. (2014). The long-term health effects of too much television: whose responsibility? *Journal of Epidemiology and Community Health,* Vol. 68 No. 10, pp. 905.

25. McMahon, W. R., Ftouni, S., Phillips, A. J. K., Beatty, C., Lockley, S. W., Rajaratnam, S. M. W., Maruff, P., Drummond, S. P. A., Anderson, C. (2020). The impact of structured sleep schedules prior to an in-laboratory study: Individual differences in sleep and circadian timing. *PLoS One*, Vol. 15 No. 8.

26. Guzmán V, Lissner L, Arvidsson L, Hebestreit A, Solea A, Lauria F, Kaprio J, Reisch L, A, Moreno L, Felső R, de Henauw S, Veidebaum T, Ahrens W, Hunsberger M(2022). Associations of Sleep Duration and Screen Time with Incidence of Overweight in European Children: The IDEFICS/I.Family Cohort. *Obesity Facts*, Vol. 15, pp. 55–61.

27. Nakshine, V. S., Thute, P., Khatib, M. N., and Sarkar, B. (2022). Increased Screen Time as a Cause of Declining Physical, Psychological Health, and Sleep Patterns: A Literary Review. *Cureus*, Vol. 14 No. 10: e30051.

28. Orbeta, R. L., Overpeck, M. D., Ramcharran, D., Kogan, M. D., Ledsky, R. (2006). High caffeine intake in adolescents: associations with difficulty sleeping and feeling tired in the morning. *J Adolesc Health*, Vol. 38 No. 4, pp. 451–453.

29. Sun, L., Li, K., Zhang, L. and Zhang, Y. (2022). Distinguishing the Associations between Evening Screen Time and Sleep Quality among Different Age Groups: A Population-Based Cross-Sectional Study. *Frontiers in Psychiatry,* Vol. 13.

Emerging Horizons: Business and Society in the Post Pandemic Era –
Brig. Dr. Rajiv Divekar et al. (eds)
© 2024 Taylor & Francis Group, London, ISBN 978-1-032-90822-9

14

Psychological Effects of Covid 19 on Employee Engagement a Comparison Between Employees Working Remotely and Employees Working in Person

Pradnya Vishwas Chitrao[1]
Professor, Symbiosis Institute of Management Studies (SIMS),
Symbiosis International Deemed University

Pravin Kumar Bhoyar[2]
Deputy Director, Symbiosis Institute of Management Studies (SIMS),
Symbiosis International Deemed University

Brig Rajiv Divekar[3]
Director, Symbiosis Institute of Management Studies (SIMS),
Symbiosis International Deemed University

Swapnil Vaidya[4]
Symbiosis Institute of Management Studies (SIMS),
Symbiosis International Deemed University

ABSTRACT

The Corona2019 lockdown in India to stop the disease from spreading changed the working culture throughout. The study aims to analyse & compare the current state of the employees operating online from home & the employees working in person on the variables of Depression, Perceived Stress, Employee Engagement & Mental Health. Comparative 2-group design is used. Sample (N=204) is collected in the online mode through Google Forms. The data is collected from people working from home (N=117) & employees working from the company (N=87) using Burn's Depression Checklist, Perceived Stress Scale, Gallup's Employee Engagement Questionnaire & Mental Health Checklist. Mean scores are compared followed by Mann-Whitney U test is applied. The findings showed that the employees working from home are more depressed, more stressed, have less employee engagement& have a bad condition of mental health than the employees working from the office. The results have various implications in the MNCs & the organizations following work from home culture.

KEYWORDS: Employee engagement, Psychological effects of Covid 19, Remote working, Working in person, Perceived stress, Mental health

[1]pradnyac@sims.edu, [2]pravink@sims.edu, [3]director@sims.edu, [4]swapnil.pgdm2021@sims.edu

DOI: 10.4324/978100355996-14

1. Introduction

The initial human manifestations of COVID-19 (Coronavirus Disease of 2019) were first made public by bureaucrats in Wuhan City, China, in December 2019. Consequently, it spread from China to various countries. Majorly, it spread from the air passengers from country to country & India was not an exception. Most countries imposed the intervention of the lockdown to control the spread of the coronavirus. India also enforced lockdown from 25th March 2020, initially for 21 days which was extended gradually. The Covid-19 pandemic changed the world throughout, and affected the way we functioned. Almost everyone in the country was stranded at homes & hence pushed to start working from home.

Today, working from home can be seen as the new normal for many employees. This major shift can affect a person in several ways. The proposed research is centred on the comparative analysis of the number of factors between the employees working from home & the employees going to the workplace to fulfil their job duties & responsibilities.

1.1 COVID-19 Pandemic & Intervention of Lockdown

A pandemic is called an epidemic when it takes place all over the world, and usually affects a lot of people. The Merriam-Webster dictionary, defines COVID-19 as a serious respiratory disease caused primarily by exposure to infectious material (e.g., respiratory diseases). and which is easily transmitted from person to person. Consequently, people need a lock to remain wherever they are, usually because of posing a risk to themselves or others if they move around without restriction. During the COVID-19 epidemic, the phrase lockdown mainly referred to rules about social distancing and isolating by remaining at home. At the beginning of April 2020, 3.9 billion people around the globe could not step out of their homes except during permitted time frames to buy essentials. By April end, around 90 percent of the people in the world were locked in the United States and in India.

1.2 Nature of Work

In this research, nature of work refers to the place from where the employee is carrying her/his duties & responsibilities. Working from home (WFH) refers to the system in which employees can work from their own homes, rather than coming physically to office. Working from the office refers to the arrangement where the employees travel from their home to the workplace or company's office to fulfil their duties & responsibilities.

1.3 Depression

Depression is a grave medical illness wherein one feels, thinks and acts in a negative manner. It creates sadness and results in a lack of interest in activities that were earlier considered as interesting. If left untreated, it can cause various emotional and physical problems and can impact one's capacity to function both professionally and also at a personal level.

1.4 Perceived Stress

Stress is a feeling of tension and pressure. Stress in small measures is often useful, and productive. Positive stress generally enhances motivation, develops the urge to adapt, and respond positively to the environment. However, stress can lead to personal injury. Stressful stressors include thelack of control or guaranty of one's life, excessive irritability, excessive changes occurring in a person's life, and absence of confidence for dealing with the issues being faced.

1.5 Mental Health

Mental health is the emotional, psychological and social state of well-being in which every person attains one's potential, copes with day to day, usual stresses of life, and is capable of fruitfully working, & contributing to society. The importance of mental health is accentuated in World Health Organization's (WHO) description of health wherein it is stated that Health is a condition of total physical, mental & social well-being & does not refer only to the lack of ailment or debility. Evidence from the World Health Organization indicates that nearly half the population in the world is afflicted by mental illness that severely affects their self-esteem, relationships & even their ability to function in everyday life (Stories, 2010).

According to Dr. Pramod Kumar there are 5 physical dimensions of mental health:

- **Headache:** A headache may manifest as a sharp pain, feeling of palpitations or dull pain. Headaches may develop slowly or abruptly and may last from one hour to several days.
- **Fatigue:** It is complete exhaustion of energy or strength. It is a feeling of lack of work capacity and decreased efficiency.
- **Sleeplessness:** Sleep disorders are all conditions that impair sleep except environmental factors.
- **Indigestion:** It is an uneasy feeling (such as pain or burning sensation) in the stomach or chest due to difficulty in digesting food.
- **Acidity:** It is a burning sensation in the central region of the chest or the upper central part of the abdomen which can make you feel angry.

Good mental health is the mental state of a person working at satisfactory levels of emotional and behavioural adjustment. But mental illness refers to all clinical mental disorders simultaneously: a health condition distinguished by disorders of thought, mood, or behaviour that are related to stress or dysfunction.

1.6 Employee Engagement

Employee engagement measures and governs employee attitudes regarding key elements of work culture. One can determine whether employees are actively involved in their work or are simply spending their time. Then, you can decide how to enhance your employees' association with their assignments and the organization. Gallup pinpointed 12 aspects of employee commitment that forecast high team performance. Executives can measure engagement by interviewing and rating their subordinates' answers to these 12 survey questions to develop a framework for their interactions with employees. E.g., occasional meetings, meeting schedules, performance reviews, and team goals.

1.7 Statement of the Problem

To analyse the effects of COVID-19 Pandemic on Depression, Soundness of Mind, Perceived Stress, Working Engagement & compare it on the employees working remotely & working in person.

1.8 Rationale & Significance of the Study

The year 2020-21 will be highlighted in history as it has changed many things throughout, especially the way we work. Working from home has become a common phenomenon for most MNCs like Google & Microsoft. Still, the question remains which is the ideal way of working – from home or the workplace. There are cons & pros of each but also there are several factors which will get affected by this nature of the job, which an organization has to consider.

Working in the new normal can be a bliss for many employees & on the other hand, it can prove to be a curse.

2. Objectives

The objectives of the research are-

1. To measure & compare the amount of Depression between the employees who were operating from home & the employees working from office premises.
2. To compute & compare the level of Perceived Tension between the employees working from home & the employees physically coming to office.
3. To measure & compare the degree of Employee Engagement between people working from home & the employees working from the office.
4. To analyse & compare the condition of Mental Health between the employees who were executing work from home & the employees operating from the company office.

3. Review of Literature

3.1 Depression

Depression is treated as the first DV in the research. Marimuthu et al. (2020) conducted a research survey of people operating from home during the pandemic in Malaysia. Out of 104 respondents interviewed, 81 respondents had a score of

3 or more out of 5 for stress and pressure on housework. In addition, a total of 81 respondents stated that they dealt with depression, depression and insomnia during COVID-19. This showed that there was a strong psychological impact on employees working from home during the COVID-19 epidemic. Dawel et al. (2020) concluded that epidemics & intervention of lockdown were strongly associated with an increase in signs of depression and anxiety, as well as also a decrease in mental well-being. These results suggest that improving social functioning and participation in community social activities are important in reducing epidemic-related effects on mental health and wellbeing.

3.2 Perceived Stress

The research suggested that social isolation may be the reason for a lot of mental health problems such as acute stress disorder, irritable moods, inability to sleep, emotional anguish, and mood disorders, despondency, worries, and nervousness (Bai et al., 2004). An Iranian research article highlighted the role of unpredictability, insecurity, disease severity, inaccurate information, and social segregation as leading to stress and psychological bitterness in the COVID-19 epidemic. The researchers emphasized the requirement for psychological assistance, especially for susceptible folks, as also the building up of social capital to alleviate the negative cognitive effects of the pandemic (Zandifer and Badrapham, 2020).

3.3 Employee Engagement

Go (2016) called for a focus on fatal errors and the downfall of working from home, the cultural differences employees face during webinars. Working from home creates a large communication gap between supervisors and subordinates that negatively affects employee engagement. The Brunswick Group (Mets, 2020) noted that companies need to develop employee retention and communication plans to help keep morale high and help their employees stay connected to theCOVID-19 pandemic. Communication with employees should be regular and frequent. Companies should encourage employees to share experiences about what they find challenging and how they may remain focused and productive.

3.4 Mental Health

The latest report by Blind, an unspecified US based accomplished network with 3.2 million confirmed users, reported that 52.9 percent of responders from organizations like Google, Facebook, Amazon, Apple, LinkedIn, and Walmart were experiencing melancholy during WFH because of communal distancing. Also, almost 56.4 percent of persons who were surveyed by Blind found they had undergone worry during WFH and social isolation. Around 53 percent said they were encountering mental wellbeing problems (Coronavirus: Why work from home no longer seems like a perk even at Google, Facebook, 2020).

A study focusing on Lockdown concluded that imposed lockdown is an unknown and distressing experience that entails remaining away from companions and family, and a moving away from normal schedules which causes psychosocial problems. Social help is most required during unfavourable times such as the corona epidemic; so, cutting off social aid by way of a mandatory lockdown plan can jeopardize a person's feeling of affinity and may considerably affect mental wellbeing (Hawryluck et al., 2004).

Another research indicated that the largescale escalation of COVID-19 could result in a psychological health crisis, more so in nations having high number of cases (Dong and Bouey, 2020) which would necessitate on a major proportion both psychosocial crisis interventions, and even the inclusion of therapy that will promote mental wellbeing in future disaster management plans. In another research (Duan and Zhu, 2020) it was found that Occidental nations have included cognitive arbitrations in their arrangements for malady eruptions.

4. Research Gap Analysis

Review of literature reflects that working from home does have some pros but it also has other repercussions. The studies mentioned are concluding that COVID-19 Pandemic has elevated levels of Depression, and Perceived Tension, & also the condition of Mental Health of the individuals is negatively affected. Also, some studies focused on employees working from home where they were found to be facing difficulties with respect to employee engagement.

Review of extensive literature suggested that scarce heed was paid to employees working from office. Hence the researchers decided to do comparative analysis between the 2 groups, i.e., the employees working from home & working from the office on the variables of Depression, Perceived Stress, Employee Engagement & Mental Health.

This is the most prominent research gap as the comparison was not done between the employees operating from home & the employees reporting physically to office during COVID-19 pandemic.

It was also found that more in-depth studies need to be conducted in India.

4.1 Variables

Independent Variable (IV):

Nature of Work (Working from the home & Working from the office)

Dependent Variables (DVs):
1. Depression
2. Perceived Stress
3. Employee Engagement
4. Mental Health

Controlled Variables:

1. Nationality
2. Employment Condition
3. White Collar Workers

Operational Definitions of the Variables:

Nature of Work (Working from the home & Working from the office)

Working from the home refers to an employee fulfilling his/her job duties & responsibilities in the online mode from his/her home.

Working from the office refers to an employee is actually going to the workplace to fulfil his/her job duties & responsibilities.

4.2 Depression

Depression is defined on the basis of 14 dimensions by David D. Burns (1989) which is given as follows:

1. Sorrow
2. Disappointment
3. Low Self Respect
4. Subservience
5. Culpability
6. Irresoluteness
7. Annoyance and exasperation
8. Loss of interest in life
9. Loss of inducement
10. Poor self-perception
11. Appetite changes
12. Loss of sexuality
13. Illness Anxiety Disorder
14. Self-destructive impulses

Perceived Stress:

Perceived Stress is operationally defined by Sheldon Cohen (1983) as how well one is dealing with stress that has occurred in the previous month.

Mental Health:

Mental health is functionally defined by Dr. Pramod Kumar (1992) as the absence of physical health & mental health symptoms.

Physical Health is operationally defined as the lack of the signs like Headache, Tiredness, Disturbed Sleep, Indigestion & Acidity.

Mental Health is operationally defined as the absence of the symptoms like Anxiety & Tension, Restlessness, Nervousness, Loneliness, Hopelessness & Anger.

4.3 Design of the Experiment

A quantitative descriptive research design is used for the study. Two groups were the employees working from home & the employees working from the office. As the research was conducted in the online mode, a snowball sampling method was used.

5. Hypotheses

1. The employees operating from their residence would have a higher level of depression than the employees working from the office.
2. The employees functioning from home would have a higher level of perceived stress than the employees working from the office.
3. The employees working from home would have a lower level of employee engagement than the employees working from the office.
4. The employees working from home would have a worse condition of mental health than the employees working from the office.

5.1 Sample

The research was conducted online. There was total 79 males & 125 females in the study. All the employees were working in India & all were white collar workers.

5.2 Tools

Total 4 standardized tools used for the current research are Burn's Depression Checklist, Perceived Stress Scale, Gallup's Employee Engagement Questionnaire & Mental Health Checklist. A Personal Data Sheet is also used to get personal information of the employees.

5.3 Personal Data Sheet

Personal Data Sheets contain sections like Name (Optional), Email id (optional), Gender, Age, is employee working from the home or working from the office, Work Experience, Name of the organization, etc.

5.4 Burn's Depression Checklist

The Burns Depression Checklist (BDC) is a very prestigiously rated scale for depression created by David Burns, MD.

The BDC version of 1984 consisted of 15 questions. The circumstances for the responses are "during the past week from today" and is scored from 0 to 4, from the range of "not at all" to "extremely".

5.5 Mental Health Checklist (MHC)

Mental health checklist computes pre-illness mental position of the person. It was developed by Dr. Pramod Kumar in 1992. The application of this scale was meant as an examination of the pre-illness mental state of a respondent. The final form of the MHC consists of 11 items -6 mental and 5 somatic, given in a 4-point rating format.

The split-half reliability came to 0.70 (N=30) having a reliability index of 0.83. The test-retest reliability was 0.65 (N=30) with a reliability index of 0.81. The retest was administered two weeks later.

5.6 Perceived Stress Scale (PSS)

PSS is used by psychologists for measuring the perception of stress in an individual's life. Sheldon Cohen created this scale in 1983. The scale has ten questions on a five-point scale for comparing an individual's perceived stress on account of circumstances or events.

The reliability scores of the PSS (all 10 items) and its two subscales showed acceptable internal consistencies by achieving the cut-off of $\alpha > 0.70$ in the sample. The PSS has shown prominent psychometric properties, having good reliability and construct validity & is proved as a unidimensional measure of perceived tension.

5.7 Gallup's Employee Engagement Questionnaire

The Gallup Workplace Audit consists of 12 items that compute employee perceptions of work characteristics. There are 5 options ranging from Strongly Agree to Strongly Disagree for each question on the Likert Scale.

5.8 Procedure for Data Collection

Google Form was used to collect the data in the online mode due to COVID-19 Pandemic. Time period to complete the data collection was 46 days starting from 1st July 2021 to 15th August 2021. Confidentiality was assured by the researcher & no individual data is reported in the research throughout.

5.9 Demographics of the Sample

The full sample size selected for the research is 204 employees & the demographics of the sample are discussed as below:

The total sample size is 204 employees out of which 117 were working from home & 87 were working from office.

The total sample size is 204 employees out of which 80 employees are below 25 years age cap. Another 80 employees are within the age bracket of 25 to 35 years. Between 36 to 45 years age bracket there are 27 employees and remaining 17 employees are above 45 years age bracket.

Out of the total sample of 204 employees, 79 are male while 125 are female employees. All 204 employees included in the sample are working from India. Out of the total sample, 79 employees were having less than 2 years of work experience. 70 employees i.e., 34.3% of the total sample are having work experience of 2 to 5 years. 26 employees are having experience of between 6 to 10 years while 29 employees have worked for more than 10 years.

5.10 Descriptive Statistics

From Table 14.2, it is evident that there is a lot of difference between the means of all 4 variables between the employees operating from home & the employees actually coming to office.

On the variable of Depression, the mean of the employees working from home is **15.70** & that of employees working from office is **6.63** which means the employees working from home are more depressed than that of the employees working from office.

On the variable of Perceived Stress, the mean of the employees working from home is **18.71** & that of employees working from office is **10.84** which means the employees working from home are more stressed than that of the employees working from office.

On the variable of Employee Engagement, the mean of the employees working from home is **40.4615** & that of employees working from office is **52.3793** which means the employees working from home are having less employee engagement than that of the employees working from office.

On the variable of Mental Health, the mean of the employees working from home is **24.8718** & that of employees working from office is **16.7241** which means the employees working from home are having bad condition of mental health than that of the employees working from office.

6. Report

Q. How are you working currently?		Depression Total Score	Perceived Stress Total Score	Employee Engage-ment Total Score	Mental Health Total Score
Working from Home	Mean	**15.70**	**18.71**	**40.4615**	**24.8718**
	N	117	117	117	117
	Std./Deviation	11.296	7.166	12.75265	8.64385
Working from Office (Going to the office for work)	Mean	**6.63**	**10.84**	**52.3793**	**16.7241**
	N	87	87	87	87
	Std. Deviation	6.425	7.317	8.45679	6.80234
Total	Mean	**11.83**	**15.35**	**45.5441**	**21.3971**
	N	204	204	204	204
	Std. Deviation	10.517	8.200	12.57541	8.86651

Test of Normality of Sample:

To test the normality of distribution, Kolmogorov–Smirnov Test is used. The findings of Kolmogorov-Smirnov Test for the sample indicated that p values of all the variables are lesser than 0.05 i.e., at 5% level of significance, and therefore Normal Distribution is not followed.

Result Table:

Kolmogorov-Smirnov test for normality

Tests of Normality			
	Kolmogorov-Smirnov[a]		
	Statistic	df	Sig.
Depression Total	.231	66	.000
Perceived Stress Scale Total	.148	66	.001
Employee Engagement Total	.192	66	.000
Mental Health	.211	66	.000

a. Lilliefors Significance Correction

Interpretation:

Initially, the investigator planned to use Student's t-test; but the results of Kolmogorov-Smirnov Test of the sample on all the variables are lesser than 0.05 ($p<0.05$). This means that data is not following the Normal Distribution Curve.

6.1 Test of Homogeneity of Variances

Homogeneous, or equal, variance is evident when the standard deviations of samples are more or less equal. But as interpreted in the last point, the Normality of Data is not followed. Hence, the investigator decided to use Mann-Whitney U test for inferential statistics which is a non-parametric test. This is discussed in the next point.

6.2 Inferential Statistics

As the sample was not following all the assumptions for Student's t-test, Mann-Whitney U Test is used which is a non-parametric test.

Interpretation:

Table 14.1, Table 14.2, Table 14.3 & Table 14.4 are the result tables of Mann-Whitney U Test for the variables Depression, Perceived Stress, Employee Engagement & Mental Health respectively. **Asymp. Sig. (2-tailed) Value** from these tables is **.000** for all the variables- Depression, Perceived Stress, Employee Engagement & Mental Health respectively. This means the difference of means on all the 4 variables is significant as all the values are less than 0.05 ($p<0.05$).

Discussion:

Overall interpretation of the results is discussed here with respect to each of the hypotheses.

There are total 4 hypotheses in the research study which are discussed here one by one.

Result Tables

Table 14.1   Mann-Whitney *U* test for depression

Ranks				
	3. Where are you currently working from?	**N**	**Mean Rank**	**Sum of Ranks**
Depression Total	Working from Home	117	124.68	14587.00
	Working from Office (Going to the office for work)	87	72.68	6323.00
	Total	204		

Test Statistics	
	Depression Total
Mann-Whitney U	2495.000
Wilcoxon W	6323.000
Z	-6.233
Asymp. Sig. (2-tailed)	**.000**

a. Grouping Variable: 3. Where are you currently working from?

Table 14.2   Mann-Whitney *U* test for perceived stress

Ranks				
	3. Where are you currently working from?	**N**	**Mean Rank**	**Sum of Ranks**
Perceived Stress Total	Working from Home	117	127.38	14903.00
	Working from Office (Going to the office for work)	87	69.05	6007.00
	Total	204		

Test Statistics	
	Perceived Stress Total
Mann-Whitney U	2179.000
Wilcoxon W	6007.000
Z	-6.988
Asymp. Sig. (2-tailed)	**.000**

a. Grouping Variable: 3. Where are you currently working from?

Depression

Mean of the first variable of Depression of the employees working from home **(M=15.70)** is much higher than the employees working from the office **(M=6.63)** & is consequential at **95%** level of significance.

As a result, the first hypothesis, **'The employees working from home would have high levels of depression than the employees working from the office'** is accepted.

Table 14.3   Mann-Whitney *U* test for employee engagement

Ranks				
	3. Where are you currently working from?	**N**	**Mean Rank**	**Sum of Ranks**
Employee Engagement Total	Working from Home	117	76.86	8993.00
	Working from Office (Going to the office for work)	87	136.98	11917.00
	Total	204		

Test Statistics	
	Employee Engagement Total
Mann-Whitney U	2090.000
Wilcoxon W	8993.000
Z	-7.204
Asymp. Sig. (2-tailed)	**.000**

a. Grouping Variable: 3. Where are you currently working from?

Table 14.4   Mann-Whitney *U* test for mental health

Ranks				
	3. Where are you currently working from?	**N**	**Mean Rank**	**Sum of Ranks**
Mental Health Total	Working from Home	117	127.15	14876.00
	Working from Office (Going to the office for work)	87	69.36	6034.00
	Total	204		

Test Statistics	
	Mental Health Total
Mann-Whitney U	2206.000
Wilcoxon W	6034.000
Z	-6.934
Asymp. Sig. (2-tailed)	**.000**

a. Grouping Variable: 3. Where are you currently working from?

Perceived Stress

Mean of the first variable of Perceived Stress of the employees working from home **(M=18.71)** is much higher than the employees working from the office **(M=10.84)** & also it is significant at the **95%** level of significance.

Thus, the second hypothesis, **'The employees working from home would have high levels of perceived stress than the employees working from the office'** is accepted.

Employee Engagement

Mean of the first variable of Employee Engagement of the employees working from home **(M=40.4615)** is much lower than the employees working from the office **(M=52.3793)** & also it is significant at the **95%** level of significance.

Thus, the third hypothesis, **'The employees working from home would have low level of employee engagement than the employees working from office'** is accepted.

Mental Health

Mean of the first variable of Mental Health of the employees working from home **(M=24.8718)** is much higher than the employees working from the office **(M=16.7241)** & also it is significant at the 95% level of significance.

Thus, the fourth hypothesis, **'The employees working from home would be having bad condition of mental health than the employees working from office'** is accepted.

7. Conclusion of the Study

The employees working from home are more depressed, more stressed, have less employee engagement & have a bad condition of mental health than the employees working from the office in the COVID-19 Pandemic in India.

8. Implications of the Study

The organizations which have the work from home culture should take care of their employees' mental health.

Organizations should conduct Employee Welfare Programs targeting to improve mental health & try to reduce the effects like Depression, Stress, Burnout, Anxiety, etc.

Organizations should provide their employees with psychological help. They can have a dedicated Counsellors for each department.

As social interactions play a vital role in maintaining the mental health as well as increasing the employee engagement, the organizations should function in informal groups having a friendly culture in the online mode.

9. Limitations of the Study

- Random sample is not used.
- The size of the sample is limited.
- The sample selected for the research belong to only India.
- All the participants in the sample are White Collar Workers.

- Pre COVID-19 pandemic data of individuals on the variables in the research was not reported.
- The investigator had no control at all in the data collection procedure as the data is collected in the online mode. Factors like environmental disturbances, noise, multitasking might have influenced the data.
- Extraneous or confounding variables like pay-cut, fear of layoffs, boredom, demotions, problems due to lockdown, family issues, especially prominent in COVID-19 pandemic are not controlled & could have influenced the levels of depression, stress, mental health & employee engagement.
- Qualitative analysis is not done due to time constraints.

10. Further Suggestions for Research

Research can be done using true experimental design using randomized sample.

Research should be conducted on a large sample.

Research needs to be implemented on Blue Collar Workers as well.

Sample with different characteristic such as different nationality needs to be tested.

Qualitative analysis should be done to support quantifications.

High levels of stress & depression, bad conditions of mental health and low levels of employee engagement can lead into less job satisfaction, high attrition rate, conflicts between the employees, low job performance, etc. These relationships need to be tested.

REFERENCES

1. Bai, Y., Lin, C., Lin, Y., Chen, J., Chue, C., Chou, P. (2004). Survey of stress reactions among health care workers involved with the SARS outbreak: Psychiatric Services.
2. Beck, A., Steer, R., and Brown, G. (1996) "Manual for the Beck Depression Inventory-II". San Antonio, TX: Psychological Corporation.
3. Burns, D. D. (1989). The Feeling Good Handbook. New York: William Morrow and Co.
4. Cohen, S., Kamarck, T., Mermelstein, R. (1983). A global measure of perceived stress. Journal of Health and Social Behavior.
5. Cohen, S., Williamson G. (1988). Perceived stress in a probability sample of the U.S. In: Spacapan S, Oskamp S, editors. The social psychology of health. Thousand Oaks, CA: Sage.
6. Coronavirus in India. Retrieved from: https://www.worldometers.info/coronavirus/country/india/
7. Coronavirus: Why work from home no longer seems like a perk even at Google, Facebook. Retrieved from: https://yourstory.com/2020/04/coronavirus-work-from-homeloneliness-anxiety-google-facebook?utm_pageloadtype=scroll

8. Dawel et al., (2020). The Effect of COVID-19 on Mental Health and Wellbeing in a Representative Sample of Australian Adults: Frontiers in Psychiatry.
9. Dong L., Bouey J. (2020). Public mental health crisis during COVID-19 pandemic, China.
10. Duan L., Zhu G. (2020). Psychological interventions for people affected by the COVID-19 epidemic. Lancet Psychiatry.
11. Go, R. (2016, May 9). The 7 deadly disadvantages of working from home: Hubstaff,
12. Hawryluck, L., et al., (2004). SARS control and psychological effects of quarantine: Emerging Infectious Diseases, Toronto, Canada.
13. Marimuthu, et al (2020). The psychological impact due to working from, home in COVID-19 Pandemic: A CASE STUDY.
14. Nair, S. (29 March 2020). "For a billion Indians, lockdown has not prevented tragedy". The Guardian.
15. Storrie, K., Ahern, K.; Tuckett, A. (2010). "A systematic review: Students with mental health problems—a growing problem". International Journal of Nursing Practice.

Note: All the tables in this chapter were made by the author.

Emerging Horizons: Business and Society in the Post Pandemic Era –
Brig. Dr. Rajiv Divekar et al. (eds)
© 2024 Taylor & Francis Group, London, ISBN 978-1-032-90822-9

15

Do Recommendations Help in Usage of Online Library Resources—Post-Covid Scenario?

Komal Chopra[1]
Symbiosis Institute of Management Studies
Symbiosis International (Deemed University),
Pune, India

Dipali More[2]
Library In-charge,
Symbiosis Institute of Management Studies,
Symbiosis International (Deemed University)
Pune, India

ABSTRACT

The purpose of the study is to evaluate the role of recommendations in usage of online library resources in post-covid scenario, The data for the study was collected from faculty of six different streams of education to understand how they recommended and what they recommended to students. Questionnaire method was used to collect the data which underwent statistical analysis. The results showed that faculty recommended various resources to students for their classroom learning and assignment but it was the quality of the online resource that determined its usage.

KEYWORDS: Library, Usage, Online resources, Faculty, Evaluation

1. Introduction

The academic library functions as a dynamic instrument of an educational institution (Cox, 2018). Academic libraries are assigned with six functions namely - (i) conservation of knowledge and ideas, (ii) teaching, (iii) research, (iv) publication, (v) extension service, and (vi) interpretation (Harland et.al, 2018).

---

[1]chopra.k@sims.edu, [2]library@sims.edu

DOI: 10.4324/978100355996-15

These functions are aligned with the mission, objective and subject area of the institution (Rampun, 2021). One of the major functions of an academic library is the disbursement of information through various resources (Atte and Ibikunle, 2017). In recent years, there has been an increasing focus on usage of online resources such as research databases, reports, articles and books in order to enable faculty and students to access information at a very rapid pace (Jessy and Rao, 2016) The growth of information technology has made it possible for the users to access information on their mobile devices (Mckie and Narayan, 2019).

Faculty are using online information resources to make their classroom session interesting as well as enhancing their research output (Allen and Taylor, 2017). Published literature on online resources has discussed the importance of online resources on academic output. It has highlighted the impact of usage of library resources on student learning (Smith, 2001). It also helps to promote student engagement in academic institutions (Salisbury and Peasley, 2018). Researchers also discussed the availability and accessibility of different library resources (Onye, 2016). The awareness of library resources also plays an impact on its usage (Wang and Bai, 2016). However, published literature does not evaluate the impact of endorsement of online resources by faculty on its usage by students and the pattern of usage.

Post-covid use of online library resources has gained importance due to availability of resources and habit of online mode of learning (Otike, 2021). The academic libraries are also providing extensive support to remote users for usage of online resources (Dube & Jacob, 2022). Hence, it's important to understand the motivational factors for using online resources in post covid scenario.

2. Literature Review

Researchers studied the various factors that affect information need of teaching staff. The finding shows that faculty who have extensive teaching and research experience make full utilization of library facilities (Behera and Satpathy, 2004). A study was done from faculty perspective to examine the attitude of faculty member toward the collaboration for online resources. The finding of research showed that the majority of faculty members had positive attitude towards collaboration (Shapiro, 2016). A group of researchers indicate that well designed endorsement program for online resources is beneficial for library staff, faculty and students and its success is dependent on the collaboration that librarian maintains with faculty and students (Core et. al., 2016). The endorsement can be done with the help of peer-to-peer interaction (O'Kelly et. al., 2015). The findings of a study make us realize that the increasing complex and strong commitment towards marketing of resources through word-of-mouth recommendations provide means for library to invest in online resources (Schimmelpfennig and Hunt, 2020).

University authorities and faculty have an important task of promoting library resources to students and researchers (Wang, 2016). That would help to spread awareness about online resources (McKie and Narayan, 2019). As demands become increasingly complex, a strong commitment to endorsement provides a means for increasing usage (Bakkalbasi, 2017). Apart from endorsements, workshops for usage of online resources in the form of training will motivate the students to use these resources (Thielen, 2018). Initially, the librarians should be trained and they would further train users of the resources (Mulongo, 2016). A researcher studied Vroom's expectancy theory to create user motivation. The theory suggested that having continuous focus on user needs and expectation and delivering resources. Another study focused on use of e-resources by faculty members and factors affecting their decision. Faculty are very positive about using library e-resources for increasing their academic productivity (Saunders, 2015).

Literature on adoption of online resources by students and faculty have highlighted the need of usage of technology (Yoon, 2016). Infrastructure, attitude, perception and expectations play an important role in adoption of technology (King and Boyatt, 2015). Studies have shown peer influence and adoption play an important role in adoption of online resources (Jung and Lee, 2020). The experience with online resources should meet the expectations of library users (Hernon and Altman, 2010).

Academic library services have explored various methods for supporting the higher education system in the post covid circumstances. Libraries have upgraded service quality, enhanced research support services, collaboration with faculty, stressing on importance of information literacy program and redesigned their digital landscape to meet the needs of users in (Sukula et. al., 2020). There is need to combine virtual and physical space is observed. Also, the need of users as "participatory" for creating user experience is included in new strategies (Panattoni, 2021). An integrated tech-led approach helped libraries continued functioning smoothly in new normal situation (Dadhe & Dubey, 2020, Abubakar, 2021). However, the current literature suffers from understanding the pattern of adoption and usage. The current study proposes to understand the patterns of adoption of online resources by students based on endorsement by faculty.

3. Research Methodology

The survey method was adopted to understand the faculty endorsement methods and its impact on usage of library information resources. The questionnaire was developed based on review of literature and sent through google form to collect the data from faculty of different streams of education such as engineering, media, healthcare, humanities, computer studies and management. The questionnaire was in two parts. First part collects general information like gender and faculty stream. Second part focuses on recommendation made by faculty members to students and its purpose. The sample size comprised of 175 respondents.

Hypothesis testing

The following hypothesis was proposed and tested

H0: Recommendation of library resources has a significant impact on usage pattern

The hypothesis was tested using SPSS software

4. Findings

The response received from 175 teaching staff to the questionnaire comprising of 98 (56%) females and 77 (43.3%) males (Table 15.1). They belong to 30 different institutes. 24 (13.72%) teaching

Table 15.1 Gender wise information

Gender	N=175	Percentage
Female	98	56.00%
Male	77	44.00%

staff from 3 Engineering institute responded whereas 20 (11.43%) teaching staff from 4 Media Communication & Design (MSD) institutes and 2 Computer Studies institute responded. In case of Health Science & Biomedical (HSB), and Humanities and Social Sciences (HSS) 20 (11.43%) teaching staff responded from 6 institutes of each faculty (Table 15.2). Major response was from management faculty where 104 (59.43%) teaching staff responded were belonging to 15 institutions. Few faculties from management institutes and engineering institute are teaching multiple subjects i.e. 24 engineering faculties are teaching 54 subjects where in management 104 faculties were covering 126 subjects.

Table 15.2 Stream wise information

Streams	Number of institutes covered	Response from faculty	Number of Subject taught by Respondents
Engineering (Eng)	3	24	54
Media Communication & Design (MC&D)	4	18	18
Health Science & Biomedical (HS&B)	2	8	8
Humanities and Social Sciences (HSS)	4	12	12
Computer Studies (Comp St)	2	9	9
Management (Mgt)	15	104	126

4.1 Awareness and Frequency of User

Teaching staff responded were totally aware about the resources available with their respective institute libraries. In order to collect the data on frequency of using library information resources by teaching staff (Table 15.3), respondent was requested to rate their frequency in 4 pointer scale i.e., once in a week, once in a month, once in a semester and once in a year. The result from the table shows that majority (79.9%) of teaching staff have utilized library information resources

Table 15.3 Frequency of usage of library resources

Frequency	N= 175	percentage
once a week	50	28.57143
once in a month	90	51.42857
once a semester	31	17.71429
once a year	4	2.285714

regularly i.e. at least once in a month (51.6%) or once a week (28.3%), very few teaching staff that hardly made use of library information resources, once in a semester (18.3%) and once in a year (1.6%).

4.2 Recommendation of Library Information Resources

The respondents are asked to indicate the purpose of recommending the online library resources to students from given choices. Table 15.1 indicates that the information resources were mostly recommended for research work (81%), Subject Studies (63%) and as reference reading (58%) that for the regular assignments (36%).

Table 15.4 Recommendation of library resources

Details	Eng	MC & D	HS & B	HSS	Comp St	Mgt	N = 175	%
1. Purpose of recommending library resources to student								
Research Work	9	7	6	6	23	91	**142**	81
Assignments	6	6	3	0	6	42	**63**	36
Additional Reading	6	3	6	3	15	69	**102**	58
Regular Studies/Subject studies	12	6	6	6	7	73	**110**	63
2. Recommendation of library resources other than syllabus								
Database	5	5	3	5	14	87	**119**	68.3
Reference Books	8	5	3	3	11	49	**79**	45
E-books	7	0	2	5	13	61	**88**	50
Case Studies	0	0	2	3	8	33	**46**	26.6
Journals and Magazines articles	6	6	3	3	20	67	**105**	60
CDs/ AVs	0	0	0	0	0	0	**3**	1.66
Books	5	2	5	5	18	53	**88**	50
3. library online resources recommended								
EBSCO	0	2	5	8	25	58	**98**	56
Emerald Insight	0	3	6	0	18	61	**88**	50
Prowess	0	0	0	0	3	24	**27**	15
Capitaline	0	0	0	0	0	11	**11**	6
JSTOR	9	6	3	6	19	33	**76**	43
Online Journals	6	3	7	4	20	48	**88**	50
Frost &Sullvian	0	0	3	0	9	23	**35**	20

The University syllabus recommends reference reading in the form of books, websites and journal article for each subject. Table 15.2 study whether teaching staff taking efforts to enhance students learning process by recommending library resources for reference reading other than that given in syllabus. The result shows that database (68.3%), Print journals and magazines articles (60%), books and e-books (50%) were recommended more than the reference books (45%), case studies (26.6%) and CDs/AVs (1.66%).

Table 15.4 further study the e-resource referrals recommendation made by teaching staff. It is found that the online journals databases like EBSCO (56%), Emerald Insight and online journals purchase by individual institute (50%), and JSTOR (43%) were majority in referral recommendation given by teaching staff irrespective of the faculty/ stream they are working in.

The influence of recommendation by teaching staff was observed through usage statistics and library feedbacks. Every year there is significant growth in utility of library information resources was found (Table 15.5). The results showed the exceptional increase in use of library resources during and post covid.

Table 15.5   Usage of information resources

Database	2014	2015	2016	2017	2018	2019	2020	2021
Emerald	23143	31264	27876	32418	32438	27434	148779	252448
EBSCO	21089	33431	86325	106851	112825	1349150	153924	3147190
Frost & Sullivan	142	342	560	860	781	743	1293	638
Prowess	3100	5174	5933	778	1664	25864	43513	54643
Economic Outlook	249	889	1743	402	1537	22822	10393	8888

Table 15.6   Results of hypothesis testing

Model Summary				
Model	R	R Square	Adjusted R Square	Std. Error of the Estimate
1	.442[a]	.195	-3.024	467123.40942

a. Predictors: (Constant), Economic Outlook, Prowess, Emerald, EBSCO

Table 15.7   Coefficient of regression

Model	Unstandardized Coefficients		Standardized Coefficients	t	Sig.
	B	Std. Error	Beta		
1	216644.396	387822.263		.559	.676
(Constant) Emerald	-70666.896	181053.481	-2.292	-.390	.763
EBSCO	57653.542	222024.429	2.017	.260	.838
Prowess	8443.510	555756.462	.059	.015	.990
Economic Outlook	644.646	183392.267	.011	.004	.998

Inference

The results clearly indicate that the usage pattern may not be driven by endorsement. Hence it is driven by the quality of online resource and its benefits to the user.

5. Discussion

Post covid has highlighted the importance of online resources amongst remote users of academic library. The excessive information available on internet and decreasing reading culture has resulted in low academic library usage (Anyaoku, 2015). Covid-19 and increased technological advancement brought in the essentiality of collaboration between faculty members and library environments (Sukula et. al., 2020). The results are in line with other studies on the topic. Faculty generally take a decision on the quality of resource and recommend the same to students (Hernon and Altman, 2010). Therefore, the quality of online resources influences its usage (Xie and Bugg, 2009). Faculty effective instructions have brought significant change in student attitude towards library information resources (Bringula, 2013). Researchers are of the view that neither librarian nor composition instruction alone can improve student research, but the close collaboration of both by designing assignment and delivering instructions will support and improve student writing and research. Faculty instructions about library information resources have improve the public image of the library and also boost the usage of library information resources and services.

6. Conclusion

Library is the main store house of quality resources and services. It provides good information services support for teaching, learning and research. It depends on the attitude of the faculty members of an academic institution as how they use these library resources and encourage students to take advantage. Faculty instruct student about where to look for information needed and how to use the library resources and service. The paper reveals that faculty making extensive use of library information resource for their research and classroom sessions. They are also influencing student attitude towards library information resources by recommending for their research assignment and day to day classroom sessions studies. This resulted in significant increase in usage of library information resources. Therefore, it is very important that library should not miss any opportunity to work with faculty and collaborate for effective use of library information resources.

REFERENCES

1. Abubakar, M. K. (2021). Implementation and Use of Virtual Reference Services in Academic Libraries during and post COVID-19 Pandemic: A Necessity for Developing Countries. *Library Philosophy and Practice* (e-journal). 4951. https://digitalcommons.unl.edu/libphilprac/4951

2. Allen, L. E., & Taylor, D. M. (2017). The role of the academic Library Information Specialist (LIS) in teaching and learning in the 21st century. *Information Discovery and Delivery*, 45(1), pp. 1–9.

3. Anyaoku, E. N. (2015). Evaluating undergraduate students' awareness and use of medical library resources: A study of Nnamdi Azikiwe University, Nigeria. *International Journal of Library Science*, 4(3), pp. 53–58.

4. Atte, S. L., & Ibikunle, G. O. (2017). Constraints to acquisition of competencies for effective information services delivery by librarians in North Western Nigerian University Libraries. *Samaru Journal of Information Studies*, 17(1), pp. 30–39.

5. Bakkalbasi, N. (2017). Assessment and Evaluation, Promotion, and Marketing of Academic Library Services. In Gilman, T (Ed.), *Academic Librarianship Today* (211), Rowman & Littlefield.

6. Behera, S. & Satpathy, S.K. (2014). Factors affecting information needs of faculty members of teachers training institutions of Odisha. *DESIDOC journal of Library and Information Technology*, 34(5), pp. 407–411.

7. Bringula, R. P. (2013). Influence of faculty-and web portal design-related factors on web portal usability: A hierarchical regression analysis. *Computers & Education*, 68, pp. 187–198.

8. Côté, M., Kochkina, S., & Mawhinney, T. (2016). Do you want to chat? Reevaluating organization of virtual reference service at an academic library. *Reference and User Services Quarterly*, 56(1), pp. 36–46.

9. Cox, J. (2018). Positioning the academic library within the institution: A literature review. *New Review of Academic Librarianship*, 24(3-4), pp. 217–241.

10. Dube, T. V., & Jacobs, L. (2022). Academic library services extension during the Covid-19 pandemic: considerations on higher education institutions in the Gauteng Province, South Africa. *Library Management*. https://doi.org/10.1108/LM-04-2022-0039

11. Dadhe, P. P., & Dubey, M. N. (2020). Library services provinces provided during COVID-19 pandemic: content analysis of websites of premier technological institutions of India. *Library Philosophy and Practice* (e-journal). 4445. https://digitalcommons.unl.edu/libphilprac/4445

12. Harland, F., Stewart, G., & Bruce, C. (2018). Aligning library and university strategic directions: A constructivist grounded theory study of academic library leadership in Australia and the USA. *New review of academic librarianship*, 24(3-4), pp. 263–285.

13. Hernon, P., & Altman, E. (2010). Assessing service quality: Satisfying the expectations of library customers. *American Library Association*.

14. Jessy, A., & Rao, M. (2016). Marketing of resources and services with emerging technologies in modern libraries: An overview. *International Journal of information dissemination and technology*, 6(1), pp. 15–20.

15. Jung, I., & Lee, J. (2020). A cross-cultural approach to the adoption of open educational resources in higher education. *British Journal of Educational Technology*, 51(1), pp. 263–280.

16. King, E., & Boyatt, R. (2015). Exploring factors that influence adoption of e-learning within higher education. *British Journal of Educational Technology*, 46(6), pp. 1272–1280.

17. Mckie, I. A. S., & Narayan, B. (2019). Enhancing the academic library experience with chatbots: An exploration of research and implications for practice. *Journal of the Australian Library and Information Association*, 68(3), pp. 268–277.

18. Mulongo, M. J. (2016). Investigation of Mobile Library user on the Expectancy T. *Research Journal of Library Sciences*, 4(5), pp. 14–30.
19. O'Kelly, M., Garrison, J., Merry, B., & Torreano, J. (2015). Building a peer-learning service for students in an academic library. *Portal. Libraries and the Academy*, 15(1), pp. 163–182.
20. Onye, U. U. (2016) Availability, Accessibility and Utilization of Library Information Resources by Students of the Federal University of Technology, Owerri (FUTO). In *Information and Knowledge Management*, 6(10), pp. 1–8.
21. Otike, F. W., Bouaamri, A., Barát, A. H., & Kiszl, P. (2021). Emerging Roles of Libraries and Librarians During and Post COVID-19 Pandemic: Challenges and Opportunities. *Handbook of Research on Information and Records Management in the Fourth Industrial Revolution*, pp. 1–16.
22. Panattoni, D. (2021). The new normal: public libraries in Italy post-covid 19. *International Information & Library Review*, 53(1), pp. 63–68.
23. Rampun, R., Zainol, Z., & Tajuddin, D. (2021). The role of training objectives for the effectiveness of training programmes in the Academic Library. *Management Research Journal*, 10(1), pp. 1–12.
24. Salisbury, F., & Peasley, J. (2018). Measuring the academic library: Translating today's inputs and outputs into future impact and value. *Information and Learning Science*, 119(1 / 2), 109–120.
25. Saunders, L. (2015). Academic libraries' strategic plans: top trends and under-recognized areas. *The journal of academic librarianship*, 41(3), pp. 285–291.
26. Schimmelpfennig, C., & Hunt, J. B. (2020). Fifty years of celebrity endorser research: Support for a comprehensive celebrity endorsement strategy framework. *Psychology & Marketing*, 37(3), pp. 488–505.
27. Shapiro, S. D. (2016). Engaging a wider community: The academic library as a center for creativity, discovery, and collaboration. *New Review of Academic Librarianship*, 22(1), pp. 24–42.
28. Sukula, S. K., Thapa, N., Kumar, M., & Awasthi, S. (2020). Reinventing Academic Libraries and Learning - Post-Covid (19) in the Perspective of Collaboration among Key Stake-holders in Higher Education: A brief Assessment and Futuristic Approach. *International Journal of Research in Library Science (IJRLS)*, 6(1), pp. 77–92.
29. Smith, K. R. (2001). New roles and responsibilities for the university library: Advancing student learning through outcomes assessment. *Journal of Library Administration*, 35(4), pp. 29–36.
30. Thielen, J. (2018). STEM Chalk Talks: Scientific Information Resource Training for All Librarians. *Science & Technology Libraries*, 37(3), pp. 290–301.
31. Wang, J. (2016). Digital collection development and sharing on a national scale: a case study of the digital library promotion project, *New Library World*, 117(11/12), pp. 678–687.
32. Wang, S., & Bai, X. (2016). University students' awareness, usage and attitude towards e-books: Experience from China. *The Journal of Academic Librarianship*, 42(3), pp. 247–258.
33. Xie, B., & Bugg, J. M. (2009). Public library computer training for older adults to access high-quality Internet health information. *Library & information science research*, 31(3), pp. 155–162.
34. Yoon, H. Y. (2016). User acceptance of mobile library applications in academic libraries: an application of the technology acceptance model. *The Journal of Academic Librarianship*, 42(6), pp. 687–693.

Note: Source for tables 1 to 4 made by the author and for table 5 to 6 SPSS software

Emerging Horizons: Business and Society in the Post Pandemic Era –
Brig. Dr. Rajiv Divekar et al. (eds)
© 2024 Taylor & Francis Group, London, ISBN 978-1-032-90822-9

16

Implications of Financial Literacy and Gender Gap in Financial Decision Making

Rahul Dhaigude[1]
Symbiosis Institute of Management Studies (SIMS),
Symbiosis International (Deemed University)
Pune, India

Naval Lawande[2]
Symbiosis Institute of Management Studies (SIMS),
Symbiosis International (Deemed University)
Pune, India

Divendra Ujagare[3]
Shri Shiv Chhatrapati College
Junnar, India

ABSTRACT

An individual is called financially literate if one has proficiency to make informed decisions related to financial management. In this modern era financial literacy is rampant and people lack knowledge which creates widespread and persistent gender indifference.

Women consistently scoreless in terms of knowledge about finances and this negatively impacts the financial wellbeing of women. The lower level of earning, relatively less work experience due to child rearing puts women in explicitly riskier situation than men.

This research paper explores whether households in the context of India are armed with enough intellect and capability and knowledge which is essential to take well informed and better decision related to savings and investments decisions and also borrowing decisions such as loans. In addition to that it finds out the gap in financial level comparing gender as parameter by using survey method and statistical tools. This study explores the wider area of importance of financial literate person in today's dynamic and changing world.

[1]rahul.dhaigude@sims.edu, [2]Naval.lawande@sims.edu, [3]d63ujagare@gmail.com

DOI: 10.4324/978100355996-16

Most recent studies done about this subject divide it into two main components- one is the subjective knowledge i.e. day to day spending decision and other is goal focused which is planning of retirement, emergency funds, children education, medical planning and royalty planning. One of the most primary reason and cannot be ignored is changing dynamics of family from Joint to nuclear which puts immense pressure on bread earner to plan for everything in advance irrespective of gender.

KEYWORDS: Financial literacy, Gender gap, women, Developing countries, Household decision making

1. Introduction

One of the biggest challenges for developing nation and emerging nation such as India is women empowerment which is only attainable if these group are financially literate and knowledgeable. For a person to take effective and intellectual decision in life one needs to have idea and knowledge about that domain especially finance. A woman when educated literally educates the whole family. Our society is always male dominated where all the decisions linked to financial management are taken care of by men and not giving enough space to women to apply her skills. In 90% of households' females are spender hence they need to be educated first. The survey by NCFE clearly exhibit that the financial literacy percentage among the women in India is quite low which needs special focus (Purohit, H., & Dwivedi, M. (2016).

Several researches have shown that there is wide gender gap when it comes to financial literacy but it is more in India due to lack of awareness and ignorance about the importance of financial knowledge in one's life. It is realised way beyond that women are more capable and better when it comes to taking care of household finances but observed evidently that they take step back when it comes to long term financial decisions and generally leaves to their male member of family. Hence it is necessary that women should be given basic financial knowledge so that they can make better decision related to savings and investments. According to surveys done women's life expectancy is higher than men which becomes one of the prime reasons to educate women as they will be burdened with supporting family in later stage of life. Also, women population in India is 50%, it will be unfair if the rest 50% only takes the decision related to investment. Other prominent reasons which influence one to delve into this kind of study is economic growth, family wellbeing, freedom from being exploited by society, self-sufficiency and driver of financial markets.

Financial ignorance not only effects an individual but also carries a significant cost for the nation as whole. This paper is structured as follows, at the outset we tried to review few of researches that has been done in this direction related to financial literacy and gender, then we turn to know if there actually exists a gender gap through a survey and interpreting and analysing it through statistic tools. Finally, the study concludes about driving major observation about the reason behind gender gap and finish the paper with few recommendations

2. Literature Review

Hilgert et al. (2003) used information from the Surveys of Consumers to find correlations between credit management practices and scores on a 28-item live test of objective financial facts. When Lusardi and Mitchell (2007) examined retired families, they found that higher levels of knowledge were linked to successful retirement planning and advanced asset financing (e.g., stocks). Knowledge has been divided into subjective and objective components in a number of recent research.

Robb and Woodyard (2011) found a significant positive correlation between self-assessed mathematical ability and subjective data such as acknowledging market and financial news. As a result, people engaged in an excessive selection of recommended financial practices, such as risk management, checking one's credit report, and maintaining an emergency fund. Subjective knowledge was far more relevant than objective information, which included concepts like portfolio diversification and compound interest. Nevertheless, objective knowledge was still a key factor in the study.

Lusardi and Mitchell (2008) observed notable gender disparities in financial knowledge, with men often demonstrating greater levels than women, using data from the Health and Retirement Study (HRS). Standard family studies theories from the mid-1900s, like Bulmer's symbolic interactionism, wherein gender roles were socially assigned specific duties, with the male role being that of economic supplier and distributor, may theoretically support these findings.

Survey by Global rating agency Standard and Poor's financial survey shows that country level financial literacy ranges from 13 percent to 71 percent. The countries such as Australia, Denmark, Netherlands, Norway, Sweden ranks higher in terms of these scores. South Asian countries ranks lower. Also, it has brought it in a very interesting concept whether the bank account holders have that knowledge and it came out that only 30% in growing economies have enough financial score to pass as financial literate.

"Savings are corelated to the level of knowledge you have and impacts a nation health significantly". Mahdzan, N.S., Tabiani, S. (2013).

Brown, Martin and Graf, Roman (2013) in their paper of financial literacy and retirement used survey of 1500 to determine whether financial literacy effects the retirement planning in Switzerland and measured it in three basic areas compound interest, inflation and risk diversification. "They measured retirement as voluntary retirement saving accounts. As a result, they found that it is comparatively higher in Switzerland Also, financial literacy and retirement planning are corelated to each other."

Mahdzan, N.S., Tabiani, S. (2013) "The Impact of Financial Literacy on Individual Saving: An Exploratory Study in the Malaysian Context" reveals major results that regularity in savings are closely related to age, gender and income. It suggests that policy makers should focus on such educations to increase the savings.

Financial Literacy Among Women in India: A Review Pacific Business Review International (Oct 2016) – "This review talks about the financial literacy in India and reveals that women are facing psychological, cultural and financial barriers to take decisions independently". It also talks about the schemes which are implemented by Government in this direction.

Does the gender gap in financial literacy continue to exist when someone retires? Ghanaian evidence. the article also discusses the distinction and Nominal scores revealed that male retirees lead in financial literacy on three of the ten questions used to assess financial literacy, while male domination was evident on seven of the questions." However, the $\chi2$ test of independence revealed that these observed nominal differences were not significant, with the exception of the loan interest rate calculation issue that favored male borrowers. By calculating the financial literacy score, the cumulative effect was shown to be statistically different for men and women, with a preference for men, according to an independent sampling t-test (Anokye M. Adam et.al.2017).

"In Our Best Interest: Women, Financial Literacy, and Credit Card Behavior," by Gary R. Mottola (2013), according to data from the National Financial Capability Study by the FINRA Investor Education Foundation, women were more likely than males to use their credit cards in expensive ways, such as by paying late fees and overdraft charges. Upon adjusting for many demographic factors, such as financial literacy and a self-reported mathematical aptitude, the disparities in credit card usage patterns based on gender were eradicated. These results imply that gender disparities in credit card management would be mitigated if men and women were equally represented in key areas where women traditionally lag behind men, such as income and financial knowledge.

Banniera, Christin, et al. (2019), by using nationally representative US data, demonstrated that women are less knowledgeable than males on the features of Bitcoin. After looking into the factors behind this difference, discovered that personality characteristics and socio demographics only account for a minor portion of the difference. About 40% of the gender disparity in Bitcoin literacy may be explained by include measures for both perceived and real financial literacy. On the other hand, digital technology experience does not bring any additional explanatory power. The findings suggest that while reducing gender disparities in financial literacy is crucial, protecting financial health in ever more digitalized financial institutions is becoming more difficult.

Wai-Sum Chan, Kee-Lee Chou, Alfred M. Wu, and Kar-Ming Yu (2015) investigated whether gender differences exist in financial literacy among Hong Kong workers using a phone survey conducted in 2012. If so, they looked at whether these differences could be attributed to gender differences in sociodemographic variables, social or psychological factors, or the results of retirement planning. The findings indicate differences in age, risk tolerance, computational ability, spousal support for retirement savings, and perceived financial awareness, in addition to gender differences in financial literacy. Multivariate data analyses indicate that gender variations in risk tolerance, computing ability, and self-reported financial knowledge could account for a portion of the gender gap in financial literacy; nevertheless, the difference persisted even after controlling for variables that were found to be associated with the gender gap.

3. Objectives

Primary
- To study financial literacy and whether there exists gender gap.

Secondary
- To study the financial awareness level among individuals and different factors affecting their financial decision making.
- To explore financial literacy and gender gap when it comes to different factors like age, educational background and working professionals.

4. Scope of Study

The study tries to find whether there exists a gender gap in terms of financial literacy, if so whether there are specific factors which can be extracted out to understand this gap. It mainly focuses on financial literacy at different age level, educational level and professional level only India. The scope of study is limited to geographical area of India as only these are considered when surveys are taken. The study tries to review only past 10 years study that are conducted in this domain as change in landscape is very evident over the years due to change in economic situation and perspective of people in terms of recognising gender equality.

It mainly covers the people in and around different regions of India and to analyse gender gap the questionnaire is built based on three parameters of finance score i.e. knowledge, attitude and behaviour which governs a person pecuniary acumen and influences his/her decision of major impact. The age group is usually above 18 assuming that they have at least attained sufficient knowledge to understand the questionnaire.

5. Limitations

- The study has geographical constraints
- The study assumes that particular question about the financial knowledge are sufficient to calculate financial score
- It also limits the sample size which may not be actual representation of the whole data
- Time constraints
- Limited access to data
- Personal or cultural bias of respondents while answering questions

6. Research Methodology

To fulfil the above objectives, Quantitative study is carried out which in turn brings out the qualitative aspects of study. The analysis is based on survey data from 309 individuals of age between 18-60 from the different area including village, city, town and rural areas. The data were collected by floating google form an in case of rural areas by face to face interviews by researcher. The survey was also implemented through telephonic interviews wherever physical reach is not possible especially rural areas. It was clearly communicated to respondents that there is no renumeration for filling out survey and it is purely for academic purpose. The survey is illustrative of population in terms of gender, age and geographic location.

This study uses primary data which is mostly used by private individuals, public organisations even by government to find out common perception among individuals. It is mailed to individuals who understand and expected to read questions comfortably. The reason for selecting this method is cheaper, unbiased of interviewer, respondents have sufficient time to answer, respondents can be reached conveniently, results are reliable.

Following are the details: -

7. Data Collection

To collect the data for this research the primary and secondary data were being used.

Primary Data: Primary data are those data which are composed first handed. Here the primary data is composed through designing a designed questionnaire and through a widely well-known method survey. The questionnaire is then sent to respondents through email and responses were recorded in excel sheet. This data is used to carry out this research successfully.

Data was collected in a systematic manner. To apprehensively complete this project, designed and structured questionnaire were identified as the main tool of data collection and it is being extensively used.

Secondary Data: It was collected through internet websites, previous research papers to understand the recent trends in financial literacy among other countries such as OCED papers were extensively analysed in order to access the and prepare the questionnaire which is comprehensive and gives meaningful insight about the level of financial literacy. Research reports from OCED, Research papers-Centre for Financial Studies were reviewed thoroughly.

Papers from well-known research data base and articles from journal available online such as Ebsco, Emerald insights, Jstor, journals.sagepub.com and google scholar.

7.1 Research Type

Depending on the kind of the study and keeping in mind the objectives of research, the descriptive kind of method is being cast-off. Descriptive study is taken up when the researcher wants to know and delve deep into understanding the awareness level of population at large. Conclusion were arrived after studying and analysing the data collected from survey. Statistical tools were extensively used for analysis of data.

7.2 Survey Method

The survey was conducted online through floating google form and e-mail was sent to them.

8. Design of Instrument

In order collect and procure information, the scholar designed an organized questionnaire. The researcher equipped a solo questionnaire according to the requirement of the data from the respondent. The questionnaire was designed after studying different methods that are adopted at global level and researched done and questions that are considered by practically reviewing what questions can maximize and grab the financial acumen of person. The questionnaire was divided into three segments according to knowledge, behaviour and attitude. For each questions score were assigned and then theses are added up to get final score.

8.1 Sampling Method

- Individuals aged between 18 and above
- Online questionnaires may be favoured because of high availability and accessibility of internet due to Digital India.
- The answers and responses from the participants will serve as the data for analsysis which will be stored in excel sheets and then advanced statistical tool by IBM Statistics will be used.
- Final completed responses- 309

8.2 Tools for Analysis

In the present study pie chart was used to present a clear picture. Also graphs and percentage analysis is used to give a pictorial and quantitative aspect of the research.

The test used to check the stated hypothesis are Independent Sample t-test. This is the tools which compares means of two sample groups to determine whether the population means are significantly different. It is type of parametric test. The variables used in this t-test are Dependent variable (test variable) and independent variable (grouping variable).

The observations taken also satisfies the assumptions which are required to run the test.

1. Dependent variable must be continuous (interval or ratio level). Here the financial score is interval scale
2. Independent variable is categorical. Here groups are Male and female.
3. There is no relationship of subject in each group. One group cannot influence the decision of another group.
4. Data collected is random data from population.
5. Normal distribution of sample is been taken care of. There is no heavily skewed data which may yield inaccurate result.
6. Since the sample size is not same. Hence the condition of equal variance assumed does not fulfil. So, Whitney t-test should be done but independent t test also gives the same result.
7. Most important requirement there is no outliers.

9. Analysis and Interpretation

The questionnaire was analysed based on simple data analysis tools such as sum, count, average etc wherever necessary, the analysis is given below:

9.1 Analysis on Data Set

There were more male responses as compared to female. 70.6% female actively responded and 29.4% male responded. The difference in data set will set stage for identifying the major gaps of financial literacy if exists.

Clearly mostly young population whether working and non-working people actively responded. They were the one who are interested in spending and investing in different financial instruments. As stated in few research papers that financial health of country can be accurately gauged by its spending pattern of young population. This data will also help in fulfilling the secondary objective of research paper.

There is good mix of every educational criteria. Among them the maximum respondents have attained undergraduate courses which reflect that at least they understand questionnaire floated to them. Salaried people top the list that means they are the ones who are actually managing their finances. Also 16.8% accounts for not working which will clarify whether financial literacy rate is linked to working and non-working class. More the data is scattered among different groups, better will be the result of analysis.

The size of the settlement can make a difference to access to services, including financial services. People living in rural areas generally devoid of knowledge and low access to financial products due to lack of available information and lack of funds and fear of losing those funds.

The first point to analyse financial behaviour is household budget.69% responded positively indicating the step towards financial inclusion.

9.2 Analysis on Financial Behaviour

9.Which of the following statements best describes you
309 responses

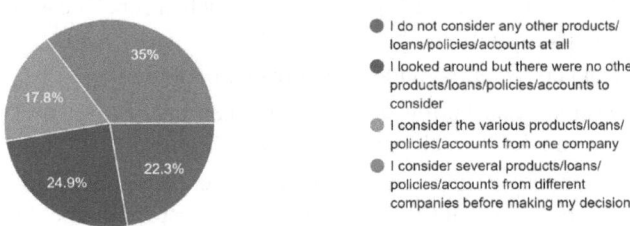

- I do not consider any other products/ loans/policies/accounts at all
- I looked around but there were no other products/loans/policies/accounts to consider
- I consider the various products/loans/ policies/accounts from one company
- I consider several products/loans/ policies/accounts from different companies before making my decision

Fig. 16.1 Awareness about self

Nearly 35% consider several products before taking decision indicates about the awareness which is widespread in today's world due to higher internet penetration and information overcrowding. Around 25% did not find alternatives rather than few basic widely advertised for example LIC policies, SBI loans etc.

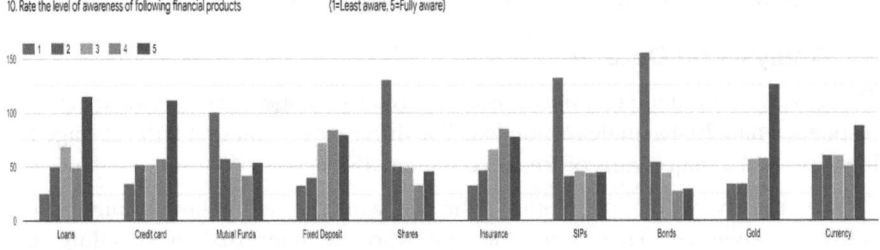

Fig. 16.2 Awareness about financial products

Mostly people were aware of Loans, Credit Cards, Gold and Insurance which are marketed widely but lot has to be done towards currency, mutual funds, SIPs, Shares. The perception of losing a lot of money in these alternative schemes and lack of proper knowledge leads to risk averse appetite.

11. Which sources of information do you feel most influenced your decision, about which one to take out
Rate the level of influence (1=Least influenced 5=Highly influenced)

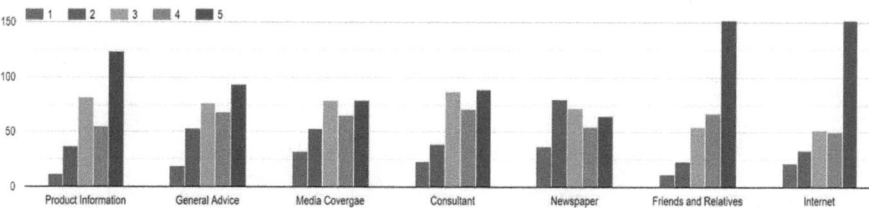

Fig. 16.3 Influencers of financial decisions

Heavy reliance on advises and recommendation of friends and relatives shows that financial decision are still the most important and trust and confidence and personal touch is required to make those. In addition to that internet has become widely popular in influencing the decision as there is excess of information available

9.3 Analysis on Financial Attitude

12. Before I buy something I carefully consider whether I can afford
309 responses

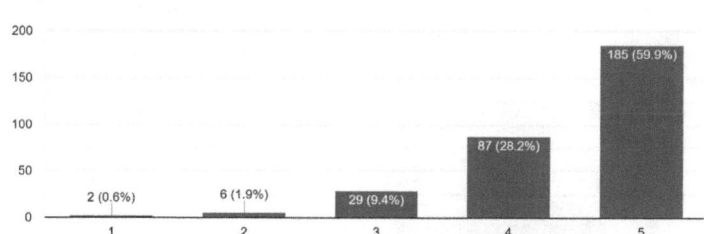

Fig. 16.4 Criteria for taking financial decision

Financial attitude reveals a lot about a person's understanding of financial decision. A well learned person will always spend his income judiciously in right place at right time and considering various criteria before making an investment decision. The first question itself answers the importance of making decision by taking into consideration whether one can afford or not.

13. I tend to live for today and let tomorrow take care of itself
309 responses

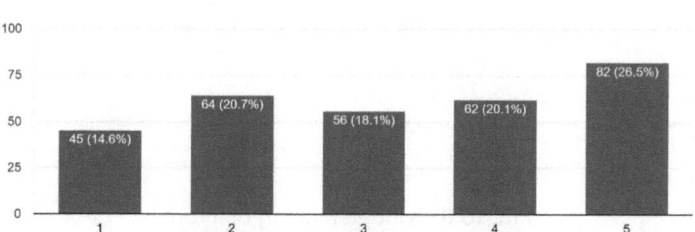

Fig. 16.5 Financial attitude

18. I set long term financial goals and strive to achieve them
309 responses

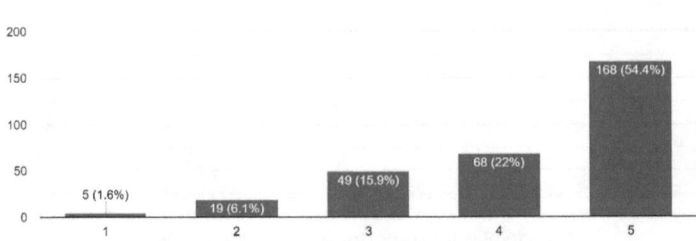

Fig. 16.6 Financial goal setting

According to Shahrabani (2012), Laily (2013), and Sundarasen, et al. (2016) the level of financial knowledge effects the behaviour in terms of financial plan. The higher the level of financial literacy, better the personal finance management. Above questions reveals that those who answered above questions correctly have higher awareness about these statements' person who sets long term objective generally scored higher.

9.4 Analysis on Financial Knowledge

20. Now imagine that the brothers have to wait for one year to get their share of the Rs.1,000 and inflation stays at 4%. In one year's time will they be able to buy
309 responses

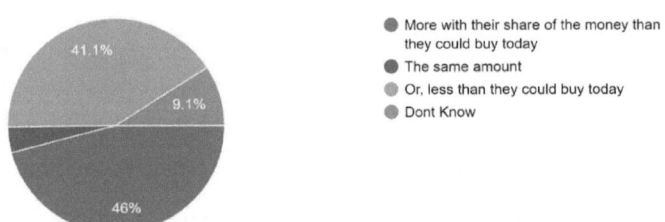

Fig. 16.7 Understanding of inflation

21. You lend Rs.25 to a friend one evening and he gives you Rs.25 back the next day. How much interest has he paid on this loan?
309 responses

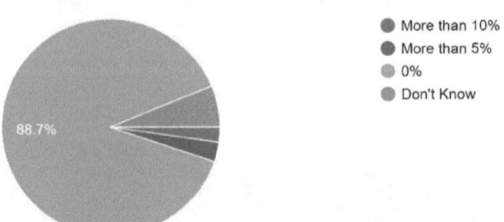

Fig. 16.8 Understanding of interest

It is key in every decision. Closely related to financial knowledge depicts one ability to manage finances and better planner.88%of the population entered it correctly depicting that most of them are at least aware.

9.5 Findings

The study conducted above gives us wide view of financial literacy rate according to variation in age, educational group and financial well-being.

1. Lower financial literacy among women:

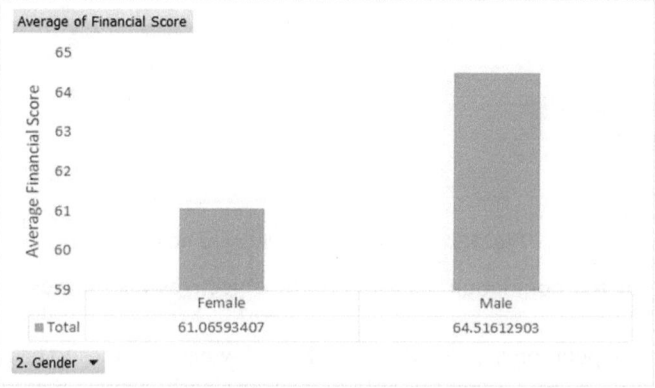

Fig. 16.9 Average financial score

As one can easily visualize the financial score is relatively less in women as compared to men.

2. Age factor as important factor to judge financial score. It was found out that in most age groups be it 25-40,40-60 or above 60. Women are not able to score well.

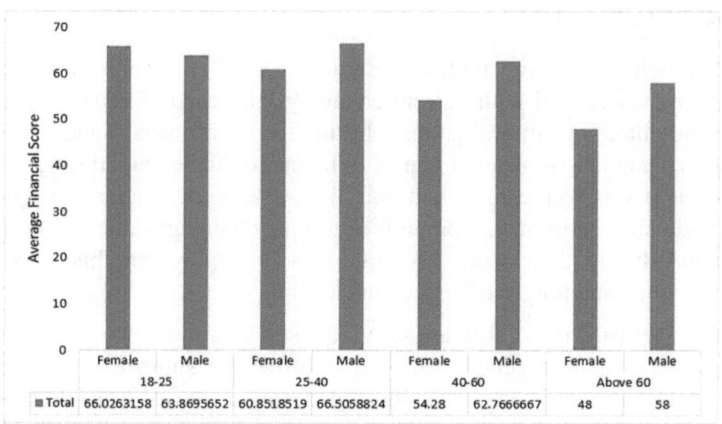

Fig. 16.10 Agewise financial score

3. Comparing working as criteria, scores are also less in this case. As we can see nearly 66% women were not able to fulfil the good score criteria

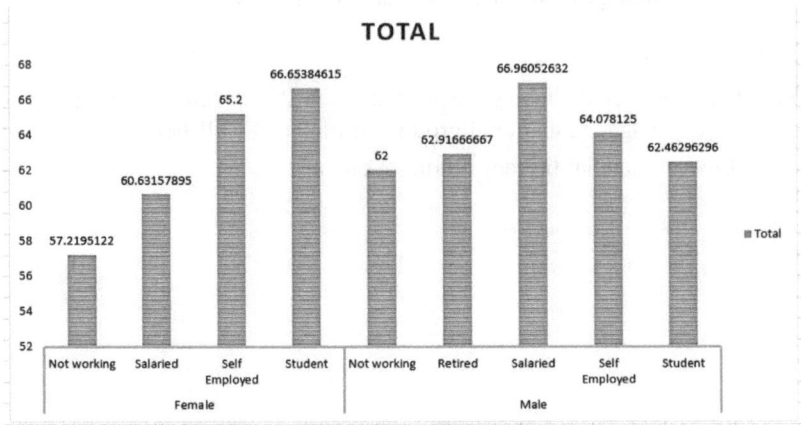

Fig. 16.11 Profession wise financial score

4. 54% of the population sets long term objectives and strives to complete them.
5. 9% of population answered "Don't Know" when it comes to basic financial questions of SI, CI and not able to answer clearly depicts that there is lack of knowledge
6. This exploratory also suggests that women take less interest in financial decisions and hence rarely concerned about matters of the same.
7. It was evident there exists a difference in mean of two groups suggests that there is widespread gap.

10. Conclusion

The skill which has become evident these days is skill of financial acumen which is very necessary to deal with current changing landscape of economy, financial markets and changing cultural pattern. In this research it was found out whether there exists a gender gap when it comes to financial literacy and through research and analysis it was well established that there does exist gender gap by using a large sample size. Moreover, women face unique challenges due to lower wages and income during their work life, interrupted employment histories due to personal reasons and longer life expectancies than men.

Also, this paper tried to put forward some realistic solutions and recommendation how can one deal with gender gap and improve the subjective knowledge of women which can only be increased through awareness level. T-test done above to find out whether there exist mean differences in financial sores of two sample size gives us the clear picture by rejecting null hypothesis. Findings also suggests that financial education seminars should more be targeted towards non-working class. Also, results have shown women of higher age have relatively lowest knowledge as compared to others which suggest that they need to be empowered because the decision related to distribution of property among family members may be the most important decision to be made.

This paper creates opportunities for others researchers to conduct the survey with different population of different sample size which needs to be taken care of.

11. Implications for Practice

Practitioners who are into financial domain such as financial planner, financial therapists and planner and policy makers who deals with such issue of managing funds and allocating them can find this paper useful while planning. Also, while planning for financial gals one needs to be aware of the behaviour of a person and what his income streams will be. This paper will truly reflect the biases while planning financial courses for different people.

This study is significant in the following ways:

- Strive to understand the financial behaviour among individuals
- Build women's financial capability.
- Change the perception of finance as an area of male expertise
- Innovate and develop new products
- How else can we encourage women to invest?
- Understanding the factors which leads to low literacy rate among women
- Understand the individuals subjective and objective knowledge about finance
- Regulators and stakeholders to design policies related to financial education

REFERENCES

1. Adam, A. M. (2017). Gender disparity in financial literacy: Evidence from homogeneous group. The Journal of Accounting and Management, 7(2).
2. Baluja, G. (2016). Financial literacy among women in India: a review. Pacific business review international, 9(4), 82–88.
3. Bannier, C., Meyll, T., Röder, F., & Walter, A. (2019). The gender gap in 'Bitcoin literacy'. Journal of Behavioral and Experimental Finance, 22, 129–134.
4. Brown, M., & Graf, R. (2013). Financial literacy and retirement planning in Switzerland. Numeracy, 6(2), 6.
5. Hilgert, M. A., Hogarth, J. M., & Beverly, S. G. (2003). Household financial management: The connection between knowledge and behavior. Fed. Res. Bull., 89, 309.
6. Jonubi, A., & Abad, S. (2013). The impact of financial literacy on individual saving: An exploratory study in the Malaysian context. Transformations in Business & economics, 12(1), 28.

7. Jonubi, A., & Abad, S. (2013). The impact of financial literacy on individual saving: An exploratory study in the Malaysian context. Transformations in Business & economics, 12(1), 28.

8. Lusardi, A., & Mitchell, O. S. (2007). Financial literacy and retirement planning: New evidence from the Rand American Life Panel. Michigan Retirement Research Center Research Paper No. WP, 157.

9. Lusardi, A., & Mitchell, O. S. (2008). Planning and financial literacy: How do women fare?. American economic review, 98(2), 413–417.

10. Mottola, G. R. (2013). In our best interest: Women, financial literacy, and credit card behavior. Numeracy, 6(2), 4.

11. Purohit, H., & Dwivedi, M. (2016). Level of awareness among rural women regarding Financial welfare schemes: A study of Tonk District.

12. Robb, C. A., & Woodyard, A. (2011). Financial knowledge and best practice behavior. Journal of financial counseling and planning, 22(1).

13. Yu, K. M., Wu, A. M., Chan, W. S., & Chou, K. L. (2015). Gender differences in financial literacy among Hong Kong workers. Educational Gerontology, 41(4), 315–326.

Note: All the figures in this chapter were made by the author.

Emerging Horizons: Business and Society in the Post Pandemic Era –
Brig. Dr. Rajiv Divekar et al. (eds)
© 2024 Taylor & Francis Group, London, ISBN 978-1-032-90822-9

17

Awareness of Health Insurance among Rural Customers—An Empirical Study

Rashmy Moray[1], Vanishree Pabalkar[2]
Symbiosis Institute of Management Studies,
Pune Symbiosis International (Deemed University)
Pune, India

ABSTRACT

The study assesses the healthcare insurance needs and examine the extent of awareness of health insurance among rural households and highlight the existing challenges prevailing in the rural segments in India. Primary data was collected through survey method using questionnaire. Non-parametric tests have been applied to obtain results. The study highlights demographic factors and existing challenges as strong determinants of health insurance needs and obstacles in the extent of awareness about several schemes, among the rural households. The outcome of the study comprehends the prevalent need of health insurance among rural households and extent of awareness about the schemes that would be helpful to the insurance companies.

KEYWORDS: Health insurance, Needs, Awareness, Challenges, Pandemic

1. Introduction

As per the twelfth five-year development strategy (2012–17), the planning commission of India stated that approximately 250 million people fall below the poverty line, out of which 200 million live in rural areas. The rapid spread of COVID-19 heightened in rural India due to the economic slowdown in the industry, leading to an increase in migrants who are villagers and rural daily-wage workers (Mitra, 2020). The rise in COVID-19 in rural India is a threat as

[1]rashmy.moray@sims.edu, [2]vanishree.p@sims.edu

DOI: 10.4324/978100355996-17

approximately 70% of the 1.3 billion Indian inhabitants reside in hamlets and have scarce means to health care (Bloomberg, 2020). COVID-19 has worsened in rural areas due to inadequate healthcare services. Amidst of pandemic with inadequate infrastructure, the well-being of the rural inhabitants is vulnerable, and health insurance is critical in such a scenario amplifying the significance of the insurance sector(Chandra, 2019). India's total healthcare expenditure has climbed to 3.6% of GDP, including the private sector, which is considered the lowest among the developing nations. According to the CARE rating agency, approximately, 8.8% of GDP is spent on public health care by OECD nations and in developed countries like the USA is 16.9%, China with a minimum of 5%, Germany & France 11.2% and Japan spends approximately 10.9%. In India, it remains way lower than the average expenditure made by the South-East Asian nations compared to developed nations where public health spending is nearly 18-20% of GDP. The GOI intends to upsurge public health expenditure to 2.5% of GDP by 2025. In India, against the pandemic crisis, additional spending is surging up despite the same substantial inefficiency, malfunctioning and dire scarcity of the health care provisions in the public sector that do not match the rising needs of the rural population.

National Health Authority announced to cover the COVID-19 treatment of the poor, rural and weaker households under Ayushman Bharat, the national insurance scheme for the poor in India. Many schemes have been initiated to meet the healthcare expenditure for those without health insurance coverage. To fight against COVID-19, the Insurance Regulatory and Development Authority of India (IRDAI) has allowed the offering of COVID-19-specific, customer-centric short-term health insurance policies for three to eleven months by the insurance establishments valid till 2021 (Dubey, 2020). Several insurance companies have launched COVID-19 insurance products based on the available information on patients' profiles, morbidity rates, cost of treatment, and other projections (Sinha, 2020). Aegon Life Insurance, in collaboration with Flipkart, launched 'life insurance with Covid-19 cover, a tie-up between HDFC Ergo General Insurance Company and Apollo Clinic and SBI General Insurance and Yes Bank, in partnership with Reliance General Insurance, launched the FD+Covid-19 cover for new fixed deposit holders (George Mathew, 2020).

2. Literature Study

Health insurance means buying an individual or collective healthcare coverage by committing to pay a stipulated amount at regular periodic intervals called a premium. It is an arrangement which tends to defer, delay, reduce or altogether avoid paying for healthcare expended by individuals and households (Akila, 2013). It covers medicinal expenditures, including hospitalization and expenses related to the disease. Several types of insurance schemes were launched in India: public, private, and community-based.

2.1 Issues and Challenges in Health Care System

Despite these initiatives, the budget allocation towards the health sector in India as a percentage of public expenditure policy is the lowest in the world. It is primarily met out of pocket (OOP) due to unregulated private markets. (Tanja, 2016) posing barriers to health care. Healthcare costs are spiralling due to demographic factors, epidemiology (rising scale of cost-intensive communicable and non-communicable diseases) and social transition (high expectations of consumers for technology-based healthcare). Only 13% of the rural inhabitants carry the means of primary health centres, 33% to sub- centre, and 9% to hospitals. Recently, the health policymakers proposed for expanding health insurance, considering it a critical element in streamlining the nation's healthcare system and as a poverty reduction agenda. In the 9th five-year plan, health insurance was given weightage considering the rising cost of hospitalization, leading to indebtedness among the rural population. Significant reform in the Indian healthcare sector is the Universal healthcare (UHC) policy as defined by WHO, to be achieved by (Devadasan N, 2014). It is observed that preventive and curative healthcare services will cover the Indian population.

Healthcare challenges in urban-rural India: Several challenges are observed in the Indian healthcare system comprising negligible healthcare awareness among the inhabitants illiteracy, w.r.t the healthcare system, and least importance towards well-being (Kasthuri, 2018). Access to a health facility is another crucial element for the rural population since urban populations are more connected to the advanced technology-based healthcare environment than their rural counterparts. Availability, supply and usage of health care services are considered to define access. Physical reach is equally considered necessary in availing the healthcare services within reach of a specified distance (Aitken, 2013). Only 37% of the rural population can avail healthcare facilities, and the more they are distant from the towns, the more vulnerable they are to the odds of diseases causing deaths. (Rao A, 2011) emphasized on shortage of healthcare personnel in India, revealing that the healthcare workforce is unevenly distributed and prefers to work in a developed infrastructural environment.

Need for health insurance. Insurance agent, and significantly less awareness about the government interventions and schemes exists among the rural segment. (Sudhir Gowda, 2015) identified that the rural population is ignorant and unaware of health insurance using the socio- demographic factors influencing their behaviour. There is a need to increase the level of awareness w.r.t their well-being and the significance of health insurance, including healthcare expenditures among rural inhabitants.

(Pradeep Panda, 2014) highlighted that comprehensive health insurance coverage is selected within households, and the head of the family takes the initiative in the states of Bihar and Uttar Pradesh under various health insurance schemes. Also, the existing poor level of awareness and socio-demographic factors are the strong determinants in taking a health insurance policy and expecting the expenditure to be covered through public health policy due to weak economic conditions. (Choutagunta, 2020) notified a fragile healthcare system of India w.r.t infrastructure for dealing with the COVID-19 outbreak. (Anant Kumar, 2020) highlighted the potential impact of COVID-19 on a rural segment in India, emphasizing inadequate rural health care system w.r.t infrastructure and the poor rural and marginalized population's inability to meet the medical costs

3. Research Methodology

An exploratory research design is adopted and with the help of existing literature, a predetermined structured questionnaire was developed, and variables were selected from the previously established studies. A five point Likert scale is casted in the survey to elicit responses. Pune district is a district in the state of Maharashtra in India. There are 15 talukas in the Pune district (including two city talukas). The 15 talukas have been classified into the 5 district sub-divisions: Baramati, Bhor, Pune, Shirur and Maval.

The random sampling technique is used as the researcher has no previous knowledge about the population. From the districts in Pune, the sample size chosen is at a 5 % margin of error and 95 % confidence interval. Slovin's formula/ approach has been applied to arrive at the representative respondents. I.e., $n = N / (1 + Ne^2)$ where n = Number of samples, N = Total population & e = Error tolerance (level). Therefore, n = N / (1 + N e2) = at 95 % confidence level, 1,000 / (1 + 1000 * 0.05^2), where = 1000/(1 + 1000 * 0.05^2) = 1000/ (1 + 1000 * 0.0025) and hence n = 1000/ (1001 * 0.0025), n = 1000/(2.5025) = 399.6. The sample size was taken as 400. Since the random sampling technique was used in collecting the responses, approximately 300, 75% (sample size) of rural households were approached for their participation in the survey. The response rate was 67 % (268 responses) which were the rural households from in and around Pune districts that were found valid, and the remaining were outliers. Frequency analysis was used to indicate the health care insurance needs of rural households in India. Fisher's test was performed to gauge the perception of health insurance needs and level of awareness and test the hypothesis. Based on the objectives to be achieved, two hypotheses were established.

Hypothesis No 1:

H_0: The health care insurance needs of rural households have no association with their demographic factors

H_1: The health care insurance needs of rural households have a meaningful association with their demographic factors

Hypothesis No 2:

H_0: The perception of the health insurance schemes among rural households has no association with their demographic factors

H_1: The perception of the health insurance schemes among rural households has an association with their demographic factors

4. Data Analysis

Data analysis has been presented in three parts. Part one introduces the demographic data of the sample in the study, Part two depicts the health care insurance needs of rural households, understanding the reasons behind not being insured, and Part three highlights the existing perception and the level of awareness prevalent among the rural population about the health insurance schemes.

Part 1: Demographic presentation of data

Table 17.1 shows that most respondents belong to the nuclear family. There is an equal number of respondents in all age groups other than 'less than 30 years'. Majorities, i.e., 81% of the respondents, are employed, few are self- employed,

Table 17.1 Demographic presentation of data

Sr. No.	Particulars	Attributes	Frequency	Percentage
1	Type of family	Joint Family	60	22.39
		Nuclear family	208	77.61
2	Age of respondents	Less than 30years	21	7.84
		Between 30-40 years	81	30.22
		Between 40-50 years	81	30.22
		Above 50 years	85	31.72
3	Primary occupation	Employed	216	80.6
		Unemployed	0	0
		Labour	0	0
		Self-employed	52	19.4
		Family-owned business	0	0
		Agriculture	0	0
		Professional	0	0
4	Number of income earners in the family	One	180	67.16
		Two	80	29.85
		Three	4	1.49
		Four	4	1.49
		Five	0	0
5	Income per annum (in Rs.)	Less than 50000	12	4.48
		50000 – 100000	76	28.36
		100000 – 150000	76	28.36
		150000 – 200000	44	16.42
		Above 200000	60	22.39
6	Annual amount spent on health care	Less than 25000	36	13.43
		25000-50000	159	59.33
		50000-750000	49	18.28
		Above 75000	24	8.96

and there are no respondents in other categories. Most families are single-income earners, very few with two-member income earners and in different types, there are a negligible number of respondents. An equal number of respondents in all income groups other than less than 50,000 years is observed. Most respondents, i.e., 59%, spend around 50,000/- on health care, and a significantly less percentage of spending is found above Rs. 50000 in the other categories.

Part 2: To understand the health care insurance needs of rural households in India

It is observed from Table 17.2 that only 9% of the sample population has a health insurance scheme. 83% responded that they do not have 'Individual Health Insurance', and very few, i.e., 17%, have 'Group Health Insurance'. 67% of the respondents have claimed the insurance, whereas 33% have not claimed the insurance. The respondents believe that health insurance is extremely important. From the table, it is clear that respondents feel the importance of health insurance; despite this, only 8.96% have a health insurance policy. The following table presents why rural households do not take health insurance policies.

Table 17.2   Health care insurance needs of rural households

S. No.	Particulars	Attributes	Frequency	Percentage
1	Health insurance scheme/policy possessed	Yes	24	8.96
		No	244	91.04
2	Type of Health Insurance policy taken	Individual Health Insurance	20	83.33
		Group Health Insurance	4	16.67
		Family Floater Health Insurance	0	0
		If any other specify	0	0
3	Claimed insurance or not	Yes	16	66.67
		No	8	33.33
4	Importance of health insurance	Somewhat important	144	53.73
		Extremely important	124	46.27

Table 17.3 shows that respondents either strongly agree or agree on the mentioned criteria in availing services in hospitals' and strongly disagree or disagree for 'Don't feel the need for insurance'. The above data shows that there is a need for well-designed health insurance schemes by considering the above factors.

Table 17.3   Reason for rural households not taking health insurance policies

Sr. No.	Particular	SD	D	N	A	SA
1	Low salary/non-availability of funds	0	4	4	76	160
2	Don't feel the need for insurance	112	132	0	0	0
3	Unaware about it	0	8	16	144	76
4	Cannot afford Insurance	0	4	0	160	80
5	Linked hospitals are not easily accessible	0	0	12	156	76
6	Difficulty in availing services in hospitals	0	0	12	156	76

SD = strongly agree, D = disagree, N = neutral, A = agree S = strongly agree

Part 3: To gauge the perception of health insurance schemes concerning the COVID-19 pandemic and contagion diseases.

Five statements are undertaken to gauge the perception of health insurance schemes, and the association of these statements with demographic data is studied in part two.

Statement 1: Implementation of such a scheme on a large scale would bring development in the rural health sector

Table 17.4 shows that the determinants for implementing such a scheme on a large scale would bring development in the rural health sector have a statistically significant association with age, number of earners, income and annual amount

Table 17.4 Implementing such a scheme on a large scale would bring development in the rural health sector

Determinants	Implementing such a scheme on a large scale would bring development in the rural health sector				Fisher Test
	Agree	%	Strongly Agree	%	p-value
Family Type					
Joint Family	32	12%	28	10%	0.6632
Nuclear Family	104	39%	104	39%	
Age					
Less than 30	9	3%	12	4%	
Between 30-40 years	49	18%	32	12%	0.02682
Between 40-50 years	45	17%	36	13%	
Above 40 years	33	12%	52	19%	
Occupation					
Employed	104	39%	112	42%	0.09094
Self-Employed	32	12%	20	7%	
Number of Earners					
ONE	96	36%	84	31%	
TWO	36	13%	44	16%	0.01519
THREE	0	0%	4	1%	
FOUR	4	1%	0	0%	
Income Per Annum					
Less than 50000	4	1%	8	3%	
50000-100000	36	13%	40	15%	
100000-150000	44	16%	32	12%	0.0006221
150000-200000	32	12%	12	4%	
Above 200000	20	7%	40	15%	
Annual Amount Spent on Health Care					
Less than 25000	16	6%	20	7%	
25000-50000	84	31%	75	28%	2.09E-01
100000-150000	28	10%	21	8%	
150000-200000	8	3%	16	6%	

spent on health care (P-value < 0.05). Family type and occupation have statistically insignificant associations with the Implementation of such a scheme on a large scale would bring development in the rural health sector (P-value > 0.05).

Statement 2: Insurance coverage offered under various schemes would give adequate coverage to fight health issues

From the above Table 17.5, it is found that all the determinants consisting, the age, family type, occupation, number of income earners and amount spent on health care for Insurance coverage offered under various schemes would give adequate coverage to fight health issues have a statistically significant association (P-value < 0.05).

Table 17.5 Insurance coverage offered under various schemes would give adequate coverage to fight health issues

Determinants	Insurance coverage offered under various schemes would give adequate coverage to fight health issues						Fisher Test
	Neutral	%	Agree	%	Strongly Agree	%	p-value
Family Type							
Joint Family	3	1%	48	18%	8	3%	0.006086
Nuclear Family	24	9%	120	45%	64	24%	
Age							
Less than 30	0	0%	13	5%	8	3%	
Between 30-40 years	8	3%	61	23%	12	4%	0.03425
Between 40-50 years	8	3%	45	17%	28	10%	
Above 40 years	12	4%	49	18%	24	9%	
Occupation							
Employed	12	4%	136	39%	68	25%	1.67E-07
Self-Employed	16	6%	32	12%	4	1%	
Number of Earners							
ONE	16	6%	116	43%	48	18%	
TWO	8	3%	48	18%	24	9%	0.002348
THREE	4	1%	0	0%	0	0%	
FOUR	0	0%	4	1%	0	0%	
Income Per Annum							
Less than 50000	4	1%	4	1%	4	1%	
50000-100000	8	3%	40	15%	28	10%	
100000-150000	0	0%	56	21%	20	7%	0.0007802
150000-200000	8	3%	28	10%	8	3%	
Above 200000	8	3%	40	15%	12	4%	
Annual Amount Spent on Health Care							
Less than 25000	0	0%	20	7%	16	6%	
25000-50000	8	3%	108	40%	43	16%	2.71E-07
100000-150000	16	6%	24	9%	9	3%	
150000-200000	4	1%	16	6%	4	1%	

Statement 3: Insurance schemes introduced will give opportunities for infrastructure development in the rural healthcare sector

Table 17.6 shows that the determinants, such as insurance schemes, will give opportunities for infrastructure development in the rural healthcare sector and have a statistically significant association with family type, number of earners and annual amount spent on healthcare (P-value < 0.05). Age, income per annum and occupation have a statistically insignificant association with Such schemes that will give opportunities for infrastructure development in the rural healthcare sector (P-value > 0.05).

Table 17.6   Insurance schemes introduced will give opportunities for infrastructure development in the rural healthcare sector

Determinants	Insurance schemes will give opportunities for infrastructure development in the rural healthcare sector				Fisher Test
	Strongly agree %	Neutral %	Agree %	Strongly Agree %	p-value
Family Type					
Joint Family	0%	6%	13%	3%	0.003656
Nuclear Family	3%	28%	27%	19%	
Age					
Less than 30	0%	3%	4%	0%	
Between 30-40 years	1%	12%	10%	6%	0.1208
Between 40-50 years	1%	10%	12%	6%	
Above 40 years	0%	9%	13%	9%	
Occupation					
Employed	3%	25%	39%	18%	0.1237
Self-Employed	0%	9%	12%	4%	
Number of Earners					
ONE	1%	27%	25%	13%	
TWO	1%	7%	12%	9%	0.02039
THREE	0%	1%	1%	0%	
FOUR	0%	0%	1%	0%	
Income Per Annum					
Less than 50000	0%	1%	3%	0%	
50000-100000	0%	10%	10%	7%	0.08629
100000-150000	1%	7%	12%	7%	
150000-200000	0%	6%	6%	4%	
Above 200000	1%	9%	9%	3%	
Annual Amount Spent on Health Care					
Less than 25000	1%	1%	7%	3%	
25000-50000	1%	25%	18%	15%	1.05E-05
100000-150000	0%	6%	11%	1%	
150000-200000	0%	1%	4%	3%	

Statement 4: There would be challenges in implementing the health insurance schemes during the pandemic

Table 17.7 shows that the determinants for implementing health insurance schemes during the current COVID-19 pandemic would face challenges, the same have a statistically significant association with age, number of earners, income per annum, occupation and annual amount spent on health care (P- value < 0.05). Only Family types with a statistically insignificant association with such schemes pose challenges in implementing the exact (P-value > 0.05).

Table 17.7 Determinants for implementing health insurance schemes

Determinants	Neutral %	Agree %	Strongly agree %	Fisher Test p-value
Family Type				
Joint Family	0%	15%	7%	0.1588
Nuclear Family	4%	49%	24%	
Age				
Less than 30	1%	5%	1%	
Between 30-40 years	3%	20%	7%	5.42E-05
Between 40-50 years	0%	21%	9%	
Above 40 years	0%	18%	13%	
Occupation				
Employed	4%	39%	28%	0.001557
Self-Employed	0%	12%	3%	
Number of Earners				
ONE	3%	40%	24%	
TWO	0%	24%	6%	1.02E-08
THREE	0%	0%	1%	
FOUR	0%	0%	0%	
Income Per Annum				
Less than 50000	3%	3%	1%	
50000-100000	13%	10%	12%	0.001314
100000-150000	21%	12%	7%	
150000-200000	13%	6%	3%	
Above 200000	13%	9%	7%	
Annual Amount Spent On Health Care				
Less than 25000	0%	6%	7%	
25000-50000	3%	42%	15%	1.05E-05
100000-150000	1%	12%	5%	
150000-200000	0%	4%	4%	

Statement 5: Health insurance schemes will improve the health of the rural population

The above table depicts the determinants for health insurance schemes that will improve the health of the rural population and have a statistically significant association with age, number of earners, income and annual amount spent on health care (P-value < 0.05). Family type and occupation have a statistically insignificant association with health insurance schemes that will advance the healthiness of the rural population (P-value > 0.05). Most of the rural households are nuclear families with single-income earners earning an average of Rs.50,000 falling in the age of 30 years, employed in private establishments with no other source of income.

Further, it is observed that negligible respondents in the study are insured and carry individual health schemes, and significantly fewer possess group or family insurance. It entails the need for penetration of health insurance among the rural population to create awareness and usage of the same. Since many respondents find it essential, it shows their understanding of the need for health care insurance, but lack of access and knowledge of such schemes is missing. It is observed that most of the respondents fall in the low-income earning category, though they feel the need for health insurance but cannot afford it. It is highly accepted that respondents need to save for health care and insurance, but facts appraised the unaware of the schemes offered.

Equally concerned about the inaccessibility of hospitals in the vicinity of their rural areas and the services offered by the health care providers. These findings emphasise the existing health financing deficiencies within the rural health sector and the prevalence of out-of-pocket expenditure systems. Since the rising cost of healthcare treatment and out-of-pocket spending is unaffordable at the rural end with the given level of income with single income earning capacity. In these circumstances, implementing national health insurance policies offered by the government in the current COVID-19 pandemic would lead to rural development. The rural population believes that implementing health insurance schemes would create opportunities for infrastructural development.

Advancement in infrastructural growth would improve livelihood and receive better healthcare services to the rural population. However, this infrastructural development is open to challenges. Since the government has limited statistics about the rural patient's demography factors, morbidity and inadequate health centres, it would be challenging to tackle primary, secondary and tertiary healthcare while taking care of prevention and health promotion.

These findings align with those (Choutagunta, 2020) (Anant Kumar, 2020), considering the facts related to the required infrastructure in the current scenario of the pandemic and any occurrences of future contagions. Empanelling and deploying private healthcare providers to rural will cost high and increase the burden not only on the government but also on the poor and vulnerable rural people. Private hospitals have expressed concerns about implementing the universal health insurance scheme.

5. Conclusion

The study intended to identify the health insurance needs and level of awareness about the health insurance schemes amongst the rural inhabitants in the event of the current COVID crisis. The study substantially supports that demography variables highly impact the need for health insurance considering the age, level of income and education and nature of employment as dominant factors. It also highlights the extent of awareness about the health insurance schemes to meet the cost of treatment among the rural poor in India. Many challenges and issues exist in the rural health sector, like low income, unaffordability, accessibility etc., in obtaining health cost protection. Universal and national health policy is expected to bridge inequalities relating to health and its access providing benefits to poor and vulnerable belts of people. Health insurance companies have a potential market if they tap t rural sector correctly by penetrating their lost cost and premium payable schemes. It is imperative to understand the rural people`s perceptions about health care requirements and develop viable, acceptable and affordable schemes accordingly.

References

1. Aitken, M. (2013). *Understanding Health Care Access in India, What is the currentSate?* IMS Institute for Healthcare Informatics. Retrieved from http://www.imshealth.com .
2. Akila. (2013). Penetration of health insurance sector in Indian market. *International Journal of Management, 3*(1), 55–67.
3. Anant Kumar, R. N. (2020). COVID Challenges and its consequences for rural health care in India. *Public health in Practise.* doi:10.1016/j.puhip.2020.100009
4. Bhattacharjee, d. M. (2020, April 3). *https://southasianvoices.org/is-indias-healthcare-system-prepared-for-covid-19/.* Retrieved from https://southasianvoices.org: https://southasianvoices.org/is-indias-healthcare-system-prepared-for-covid-19/
5. bloomberg. (2020, June 22). *https://timesofindia.indiatimes.com/india/new-coronavirus-hotspots-are-emerging-in-rural-villages-across-india/articleshow/76509700.cms.* Retrieved from https://timesofindia.indiatimes.com: https://timesofindia.indiatimes.com/india/new-coronavirus-hotspots-are-emerging-in-rural-villages-across-india/articleshow/76509700.cms
6. Chandra, H. (2019, October 31). *https://theprint.in/health/at-1-28-gdp-india-expenditure-on-health-still-low-although-higher-than-before/313702/.* Retrieved from https://theprint.in: https://theprint.in
7. Choutagunta, S. R. (2020, April). Assessing Healthcare Capacity in India. *Mercatus Working Paper.* Retrieved from https://mercatus.org/publications/covid-policy-brief-series/assessing -healthcare-capacity-india

8. Devadasan N, G. S. (2014). Monitoring and Evaluating Progress Towards Universal HEalth Coverage in India. *PLOS Medicine, 11*((9)). doi:10.1371/journal. pmed.1001697

9. Fitch. (2020, May 14).

10. George Mathew, S. S. (2020, June 2). *https://indianexpress.com/article/business/ only-5600-health-insurance-claims-coronavirus-6438004/*. Retrieved from https:// indianexpress.com: https://indianexpress.com

11. Indumathi K, H. S. (2016). Awareness of health insurance in a rural population of Bangalore, India. *International Journal of Medical Science and Public Health, 5*(10). doi:10.5455/ijmsph.2016.15042016476

12. Karan, A. S. (2014). Moving to Universal Coverage? Trends in the Burden of Out- of Pocket Payments for health care across Social Groups in India. *PLoS one 9, 9 (8).* doi: 10.1371/journal.pone.0105162

13. Kasthuri, A. (2018). Challenges to Healthcare in India - The Five A's. *Indian Journal of Community Medicine, 43(3)*, 141-143. doi:10.4103/ijcm.IJCM_194_18

14. Mitra, S. (2020, March 2020). *idr online.* Retrieved from https://idronline.org: https:// idronline.org/the-implications-of-covid-19-for-rural-india/

15. Parulekar, H. T. (2013). Health insurance: Is Indian rural population aware? *International Journal of Applied Basic Medical Research*, 132. doi: 10.4103/2229-516X.117100

16. Pradeep Panda, A. C. (2014). Enrolment in community-based health insurance schemes in rural Bihar and Uttar Pradesh, India. *Health Policy and Planning*, 960-974. doi:10.1093/heapol/czt077

17. Rao A, R. K. (2011). Human Resources for health in India. *Lacent*, 587–98. doi:10.1016/S0140-6736(10)61888-0

18. Sinha, S. (2020, June 17). *https://www.financialexpress.com/money/insurance/how-covid-19-may-impact-health-insurance-industry-in-india/1994426/*. Retrieved from https://www.financialexpress.com: https://www.financialexpress.com

19. Sudhir Gowda, C. M. (2015). Awareness about health insurance in rural population of South Ind. *International Journal of Community Medicine and Public Health*, 648–650 . doi:10.18203/2394-6040.ijcmph20151064

20. Tanja, M. N. (2016). Health insurance in India: what do we know and why is ethnographic research needed. *ANTHROPOLOGY & MEDICINE, 23*(1), 102–124. doi:http://dx.doi.org/10.1080/13648470.2015.1135787

Note: Tables 17.1 and 17.5 were made by the author and Table 17.2, 17.3, 17.4, 17.6 and 17.7 were compiled by the author.

Emerging Horizons: Business and Society in the Post Pandemic Era –
Brig. Dr. Rajiv Divekar et al. (eds)
© 2024 Taylor & Francis Group, London, ISBN 978-1-032-90822-9

A Systematic Review on Effectuation and Causation: Applying Antecedents, Decisions, and Outcomes (ADO) Framework

18

Sunakshi Gupta[1], Aubid Hussain Parrey[2]
The Business School, University of Jammu
J&K, India

Suchita Jha[3]
Symbiosis Institute of International Business
Pune, India

ABSTRACT

This research highlights the role of decision logics in entrepreneurship research by systematically analyzing the literature based on the ADO approach (antecedents, decisions and outcomes) of effectuation and causation. Based on the extensive coverage of 35 years of data from 1988 to 2022, bibliometric analysis was conducted followed by content analysis. The results revealed that this area of research showed a positive trend in terms of increasing publications from the year 2006 because this theory of decision-making gained practical importance in entrepreneurship research worldwide and the USA contributed the maximum in the number of publications over the years. The key theories, methods, and outcomes were identified through a systematic review of notable studies. This research adds to the existing knowledge in the field of effectuation and causation and covers a span of 35 years of research in this area. This study was limited to business, management and accounting subject areas and only journal articles were covered in this study. Many areas of this research field remain unexplored and future studies can be conducted by using various other theories concerning decision-making logics. This study shall help potential entrepreneurs identify which decision logic (effectually or causally) leads to successful venture creation through literature analysis. This study will further provide insight to successful or expert entrepreneurs to better understand the antecedents that impact decision-making logic and further lead to desirable outcomes.

KEYWORDS: Causation, Content analysis, Decision-making logics, Effectuation, Entrepreneurship

[1]071sunakshi@gmail.com, [2]checkaubidhussain@gmail.com, [3]suchita.jha@siib.ac.in

DOI: 10.4324/978100355996-18

1. Introduction

This study highlights the factors affecting effectuation and causation decision-making logics and the outcomes of using these decision logics for achieving the desired venture performance by applying the ADO framework. This study reviews the empirical and theoretical research from 1988-2022 to understand the factors affecting effectuation and causation, the methodologies involved, and outcomes. The prior studies provided a systematic synthesis of the literature with significant gaps emphasizing the importance of understanding the antecedents or consequences of effectuation only, with no focus on causation. The seminal articles related to the theory of effectuation were analysed using content analysis, where effectuation was merely considered a theory, ignoring the factors that impact effectuation and causation. This research addresses all these gaps by systematically analysing the literature using the ADO framework and bibliometric analysis.

2. Literature Review

Effectuation offers an original perspective on entrepreneurship research by analyzing how applying the causation-based decision-making model to entrepreneurial activity applies to all situations (Zhang et al., 2023). Successful entrepreneurs don't make plans; instead, they make the most of unforeseen opportunities and grow as a result of uncertainty. Rather, Sarasvathy (2001a) contended that people employ effectuation reasoning in decision-making and opportunity exploration. Decision-making logic can be employed simultaneously as a component of human thinking, according to Sarasvathy (2001a), even when making decisions across different settings. A paradigm change in our view of entrepreneurs' roles has resulted from effectual reasoning in dealing with the contingent environment (Benz & Baum, 2023). To make decisions under uncertain circumstances, expert or experienced entrepreneurs employ an effectual approach rather than a causal logic Sarasvathy (2001b). This approach presents a conflict between entrepreneurs who place more value on planning and those who use their resources to complete tasks. Various theoretical and empirical investigations analyse the theoretical and conceptual differences between the two decision-making logics: effectuation and causation (Cowden et al., 2022; Zhang et al., 2023).

The research questions presented in the research are:

1. *What are the theoretical concepts related to effectuation and causation?*
2. *What are the factors and methodological trends studied in effectuation and causation?*
3. *What are the content dimensions of two decision-making logics?*

4. *What is the future research agenda, and how can the ADO approach be applied in effectuation and causation research?*

This study offers an extensive analysis of effectuation and causation research conducted over 35 years, investigating the underlying causes or consequences of using these two decision-making logics, highlighting the theoretical and empirical contributions in the field, and finally the outcomes of the research that pave the way for future research.

Effectuation and causation found their foundations in the work of Sarasvathy (2001b) at Carnegie Mellon University. Entrepreneurial decision-making can be characterized as a pre-firm process, according to Sarasvathy's (2001a) study. An entrepreneur must choose between starting a business and rejecting an idea. Resources, stakeholders, the environment, and an entrepreneur are the four interconnected circles that make up the process (Sarasvathy, 2001b, 2001a) of entrepreneurship. The characteristics of the four creative entrepreneurial decision options, or logic, are as follows: Initially, each instance encompasses one of the four domains of the entrepreneurial process. Every pre-firm is faced with decisions starting from each of the four categories. Secondly, even though each entrepreneurial decision can originate in any one of the four spaces, each decision has elements from each of the four domains. Thus, it is possible to analyze or illustrate entrepreneurial decisions concerning all four domains only marginally. Thirdly, according to Dew et al. (2009) and Read et al. (2009), there is no set sequence in which the pre-firm might be forced to make innovative decisions. Two main research issues are addressed in the study by Sarasvathy (2001a), with an emphasis on the reasoning techniques used by seasoned entrepreneurs. The initial inquiry concerned recognizing shared and distinct criteria in the decision-making process of entrepreneurs throughout the establishment and development of a new business. The second research question focused on the belief of experienced entrepreneurs regarding forecasting the success of a new endeavour. This theoretical investigation of effectuation and causation led to the conclusion that the effectuation-causation theory was based on five fundamental principles (Sarasvathy, 2001b, 2001a), that was bird in hand principle, affordable loss principle, crazy quilt principle, lemonade principle and pilot in the plane principle.

3. Methodology

The present study follows a mixed review in which both bibliometric and framework-based reviews were used. The bibliometric review reveals the year-wise trend in effectuation and causation, common keywords used, most cited authors, country-wide data, universities contributing the maximum in this area, and the area of research contribution. The framework used in this review is ADO: Antecedents, decisions, and Outcomes (Paul & Criado, 2020). The complete SLR process adopted (Nolan & Garavan, 2016) for the research is shown in Fig. 18.1. PRISMA was used for reporting the systematic literature review (Page et al., 2021), with inclusion and exclusion criteria as depicted in Fig. 18.2.

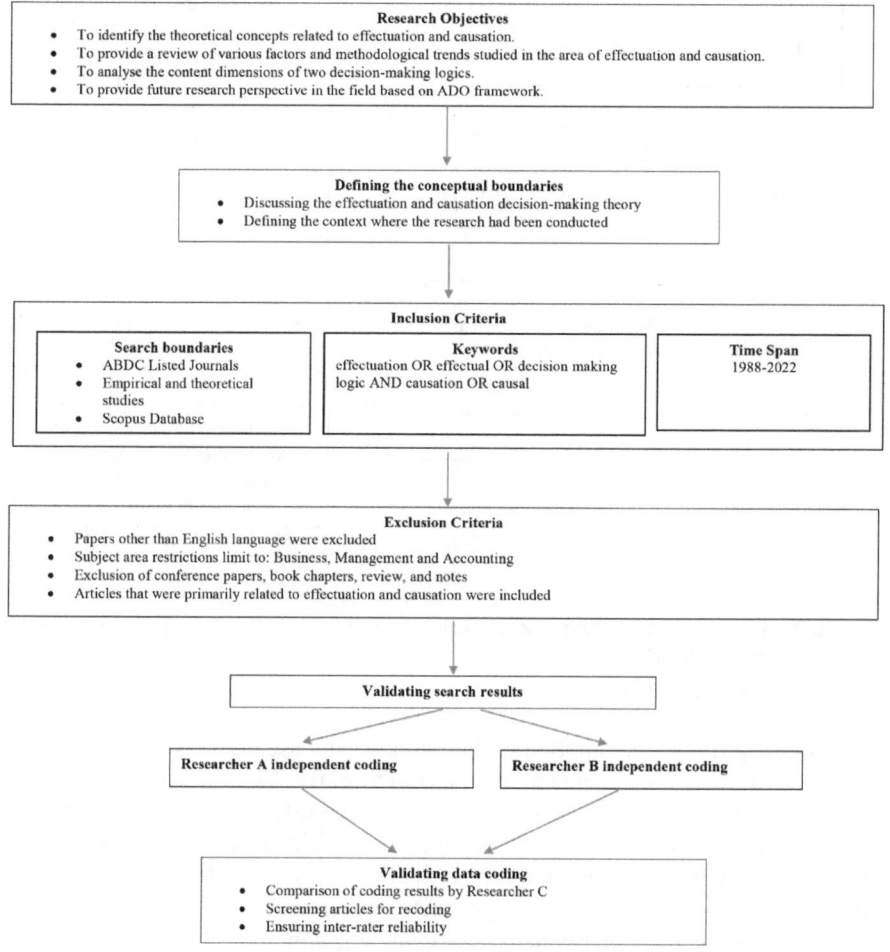

Research Objectives
- To identify the theoretical concepts related to effectuation and causation.
- To provide a review of various factors and methodological trends studied in the area of effectuation and causation.
- To analyse the content dimensions of two decision-making logics.
- To provide future research perspective in the field based on ADO framework.

Defining the conceptual boundaries
- Discussing the effectuation and causation decision-making theory
- Defining the context where the research had been conducted

Inclusion Criteria

Search boundaries	Keywords	Time Span
• ABDC Listed Journals • Empirical and theoretical studies • Scopus Database	effectuation OR effectual OR decision making logic AND causation OR causal	1988-2022

Exclusion Criteria
- Papers other than English language were excluded
- Subject area restrictions limit to: Business, Management and Accounting
- Exclusion of conference papers, book chapters, review, and notes
- Articles that were primarily related to effectuation and causation were included

Validating search results

Researcher A independent coding   **Researcher B independent coding**

Validating data coding
- Comparison of coding results by Researcher C
- Screening articles for recoding
- Ensuring inter-rater reliability

Fig. 18.1 Detailed SLR process

Source: Made by the authors

The initial step involved searching the database using the query command (TITLE-ABS-KEY (effectuation OR effectual OR decision AND making AND logic AND causation OR causal)). Following the search, 409 papers from 1988 to 2022 were found; the accuracy of the data was checked in each document. In the second step, restrictions on the Scopus database were applied with the inclusion of articles only (document type), journals (source type), and articles in the English language, resulting in 270 records. Then the bibliometric analysis of 270 articles was carried out. VOS viewer software was used for mapping and visualisation of data.

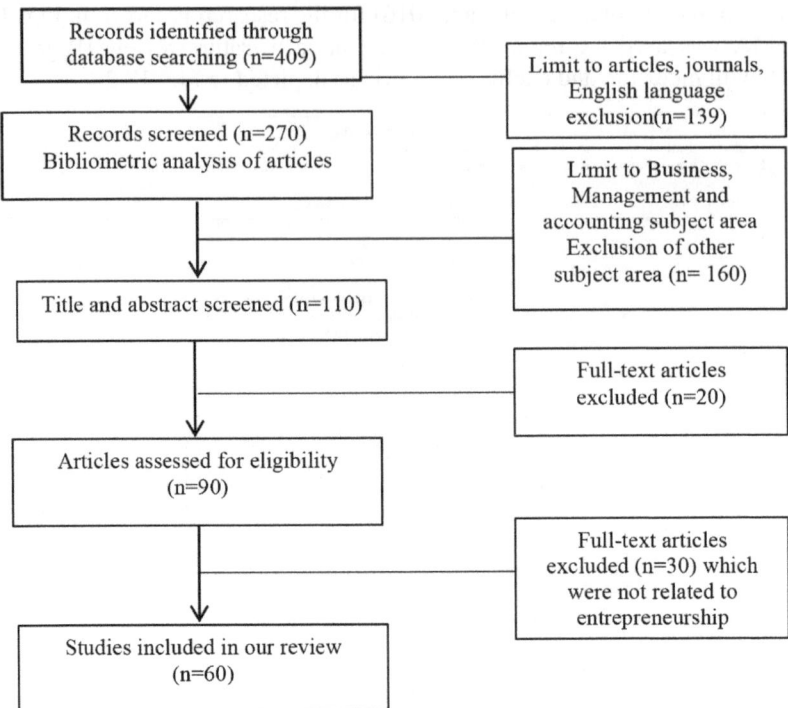

Fig. 18.2 Flowchart of inclusion and exclusion criteria of review papers using prisma method

Source: Made by the authors.

In step three, limits were applied to the Scopus database on the subject area that included Business, Management, and Accounting, resulting in 110 records. The analysis of 110 articles was conducted based on the title and abstracts that fit the study's objective by three researchers parallelly. This analysis yielded 90 articles that were found to be suitable for further analysis excluding 20 articles that were related to healthcare management, production economics, project management, supply chain management, financial management, economics, operation research, mathematical & and engineering sciences, education, and training. In step four, abstracts of 90 articles were analysed thoroughly by three researchers to select articles related to entrepreneurship. Finally, the content analysis of 60 articles was done based on the entrepreneurship area.

4. Results

The annual trend of research papers published in the field of causation and effectuation, with a minimum number of publications recorded (2 articles) in 1988. Then gradually the publications increased in the year 2006. The highest number of publications was witnessed in 2021, with 37 articles, as shown in

Fig. 18.3. During the first decade (1988-1999), there were about 23 publications, and the second decade (2000-2009) witnessed 38 publications. From 2010 to 2019, there were 115 publications in this area, followed by 83 publications from 2020 to 2022, which proved that this area of research gained tremendous attention from researchers globally.

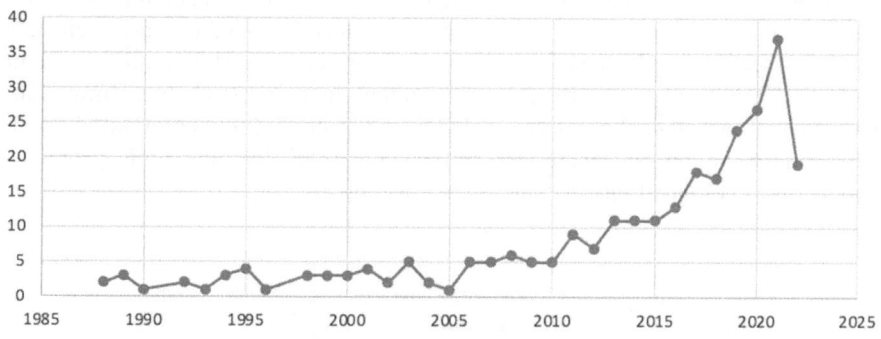

Fig. 18.3 Publications per year

Source: Adapted from Scopus database

The Fig. 18.4 shows the relationship of the keyword from 2005 to 2020. The most commonly used keyword is decision making, with a total link strength of 515, and the average year of publication is 2012. The logic keyword has the second highest link strength of 113 with an average year of publication in 2006, followed by effectuation with a total link strength of 82 and an average year of publication in 2019. From 2018 to 2020 the most commonly used keywords were causation, effectuation, international new venture, innovation, performance assessment, uncertainty, and entrepreneur.

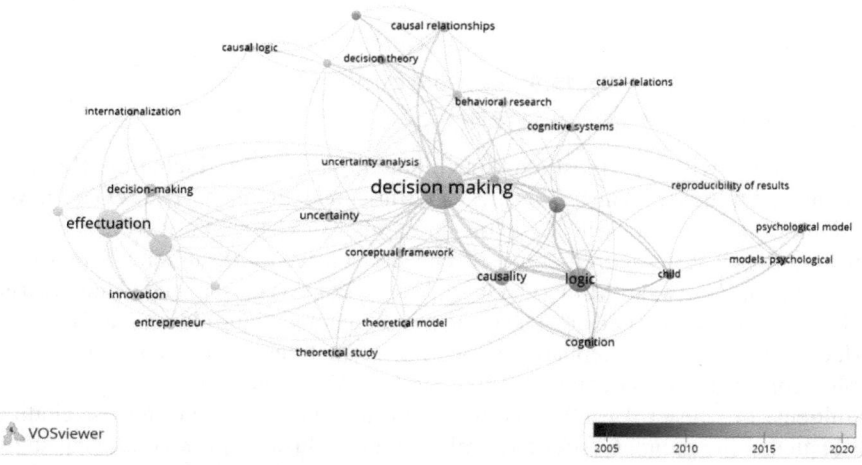

Fig. 18.4 The association of keywords over the years

Source: Adapted from Vos Viewer software

The most frequently used keywords in the literature relating to causation and effectuation are shown in Fig. 18.5. A minimum of five times per term was used for the analysis, which used 44 keywords. The entire keyword list is divided into four clusters by the software. The keyword decision-making, included in cluster 1, is frequently used (red-coloured cluster). Artificial intelligence, behavioural research, causal logic, cognitive systems, international entrepreneurship, and other terms are included in Cluster 1 (red-coloured cluster). Cluster 2 (the green cluster) is more associated with causation, effectuation, entrepreneurship, innovation, and so forth. Cognition, environmental management, human knowledge, simulation, uncertainty, and other themes are included in Cluster 3 (blue-coloured cluster). Cluster 4 (the yellow cluster) focuses more on judgment, learning, logic, problem-solving, psychological models, and other concepts.

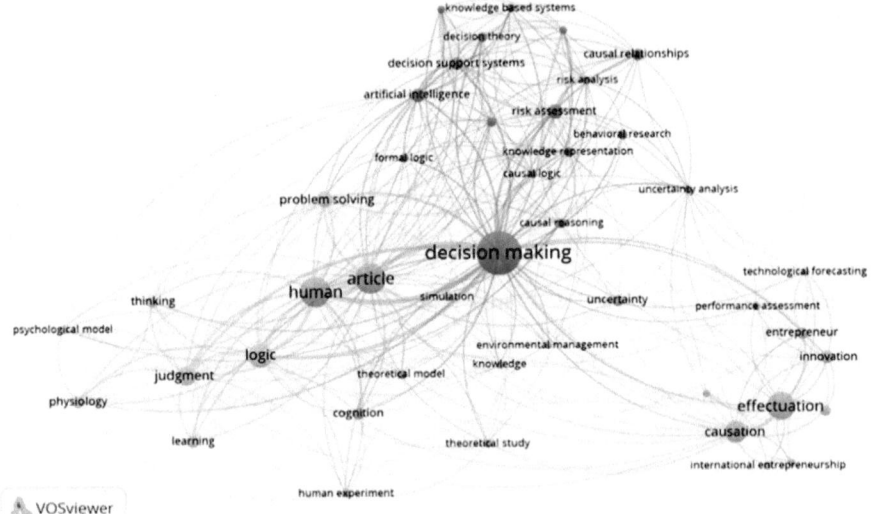

Fig. 18.5 Keyword cluster analysis

Source: Adapted from Vos Viewer software

The authors with the most citations jointly have 1624, including Berends, Reymen, Stultiens, Zhang, Mauer, Van Burg, and Stephan. The VOS viewer output gives 6 clusters with 29 items and a total link strength of 317, as shown in Fig. 18.6. Cluster 1 (red-coloured cluster) consists of 7 authors: Sarasvathy, Saarenketo, Ciszewska-Mlinaric, Obloj, Wasowska, Arvidsson, and Coudounaris. Cluster 2 (green-coloured cluster) is the largest among all the clusters, as Berends, Mauer, Van burg, and Stephan has the highest citations in this cluster. Cluster 3 (blue-coloured cluster) comprises five authors: Cui, Feng, Zhang, Reymen, and Stultiens. In Cluster 4 (yellow-coloured cluster), Ojala has the highest citation (97) among the group. Cluster 5 (purple-coloured cluster) is the same as cluster 4 with four authors: Laskovaia, Morris, Shirokova, and Wang. Cluster 6 (light blue coloured cluster) is the smallest among all the clusters with two authors, Zhang and Wang.

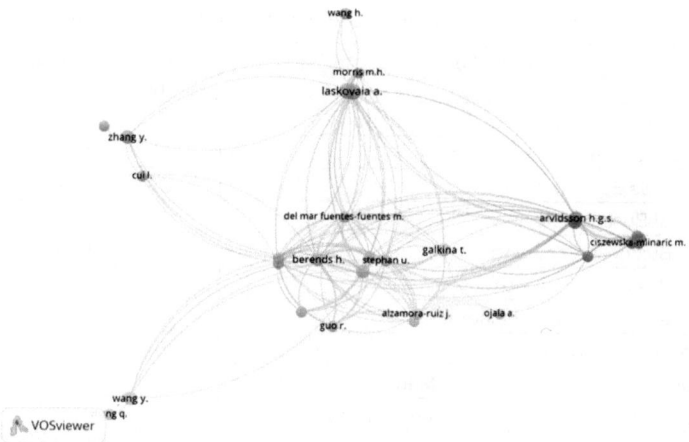

Fig. 18.6 Author analysis

Source: Adapted from Vos Viewer software

The VOS viewer software can be used to find out how many times a particular source has been cited. Figure 18.7 displays the network diagram of the most frequently cited sources. For the analysis, the minimum number of documents and citations for each source was chosen to be two respectively. The output had a total of 4 clusters with 16 elements and a total of 67 links. According to Table 18.1, the journals with the most citations are Technological Forecasting and Social Change (303 citations), Strategic Entrepreneurship Journal (237 citations), and Small Business Economics (188 citations).

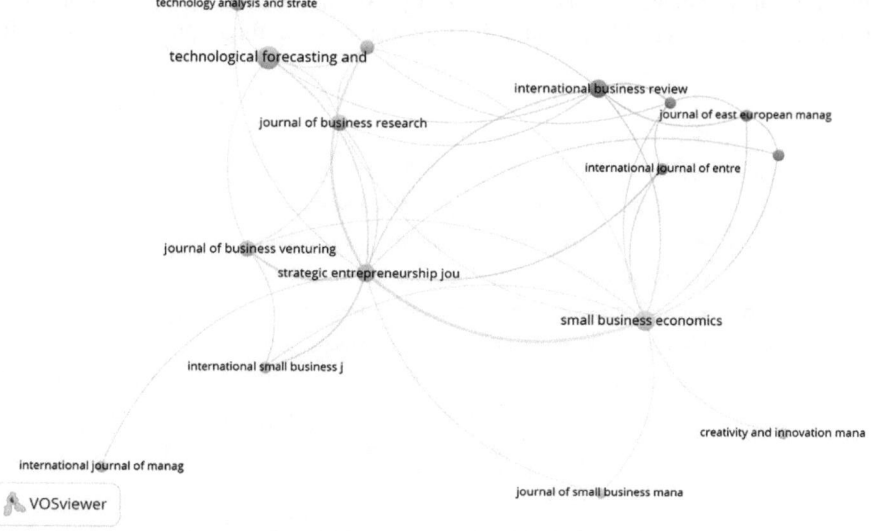

Fig. 18.7 VOS viewer output for most cited sources

Source: Adapted from Vos Viewer software

Table 18.1   Most cited sources with total link strength

Journal(s)	Total Link Strength	Citations	Docu-ments
Technological Forecasting and Social Change	8	303	8
Strategic Entrepreneurship Journal	36	237	5
Small Business Economics	21	188	6
International Business Review	11	158	5
Journal of Business Venturing	9	118	4
Journal of Business Research	7	83	4
Creativity and Innovation Management	1	82	2
European Business Review	6	55	2
International Entrepreneurship and Management Journal	12	44	3
Journal of East European Management Studies	5	27	2
International Journal of Entrepreneurship	3	14	2
Journal of Small Business Management	2	14	2
International Small Business Journal: Researching Entrepreneurship	5	9	2
Technology Analysis and Strategic Management	3	8	3
International Journal of Managing Projects in Business	1	5	2
International Journal of Entrepreneurial Venturing	4	4	2

Source: Adapted from Vos Viewer software

The roots of effectuation and causation can be traced back to Carnegie Mellon University's research on the entrepreneurial decision-making process (Sarasvathy, 2001b). Figure 18.8 shows that Laskovaia and Shirokova have the maximum number of publications (4), followed by Arvidsson, Berends, Coudounaris, Galkina, Hagmayer, Mauer, and Papageorgiou with three publications each.

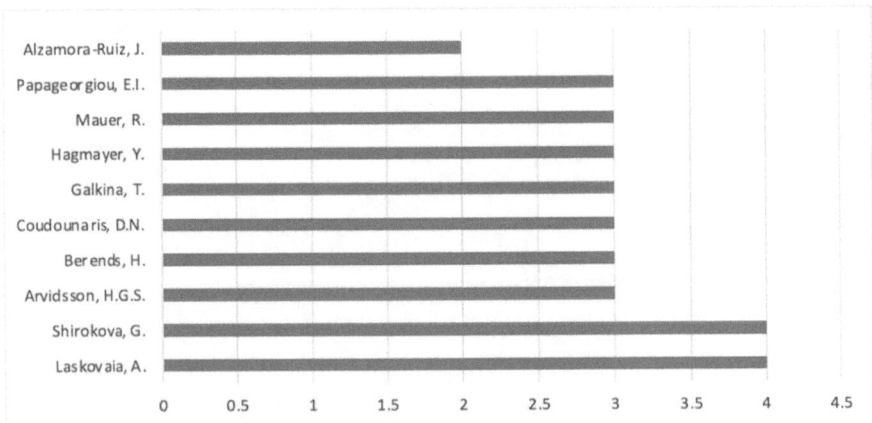

Fig. 18.8   Number of articles per author

Source: Adapted from Scopus database

Figure 18.9 depicts the universities contributing the most in several publications over the years. The Vaasan Yliopisto (Finland), Vrije Universiteit Amsterdam (Netherlands), and University College London (England) are among the top universities based on several articles published.

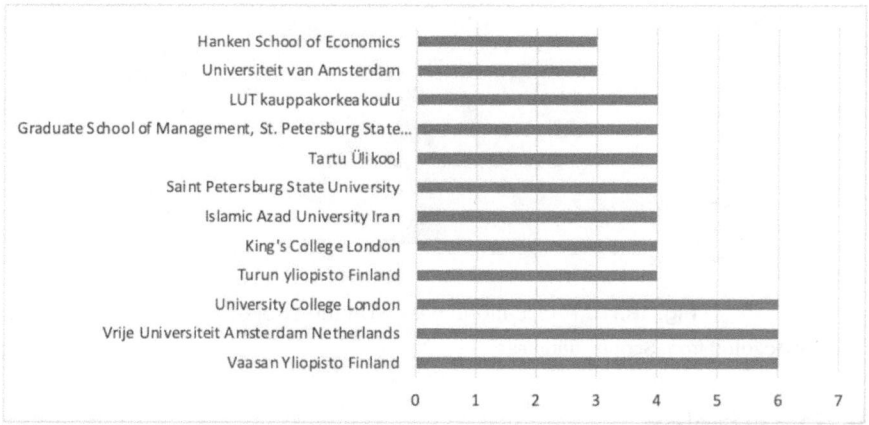

Fig. 18.9 Publications by organizations

Source: Adapted from Scopus database

In the field of effectuation and causation, with the most significant number of publications, the United States contributes 17% of the overall production. The United Kingdom contributed the second-highest percentage (11%) in the number of publications, followed by China with a 7% contribution, as shown in Fig. 18.10. Majorly the research in the area of effectuation and causation was carried out in Business, Management, and Accounting with 110 documents (22%) followed by Computer Science with 58 documents (11%) Psychology and Social Sciences (10% each) as shown in Fig. 18.11.

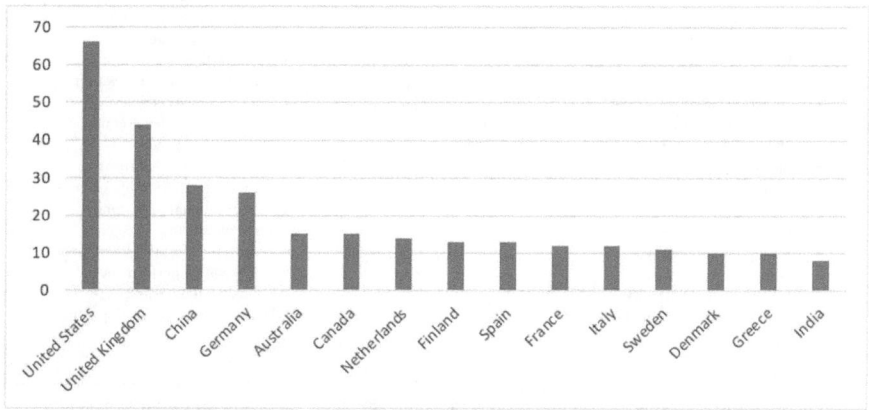

Fig. 18.10 The research contribution of countries

Source: Adapted from Scopus database

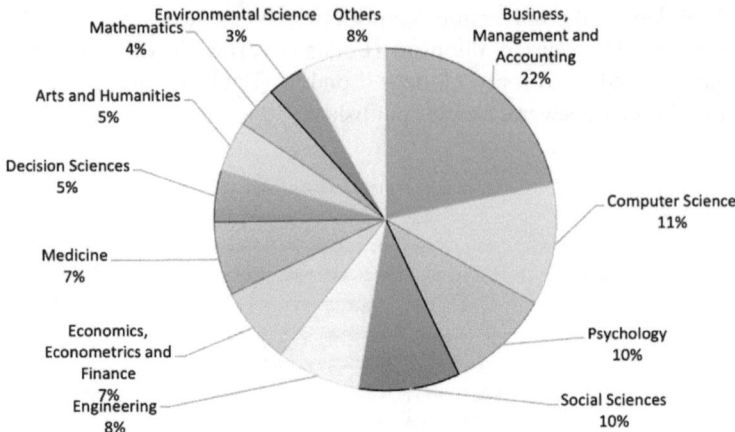

Fig. 18.11 Publications based on the subject area

Source: Adapted from Scopus database

5. Discussion

The review elaborates on the role of antecedents, decision characteristics, and outcomes in the research and offers specific directions for future researchers in this area of entrepreneurship based on the ADO framework (Paul & Criado, 2020). This study is the first to highlight the antecedents and consequences of effectuation and causation decision-making logics used in entrepreneurship research, as shown in Fig. 18.12.

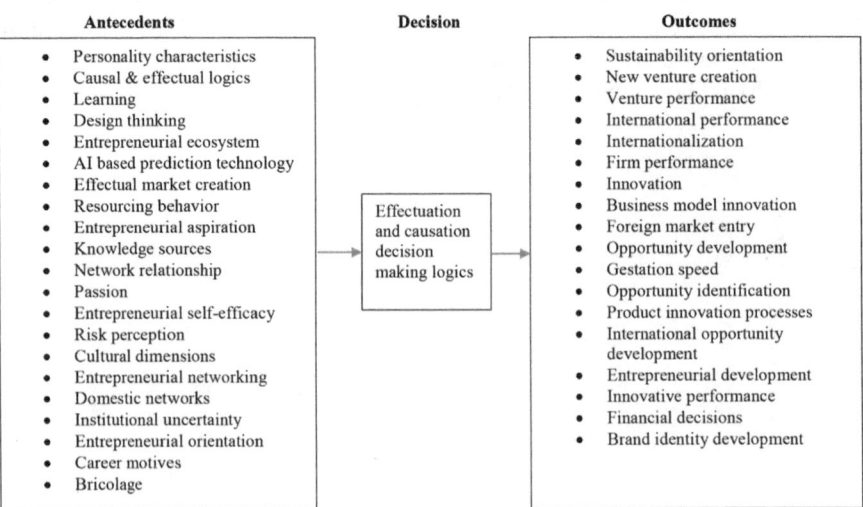

Fig. 18.12 Antecedents, decisions and outcomes (ADO)

Source: Made by the authors

5.1 Implications

Theoretical Implications

The researchers contributed to effectuation and causation decision logic based on empirical and theoretical evidence (Frese et al., 2020). However, less has been contributed to understanding the contextual factors (Galavotti et al., 2021) and their impact on decision logic. The present study is significant for understanding the theoretical and empirical evidence of antecedents, decision characteristics, and outcomes that entrepreneurs achieve based on using effectuation and causation research. This study shall help potential entrepreneurs identify which decision logic (effectually or causally) leads to successful venture creation through literature analysis and therefore bridging the gap identified in previous research studies (Mendes et al., 2019; Munteanu et al., 2022). This study will further provide insight to successful or expert entrepreneurs to understand better the antecedents identified through the theoretical lenses that impact decision-making logic and lead to desirable outcomes. The theory of decision-making logic: effectuation and causation can provide a strong foundation to carry out research in this area of entrepreneurship and provide a theoretical foundation for the area of entrepreneurship research for conducting scholarly work. This theory can provide global insights to researchers to differentiate between expert and novice entrepreneurs' decision choices (Dew et al., 2009; Ruiz-Jiménez et al., 2021) based on explicit literature. This study has analysed theoretical and empirical research in the field, therefore addressing the gap in the study (Zhang et al., 2019, 2023).

Managerial Implications

From a practical perspective, this review provides a deep insight into how entrepreneurs use specific heuristics to deal with uncertainty (Mensah et al., 2021). Environmental uncertainties play a very vital role in shaping the entrepreneurial culture. This research shall broaden the perspective of entrepreneurs in understanding the different factors that influence their ventures/firm performance (Shirokova et al., 2021; Yu et al., 2018). The managers can lead the organisations using decision logic based on this theory in conditions of uncertainty to better channel the organisation's output.

One of the antecedents of these two decision-making logics i.e., effectuation and causation is based on AI-driven technology, which shall empower entrepreneurs to add value to their products by taking leverage upon technological advancements (Alzamora-Ruiz, del Mar Fuentes-Fuentes, et al., 2021) even in uncertain times. Entrepreneurial activities help create wide networks among social groups and increase the firm's adaptability in the environment; this study shall help develop a social linkage.

Novice entrepreneurs might begin their business by minimizing losses and leveraging opportunities provided by the principles of effectuation that deal with available means. This is illustrated well in the empirical investigations conducted in the context of SMEs and new venture performances (Ruiz-Jiménez et al., 2021). These decision logics i.e., effectuation and causation used by entrepreneurs depend upon the size of the firm, development stage, resources, and other environmental factors (Zhang et al., 2019, 2023).

6. Conclusion

This review conducted a systematic analysis from 1988 to 2022 based on the Scopus database, which yielded 409 documents. Further, the bibliometric analysis of 270 articles was conducted using VOS viewer software. The results proposed that in 2006, there were more publications than in any previous year. With 37 articles published, 2021 saw the most publications, demonstrating the global scholars' intense interest in this field of study. The most commonly used keyword in the literature is decision making, with total link strength of 515, and the average year of publication is 2012. From 2018-2020 most commonly used keywords in the literature were causation, effectuation, international new venture, innovation, performance assessment, uncertainty, and entrepreneur. The authors with the maximum number of citations were Berends, Reymen, Stultiens, Zhang, Mauer, Van burg, and Stephan, totalling 1624 citations. The journals with the most citations were Technological Forecasting and Social Change (303 citations), followed by Strategic Entrepreneurship Journal (237 citations) and Small Business Economics (188 citations). Laskovaia and Shirokova had the maximum number of publications. The Vaasan Yliopisto (Finland), Vrije Universiteit Amsterdam (Netherlands), and University College London (England) were among the top universities that published the maximum number of articles. The USA had the leads in the number of publications in the area of effectuation and causation. Business, management, and accounting subject area contributed the maximum to this field with 110 articles. The content analysis was based on the ADO framework, which elaborated on the antecedents used by different researchers in understanding decision-making logic. The content analysis comprised the type of article, theories used, methods, and outcomes of the research. The literature on effectuation and causation will expand the existing body of knowledge through this research. It will provide insights to researchers to further study this area.

Limitations

This attempt at a systematic review in the field can only be considered partially exhaustive, the author acknowledges, considering the length of the study. As a result, the study's findings cannot be applied to the whole field as it is limited to business, management, and accounting subject areas. In light of this, a systematic literature review will work as a qualitative resource for future researchers interested in decision-making logics (effectuation and causation) and the interaction between antecedents and decision characteristics to accomplish desired results.

REFERENCES

1. Alzamora-Ruiz, J., del Mar Fuentes-Fuentes, M., & Martinez-Fiestas, M. (2021). Together or separately? Direct and synergistic effects of Effectuation and Causation on innovation in technology-based SMEs. *International Entrepreneurship and Management Journal, 17*(4), 1917–1943. https://doi.org/10.1007/s11365-021-00743-9

2. Benz, S. H., & Baum, M. (2023). What predicts effectuation preferences Disentangling individual and environmental factors and illuminating decision criteria. *International Journal of Entrepreneurial Venturing, 15*(1), 91. https://doi.org/10.1504/IJEV.2023.129283

3. Cowden, B., Karami, M., Tang, J., Ye, W., & Adomako, S. (2022). The spectrum of perceived uncertainty and entrepreneurial orientation: Impacts on effectuation. *Journal of Small Business Management*, 1–34. https://doi.org/10.1080/00472778.2022.2051179

4. Dew, N., Read, S., Sarasvathy, S. D., & Wiltbank, R. (2009). Effectual versus predictive logics in entrepreneurial decision-making: Differences between experts and novices. *Journal of Business Venturing, 24*(4), 287–309. https://doi.org/10.1016/j.jbusvent.2008.02.002

5. Frese, T., Geiger, I., & Dost, F. (2020). An empirical investigation of determinants of effectual and causal decision logics in online and high-tech start-up firms. *Small Business Economics, 54*(3), 641–664. https://doi.org/10.1007/s11187-019-00147-8

6. Galavotti, I., Lippi, A., & Cerrato, D. (2021). The representativeness heuristic at work in decision-making: Building blocks and individual-level cognitive and behavioral factors. *Management Decision, 59*(7), 1664–1683. https://doi.org/10.1108/MD-10-2019-1464

7. Mendes, F. F., Mendes, E., & Salleh, N. (2019). The relationship between personality and decision-making: A Systematic literature review. *Information and Software Technology, 111*, 50–71. https://doi.org/10.1016/j.infsof.2019.03.010

8. Mensah, E. K., Asamoah, L. A., & Jafari-Sadeghi, V. (2021). Entrepreneurial opportunity decisions under uncertainty: Recognizing the complementing role of personality traits and cognitive skills. *Journal of Entrepreneurship, Management and Innovation, 17*(1), 25–55.

9. Munteanu, D. R., Vanderstraeten, J., van Witteloostuijn, A., & Cambré, B. (2022). A systematic literature review on SME internationalization: A personality lens. *Management Review Quarterly*. https://doi.org/10.1007/s11301-022-00279-4

10. Nolan, C. T., & Garavan, T. N. (2016). Human Resource Development in SMEs: A Systematic Review of the Literature: Human Resource Development in SMEs. *International Journal of Management Reviews, 18*(1), 85–107. https://doi.org/10.1111/ijmr.12062

11. Page, M. J., McKenzie, J. E., Bossuyt, P. M., Boutron, I., Hoffmann, T. C., Mulrow, C. D., Shamseer, L., Tetzlaff, J. M., Akl, E. A., Brennan, S. E., Chou, R., Glanville, J., Grimshaw, J. M., Hróbjartsson, A., Lalu, M. M., Li, T., Loder, E. W., Mayo-Wilson, E., McDonald, S., … Moher, D. (2021). The PRISMA 2020 statement: An updated guideline for reporting systematic reviews. *Systematic Reviews, 10*(1), 89. https://doi.org/10.1186/s13643-021-01626-4

12. Paul, J., & Criado, A. R. (2020). The art of writing literature review: What do we know and what do we need to know? *International Business Review*, *29*(4), 101717. https://doi.org/10.1016/j.ibusrev.2020.101717

13. Read, S., Dew, N., Sarasvathy, S. D., Song, M., & Wiltbank, R. (2009). Marketing under Uncertainty: The Logic of an Effectual Approach. *Journal of Marketing*, *73*(3), 1–18. https://doi.org/10.1509/jmkg.73.3.001

14. Ruiz-Jiménez, J. M., Ruiz-Arroyo, M., & del Mar Fuentes-Fuentes, M. (2021). The impact of effectuation, causation, and resources on new venture performance: Novice versus expert entrepreneurs. *Small Business Economics*, *57*(4), 1761–1781. https://doi.org/10.1007/s11187-020-00371-7

15. Sarasvathy, S. D. (2001a). Causation and Effectuation: Toward a Theoretical Shift from Economic Inevitability to Entrepreneurial Contingency. *The Academy of Management Review*, *26*(2), 243. https://doi.org/10.2307/259121

16. Sarasvathy, S. D. (2001b). Effectual Reasoning in Entrepreneurial Decision Making: Existence and Bounds. *Academy of Management Proceedings*, *2001*(1), D1–D6. https://doi.org/10.5465/apbpp.2001.6133065

17. Shirokova, G., Morris, M. H., Laskovaia, A., & Micelotta, E. (2021). Effectuation and causation, firm performance, and the impact of institutions: A multi-country moderation analysis. *Journal of Business Research*, *129*, 169–182. https://doi.org/10.1016/j.jbusres.2021.02.045

18. Yu, X., Tao, Y., Tao, X., Xia, F., & Li, Y. (2018). Managing uncertainty in emerging economies: The interaction effects between causation and effectuation on firm performance. *Technological Forecasting and Social Change*, *135*, 121–131. https://doi.org/10.1016/j.techfore.2017.11.017

19. Zhang, Y., Cui, L., Zhang, G., Sarasvathy, S., & Anusha, R. (2019). An Exploratory Study of Antecedents of Entrepreneurial Decision-Making Logics: The Role of Self-Efficacy, Optimism, and Perspective Taking. *Emerging Markets Finance and Trade*, *55*(4), 781–794. https://doi.org/10.1080/1540496X.2018.1478283

20. Zhang, Y., Li, Z., Sha, Y., & Yang, K. (2023). The impact of decision-making styles (effectuation logic and causation logic) on firm performance: A meta-analysis. *Journal of Business & Industrial Marketing*, *38*(1), 85–101. https://doi.org/10.1108/JBIM-08-2021-0378

Emerging Horizons: Business and Society in the Post Pandemic Era –
Brig. Dr. Rajiv Divekar et al. (eds)
© 2024 Taylor & Francis Group, London, ISBN 978-1-032-90822-9

19

A Study of the Relationship Between Shoppers' Demography and Online Store Preference Post COVID-19

Smita Mehendale[1]
Assistant Professor,
Symbiosis Institute of Management Studies (SIMS),
Symbiosis International Deemed University,
Pune, India

Aakash Kamble[2]
Flame University, Lavale, Pune, India

ABSTRACT

Online shoppers of a particular e-store exhibit specific demographic characteristics which distinguish them from shoppers of other online retail stores. This study examines the relationship between demographic characteristics and preference for a specific online store. Demographic characteristics of age, education, occupation and annual household income in (Rs.) are the most commonly studied in the case of retailing, which have also been considered for this study. A sample of 586 respondents was collected across India through a survey using a structured questionnaire. Chi-square tests established associations between variables measuring select demographic characteristics and store preference. The study found that demographic variables are significantly associated with online shopping preferences.

KEYWORDS: Online shopping, Online store preference, Age, Education, Occupation, Income

1. Introduction

The Indian e-commerce sector is currently moving from infancy to the next phase of growth. In the last decade, the market has witnessed exponential growth, and

[1]smita.m@sims.edu, [2]kamble.aakash@outlook.com

DOI: 10.4324/978100355996-19

predictions for the future are consistent with the past. But that is still the tip of the iceberg as online channels, especially in retail, are a small portion of the overall retail sector; hence scope for growth is immense. Online retail has shown the highest and most consistent growth.

Indian online retail is poised to be the world's fastest-growing market. E-retail is currently a minuscule portion of the overall retail sector in India. Currently, at 3.4% of the overall retail sector (Salman, 2020), the online retail segment of e-commerce was expected to grow 31% to reach 32.70 billion in 2018 and touch US$60 billion in 2020. In addition, the share of Retail currently accounts for 10% of India's GDP and 8% of employment (Chandra, n.d.).

The Indian ecosystem for retail is robust and all set to launch the next glorious phase of growth for e-retailing. One reason for the phenomenal growth story of Indian e-retailing is the increase in internet users from 4% in 2007 to 52.09% in 2019 (Ibef, 2020). The internet users in India (in numbers) in 2020 was 700 million and may reach the mark of 974 million users by 2025 (projected) (Keelery, 2020). This data shows tremendous potential for growth for businesses relying on the internet to deliver products and services. India has been ranked second only to China in terms of potential for the online market worldwide. In India, this rise in the projected number of users of internet comes not just from urban areas but also rural areas. In addition, digital buyers in India are estimated to touch 100-110 million in 2020 (Soni, 2020). The internet penetration in India in 2019 was 36%, which signals room for further growth. In fact, in absolute numbers, India was expected to surpass USA (Pwc, 2014). This offers an excellent opportunity for online players. Coupled with this, the swelling number of smartphone users in India is also a factor in the rise of online retailing. COVID-19 offered an excellent opportunity to online retailers as customer groups who had not shopped online earlier also started shopping for limited product categories online. Also, shoppers started buying categories of products earlier that they bought offline only during the COVID-19 lockdown.

Flipkart currently leads the Indian online retail space along with Myntra, its fashion apparel subsidiary. Originally homegrown, it started operation in 2007 as a bookseller, but later in 2018, Walmart acquired a significant stake with an investment of $16 billion. With the entry of Walmart into this space, amazon has lost its edge as an international player with deep pockets. Amazon is an American organization that started operations in 1994 in the US. It made a soft entry into India with jungle.com, a price comparison website. It launched amazon.in in June 2013, surprising experts with an organic approach to India as against widely expected inorganic entry.

This study was undertaken to understand the relationship between online store preference for amazon or flipkart and demographic characteristics like age, education, occupation and household income of online shoppers post-COVID-19.

2. Literature Review

India tops the world list of young demographic population (Insightsonindia, 2020; Policy Circle Bureau, 2022). As against the higher median age in developed countries, India's median age is 22 (Ghosh. 2020), which offers a massive opportunity for online retailing since past research confirms that younger generations are more internet savvy and confident in shopping online than their predecessors. There has been growth in literacy levels in India from 1951 at just 18.3% to 74.4 in 2018 (TIMESOFINDIA.COM, 2022). This growth is accompanied by growth in digital literacy which has led to increased penetration of online retailing.

Researchers have agreed that individual (shopper) characteristics influence preference for a store. These attributes include demographic, socioeconomic, psychographic and geographic factors. Carpenter and Moore (2006) concluded in their research that the characteristics of customers have a significant impact on predicting consumption behaviours in the context of a retail store. Past researchers confirmed that online shopping behaviour is highly influenced with demographic factors (Bawa & Ghosh, 1999; Leszczyc et al., 2000) also confirm that standard demographic variables are significant predictors of the "shopping behaviour of the household". Other similar studies on influence of demographic variables in the context of retail stores confirmed their impact on the timing of the visit to store (Kahn & Schmittlein, 1989), devising promotional strategies for retail (Pattanaik et al., 2017) and preference for a particular store (Kau & Ehrenberg, 1984). Hence, retailers consider the demographics of customers as essential for developing strategies for retailers.

Demographic factors commonly considered for research in retail include occupation, education, income and age (Arnold & Reynolds, 2003; Sinha & Banerjee, 2004; Zeithaml, 1988). These factors are also closely related to each other and hence studied together to understand the demographic profiles of online shoppers. A field study by Zeithaml (1988) examined the extent of influence of demographic factors, namely age, status of marriage, income, gender, and work status, on variables related to retail shopping (e.g., amount of money spent, number of times of visits to supermarket in a week. Similarly, Fox et al. (2004) drew a comparison between demographic profiles of shoppers of supermarket and warehouse club shoppers. They found that age, education and income levels differed for the two types of retailers. One of the critical metrics in retail is the time spent in retail stores, which according to a study, is influenced by age, education, occupation, level of income, marital status and gender (Bellman et al., 1999; Forsythe and Bailey, 1996; Slyke et al., 2002). Advancing age is also an indication of family status and career growth, leading to increased and diversified online purchases (Bauboniené & Gulevičiūtė, 2015). Although studies have been conducted on online store preference, but have not focused on demographic characteristics as determinants of store preference. This study is undertaken to indicate the influence of select demographic factors on e-retail store preference, amazon and flipkart.

Most studies on age and online shopping conclude that age is a predictor of online shopping preference. Contradictory findings also exist in the literature. A study by Safitri et al. (2018) concluded that Gen Y might not be fully aware of online shopping. However, age group is an essential factor in online shopping preferences, as concluded by past studies (Richa 2012). Another study concluded that age group, along with education, plays a significant role in choosing online stores for shopping. Haver (2008) also concluded that younger groups segments based on age are more likely to be conversant with online shopping and hence develop online shopping preferences. Trocchia and Janda, (2000) found the younger generation to be more conversant with the internet and hence better informed and more critical in evaluating online services like retailing. This could be the result of better education and choice of profession (Kanchan et al., 2015). Singh and Sailo (2013), in their study, concludes that service class, in particular, professionals in government service are more likely to use the internet and internet services like online retailing. Bellman (1999) also suggested the influence of age, income and education on the choice of online shopping.

Therefore,

H1: There is an association between Online Store Preference and Age

H2: There is an association between Online Store Preference and Education

H3: There is an association between Online Store Preference and Occupation

H4: There is an association between Online Store Preference and Income

3. Methodology

A sample of 586 was collected from across India for this survey during December 2021 and February 2022. Qualitative factors like availability of resources and time and significance of the study were considered while deciding on sample size (Malhotra & Birks, 2007; Malhotra & Dash, 2010). Demographic studies are justified with a large sample size; hence a large sample was collected based on the online store preference of shoppers. The quota sampling method, a non-probability method of sampling has been used for this study. The questionnaire collected categorical data on age, occupation, income, education and store preference (amazon and flipkart). Since those shoppers online are internet savvy, the survey was conducted online by sending emails or WhatsApp links. Also, since the sample was collected across India, online surveys have a wider reach and were found to be a suitable method for this study. This study used the Chi-square test of independence to understand the demographic variables' relationships with online shopping behaviour based on groups of respondents with store preferences of either amazon or flipkart. Effect size calculation is done with Phi (for 2 * 2 table) or Cramer's V (more than two categories). The data collected was analyzed using IBM SPSS 22.

4. Data Analysis

Retail store preferences and demographic characteristics of shoppers are studied together to better understand a phenomenon. Thus, demographic variables have significance in this study. The formulated hypothesis tries to establish an association between online store preference (amazon or flipkart) and demographic characteristics. The demographic factors considered in this study to understand their impact on the store preference are age, gender, education, occupation and annual household income in (Rs.) to test whether there is any association between the demographic variables and Store Preference, Chi-square test of independence was applied.

H1: There is an association between Online Store Preference (amazon or flipkart) and age.

A chi-square test of independence was carried out for comparing the demographic variable in age categories and Preferred Store (amazon or flipkart) (Table 19.1)

Table 19.1 Age and preferred store

			Preferred_str		Total
			Amazon	**Flipkart**	
Age	18 – 25yrs	Count	46	77	123
		% within Age	37.4%	62.6%	100.0%
	26 – 35yrs	Count	185	165	350
		% within Age	52.9%	47.1%	100.0%
	36 – 45yrs	Count	58	14	72
		% within Age	80.6%	19.4%	100.0%
	46 yrs and above	Count	4	37	41
		% within Age	9.76%	90.2%	100.0%
Total		Count	293	293	586
		% within Age	50.0%	50.0%	100.0%

Table 19.2 reveals that a significant interaction was found ($\chi2$ (3, n = 586) = 62.406, p < .05). Hence, it is concluded that the variable age has a significant association with online store preference for amazon and flipkart. The effect size of the significance was calculated using Cramer's V (more than 2 * 2 table) and was found to be 0.33 which is substantial.

A post-hoc analysis was carried out with Bonferroni Chi-Square Residual Analysis (Table 19.3). The Bonferroni corrected p value (.05/8 = .0063) was considered to

Table 19.2 Chi-square tests for age and preferred store

	Value	Df	Asymp. Sig. (2-sided)
Pearson Chi-Square	62.406[a]	3	.000
Likelihood Ratio	68.543	3	.000
Linear-by-Linear Association	.226	1	.634
N of Valid Cases	586		

a. 0 cells (0.0%) have expected count less than 5. The minimum expected count is 20.50.

Table 19.3 Bonferroni chi-square residual analysis

Gen	Df	$\chi 2$ value	Adj p value
18 - 25 yrs – amazon	3	9.86	.0198
26 - 35 yrs – amazon	3	2.82	.4198
36 - 45 yrs – amazon	3	30.69	.0000
45 yrs and above – amazon	3	28.52	.0000
18 - 25 yrs – flipkart	3	9.86	.0198
26 - 35 yrs – flipkart	3	2.82	.4198
36 - 45 yrs – flipkart	3	30.69	.0000
45 yrs and above – flipkart	3	28.52	.0000

determine significant differences. Age group of 36 to 45 yrs -amazon, age group of 46 yrs and above -amazon, age group of 36 to 45 yrs – flipkart and 46 yrs and above -flipkart were found to be significantly different. Age group of 46 yrs and above have a clear preference for flipkart whereas age group of 36 to 45 yrs has a clear preference for amazon.

H2: There is an association between Online Store Preference (amazon or flipkart) and education

A chi-square test of independence was carried out for comparing demographic variable, Education (Primary/Secondary, Diploma, Bachelor's/ Graduate Degree, Postgraduate Degree, Doctorate and Others) and Preferred Store (amazon or flipkart) (Table 19.4).

Table 19.4 Education and preferred store

			Preferred_str		Total
			Amazon	Flipkart	
Education	Primary/Secondary/ Diploma/Graduate	Count	111	135	246
		% within Preferred_str	37.9%	46.1%	42.0%
	Postgraduate/ Doctorate	Count	182	158	340
		% within Preferred_str	62.1%	53.9%	58.0%
Total		Count	293	293	586
		% within Preferred_str	100.0%	100.0%	100.0%

Table 19.5 reveals that a significant interaction was found ($\chi2$ (5, n = 586) = 4.036, p <.05). Hence, it is concluded that the demographic variable Education (Primary/Secondary/Diploma/ Graduate Degree and Postgraduate Degree/ Doctorate) has a significant association with online store preference for amazon and flipkart. Table 19.5 shows that counts of respondents with education up to Primary/Secondary/Graduate/Diploma have a clear preference for flipkart as against Postgraduate Degree holders who prefer amazon. The Cramer's V value of 0.08 shows negligible effect.

Table 19.5 Chi-square test for education and preferred store

	Value	df	Asymp. Sig. (2-sided)
Pearson Chi-Square	4.036[a]	1	.045
Continuity Correction[b]	3.706	1	.054
Likelihood Ratio	4.041	1	.044
Fisher's Exact Test			
Linear-by-Linear Association	4.029	1	.045
N of Valid Cases	586		

a. 0 cells (0.0%) have expected count less than 5. The minimum expected count is 123.00.
b. Computed only for a 2 x 2 table

H3: There is an association between Online Store Preference (amazon or flipkart) and occupation

A chi-square test of independence was carried out for comparing demographic variable Occupation (Salaried Employee, Self-employed, Homemaker, Student, Retired and Unemployed) and Preferred Store (amazon or flipkart) (Table 19.6).

Table 19.6 Occupation and preferred store

			Preferred_str		Total
			Amazon	Flipkart	
Occupation	Salaried Employee	Count	205	142	347
		% within Occupation	59.1%	40.9%	100.0%
	Self Employed	Count	35	34	69
		% within Occupation	50.7%	49.3%	100.0%
	Home Maker	Count	19	22	41
		% within Occupation	46.3%	53.7%	100.0%
	Student	Count	26	51	77
		% within Occupation	33.8%	66.2%	100.0%
	Retired	Count	5	37	42
		% within Occupation	11.9%	88.1%	100.0%
	Unemployed	Count	3	7	10
		% within Occupation	30.0%	70.0%	100.0%
Total		Count	293	293	586
		% within Occupation	50.0%	50.0%	100.0%

Table 19.7 reveals that a significant interaction was found (χ2 (5, n=586) = 45.770, p <.05). Hence, it is concluded that the demographic variable Occupation (Salaried Employee, Self-employed, Homemaker, Student, Retired and Unemployed) has a significant association with Preferred Store (amazon and flipkart). Table 19.6 shows that counts of respondents with occupation of Homemaker and Self-employed not being different in terms of preference and the count of Unemployed being less than 10 for any meaningful comparisons.

Table 19.7 Chi-square test for occupation and preferred store

	Value	Df	Asymp. Sig. (2-sided)
Pearson Chi-Square	45.770[a]	5	.000
Likelihood Ratio	49.210	5	.000
Linear-by-Linear Association	42.066	1	.000
N of Valid Cases	586		
a. 0 cells (0.0%) have expected count less than 5. The minimum expected count is 5.00.			

The Bonferroni adjusted chi square residual analysis (Table 19.9), shows the adjusted p value after Bonferroni correction and it is compared with p < .0042 (.05/12 = .0042). Significant difference was found in the preference of online stores for Salaried Employees and Retired people and Salaried Employees have a clear preference for amazon and retired people have a clear preference for flipkart. Also, Cramer's V is .28 which shows large effect (Table 19.8).

Table 19.8 Symmetric measures

		Value	Approx. Sig.
Nominal by Nominal	Phi	.279	.000
	Cramer's V	.279	.000
N of Valid Cases		586	

H4: There is an association between Online Store Preference (amazon or flipkart) and Annual Household Income (in Rs.)

A chi-square test of independence was carried out for comparing demographic variable Household Annual Income (in Rs.) with categories (Below 5,00,000lacs; 5,00,001 – 10, 00,000 lacs; 10,00,001 – 15,00,000 lacs; 15,00,001 – 20,00,000 lacs; Above 20,00,001) and Preferred Store (amazon or flipkart) (Table 19.10).

Table 19.11 reveals that a significant interaction was found (χ2 (4, n=586) = 77.534, p <.05). Hence it is concluded that the demographic variable Household Annual Income (in Rs.) with categories (Below 5,00,000lacs; 5,00,001 – 10, 00,000 lacs; 10,00,001 – 15,00,000 lacs; 15,00,001 – 20,00,000 lacs; Above 20,00,001) has

Table 19.9 Occupation_ bonferroni chi-square residual analysis

Occupation	Df	χ2 value	Adj p value
Salaried Employee_amazon	5	28.09	0.0000
Self Employed_amazon	5	.02	1.0000
Home Maker_amazon	5	.24	0.9986
Student_amazon	5	9.36	0.0954
Retired_amazon	5	26.21	0.0001
Unemployed_amazon	5	1.64	0.8966
Salaried Employee_flipkart	5	28.09	0.0000
Self Employed_flipkart	5	.02	1.0000
Home Maker_flipkart	5	.24	0.9986
Student_flipkart	5	9.36	0.0954
Retired_flipkart	5	26.21	0.0001
Unemployed_flipkart	5	1.64	0.8966

Table 19.10 Household annual income (Rs.) and preferred store

			Preferred_str		Total
			Amazon	Flipkart	
Hsehold An_ income	Below 5,00,000	Count	59	135	194
		% within HseholdAn_ income	30.4%	69.6%	100.0%
	5,00,001 - 10,00,000	Count	89	86	175
		% within HseholdAn_ income	50.9%	49.1%	100.0%
	10,00,001 - 15,00,000	Count	54	53	107
		% within HseholdAn_ income	50.5%	49.5%	100.0%
	15,00,001 - 20,00,000	Count	32	9	41
		% within HseholdAn_ income	78.0%	22.0%	100.0%
	20,00,001 & above	Count	59	10	69
		% within HseholdAn_ income	85.5%	14.5%	100.0%
Total		Count	293	293	586
		% within HseholdAn_ income	50.0%	50.0%	100.0%

Table 19.11 Household annual income (Rs.) and preferred store (amazon or flipkart)

	Value	Df	Asymp. Sig. (2-sided)
Pearson Chi-Square	77.534[a]	4	.000
Likelihood Ratio	82.878	4	.000
Linear-by-Linear Association	71.604	1	.000
N of Valid Cases	586		

a. 0 cells (0.0%) have expected count less than 5. The minimum expected count is 20.50.

a significant association with Preferred Store (amazon and flipkart). Cramer's V was used to interpret the effect size (Table 19.8) which was 0.36 and found to be large effect (Cohen, 2012)

Table 19.10 shows that respondents with Household Annual Income (in Rs.) of 5,00,001 – 10, 00,000 lacs and 10,00,001 – 15,00,000 lacs do not have much difference in store preference. But respondents with Household Annual Income (in Rs.) of Below 5,00,000/- have a clear preference for flipkart as against those with Household Annual Income (in Rs.) in the range of 15,00,001 - 20,00,000 and those above 20,00,001 lacs have a clear preference for amazon.

Table 19.12 Symmetric measures

		Value	Approx. Sig.
Nominal by Nominal	Phi	.364	.000
	Cramer's V	.364	.000
N of Valid Cases		586	

To confirm the same, Bonferroni Adjusted Residual Analysis was done (Table 19.13). The adjusted residuals in table were squared to arrive at chi square value. The corresponding p value was calculated in SPSS using significance function for chi square. Finally, the chi square p-value was compared with the Bonferroni corrected p-value (.05/10 = .005). The adjusted p-value shows that respondents with income below Rs.5,00,000 had a clear preference for flipkart and respondents with income of Rs. 20,00,000 and above preferred amazon.

Table 19.13 Income_ bonferroni chi-square residual analysis

Income	Df	$\chi2$ value	Adj p value
Below 5,00,000_amazon	4	44.49	0.0000
5,00,001 - 10,00,000_amazon	4	0.07	0.9994
10,00,001 - 15,00,000_amazon	4	0.01	1.0000
15,00,001 - 20,00,000_amazon	4	13.84	0.0078
20,00,001 & above _amazon	4	39.44	0.0000
Below 5,00,000_flipkart	4	44.49	0.0000
5,00,001 - 10,00,000_flipkart	4	0.07	0.9994
10,00,001 - 15,00,000_flipkart	4	0.01	1.0000
15,00,001 - 20,00,000_flipkart	4	13.84	0.0078
20,00,001 & above _flipkart	4	39.44	0.0000

Table 19.14 Hypothesis testing outcomes

H1-4: There is an association between Online Store Preference and Demographic Characteristics (Age, Education, Occupation and Household Annual Income in Rs.)					
Hypothesis	**Relationship**	**$\chi 2$ Value**	**df**	**Asymptotic Significance (2-sided) p-value (.05)**	**Decision**
H1	H1 - Age -> Store Preference	62.406	3	0.000	Supported
	H2 - Education -> Store Preference	13.749	5	0.017	Supported
	H3 - Occupation -> Store Preference	45.770	5	0.000	Supported
	H4 - Annual Household Income in Rs. -> Store Preference	77.534	4	0.000	Supported

5. Discussion

Chi-square test results show that all the hypothesis from H1 to H4 were supported. All the demographic characteristics under study i.e., age, education, occupation and household annual income (Rs.) are associated with online store preference.

The tests revealed that younger age group between 18 to 25 yrs and age group above 46 yrs have a clear preference for flipkart whereas those in the age group of 26 to 35 yrs and 36 to 45 yrs have a clear preference for amazon. Education is also found to be associated with online store preference. The study showed that respondents with Bachelor's/ Graduate Degree have a clear preference for flipkart as against Postgraduate Degree holders who prefer amazon. Analysis of Employment Status (Salaried Employee, Self-employed, Homemaker, Student, Retired and Unemployed) showed that respondents who are Salaried Employees have a preference for amazon as against Students and Retired people who prefer flipkart.

Finally, the study establishes an association between respondents Household Annual Income (in Rs.) (Below 5,00,000 lacs; 5,00,001 – 10, 00,000 lacs; 10,00,001 – 15,00,000 lacs; 15,00,001 – 20,00,000 lacs; Above 20,00,001) and online store preference. Respondents with Household Annual Income (in Rs.) of Below 5,00,000/- have a clear preference for flipkart as against those with Household Annual Income (in Rs.) in the range of 15,00,001 - 20,00,000 and those above 20,00,001 lacs have a clear preference for amazon. The other income categories did not show any clear preference for either amazon or flipkart.

The findings of this study on demographic variables clearly show that understanding of demographic variables and their influence on Online Store Preference is very important for online retailers to create differentiated offerings. This study only indicates that differentiated offerings based on demographic variables could help create brand preferences amongst customers. Further investigation may be required through advanced statistical techniques like cluster analysis to establish clear demographic characteristics of customers of competing brands.

REFERENCES

1. Arnold, M. J., & Reynolds, K. E. (2003). Hedonic shopping motivations. Journal of retailing, 79(2), 77–95.
2. Baubonienė, Ž., & Gulevičiūtė, G. (2015). E-commerce factors influencing consumers 'online shopping decision. Social technologies, 5(1), 62–73.
3. Bawa, K., & Ghosh, A. (1999). A model of household grocery shopping behavior. Marketing letters, 10, 149–160.
4. Bellman, S., Lohse, G. and Johnson, E. (1999).,, Predictors of online buying behaviour, "Communications of the ACM, 42 (12), 32–38.
5. Carpenter, J. M., & Moore, M. (2006). Consumer demographics, store attributes, and retail format choice in the US grocery market. International Journal of Retail & Distribution Management, 34(6), 434–452.
6. Chandra, S. (n.d.) Retail & E-commerce. Invest India. https://www.investindia.gov.in /sector/retail-e-commerce
7. Forsythe, S. M., & Bailey, A. W. (1996). Shopping enjoyment, perceived time poverty, and time spent shopping. Clothing and Textiles Research Journal, 14(3), 185–191.
8. Fox, E. J., Montgomery, A. L., & Lodish, L. M. (2004). Consumer shopping and spending across retail formats. The Journal of Business, 77(S2), S25–S60.
9. Ghosh, M. D. (2020, February 23). Youth can be a clear advantage for India. https://www.thehindu.com/. Retrieved August 20, 2022, from https://www.thehindu.com/opinion/lead/youth-can-be-a-clear-advantage-for-india/article30897179.ece
10. Haver, K. (2008). Why be on the internet. Furniture Today, 33(17), 2–3.
11. Ibef, (2020, July). E-commerce Industry in India. https://www.ibef.org/industry/ecommerce.aspx#:~:text=The%20Indian%20E%2Dcommerce%20market,38.5%20billion%20as%20of%202017.&text=India's%20E%2Dcommerce%20revenue%20is,the%20highest%20in%20the%20world.
12. Insightsonindia. (2020, February 26). Insights into Editorial: Youth can be a clear advantage for India. https://www.insightsonindia.com/. Retrieved August 26, 2022 from https://www.insightsonindia.com/2020/02/26/insights-into-editorial-youth-can-be-a-clear-advantage-for-india/
13. Kahn, B. E., & Schmittlein, D. C. (1989). Shopping trip behavior: An empirical investigation. Marketing letters, 1, 55–69.
14. Kanchan, U., Kumar, N., & Gupta, A. (2015). A study of online purchase behaviour of customers in India. ICTACT Journal on Management Studies, 1(3), 136–142.
15. Keelery, S. (2020, August 03). Number of internet users in India 2015-2025, Statista. https://www.statista.com/statistics/255146/number-of-internet-users-in-india
16. Keng, K. A., & Ehrenberg, A. S. (1984). Patterns of store choice. Journal of Marketing Research, 21(4), 399–409.
17. Leszczyc, P. T. P., Sinha, A., & Timmermans, H. J. (2000). Consumer store choice dynamics: an analysis of the competitive market structure for grocery stores. Journal of Retailing, 76(3), 323–345.
18. Malhotra, N. K., & Dash, S. J. M. R. (2010). An applied orientation. Marketing Research, 2, 93–98.

19. Malhotra, N., & Birks, D. (2007). Instructor's Manual. Pearson Education.
20. Pattanaik, S., Mishra, B. B., & Moharana, T. R. (2017). How consumer demographics is associated with shopping behaviour? A study on Indian consumers.
21. Policy Circle Bureau. (2022, July 15). Demographic dividend: Can India benefit from its young population. Policy Circle Bureau. Retrieved August 30, 2022, from https://www.policycircle.org/economy/demographic-dividend-india
22. PwC (2014). eCommerce in India Accelerating growth. https://www.pwc.in/assets/ pdfs/ publications/2015/ecommerce-in-india-accelerating-growth.pdf
23. Richa, D. (2012). Impact of demographic factors of consumers on online shopping behaviour: A study of consumers in India. International Journal of Engineering and Management Sciences, 3(1), 43–52.
24. Safitri, J., Rini, E. S., Ginting, P., & Lubis, A. N. (2018, January). The Role of Buying Motivation in Moderating Online Shopping Behaviour. In 1st Economics and Business International Conference 2017 (EBIC 2017) (pp. 353–357). Atlantis Press.
25. Salman, S.H. (2020, June 11). India's e-commerce market to see 300mn shoppers by 2025. Livemint. https://www.livemint.com/industry/retail/india-s-e-commerce-market-to-see-300-mn-shoppers-by-2025-11591894031861.html
26. Singh, A. K., & Sailo, M. (2013). Consumer behavior in online shopping: a study of Aizawl. International Journal of Business & Management Research, 1(3), 45–49.
27. Sinha, P. K., & Banerjee, A. (2004). Store choice behaviour in an evolving market. International Journal of Retail & Distribution Management, 32(10), 482–494.
28. Soni, S. (2020, June 16). Amazon, Flipkart, other e-retailers' GMV to grow 4X by 2020 as small towns drive e-commerce ahead, Financial Express. https://www. financialexpress.com/industry/sme/indias-e-commerce-user-base-to-grow-to-300-350-million-shoppers-by-2025-from-100-110-million-in-2020/1993274/
29. TIMESOFINDIA.COM. (2022, August 14). 75 years, 75% literacy: India's long fight against illiteracy. The Times of India. https://timesofindia.indiatimes. com /india/75-years-75-literacy-indias-long-fight-against-illiteracy/article show/93555770.cms
30. Trocchia, P. J., & Janda, S. (2000). A phenomenological investigation of Internet usage among older individuals. Journal of Consumer Marketing, 17(7), 605–614. https://doi.org/10.1108/07363760010357804
31. Van Slyke, C., Comunale, C. L., & Belanger, F. (2002). Gender differences in perceptions of web-based shopping. Communications of the ACM, 45(8), 82–86.
32. Zeithaml, V. A. (1988). Consumer perceptions of price, quality, and value: a means-end model and synthesis of evidence. Journal of marketing, 52(3), 2–22.

Note: Table 19.1, 19.2, 19.4, 19.5, 19.6, 19.7, 19.8, 19.10, 19.11, 19.12 and 19.14 were SPSS output of data collected by the authors and Table 19.3, 19.9, 19.13 were authors compilation.

Emerging Horizons: Business and Society in the Post Pandemic Era –
Brig. Dr. Rajiv Divekar et al. (eds)
© 2024 Taylor & Francis Group, London, ISBN 978-1-032-90822-9

20

Effectiveness of Artificial Intelligence on Online Retail Sector in Indian Context— Consumer Behavior Patterns Perspective

N. Suma Reddy[1]

Research Scholar,
Mittal School of Business,
Lovely Professional University, Phagwara, Punjab

Associate Professor
Commerce Department, St. Ann's College for Women,
Mehdipatnam, Hyderabad

Pooja Khanna[2], Sabina Verma[3]

Mittal School of Business,
Lovely Professional University, Phagwara, Punjab

**Pravin Kumar Bhoyar[4],
Komal Chopra[5]**

Symbiosis Institute of Management Studies,
Symbiosis International (Deemed University)
Pune India

ABSTRACT

This article's objective is to investigate whether artificial intelligence can affect Indian consumers' online shopping habits. The entire research is relied upon the quantitative exploration method. Through the primary data sources, the crucial data was gathered. The convenience sampling method was used. There were 450 participants in the sample, of which 396 provided thoughtful responses. The analysis is done with SPSS 22. The findings demonstrated a strong correlation between consumer behavior patterns and AI. Furthermore, the first hypothesis is supported by the fact that the r value is 0.951, which shows that the proposed model definitely aids in predicting the relative weightage of AI on consumer behavioral patterns. Online retailers are advised by the analysis to employ artificial intelligence (AI) at every point of the consumer experience, including need assessment, data search and retrieval, and digital platform pre- and post-purchase decision-making.

[1]nsumareddy70@gmail.com, [2]pooja.28675@lpu.co.in, [3]Vermasabina11@yahoo.com,
[4]pravink@sims.edu, [5]chopra.k@sims.edu

DOI: 10.4324/978100355996-20

KEYWORDS: Artificial intelligence (AI), Consumer buying behaviors, Online retailers, Consumer journey, Data-driven decisions

1. Introduction

The business in the retail sector through AI intervention will climb to 20 billion dollars by 2027, according to the most recent poll in marketing analytics. The implementation of AI in retail is altering the way businesses manage their activities in a new era of expanding business systems, providing better outcomes, and attracting customers in the digital world. In addition, the role of multichannel or omni-channel retailing methodologies, untapped opportunities to increase sales effectiveness, requests from businesses to streamline business interactions, and growing needs to improve end-client experiences and make the most of market factors are all contributing to the growth of global man-made brainpower in the retail market.

The computerization of retail operations becomes necessary to compete in niche market sectors; these advancements have a few ramifications for advertising exercises to improve their exhibition. One of these advances is artificial intelligence (AI), which gives advertisers the ability to better organize, concentrate on, and rework marketing activities. By focusing on the invention, streamlining, and delivery of significant value, artificial intelligence (AI) benefits consumers, advertisers, and every part of society, AI gives marketers new strategies and resources to help them accomplish their objectives.

Recently, Artificial intelligence has become an emerging trend in a variety of industries. Simulated intelligence fundamentally alters the concept of advertising, and It significantly alters the way that consumers and businesses engage. Because of this, marketers should be ready for the innovations to come with the advent of artificial intelligence; understanding how AI will affect advertising is crucial. However, the lack of in-depth research on how artificial intelligence affects consumer behavior discourages advertisers from implementing such innovation. Marketers need to think about how artificial intelligence (AI) could be unified with their marketing to forecast and modify the behavior of consumers across the customer journey, from demand recognition to data search, evaluation, and buying independent direction to post-purchase behavior.

Whether online or offline, AI can compel a great deal of unique information from a variety of sources, including images, videos, and data on customer behavior and response. When a customer makes a purchase from a retailer, the store may retain a variety of data, including natural information, customer data (such as age, orientation, and ethnicity), and data based on value (such as the cost of the item and quantity). A purposeful ID reaction of shopper discounting behavior is necessary in order to hypothesize an item's interest more effectively and unambiguously.

To address this issue, organizations are deploying "progressed and solid information mining calculations" to store and evaluate results in order to improve execution with information examination. Accordingly, information executives are one of the biggest issues and an emerging field too in the retails business. Does AI affect customers' buying behavior with regard to online retailing? Is the predetermined question that this study is concerned with answering? Do customers heed recommendations made by AI frameworks used in the stores they control while making purchases?

2. Literature Review

Standish and Ganapathy, (2020): It was emphasized that, despite recent advances in AI technology, the field is still in its infancy. A growing portion of retailers have started experimenting with AI, yet many are feeling the loss of the full benefit of extending the innovation throughout the value chain The large number of AI applications, both in development and now available, adds to retailers' confusion and dismay on which developments in AI to invest in.

Davenport et al. (2019): The study highlighted that internet shops concur that AI is capable of accurately predicting the demands and requirements of their clients. Because of this, a few online retailers have started offering shipments after purchasing. They use artificial intelligence (AI) to determine client preferences and send these products without requiring typical requests from customers, giving them the freedom to purchase or return items they don't need. Customers submit orders in this scenario after obtaining the products they have requested. When it comes to anticipating customer requests for deliveries, Given that it delivers things to the closest delivery place, Amazon is an ideal example. This change to the action plan could affect how customers behave and how shops advertise. As a result, AI can recognize needs from the initial stage. AI can comprehend clients' arising needs and needs, and afterward proposes suitable proposals with regards to internet retailing.

Jarek and Mazurek (2018): The study demonstrated that AI is an important aspect of the way that movement is displayed. The retail industry is a prime example of how artificial intelligence is having an impact, as shown by the frequent client contacts that yield a plethora of data on customer credits and swaps.

Kietzmann (2017): Advertisers base their decision on their promoting techniques and deal predictions on their experiences with consumer buying behavior. Such knowledge is used by artificial intelligence to advise retailers on item displays and inventorying. Thus, it is crucial to understand the customer journey; AI can help advertisers with this understanding and help them reach customers at various stages of the customer journey. It's crucial to recognize the crucial role that AI can play at every level of the purchasing process to understand what it means for consumers. Consequently, the database of client information never stops growing in size, speed, variety, and accuracy. Such an informational evolution could be transformed into useful consumer knowledge with the help of computer-based intelligence.

Daugherty & Wilson (2016): Deep learning can be useful for AI techniques such as task augmentation, automation, profiling, and customisation. These technologies provide a variety of opportunities for consumer-brand interactions because they are built on the information generated by big data analysis. Deep learning, for example, is used in retail settings to enhance task assignment and scheduling through the results of data mining and profiling. This enhances customer happiness and staff management.

Avinaash (2015): These data are analyzed by AI, which then instantly offers the clients personalised recommendations. Quill is a perfect example of how artificial intelligence (AI) methods such as algorithms, natural language processing (NLP), and predictive analytics can be utilised to gather context-specific information about users from brand data. Because it will change the way retailers market to customers and how they behave, AI is the technology that marketers will adopt.

Alpaydin (2014): AI needs machine learning to function. Any automated system, like AI, needs The ability to discover and learn from the world as humans do in order to survive in an unpredictable environment. Indeed, AI will be a dominant player in the market credits to deep learning, natural language processing and machine learning.

3. Objectives of the Study

The main goal is to establish a connection between artificial intelligence and online consumer purchasing behaviour; the secondary purpose is to determine how well demographic characteristics such as age, gender, level of education, and yearly income influence online shopping behaviour.

4. Conceptual Model

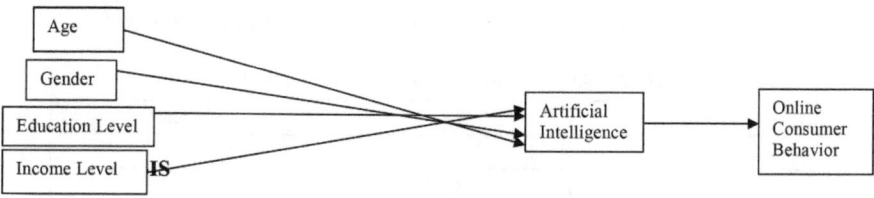

Fig. 20.1 Research model

Source: prepared by Author

Hyothesis-1: There exists a significant association among Artificial intelligence and online consumer behavior.

Hypothesis 2: There are significant positive differences between online consumer behavior and variables like age, gender, and Educational and Income level.

5. Methodology

The study approach that was selected was descriptive research, which only uses quantitative instruments to achieve the stated goals. An online survey was used to collect primary data in order to assess how artificial intelligence is affecting consumer behavior. The questionnaire was modified based on several research evaluations, and it has 10 items that represent artificial intelligence and 8 items that characterize consumer behavior. Likert scale of 1 being the least and 5 being the highest were recorded. Non-probability sampling was the sampling approach employed. Sampling technique used to collect the data was convenience sampling . The sample in this study consisted of 450 individuals. The validity of the questionnaire was checked and evaluated. Both the content and the construct validity were found to be satisfactory. Out of all the responses that were collected, 396 were found to be valid in all aspects. Data collected was analysed using SPSS.

6. Results and Discussion

Cronbach's alpha can be used to assess the reliability of each construct, which has a distinct number of assertions. This model focuses on two constructs: artificial intelligence (AI) and online consumer behavior (OCB).

Table 20.1   Test of reliability

Variables	Alpha value (Cronbach)	Item number
AI	0.979	10
OCB	0.963	8

Source: prepared by Author

AI and OCB both have high dependability coefficients of 0.978 and 0.963, The surveys are deemed dependable since the internal consistency determined by utilizing the adjusted correlations and Cronbach's alpha both exceed 0.5.

Table 20.2   Association between constructs (pearson)

	AI	OCB
AI		
Sig. value	0.00	
OCB	0.987**	
Sig. value	0.0000	

Source: prepared by Author

In Table 20.2, the variables have a positive correlation with one another.

A. Testing the First Hypothesis-1

Hyothesis-1: There is a strong positive relationship with respect to artificial intelligence and online consumer behavior.

Table 20.3 ANOVA

factor	Sum of Sqs	Value of df	Value of Mean Square	Fvalue	Value of P
	289.615	1	288.51	8727.07	
OCB	12.639	395	.034		0.000a
	301.258	396			

Source: prepared by Author

In Table 20.3, The model demonstrates that OCB and AI have a significant relationship. .000 is the significant level. The positive numbers demonstrate that the relationship is positive.

Table 20.4 Regression analysis

	Coefficients (Un)		Coefficients (Std)	t	Sig value
	Beta	Std. Error	Beta		
(Const)	.102	.040		2.528	.012
AI	.957	.010	.979	93.413	.000

Source: prepared by Author

The significance of the resource coefficient is demonstrated by the AI basic regression model's coefficient in Table 20.4 .000 is seen as noteworthy.

B. H2 test

Hypothesis-2: There exists a significant difference value between online behavior of consumers and the variables like age, gender, and Educational and Income level.

The tests employed are The Mann-Whitney U test and the Kruskal Wallis

Table 20.5 Table for mann-whitney test for OCB as per gender

Mean Rank	G		M W U value	W	Z
OCB	M	F	56.15	27.351	-11.73
	131.5	264.6			

Source: prepared by Author

With a Sig (0.000) 0.05 value in Table 20.5, hypothesis 2 is validated.

Table 20.6   Tabulation of kruskal-wallis test for OCB as per age

Mean Rank	Age 18-24	Age 25-29	30 and above	Chi-Square	DOF
OCB	185.65	304.2	118.02	225.18	2

Source: prepared by Author

We accept the alternate hypothesis

Table 20.7   Tabulation of KI-W test for OCB as per educational level

Mean Rank	Pre-University	University	Post Graduate	Chi-Square	DOF
OCB	248.44	138.51	328.02	225.02	2

Source: prepared by Author

We accept the alternate hypothesis.

Table 20.8   Tabulation of K-W test for OCB as per income level

Mean Rank	Less than 5L	5L-10L	10L and above	Chi-Square	DOF
OCB	151.5	287.56	174.86	112.37	2

Source: prepared by Author

We accept the alternate hypothesis.

C. Using SEM to test the validity of the Conceptual Model Developed

To determine whether the data supported the research hypotheses, a SE Model was conducted using the AMOS v22 application. This study's structural model specifies how AI affects consumer behaviour and how different constructs interact. Structural equation modelling or SEM can be used to verify the structural relationship in a structural model. Following are the attributes of the research model: One build included both endogenous OCB and exogenous AI.

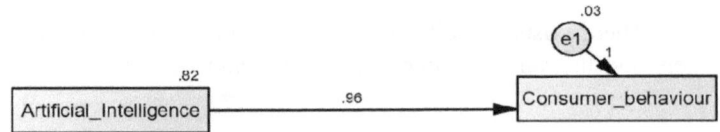

Fig. 20.2   Assessment of SEM

Source: prepared by Author

The parameter estimate comes out to be significant and has the predicted sign, indicating that the hypothesis is supported (e.g., positive effect).

Table 20.9   Assessment of SEM

Hypotheses				Estimate	S.E	C. R	P	Results
H1	OCB	<---	AI	.957	.010	93.54	***	supported

Source: prepared by Author

Moving on to the estimated parameters that represent the research hypothesis, Table 20.9 indicates that the constructs' associations' signs reflect the relationship that has been hypothesized. Furthermore, there is a 0.000 route coefficient from AI to OCB. This indicates that the hypothesis is supported and that AI does have an impact on customer behaviour. Hence, we accept H1

7. Findings

The following benefits and applicability of the structured model:

1. Better degree rates for the reliability of all model constructs range from (0.979 to 0.963) according to Cronbach's alphas.
2. Every construct shows a significant correlation with each other at the 0.01 level, and every variable has a positive correlation with every other variable.
3. Artificial intelligence and OCB have a positive link that influences the model's ability to represent the range of buyer behaviour by 95.8%.
4. Structural equation model analysis was used to validate the first hypothesis

8. Conclusion

The digital revolution in retail activities is necessary to be competitive in ever-evolving markets. One of these technologies that helps marketers better understand and target consumers is artificial intelligence (AI). AI profoundly transforms the way that marketing is done, as well as how customers engage with organizations. They should be well aware of how they can use AI to predict and modify OCB at every stage of the consumer journey in their advertising efforts. This research describes the impact of AI on OCB in the web-based retailing industry in order to assist online merchants in determining the level to which their customers follow their commendations. An overview of artificial intelligence, including its various degrees and applications, is given by the investigation. The study also covers the role of AI on purchase behavior of consumers, highlighting the various stages of the shopping process, including need recognition, data search, and pre- and post-purchase review.

REFERENCES

1. R. Arthur. Macy's Teams with IBM Watson for AI-Powered Mobile Shopping Assistant. Forbes.com, 2016.
2. F. Bertacchini, E. Bilotta, P. Pantano. Shopping with a robotic companion. Computers in Human Behavior, 2017, 77: 382–395.
3. J. Bowman. How Artificial Intelligence is transforming the retail conversation. The Store WPP in partnership with IBM, 2017.
4. C. Chan, H. Lau, Y. Fan. IOT Data Acquisition in Fashion Retail Application: Fuzzy Logic Approach. In International Conference on Artificial Intelligence and Big Data, 2018.

5. D. Grewal, S. Motyka, M. Levy. The Evolution and Future of Retailing and Retailing Education. Journal of Marketing Education, 2018, 40(1): 85–93.

6. D. Grewal, A. Roggeveen, J. Nordfält. The Future of Retailing. Journal of Retailing, 2017, 93(1): 1–6. IFR. Service Robots. International federation of robotics, 2016.

7. J. Gubbi, R. Buyya, S. Marusic, M. Palaniswami. Internet of Things (IoT): A vision, architectural elements, and future directions. Future Generation Computer Systems, 2013, 29(7): 1645–1660.

8. C. Hsu, C. Yeh. Understanding the factors affecting the adoption of the Internet of Things. Technology Analysis & Strategic Management, 2016, 29(9): 1089–1102.

9. S. Kamble, A. Gunasekaran, H. Parekh, S. Joshi. Modeling the internet of things adoption barriers in food retail supply chains. Journal of Retailing and Consumer Services, 2019, 48: 154–168.

10. G. Molnar, Z. Szuts. The Role of Chatbots in Formal Education. 2018 IEEE 16th International Symposium on Intelligent Systems and Informatics (SISY), 2018.

11. W. Reinartz, N. Wiegand, M. Imschloss. The Impact of Digital Transformation on the Retailing Value Chain. SSRN Electronic Journal, 2018.

12. R. Seranmadevi, A. Senthil Kumar. Experiencing the AI emergence in Indian retail – Early adopters approach. Management Science Letters, 2019: 33-42.

13. J. van Doorn et al. Domo Arigato Mr. Roboto", Journal of Service Research, 2016, 20(1): 43–58.

14. N. Verma, J. Singh. A comprehensive review from sequential association computing to Hadoop-Map Reduce parallel computing in a retail scenario. Journal of Management Analytics, 2017, 4(4): 359–392.

15. Y. Li, H. Fleyeh. Twitter Sentiment Analysis of New IKEA Stores Using Machine Learnin. In 2018 International Conference on Computer and Application (ICCA), Sweden, 2018.

16. G. Santoro, F. Fiano, B. Bertoldi, F. Ciampi. Big data for business management in the retail industry. Management Decision, 2018. Available: 10.1108/md-07- 2018–0829

17. Bradlow, E. M. (2017). The Role of Big Data and Predictive Analytics in Retailing. Journal of Retailing. ISSN 0022–4359; Pages 74–95

18. Brougham D, H. (2018). Smart Technology, Artificial Intelligence, Robotics, and Algorithms (STARA): Employees' perceptions of our future workplace. ISSN 1873–3271; Pages 239–257

19. Camisón, C. &. (2009). Capabilities and propensity for cooperative internationalization. International Marketing Review. ISSN 0265–1335; Pages 124–150

20. Grewal, D. R. (2017). The Future of Retailing. Journal of Retailing ISSN 1523–035X; Pages 1–6

21. Felix Weber (2019) State-of-the-art and adoption of artificial intelligence in retailing. Digital policy regulations and Governance ISSN 2398–5038

22. Guo, Z. W. (2011). Applications of artificial intelligence in the Apparel Industry. Textile research journal ISSN 1871–1892

23. Hirchman, E. H. (1982). The Experiential Aspects of Consumption: Consumer fantasies, feelings and fun. Page 132–140

24. HJP, P. E. (2011). Advanced Technologies Management for Retailing: Frameworks and Cases. Hersey, Pennsylvania: IGI Global.

25. Kephart, J. H. (2000). Dynamic pricing by software agents. Computer Networks Pages 732–751

26. Kumar, V. A. (2017). Future of Retailer Profitability: An Organizing Framework. Journal of Retailing. ISSN: 0022–4359; Pages 96–119
27. Lemon, K. V. (2016). Understanding Customer Experience throughout the Customer Journey. Journal of Marketing ISSN 0022–2429; Page 69–96
28. Russell S, D. D. (2015). Research Priorities for Robust and Beneficial Artificial Intelligence. Ai Magazine (AI MAG) ISSN 0738–4602; Page 105–114
29. Shankar, V. (2018). Big Data Analytics in Retailing. Marketing Intelligence Review. ISSN 2628–166X; Pages 37–40
30. Tussyadiah IP, Z. F. (2017). Attitude toward Autonomous On-Demand Mobility: The Case of Self-Driving Taxi. Information and Communication Technologies in Tourism 2017 ISBN978-3-319-51168-9; Pages755–766
31. Walker RH, C.-L. M. (2002). Technology-Enabled Service Delivery: An Investigation of Reasons Affecting Customer Adoption and Rejection. International Journal of Service Industry Management, ISSN: 0956–4233; Pages 91–106
32. Watson, H. (2014). Big Data Analytics: Concepts, Technologies and Applications. Communications of the Association for Information Systems ISSN 1529–3181; Pages 1247–1268.